Llyn Cerrig Bach

Estimated position of assemblage's original location (derived from Fox 1947a: fig.2)

Bedrock ridge which would have formed an elongated island of drier ground within the ancient bog or lake of Llyn Cerrig Bach.

Aerial photograph of Llyn Cerrig Bach (looking southeast) (RAF)

LLYN CERRIG BACH

A STUDY OF THE COPPER ALLOY ARTEFACTS FROM THE INSULAR LA TÈNE ASSEMBLAGE

By Philip Macdonald

with contributions by
Kilian Anheuser, Tony Daly, Mary Davis, Jim Wild and Tim Young

Published for the Board of Celtic Studies and
Amgueddfa Cymru – National Museum Wales

UNIVERSITY OF WALES PRESS
CARDIFF
2007

British Library Cataloguing-in-Publication Data
A catalogue record for this book is available from the British Library.

ISBN 978-0-7083-2041-9

www.wales.ac.uk/press

Printed in Malta by Gutenberg Press Limited, Tarxien

For Siobhan and Charlotte

Contents

List of figures   ix

List of plates   x

List of tables   xi

Preface   xiii

Acknowledgements   xv

1   Introductory remarks   1

2   The copper alloy horse furniture and vehicle fittings excluding the bridle-bits   8

3   The copper alloy bridle-bits   52

4   The copper alloy artefacts excluding the horse furniture, vehicle fittings and pieces of artistic merit   88

5   Artefacts of artistic merit   117

6   The source and date of the assemblage (*with a contribution by Mary Davis*)   152

7   Concluding remarks   171

Appendix 1   Tabulated list and concordance table for the Llyn Cerrig Bach assemblage   190

Appendix 2   Metallurgical analysis of the copper alloy artefacts in the Llyn Cerrig Bach assemblage *Kilian Anheuser, Mary Davis and Philip Macdonald*   199

Appendix 3   Field survey at Llyn Cerrig Bach *Philip Macdonald and Tim Young*   207

Catalogue of the copper alloy artefacts from Llyn Cerrig Bach   217

Bibliography   259

Index   289

Figures

1   Location map: find-spot of the Llyn Cerrig Bach assemblage   3
2   Coiled decorative strips: thickness/density index plotted against width   113
3   Crescentic decorative plaque (No. 47)   124
4   Details of the design from the crescentic plaque (No. 47) replicated on
    other pieces of metalwork   125
5   Decorative elements of the shield boss mount (No. 48)   128
6   The Barmouth miniature shield   135
7   Topographic map of the primary site and its immediate environs   209
8   Geophysical survey: resistivity profiles   211
9   Results of the magnetometry survey   213
10 Llyn Cerrig Bach: map of RAF Valley, showing the extent of the area
    cultivated during 1942 and the area apparently covered by freshly-spread
    peat (13 November 1942), within which the tertiary site probably lies   215
11 Terrets (Nos 1–3); linchpin (No. 8); ring (No. 9)   237
12 Nave hoops (Nos 4–7)   238
13 Three-link bridle-bit (No. 10): detail of central link; three-link bridle-bit
    (No. 11): detail of decorative roundel   239
14 Three-link bridle-bits (Nos 12–15)   240
15 Rein-rings (Nos 16–20); ring (No. 21)   241
16 Two-link bridle-bit (No. 22); three-link bridle-bit of Irish type (No. 23) 242
17 Globular cauldron fragment (No. 24)   243
18 Globular cauldron fragment (No. 25)   244
19 Hemispherical cauldron fragment (No. 26)   245
20 Scabbard mouth (No. 27); probable scabbard or sheath-binding (No. 28);
    pommel (No. 29); cylinder (No. 30); sheet fragments (Nos 32–34)   246
21 'Trumpet' fragment (No. 31)   247
22 Coiled decorative strips (Nos 35–43)   248
23 Bean-shaped plaques (Nos 44–45); decorative curved plate (No. 46); so-called
    horn-cap (No. 49)   249
24 Crescentic decorative plaque (No. 47)   250
25 Shield boss mount (No. 48)   251
26 'Square' plaques (Nos 50–52); rectangular plaques (Nos 53–54); tri-disc (No. 55) 252

Plates

Plate 1   Aerial photograph, December 1940 [National Archives and Records
          Administration, Cartographic and Architectural Branch, USA]   253
Plate 2   Aerial photograph, April 1942 [Central Register of Air Photography
          for Wales, Medmenham]   254
Plate 3   Aerial photograph, November 1942 [Central Register of Air Photography
          for Wales, Medmenham]   255
Plate 4   Aerial photograph, detail of November 1942 [Central Register of Air
          Photography for Wales, Medmenham]   256
Plate 5   X-Radiographic images of (a) the double-cordoned nave hoop (No. 6),
          (b) the 'vase-headed' linch-pin (No. 8) and (c) the three-link bridle-bit of
          Irish type (No. 23)   257
Plate 6   Shield boss mount (No. 49): (a) prior to conservation (c.1944) and
          (b) after reshaping   258

Colour Plates

(Plates 1a–4 between pages 224 and 225)

Frontispiece   Aerial photograph of Llyn Cerrig Bach [RAF]   ii
Colour Plate 1a   Globular cauldron fragment (No. 25)
Colour Plate 1b   'Trumpet' fragment (No. 31)
Colour Plate 2a   Crescentic decorative plaque (No. 47)
Colour Plate 2b   Swastika design on so-called horn-cap (No. 49)
Colour Plate 3   Shield boss mount (No. 48)
Colour Plate 4   So-called casket ornament (Nos 50–55)

Tables

1   Group I terrets   14
2   Group II terrets   17
3   A selection of examples of insular La Tène metalwork embellished with
    pseudo-stitch decoration   24
4   Copper alloy nave hoops   27
5   'Vase-headed' linch-pins from Britain   39
6   So-called miniature terrets   45
7   Three-link bridle-bits of the British Iron Age (excluding the examples from
    Llyn Cerrig Bach)   57
8   Two-link bridle-bits of the British Iron Age   75
9   Later Iron Age cauldrons from Britain and Ireland   93
10 Cast copper alloy scabbard mouths from La Tène III swords   99
11 Characteristics of the coiled decorative strips   111
12 The diameters of the fixing holes on the decorative crescentic mount (No. 47)   120
13 So-called horn-caps   140
14 Selection of Iron Age and Romano-British 'casket' ornament   147
15 Frequency of Northover's copper alloy impurity patterns in the Llyn Cerrig
    Bach assemblage   155
16 Radiocarbon dates from the Oxford Radiocarbon Accelerator Unit   169
17 Concordance table of the known contents of the Llyn Cerrig Bach assemblage   192
18 Metallurgical analyses of the copper alloy artefacts from the Llyn Cerrig Bach
    assemblage   202
19 Three-link bridle-bit (No. 11): lengths of the design components of the
    side-links   221

Preface

The collection of metalwork from Llyn Cerrig Bach, Anglesey, is one of the most important assemblages of early Iron Age metalwork known from the British Isles. It was discovered during construction work at RAF Valley during the Second World War and was first published by Sir Cyril Fox, then Director of the National Museum of Wales, in a landmark volume in 1947. Fox's report represented a significant advance in the standard of reporting of ancient metalwork, the study of insular La Tène art and the interpretation of prehistoric depositional practices.

This volume, published on the sixtieth anniversary of Sir Cyril Fox's original report and in the Museum's centenary year, is the outcome of a research project initiated in 1994 by Professor William Manning and funded by the Board of Celtic Studies of the University of Wales. Facilities for study were provided by the Department of Archaeology & Numismatics, Amgueddfa Cymru – National Museum Wales, where the collection is housed and displayed, and the project represents a successful partnership between the university and museum sectors in researching archaeological artefacts. Philip Macdonald, the author of this work, was employed as a Research Assistant to prepare a catalogue of the copper alloy artefacts from the assemblage, and the material subsequently formed the basis of his doctoral research. This re-evaluation of the Llyn Cerrig Bach assemblage builds upon Sir Cyril Fox's original study. Survey at the site has provided a context for the assemblage's interpretation and an exhaustive typological study, coupled with the results of a comprehensive programme of metallurgical analysis, has identified a hitherto unrecognized phase of deposition at the site continuing into the Roman period.

The present volume has been published jointly by Amgueddfa Cymru – National Museum Wales and the Board of Celtic Studies of the University of Wales.

Michael Houlihan
Director General
Amgueddfa Cymru – National Museum Wales

Professor Geraint H. Jenkins
Chairman, Board of Celtic Studies

Acknowledgements

This monograph is the result of a research project to re-assess the copper alloy artefacts from the Llyn Cerrig Bach assemblage, which eventually formed the subject of a doctoral thesis. This research was greatly aided by the supervision of Professor W. H. Manning whose constant support and advice I am most grateful for: he read several drafts of this report and has made numerous valuable comments and suggestions for its improvement. I am grateful to the Board of Celtic Studies for funding the initial part of the research. Facilities for study were generously provided by the Department of Archaeology & Numismatics, Amgueddfa Cymru – National Museum Wales and the School of History and Archaeology, Cardiff University, and I am grateful to the staff of both institutions for their support and encouragement throughout the course of my studies.

I am particularly grateful to those individuals who have directly contributed to this volume. Tony Daly not only provided the excellent illustrations of the assemblage but also offered many insightful comments on the artefacts that he drew. Mary Davis made a significant contribution to the project by undertaking the bulk of the metallurgical study of the assemblage. Tim Young's assistance in undertaking field survey at Llyn Cerrig Bach contributed significantly to my appreciation of the assemblage's context and also had a profound and lasting effect on my whole approach to archaeological fieldwork. The assistance of Kilian Anheuser in undertaking the metallurgical analyses and Jim Wild in providing photographs of the assemblage is also greatly appreciated.

Ken Brassil, Evan Chapman, Adam Gwilt and Niall Sharples all read sections of the text and I am grateful to them all for their many helpful comments. I would like to thank Alan Lane for his support and advice throughout the duration of the project. My especial gratitude is extended to Richard Brewer for both his encouragement and his vital assistance in bringing this volume to publication.

It is a pleasure to thank the many people who provided support and assistance during the course of this project. They include Ian Armit, Amin Barzanji, Nigel Blackamore, Angie Bolton, Dr S. G. E. Bowman, Peter Brabham, Sally Budd, J. Clements, Jonathan Cotton, Peter Crew, Gareth Darbyshire, John A. Davies, Colm Donnelly, Catherine Duigan, Elizabeth Edwards, Gareth Edwards, D. Elliot, Andrea Firth, Andrew Fitzpatrick, Lady Aileen Fox, Margaret Hughes, Wing Commander H. W. Griffiths, Alun Gruffydd, Alison Harle Easson, Rachel Harris, Ciorstaidh Hayward Trevarthen, Nick Herepath, J. D. Hill, Katie Hinds, Natasha Hutcheson, G. Iwan Huws, Ralph Jackson, Colin Jones, Michael Lewis, Mark Lodwick, Frances Lynch, Stewart Lyon, Claire Mason, Paul Nicholson, Peter Northover, John Ó Néill, N. A. Payne, Flight Lieutenant John

ACKNOWLEDGEMENTS

Phillips, Josh Pollard, A. J. N. W. Prag, Katherine Reidy, Owain T. P. Roberts, R. A. Rutland, Chris Salter, J. D. Scourse, Babita Sharma, Ian Stead, Anne Venables, Elizabeth Walker, Sara Wear, Janet Webster, Peter J. Woodward, Sally Worrell and Mike Yates.

My thanks are extended to Dafydd Jones and the staff of the University Wales Press for their hard work in preparing this volume for publication. I am also pleased to acknowledge the financial assistance of the Board of Celtic Studies and Amgueddfa Cymru – National Museum Wales in publishing this report.

On a personal level, my especial thanks are extended to Siobhan Stevenson for her constant advice, encouragement and patience.

Philip Macdonald
Belfast, April 2006

1

Introductory Remarks

The Llyn Cerrig Bach assemblage is one of the most important collections of La Tène metalwork discovered in the British Isles. It came to light during construction work in 1942 at RAF Valley in north-west Anglesey when it was disturbed during the extraction of peat from the Cors yr Ynys bog located on the southern margin of Llyn Cerrig Bach (Figure 1). A total of 180 iron and copper alloy artefacts are known to have been recovered from the airfield, of which all but four are now in the collection of the National Museum of Wales. Of the 180 pieces of metalwork, five are demonstrably modern, four are possibly modern and one is possibly medieval in date; the remainder are ancient (see Appendix 1). The assemblage consists of a wide range of artefact types, mostly military equipment, vehicle fittings and items of harness, but also includes a number of tools, decorative mounts and fittings. In addition to the metalwork, the assemblage included a large amount of animal bone, of which only a small sample was collected. The assemblage was originally published by Cyril Fox in a landmark volume for insular La Tène metalwork and art studies (Fox 1947a). The copper alloy artefacts from the assemblage form the subject of this study.

The discovery at Llyn Cerrig Bach and previous research on the assemblage

For security reasons, Fox only wrote a brief account of the circumstances surrounding the discovery at Llyn Cerrig Bach (1947a: 1–4). It is possible, however, to reconstruct a more detailed account from copies of correspondence concerning the find which are held by the National Museum of Wales (accession nos. 44.32 and 44.294), various surveys and plans of the area (including the *c.*1840 tithe map and Greenly's geological survey of *c.*1900) and aerial photographs of the site taken during the war: Luftwaffe images from December 1940 (Pl. 1) (National Archives and Records Administration, Cartographic and Architectural Branch, USA, RG373 GX-12041 SD, frame 546 23) and RAF images from April 1942 (Pl. 2) (Central Register of Air Photography for Wales, Medmenham, H1 4/489 1PRV, frames 46, 47, 48), November 1942 (Pls 3 and 4) (Central Register of Air Photography for Wales, Medmenham, NLA/53 1PRV, frames 2004, 1004) and August 1945 (Central Register of Air Photography for Wales, RAF 106BUK655).

RAF Valley is located on part of the former Tywyn Trewan dune system on the west coast of Anglesey. There are several dune systems on the western coast of Anglesey, most of which confine wetlands on the poorly drained glaciated bedrock of their inland margins. The modern lake now known as Llyn Cerrig Bach (NGR SH306766) is located on the edge of such a wetland area. It is situated inland from the northern part of the Tywyn Trewan dunes, about 1.5 kilometres from the coast and the southern entrance of the tidal channel Afon Cymyran which separates Holy Island from the mainland of Anglesey (Fox 1947a: 1, fig. 1). The wetlands extend, as a series of bogs and lakes, to the north and east of Llyn Cerrig Bach. The coastward extent of these wetlands during antiquity is unknown, although it is reasonable to assume that they were more extensive than at present, having been overridden by the advancing dune system in historical times. The underlying geology of the area consists of steeply dipping Pre-Cambrian schists, intruded by bodies of gabbro (Smith and Neville George 1961: fig. 2). One of these gabbro intrusions forms the topographic ridge known as Craig y Carnau which defines the northern edge of the Tywyn Trewan dune system and runs north-eastwards from the coast at Cymyran towards Llyn Cerrig Bach. It is the northern edge of this feature which forms the 'rock platform' adjacent to Llyn Cerrig Bach described by Fox (1947a: 1–4). The modern Llyn Cerrig Bach, and a smaller lake to the south-east, are situated between the Holyhead to Bangor railway line and the road which skirts the northern perimeter of RAF Valley. These lakes are not natural but are the flooded remnants of the basin created by the extraction of peat at the Cors yr Ynys bog in 1942. Prior to the early twentieth century a single lake, also known as Llyn Cerrig Bach, existed to the south-east of the modern lake. It is not certain whether the lake had a glacial origin or was formed as a result of changes in drainage patterns caused by blockages of estuarine areas by wind-blown sand (Robinson 1980: 58; Roberts 2002: 33). The condition of the artefacts in the assemblage is inconsistent with their deposition in a marine environment (*pace* Roberts 2002: 36), indicating that by the Iron Age the lake and its surrounding wetlands formed a freshwater burial environment. The name Llyn Cerrig Bach, which means the lake of the small stones, is probably not of any great antiquity being apparently derived from the name of a nearby farmstead called Cerig Bach. As a result of drainage associated with the construction of the railway line, the lake had almost silted up by the beginning of the Second World War and was finally drained by the war-time peat extraction. The topography of the area was further altered, following the peat extraction, by the infilling of the southern parts of the original lake and dredged bog with sand and stone during the expansion of the airfield between October 1943 and October 1944. This infilling has resulted in the modern ground surface being 2.5 metres higher than the surface of the bog prior to the peat extraction. The road which defines the northern perimeter of RAF Valley and cuts through the northern end of Fox's 'rock platform' was built shortly before March 1945.

During the construction of the airfield at RAF Valley the Tywyn Trewan sand dunes were mechanically flattened to accommodate the runways. As a result of bulldozing the dune system, the vegetation that had previously stabilized the dunes was destroyed. Consequently, wind-blown sand became a major problem at the airfield. To solve this problem, peat from the wetlands adjacent to the airfield was mechanically excavated, dried on higher ground adjacent to the sites of extraction and then transported to the

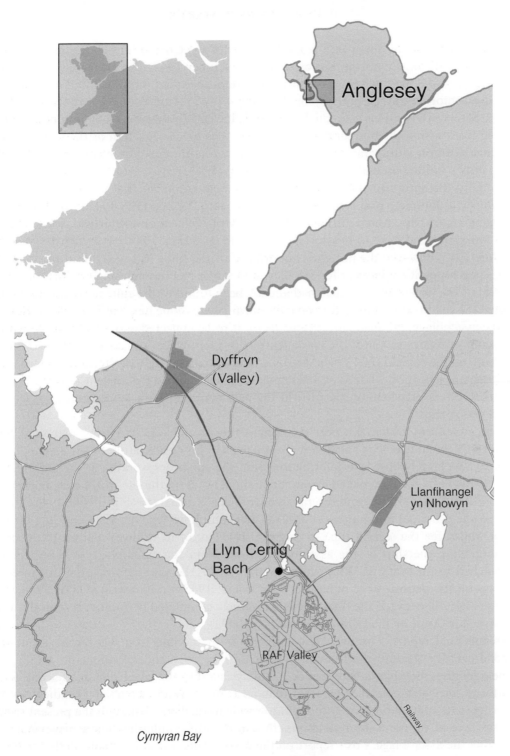

Figure 1: Find-spot of the Llyn Cerrig Bach assemblage

airfield, harrowed and sown with grass. That part of the Cors yr Ynys bog containing the Llyn Cerrig Bach assemblage was excavated in October 1942. The estimated location of the peat deposits in which the assemblage was deposited was published by Fox in a plan based on information supplied by the Ministry of War Transport (Fox 1947a: 3, fig. 2; NGR SH30607649). This estimated position is located to the south of the modern Llyn Cerrig Bach within the boundary of the airfield. The precise location of the assemblage's original position within the bog remains unknown, although Fox records that it came from only a limited area of the Cors yr Ynys bog (1947a: 3).

Initially, the antiquity of the metalwork contained within the peat was not recognized. Famously, a complete iron tyre was thrown back into the bog (Fox 1947a: 3) and one of the gang-chains, discovered during the harrowing of the peat on the airfield, was retained by a workman and used to tow lorries out of the mud (Fox 1947a: 1; Lynch 1970: 249). By July 1943, however, the potential importance of the finds was recognized by Mr J. A. Jones, the resident engineer at RAF Valley, who wrote to Fox enclosing an illustration of several of the iron artefacts which had already been found whilst cultivating the peat. Fox visited the site in August 1943 for two days during which time he established the antiquity of the assemblage and made arrangements for it to be collected and sent to the National Museum of Wales in Cardiff. Consequently, the assemblage was collected by workmen working on the airfield (Fox 1947a: 2–3). Fox estimated that the collected assemblage only represented a portion of the total assemblage spread across the airfield (1947a: 2). No record survives of where on the airfield the peat containing the finds from Llyn Cerrig Bach was spread.

The area from which the peat containing the assemblage had been extracted was flooded by the time of Fox's first visit. Consequently, his appreciation of the assemblage's context was largely based on information from the engineers working at the airfield. By March 1944 Fox had completed a number of short notes on the site which were published in both *The Times* (1944a) and several archaeological journals (1944b; 1944c; 1944d). The text of the principal interim report (1945a) was completed by June 1944 and Fox visited RAF Valley for the second time in August 1944, largely to resolve legal problems concerning the ownership of the assemblage. Finds from the assemblage were still being dispatched to the National Museum in January 1945, the year in which the two interim reports on the deposit were published (Fox 1945a; 1945b). Fox revisited RAF Valley in March 1945. The text of the final report was largely completed by August 1946 and it was published in April of the following year (Fox 1947a).

In the final report, Fox dated the assemblage to the late Iron Age, from about the second century BC until the Roman invasion of Anglesey under Paulinus in AD 60. He concluded that the objects had been deliberately cast into the lake from an adjacent 'rock platform', probably episodically rather than as a single event, as part of Druidical votive offerings to a supernatural deity thought to reside in the lake. Although the present study revises several of Fox's interpretations, this in no way diminishes his achievements in studying the assemblage. Fox's report on the assemblage was a landmark study for three reasons. First, it marked a major advance in the standard of the reporting of ancient metalwork and is still cited as a source for the study of the British Iron Age. The format that Fox used became a standard for publishing assemblages of archaeological metalwork (for example, see Piggott 1952–3; Burley 1955–6) and much of the report's content can still be accepted as valid. Secondly, it was a significant contribution to the study of insular La Tène art. Fox's appreciation of the insular La Tène art in the assemblage was accurately described, shortly after the report's publication, as demonstrating 'a vivid aesthetic percipience . . . balanced by a field archaeologist's solid appreciation of the detailed evidence necessary in forming any chronological scheme of art styles' (Piggott 1950: 2). The continuing influence of Fox's work is reflected in the assemblage effectively being used to define one half of Stead's insular La Tène art sequence (Stead 1985a: 21–2; 1996: 32–4). Finally, Fox's view that the Llyn Cerrig Bach assemblage was the product of votive deposition also marked a significant development in the interpretation of prehistoric depositional practices.

Other than Fox's report, the only detailed account of the assemblage is that given by Lynch in her important survey of prehistoric Anglesey (Lynch 1970: 249–78). Lynch's excellent account updated Fox's report on the assemblage by refining the dating of several of the items in the hoard and illustrating several artefacts which had reached the National Museum too late to be drawn for Fox's report. Since Fox wrote his account of the assemblage the view that almost the entirety of the assemblage was manufactured outside of Wales has been questioned (Savory 1968: 20–1; Lynch 1970: 255; Savory 1970: 46; 1973; 1976a: 29, 49) and his arguments concerning the sources of the assemblage have been critically reviewed (Spratling 1972: 339–44). Specific research on the artefacts has been limited. Lynch published a note on a spearhead which had remained in private hands, but is now at Oriel Ynys Môn (Lynch 1969–70) and Savory wrote an account of a previously unrecorded stamp on one of the sword blades (Savory 1966a). Several of the artefacts from the assemblage have been included in studies of specific artefact types. Most notably these include: the two iron tongs (Fell 1990: 325, 327, nos. 39 and 43, fig. A.5; Darbyshire 1996: 24–5, 32–3, nos. B4, B18, figs. 14, 20), the so-called horn-cap (Peckham 1973: 9), the two iron gang-chains (Thompson 1993: 60–74, illus. 9–13), the sword and scabbard fragments (Piggott 1950: 6–10, 22, 26, 28) and the bridle-bits (Palk 1984: 32–5, 42, 58, nos. DJ22–DJ28, SJ5, LL1–LL2). The copper alloy artefacts from the assemblage were also discussed in Spratling's account of the decorated bronzes of the late Iron Age of southern Britain (1972). This important study includes discussions of the terrets (1972: 26–7, nos. 10–11, 22), nave hoops (1972: 82–3, nos. 140–3), 'vase-headed' linch-pin (1972: 339–40, no. 112), bridle-bits (1972: 86, 89–90, 93–4, 99–100, nos. 153–7, 169), cauldron fragments (1972: 237, 265, nos. 427–8), scabbard fittings (1972: 160, nos. 269–70), pommel (1972: 158, no. 294), decorative mounts (1972: 177–8, nos. 324–5), shield boss mount (1972: 173–9, no. 308), so-called horn-cap (1972: 67–8, 71–5, no. 131) and 'casket' ornament (1972: 239–40, 269, nos. 437A–439, 453), as well as the assemblage in general (1972: 339–46). Several artefacts from the assemblage were featured in Jope's survey of insular La Tène art (2000), including the terrets (2000: 309, pl. 290.n–o), linch-pins (2000: 314, 315, pl. 301.a, f), bridle-bits (2000: 153, 302, 304, pls 273.o–p, 275.e and 280.a), 'trumpet' fragment (2000: 112, 147, 164, 252, pl. 203.f–h), coiled decorative strip (2000: 282, pl. 206.g), crescentic mount (2000: 115, 183, 197, 271, pl. 184), shield boss mount (2000: 70, 182, 249, pl. 90), so-called horn-cap (2000: 316, pl. 302.e), iron scabbard fragment (2000: 278, pl. 206.g) and iron tongs (2000: 217–18, 320, pl. 311.c–d). The ironwork from the assemblage has been the subject of several metallurgical studies. Metallurgical analyses of a link from one of the gang-chains (Fox 1947a: no. 60) and one of the tyre fragments were commissioned by Fox for inclusion in his final report on the assemblage (Fox 1947a: 75–6, 84). McGrath analysed five samples taken from four of the sword blades (1968). Metallurgical samples have also been taken from one of the currency bars (Fox 1947a: no. 130), one of the nave hoops (Fox 1947a: no. 126) and two other tyre fragments (Fox 1947a: nos. 27, 112c) (A. Gwilt pers. comm.). Two limited programmes of metallurgical analysis have also been conducted on the copper alloy artefacts from the assemblage. The first set of analyses were conducted by Messrs Minton, Treharne and Davies Ltd. (Savory 1971: 66) and the second set of analyses was undertaken by Northover (1991a) (for a discussion of these analyses see Chapter 6).

In 1994 the Board of Celtic Studies initiated a research project to re-evaluate the Llyn Cerrig Bach assemblage. This monograph is the principal outcome of that research project. In addition to a typological study of the copper alloy artefacts from the assemblage, the project also included a programme of metallurgical analyses of the copper alloy artefacts from the assemblage (see Appendix 2), radiocarbon dating of the animal bone assemblage (Hedges *et al.* 1998: 236) and survey work at the original site (Macdonald and Young 1996; see also Appendix 3).

Structure of the monograph

The study of the copper alloy artefacts from the Llyn Cerrig Bach assemblage forms the subject of this monograph. Including the composite artefacts manufactured from both iron and copper alloy, the total number of copper alloy artefacts from the assemblage is fifty-six. The manufacture, classification and date of these copper alloy artefacts is discussed in Chapters 2–5. Chapter 2 details the items of horse furniture and vehicle fittings (Nos. 1–9), excluding the bridle-bits which form the subject of Chapter 3 (Nos. 10–23). Chapter 4 details the miscellaneous artefacts (Nos. 24–46) while Chapter 5 is concerned with the artefacts of artistic merit (Nos. 47–55). Discussions on the so-called Gussage-Bury Hill tradition and pseudo-stitch decoration are incorporated into Chapter 2, whilst a short critique of insular La Tène art classification and chronology prefixes Chapter 5.

The final two chapters are more discursive. Chapter 6 is concerned with an assessment of the sources and date of the assemblage. As well as a critical review of approaches to insular La Tène chronology and provenancing studies, it includes short discussions of the ironwork and the animal bone from the assemblage, as well as a consideration of the metallurgical study of ancient copper alloys. Chapter 7 summarizes the conclusions of the previous chapters and puts forward an interpretation of the character of deposition at

Llyn Cerrig Bach with reference to both a survey of comparable sites and the relevant Classical sources. In addition to the catalogue of the copper alloy artefacts and the accompanying illustrations and photographic plates are three appendices. Appendix 1 forms a tabulated list and concordance table for the assemblage; Appendix 2 is a report on the programme of metallurgical analyses conducted on the copper alloy artefacts from the assemblage as part of the Board of Celtic Studies research project; while Appendix 3 is an account of the survey work undertaken at Llyn Cerrig Bach in 1995.

New drawings of the copper alloy artefacts have kindly been prepared for this monograph by Mr Tony Daly of the Department of Archaeology & Numismatics, National Museum Wales (Figures 11 to 26). The illustrations prepared for the original report on the assemblage (Fox 1945a; 1947a), and used selectively in subsequent publications (for example: Fox 1958; Savory 1976a), were drawn by Mr C. O. Waterhouse during 1943 and 1944. Waterhouse's illustrations conform to the conventions of the time which allowed for greater freedom of expression and a higher degree of interpretation on the part of the artist than would now be acceptable. Whilst being well executed illustrations they do not meet the high standards of technical draughtsmanship required in modern archaeological reports and consequently it has been necessary to produce a new set of drawings. The new illustrations are of an excellent quality and represent the artefacts as they currently are, showing both the ancient and the modern damage. They are of a high enough standard to allow future scholars to challenge the interpretative views put forward in this account without recourse to studying the artefacts themselves. A new set of photographs of the assemblage has also kindly been prepared by Mr Jim Wild of the Photography Department, National Museum Wales (Col. Pls 1–4).

A number of technical terms are employed in this report. Within the study of prehistoric metalwork there is some confusion over the use and meaning of several of these terms. The definitions followed for the usage of scribers, gravers, scorpers and tracers as well as the character of incised, engraved, chased and scribed lines is derived from Lowery, Savage and Wilkins (1971). Other definitions relating to metalworking techniques, such as repoussé, casting and striking, are taken from Hodges (1989: 64–79). Unless defined otherwise any reference to a decorative or art motif is taken from MacGregor's grammar of ornament (1976: pp. xvii–xix). References to the provenance of individual artefacts discussed in the monograph are to the counties as they existed before 1974. Within the study of ancient metalwork there is also a problem of inappropriate nomenclature based on now discredited provenances and interpretations. This occurs on both a specific level, where an individual piece is known by an invalid provenance (for example, the Brentford 'horn-cap'), and a general level, where a find-type is named after a now discredited or problematic functional interpretation (for example, casket ornament). Although such names are now considered misleading, their use is perpetuated for the sake of continuity with previous references in the archaeological literature. Within this report such instances of inappropriate nomenclature are designated by either the qualifying prefix 'so-called' or, where the use of this prefix is considered clumsy, simply by placing the name in inverted commas (for example, 'casket' ornament, or the so-called Brentford 'horn-cap').

2
The Copper Alloy Horse Furniture and Vehicle Fittings Excluding the Bridle-Bits

Terrets

There are three terrets from the assemblage (Nos. 1–3). Terrets are harness loops which were fixed to the yoke of horse-drawn vehicles and through which the reins were collected and passed. Excluding brooches, they are probably the most common surviving, copper alloy artefact type from the British Iron Age; over two hundred examples are known (Spratling 1972: 25–54, nos. 1–105, figs. 1–37; MacGregor 1976: 38–48, 60–72, nos. 46–127) and evidence from metalworking sites, such as Gussage All Saints, Dorset (Spratling 1979: 140; Foster 1980: 37) and Weelsby Avenue, Grimsby, Lincolnshire (Foster 1995: 51–3, table 1), suggests that they were manufactured in large numbers. Several distinct types are recognizable and three typological schemes have been proposed to classify them (i.e. Leeds 1933a: 118–26; Spratling 1972: 25–40; MacGregor 1976: 41–8). Much has been written on the number of terrets required to form a set and how those sets were arranged on the yoke. Leeds first argued, with reference to harness from the Stanwick and Polden Hill hoards, that a harness set consisted of four smaller and one larger terret (1933a: 121–2) and this view is widely accepted (Spratling 1972: 42; MacGregor 1976: 39; Spratling 1979: 134; Stead 1991a: 50). Evidence recovered from the excavation of vehicle burials in East Yorkshire suggests that the four smaller terrets were positioned across the yoke to accommodate the reins and the larger terret was probably set centrally on the yoke and held the straps which secured the yoke to the pole (Savory 1973: 37; Stead 1991a: 50). Although this arrangement may have been the norm, the recent excavation of an Iron Age vehicle burial from Newbridge, near Edinburgh, in which only four terrets (all simple iron rings) were recovered, suggests that the use of a larger terret to unite the yoke and pole was not universally adopted (cf. Carter and Hunter 2003: 532).

Terrets are almost wholly a British phenomenon; only one example is known from Ireland, a flat-topped knobbed terret from Co. Antrim which is probably a British import (Jope 1950: 59, fig. 1.3; 1955: 37; Spratling 1972: 25, 38–9; Raftery 1983: 80, no. 235, fig. 99; 1984: 57–9, fig. 38.2; 1994: 106, fig. 57.b), and there are only a few recorded examples from the Continent (for references see Ward Perkins 1939: 187; Spratling 1972: 25 and Piggott 1983: 220–1, 223). Although MacGregor traces the ultimate origin of the terret to the Near East (1976: 40), the terrets of the British Iron Age probably developed directly from insular, late Bronze Age prototypes such as those in the Parc-y-Meirch hoard,

Denbighshire (Piggott 1983: 177, 223). An indigenous origin would explain why British terrets show little evidence of Continental influence (Spratling 1972: 25, 54).

The terrets from Llyn Cerrig Bach are described in the catalogue, but a few observations comparing and contrasting their form and character are made here. All three are of cast, copper alloy, although one has an iron attachment bar (No. 1). Fox considered that the iron attachment bar originally formed a tang (1947a: 79), but this is uncertain. The bar's lower edge is incomplete and it is not possible to ascertain its original form. Of the other two terrets one has a tang (No. 2) and the other does not (No. 3). Decoration is present on the upper part of the smallest terret (No. 3) in a style termed pseudo-stitching, which imitates leatherwork. It consists of a border of punched dots set immediately below the step-like groove on either side of the terret and a raised, wavy line set within a sunken ridge on the top of the terret (pseudo-stitch decoration is discussed below). Located on the underside of the attachment bar, between the tang and one of the moulded collars, of the largest terret (No. 2) are five tiny circular depressions which superficially resemble punch marks (diameter approximately 0.5–1.0 mm). Their function, if any, is unknown. It is unlikely that they were intended to form a decorative motif because they are positioned on a part of the terret which would not have been visible when in use. It is probable that they are casting flaws. Two of the depressions contain a light brown substance which is possibly a residual trace of the material that the terret was fixed into, presumably either leather or wood.

Wear facets are visible on the inner edges of all three terrets (Figure 11). On the first (No. 1) they are present above the collars on the internal edges of both sides, although one of the facets is considerably larger than the other (Fox only noted the larger facet cf. Fox 1947a: 36). On the second (No. 2) they occur on the inner side of the collars on both sides and on the internal edge above the collar on one side. On the third (No. 3) wear facets are visible on the inner side of one of the collars and on the internal edge of the terret immediately above the worn collar. Wear facets on one side of the internal edge as well as the upper part of the collars are a common and diagnostic feature of terrets. These distinctive wear patterns are caused by the movement of the reins through the terret. They are frequently more pronounced on one side because the reins did not pass straight from the bit-rings to the driver, but were subtended at an angle through the terrets mounted on the yoke. The recognition of this distinctive wear pattern on one side of the smallest terret (No. 3) is, as previously noted (Lynch 1970: 265), evidence that it is a terret and not another type of harness fitting as has been previously argued because of its small size (Fox 1947a: 37; Savory 1976a: 33).

The evidence for metalworking from Gussage All Saints, Dorset (Spratling 1979; Foster 1980) and Weelsby Avenue, Grimsby, Lincolnshire (Foster 1995), combined with examination of the terrets, provides an insight into their manufacture. The terrets were cast by the lost-wax, or *cire perdue*, method. At Gussage All Saints examination of the terret mould fragments revealed that the casting-gates of the moulds led into the attachment bar indicating that the terrets were cast upside down with the bar uppermost (Spratling 1979: 134, fig. 100.2; Foster 1980: 13). In contrast, the casting-gates of the mould fragments from Weelsby Avenue were connected to the loop of the terret, indicating that the terrets were cast the other way up (Foster 1995: 53, fig. 25). The terrets from Llyn Cerrig Bach were arguably manufactured using both methods. One of the mould fragments from Gussage All Saints (no. 5878) contained a rectangular cutting at the junction of the attachment bar and casting-gate which would have resulted in the casting of a rectangular projection, or tang, similar to that on one of the Llyn Cerrig Bach terrets (No. 2) (Foster 1980: 13, fig. 6, pl. 7). The terret with the iron attachment bar (No. 1) must have been cast through a gate connected to its loop. The attachment bar would have been forged separately and then incorporated into the wax model of the terret which formed the basis for the mould; consequently, it would be impossible for the casting-gate to have been connected to the attachment bar. The significance of this variation in manufacturing technique is difficult to evaluate. Although at Gussage All Saints and Weelsby Avenue separate casting techniques were rigidly adhered to at each site, it does not necessarily follow that the terrets from Llyn Cerrig Bach are therefore products of different craftsmen or workshops.

No evidence exists to suggest how the third terret (No. 3) was cast, however, its pseudo-stitch decoration is of interest. The step-like grooves on either side of the terret and the sunken ridge on its top are cast features while the borders of punched dots set below the step-like grooves and the raised, wavy line within the sunken ridge were probably added afterwards. Fox, influenced by Plenderleith's examination of several pieces of harness from the assemblage, considered both the wavy line and punched dot decoration to represent the riveted junctions of three copper alloy strips which encased the iron core of the terret (Fox 1947a: 37; see also Lynch 1970: 265). Examination of the object indicates this is not the case; the terret is a solid casting and contains no iron core, and the wavy line and punched dot border are not the junctions of overlapping strips, but decorative embellishments of the original casting designed to imitate the stitched seams of leatherwork. The punch dot borders consist of 44 dots on one side and 42 on the other. The dots were applied at generally even intervals, although on both sides of the terret there are a few irregularly placed examples. The raised, wavy line in the sunken ridge was produced by 78 separate punch marks alternately set on either side of a raised line within the sunken ridge which was probably a cast feature. Possibly analogous mould fragments for terrets with a raised line within a sunken ridge were found at Gussage All Saints (Foster 1980: 10, Var. IV/V, pl. 2). The application of the punch dots served to raise further the line and produce its sinuous character.

Classification

The first classificatory scheme to be proposed for the British terrets was that of Leeds who identified eight different types: Type 1 'simpler examples'; Type 2 'broad enamel type'; Types 3 and 4 'lipped terrets'; Types 5 and 6 'terrets with rounded or flat-topped knobs'; Type 7 'terrets with round knobs'; and Type 8 'plain type with enclosed iron bar' (1933a: 118–26). Although Leeds did not explicitly define his groupings, the Llyn Cerrig Bach terrets are all examples of his Type 1. MacGregor adapted Leeds's scheme for her own classification by splitting his Type 1 into 'simple loops and terrets' and 'ribbed terrets', amalgamating his Types 5 and 7 into a 'knobbed terrets' group and renaming his Types 2, 3, 4, 6 and 8 'crescent terrets', 'lipped terrets', 'winged terrets', 'platform terrets' and 'massive terrets' respectively (1976: 38–9). MacGregor classified the Llyn Cerrig Bach terrets within her 'simple loops and terrets' grouping (1976: 62).

In comparison to the Leeds and MacGregor schemes that proposed by Spratling was more complex and, at least in terms of defining the Llyn Cerrig Bach terrets, of more use. Spratling outlined eleven groups: Group I: simple form; Group II: thick ringed terrets; Group III: ribbed terrets; Group IV: multi-knobbed terrets; Group V: lipped terrets; Groups VI and VII: winged terrets; Group VIII: flat-ringed terrets; Group IX: knobbed terrets; and the unnumbered groups: miscellaneous forms and the so-called mini-terrets (1972: 25–53). MacGregor's simple loops and terrets grouping was split into Spratling's Group I, Group II and so-called mini-terrets. Spratling classified two of the Llyn Cerrig Bach terrets within his Group I: simple form type (Nos. 1–2; Spratling 1972: 26, 341, 383–4, nos. 10–11, fig. 3) and one in his Group II: thick ringed type (No. 3; Spratling 1972: 26–7, 341, 387, no. 22, fig. 5).

The scheme used here to place the Llyn Cerrig Bach terrets within their typological context is essentially a refinement of part of Spratling's classification. A re-evaluation of the entire typology falls outside the parameters of the present study, however, new definitions are proposed for the Group I and Group II terrets as well as the so-called mini-terrets. The Group I and II terrets are discussed because it is within these types that the Llyn Cerrig Bach terrets are classified. Although there is no example from Llyn Cerrig Bach, the so-called mini-terrets are discussed in the section on the 'vase-headed' linch-pin (No. 8) because of their association with this type (see below).

Group I terrets are of a simple form. They vary from D-shape to near circular in outline, contain a pair of stops at each end of an attachment bar, and their loop thickens towards the stops, although the degree of this thickening varies. They are mostly plain, although some contain simple decoration and are tanged. They are over 35 mm in width. A possible subgroup of Type I terrets, represented by two metal detector finds from Aldridge, Staffordshire and Kessingland, Suffolk, has the type's usual simple form embellished by the addition of a bar extending from the top of one of terret's collars. This additional bar is narrow, runs parallel with the attachment bar and possibly formed a guide for the straps which fixed the terret to the yoke. Group II terrets are of a thick ringed form. They vary from oval to near circular in shape, contain a pair of stops at each end of an attachment bar, and their loops are both markedly thick and of an even thickness. Although some examples are plain, most contain some form of simple decoration. None of the Group II terrets have tangs and all are over 35 mm in width. The so-called mini-terrets vary from D-shape to near circular in outline, contain a pair of stops at each end of an attachment bar, and their loops variously thicken or thin towards the stops, or are of even thickness. They are mostly plain although some have simple decoration. Some are flat at the back, none are tanged and all are 33 mm or less in width.

Group I terrets

There are at least fifty-eight Group I terrets known from Britain (Table 1). The dating evidence for the group does not provide a narrow chronological range for the type. The terrets from Aldridge, near Brampton, near Butterwick, Castleford, Ellingham, Great Ellingham, Kessingland, Little Houghton, Long Stratton, South Walsham, near Stoke Holy Cross and Waltham are all unassociated metal detector finds. The Ardoch terret was recovered from the Roman fort and, although its precise context and associations are unrecorded, it was presumably associated with one of the two phases of the fort's occupation. Ardoch was initially occupied during the Flavian period, probably not before AD 79 or 80 and then abandoned by about AD 90; it was then reoccupied during the Antonine period between c.139 and 165 (Breeze 1982: 52; Maxwell 1989: 114–18, 165–9). The Baginton terret was recovered from a post-fort plough soil; activity at the site dates from c. AD 60 until late in the Roman period, although the main phase of occupation occurs between c. 60 and 79 (Hobley 1966–7: 69, 76). The terrets from Bury Hill were recovered from a pit dated to the late second to early first centuries BC (Cunliffe and Poole 2000: 24, 41, 45, table 2.3). The archaeological context of the Camerton collection is uncertain, but Jackson has persuasively argued that a large part of it was derived from an early military 'closure' hoard of scrap dating to around the mid first century AD (R. Jackson 1990: 18–23). The Carlisle terret was recovered from a context dating from the late first to the early second century AD (Caruana 1990: 128). One of the terrets from Cirencester is an unassociated find (G. Webster 1982: no. 102) while the other was recovered from a mid first-century AD context (G. Webster 1982: no. 103). Of the four terrets from Colchester, one is a chance find from the Sheepen Farm site (Hawkes and Hull 1947: 330, no. 2; Spratling 1972: 381, no. 1) which has a c. AD 10–60 floruit (Haselgrove 1989: 80); two are chance finds from unrecorded locations (Spratling 1972: 381: nos. 2–3); and the fourth was recovered from a Boudiccan destruction deposit at the St Nicholas church site (Spratling 1972: 382, no. 4). The discovery of the Corbridge terret is unrecorded, however, it is presumably associated with the fort, which was founded c. AD 86 and demolished in the mid second century, although occupation at the site continued into the late Roman period (Bishop and Dore 1988: 140, 294). The context of the Dunure terret is unknown. The Fishbourne terret was recovered from an occupation level dating from c. AD 100 to 280 (Cunliffe 1971a: 154). Dating of the East Yorkshire burial evidence is complex and imprecise (for a comprehensive discussion see Stead 1991a: 179–84). The vehicle burial tradition, which includes the Garton Station and Hunmanby Group I terrets, probably started at some point in the fourth to third centuries BC and apparently ended before the mid first century BC (Stead 1991a: 184; Wait 1995: 499). The Glastonbury lake village terret was recovered from the third 'floor' of Mound LXV which has been dated to the middle phase (225–175 BC) of the site's occupation (Coles and Minnitt 1995: 78–9; 200; but see Haslegrove 1997: 60). The Hod Hill example was recovered from an occupational horizon dated by associated pottery to the first century AD (Richmond 1968: 39). The Hunsbury terret is a chance find from the interior of the hillfort. Although Hunsbury was constructed at some time between the eighth and fourth centuries BC, the main period of the site's occupation was the second to first centuries BC (D. Jackson 1993–4: 18) and it is during this period that the deposition of the nave hoops probably occurred. There is no evidence to suggest that activity at Hunsbury continued into the Roman period (A. Gwilt pers.comm.). The Kirmington example is a chance find from a late Iron Age and Roman settlement (Spratling 1972: 282). The discovery of the Maryport terret is unrecorded, although the terret was probably associated with the Roman fort the foundation of which is usually dated to the early Hadrianic period (Jarrett 1976; Breeze 1982: 91; Wilson 1997b: 21–2). The chronology and sequence of the Cumbrian coastal defences are poorly understood, and while some have argued that the presence of an unrecognized Flavian or Trajanic fort at Maryport is probable (Shotter 1996: 72, 78; Caruana 1997: 48–9) for others this remains only a tentative hypothesis (Wilson 1997b: 23). The manufacture and deposition of the Middlebie hoard is dated to the second half of the first century AD (MacGregor 1976: 179–80; but see Hunter 1997: 109). Although its precise context is unknown the Muircleugh terret was associated with four knobbed terrets, a type which ranges in date from at least the mid first century AD to the third, if not fourth, century AD (MacGregor 1976: 46). The best evidence for dating the Polden Hill hoard, which contains seven Group I terrets, is provided by three brooches (Brailsford 1975a: 228–9, nos. 1–3, fig. 6.a–c) which are probably Neronian and certainly date to the third quarter of the first century AD (J. Webster pers. comm.). The South Cadbury terret was a chance find from the hillfort and could date from any point in the site's occupation during the Iron Age to the second half of the first century AD (Barrett *et al.* 2000a: 169–78). The Stanwick hoard, which contains three Group I terrets, is approximately dated to the mid first century AD (Fitts *et al.* 1999: 48). The Torwoodle terret was reportedly recovered from a floor level of the broch and, although a pre-Roman date is possible, the site is Flavian and was probably abandoned before the Antonine re-advance into Scotland (MacGregor 1976: no. 60). The context of the Wilderspool terret is unknown, but the site has an initial military phase dating from *c.* AD 80 which was superseded by an industrial settlement by the late first century AD which possibly continued until the late third century (Thompson 1965: 18–19).

The review of the archaeological contexts and associations of the Group I terrets suggests they possibly range in date from the fourth or third century BC to some point in the Roman period. Some examples were recovered from exclusively pre-Roman contexts, while others were recovered from Roman sites and, while the floruit of the type cannot be extended beyond the second century AD with certainty, the group is a genuinely long-lived phenomenon. The recovery of several Group I terrets from Roman military sites in northern Britain is an interesting phenomenon, and while it is possible that the terrets from Ardoch, Baginton, Carlisle, Corbridge and Wilderspool could date to the late first century AD, the terret from Maryport (as well as the example from Fishbourne) suggests that the type remained in vogue until at least the second quarter of the second century AD. The occurrence of other types of metalwork, which otherwise would be dated to the late Iron Age or mid first century AD, in northern Antonine military contexts is not unknown;

TABLE 1: Group I terrets

Provenance	References
Ardoch, Perthshire	Anderson 1897–8: 461–2, fig. 11; Anon. 1897–8: 56; MacGregor 1976: 41, 60, no. 46
'The Lunt', Baginton, Warwickshire	Hobley 1966–7: 118, fig. 22.10; MacGregor 1976: 60
near Brampton, Norfolk	Portable Antiquities Recording Scheme Ref. NMS1515
Bury Hill, Hampshire (2)	Cunliffe 1995: 34, 38, fig. 16.1–2; Cunliffe and Poole 2000: 47–50, nos. 1.1–1.2, fig. 2.29, pl. 2.8
near Butterwick, North Yorkshire	Portable Antiquities Recording Scheme Ref. YORYM-F941B6
Camerton, Somerset	R. Jackson 1990: 33, no. 58, pl. 6
Carlisle, Cumberland	Caruana 1990: 128, no. 69, fig. 112
Castleford, West Yorkshire	Portable Antiquities Recording Scheme Ref. SWYOR-4C3512
Cirencester, Gloucestershire (2)	G. Webster 1982: 112, nos. 102–3, fig. 36
Colchester, Essex (4)	Hawkes and Hull 1947: 330, pl. XCIX.2; Spratling 1972: 381–2, nos. 1–4, figs. 1–2; MacGregor 1976: 42, 62
Corbridge, Northumberland	MacGregor 1976: 41, 62, no. 50
Dunure, Ayrshire	MacGregor 1976: 62, no. 51
Fishbourne, West Sussex	Cunliffe 1971b: 118, no. 146, fig. 51; Spratling 1972: 382, no. 5, fig. 2
Garton Station, East Yorkshire (4)	Brewster 1971: 290–1; Stead 1991a: 47, 219, fig. 39.1–4
Gillingham, Norfolk	Hutcheson 2004: 113, 130, no. 76
Glastonbury, Somerset	Bulleid and Gray 1911: 229, 231, no. E8, pl. XLIII; Spratling 1972: 26, 382, no. 6, fig. 2; Coles and Minnitt 1995: 79, no. E8
Great Ellingham, Norfolk	Hutcheson 2004: 113, 130, no. 77
Hod Hill, Dorset	Richmond 1968: 39, fig. 31; Spratling 1972: 27, 383, no. 7, fig. 2
Hunmanby, East Yorkshire	Sheppard 1907: 485, pl. opp. p. 487; Stead 1965a: 42, 94, 114, fig. 24.1; Stead 1979: 50–2, 102, fig. 17.1
Hunsbury, Northamptonshire	Fell 1936: 63, no. 3, pl. II.A.3; Spratling 1972: 383, no. 8, fig. 2
Kirmington, Lincolnshire	Whitwell 1966: fig. 3.b.19; Spratling 1972: 26, 383, no. 9, fig. 2
Little Houghton, Northamptonshire	Portable Antiquities Recording Scheme Ref. RAH1564
Llyn Cerrig Bach, Anglesey (2)	Nos. 1–2 (see catalogue entries for full bibliographical references)
Long Stratton, Norfolk	Hutcheson 2004: 113, 130, no. 74
Maryport, Cumberland	Bailey and Haverfield 1915: pl. XI.a; MacGregor 1976: 41, 62, no. 54; J. Webster 1986: 57, no. 20, fig. 3
Middlebie, Dumfriesshire (4)	Wilson 1863b: 157–8, fig. 139, pl. XI; Anon. 1893–4: 237; Childe 1935: 230, pl. XV; MacGregor 1976: 62, nos. 55–8
Muircleugh, Berwickshire	Anon. 1920–1: 17–19, fig. 4; MacGregor 1976: 62, no. 59
Polden Hill hoard, Somerset (7)	Harford 1803: 92, no. 4, pl. XXI.5; Spratling 1972: 26, 385–6, nos. 15–17, fig. 4; Brailsford 1975a: 223, fig. 4.e, pl. XVII.d–e
South Cadbury, Somerset	Bulleid and Gray 1911: 229–30, fig. 45.C; Gray 1913: 11–12, fig. 1; Spratling 1972: 26, 386, no. 18, fig. 4; Foster 1980: 10
South Walsham, Norfolk	Hutcheson 2004: 113, no. 73
Stanwick, North Yorkshire (3)	MacGregor 1962: 24, 46, nos. 62–4, fig. 10; 1976: 42, 62
near Stoke Holy Cross, Norfolk	Portable Antiquities Recording Scheme Ref. NMS-FF9E47

Torwoodle, Selkirkshire	J. Curle 1891–2: 80, fig. 10; Childe 1946: 93, fig. 22; Piggott 1950–1: 108–9; MacGregor 1976: 41, 62, no. 60
Waltham, Kent	Portable Antiquities Recording Scheme Ref. KENT4775
Wilderspool, Cheshire	Thompson 1965: 82–3, fig. 20.24; MacGregor 1976: 62
Unprovenanced (Ashmolean Museum)	Spratling 1972: 386, no. 19, fig. 2; MacGregor 1976: 62
Additional bar subtype	
Aldridge, Staffordshire	Portable Antiquities Recording Scheme Ref. WMID-CBB883
Kessingland, Suffolk	Portable Antiquities Recording Scheme Ref. SF7546

for example, the harness strap junction recovered from a late Antonine deposit at Kinneil fortlet (G. Webster 1996) which is paralleled by a mount from the mid first century AD Seven Sisters, Glamorgan assemblage (Davies and Spratling 1976: 131, nos. 17–18, figs. 7–8; Taylor and Brailsford 1985: 257, nos. 27–8, fig. 6). The explanation for this phenomenon is not obvious; it has been suggested that native craftsmen produced decorative equipment of native form for the Roman army (G. Webster 1990: 293), but that this practise did not continue into the second century and that the number of pieces occurring in second century AD contexts in northern Britain is too great for them to have all been heirlooms at the time of their deposition (G. Webster 1996: 319–20). Although the Group I terrets are all of a simple form they are not a homogeneous group: they range in size from the Wilderspool example (width 38 mm) to the Great Ellingham terret (width 92 mm); some are decorated, such as the Glastonbury, Hod Hill, Hunsbury and Stanwick examples, while the majority are not; and they vary from being D-shaped, like the Glastonbury example, to near circular in shape, like the Fishbourne example. This absence of significant uniformity is presumably a result of the group's considerable longevity.

The two Group I terrets from Llyn Cerrig Bach are relatively large; being 72 mm (No. 1) and 85 mm (No. 2) in width. The only similar sized examples are the Great Ellingham terret (width 92 mm) noted above, one of the Colchester terrets (width 89 mm), and the South Cadbury (width 70 mm) and Baginton (width 70 mm) terrets. The Llyn Cerrig Bach examples are typical in being undecorated and near circular in shape. The iron connecting bar of one of the Llyn Cerrig Bach terrets (No. 1) is unique, although the attachment bars of the Hunmanby, Hunsbury and one of the Middlebie terrets are missing, suggesting that they were probably made of iron which has preferentially corroded away. The tang on the other Llyn Cerrig Bach Group I terret (No. 2) is an unusual, but not unique, feature. A tang is also present on the Wilderspool terret and slight protuberances on the connecting bars of the Ardoch, Corbridge, Maryport and Stanwick terrets have previously been considered 'rudimentary' tangs (MacGregor 1976: no. 54). The potential significance of these characteristics is discussed below.

Despite the lack of standardization within the Group I terrets Spratling considered it possible to pick out Group I terrets which resemble each other and are therefore possibly products of the same local workshops (1972: 26). These possible Group I variant forms included the Glastonbury and South Cadbury examples, those from the Polden Hill hoard, and those from Llyn Cerrig Bach (Nos. 1–2) (Spratling 1972: 26). The significance of this Llyn Cerrig Bach variant form is, however, problematic. As noted above, the Llyn Cerrig Bach examples were probably cast by different methods, which studies of insular La Tène foundry deposits have not yet demonstrated were practised together, undermining the local workshop model suggested by Spratling.

Within the Group I classification, characteristics such as unemphasized collars, a curved attachment bar, small size and the use of iron have all been suggested as indicative of an early date (Spratling 1972: 53; MacGregor 1976: 41). Unemphasized collars occur on the chance find from the Sheepen Farm site, Colchester, the examples from Cirencester, the Polden Hill hoard, the Muircleugh, Torwoodle and Wilderspool terrets and the unprovenanced example from the Ashmolean Museum. None of these have a date which demonstrably pre-dates the mid first century AD. The only Group I terret which definitely has an iron component is the example from Llyn Cerrig Bach which has an iron attachment bar (No. 1). As noted above, the attachment bars of the Hunmanby, Hunsbury and one of the Middlebie terrets are missing, presumably because they were originally iron which has preferentially corroded. Of these only the Hunmanby example is demonstrably early. Strongly curved attachment bars occur on one of the chance finds from Colchester, and the Fishbourne, Hod Hill, South Cadbury and Corbridge terrets, as well as one from Llyn Cerrig Bach (No. 2). Where datable these are of a first century AD date or later. The Group I terrets of small size (width under 45 mm) include the Kirmington, Muircleugh and Wilderspool examples, one from the Stanwick hoard and the unprovenanced example in the Ashmolean Museum. None of these demonstrably pre-date the mid first century AD. Thus, with the exception of the Hunmanby terret, which possibly had an iron attachment bar, none of the definitely early Group I terrets have unemphasized collars, iron components, curved attachment bars or a small size, suggesting that these criteria are not, in fact, meaningful indicators of an early date.

Group II terrets

The Group II terrets (Table 2) can be divided into two, relatively uniform, subtypes on the basis of their size. The smaller subtype consists of the Bury Hill (widths 39, 42 and 47 mm), Hod Hill (width 42 mm), Hunsbury (width 44 mm), Llyn Cerrig Bach (width 35 mm) and Meare (widths 35 and 38 mm) terrets; while the larger subtype consists of the Mill Plain (width 59 mm), probable north-west Suffolk (width 56 mm) and Bishop Wilton (width 78 mm) terrets. In general, terrets of the smaller subtype are less elaborately decorated than those of the larger subtype. Of the smaller Group II terrets the Llyn Cerrig Bach example (No. 3) is similar to the Bury Hill, Hunsbury and one of the Meare (Gray and Bulleid 1953: 221, pl. XLIX, no. E172; Spratling 1972: 26, 387, no. 23, fig. 5) terrets in having a curved connecting bar and also similar to the Bury Hill terrets in being embellished with pseudo-stitch decoration. The larger subtype is equivalent to Spratling's Mill Plain type (1979: 134), or Foster's Variety XI (1980: 11, fig. 3), which Cunliffe has argued is part of a Gussage-Bury Hill tradition (Cunliffe 1995: 34; the significance of this grouping is discussed below).

TABLE 2: Group II terrets

Provenance	References
Bishop Wilton, East Yorkshire	Clarke 1951: 216; Spratling 1972: 27; MacGregor 1976: 41, 60, no. 47
Bury Hill, Hampshire (3)	Cunliffe 1995: 34, 38, fig. 16.3–5; Cunliffe and Poole 2000: 50, nos. 1.3–1.5, fig. 2.29
Hod Hill, Dorset	Brailsford 1962: 17, no. I128, fig. 14; Spratling 1972: 26, 386, no. 20, fig. 5; MacGregor 1976: 62
Hunsbury, Northamptonshire	Fell 1936: 63, no. 2, pl. II.A.2; Spratling 1972: 26, 387, no. 21, fig. 5; MacGregor 1976: 62
Llyn Cerrig Bach, Anglesey	No. 3 (see catalogue entry for full bibliographical references)
Western Meare lake village, Somerset (2)	Gray and Bulleid 1953: 221, nos. E172–173, pl. XLIX; Spratling 1972: 26, 387–8, nos. 23–4, fig. 5; MacGregor 1976: 62
Mill Plain, Hampshire	Spratling 1972: 26–7, 388, no. 25, fig. 6; MacGregor 1976: 62
North-west Suffolk (?)	Leeds 1933a: 27; Clarke 1939: 70–1, 110; 1951: 216–17; Spratling 1972: 27, 389, no. 26, fig. 6; 1979: fig. 100.5

The dating evidence for the Group II terrets is imprecise. The Bury Hill terrets were recovered from a pit dated from the late second century BC to the early first century BC (Cunliffe and Poole 2000: 24, 41, 45, table 2.3). The example from Hod Hill is a chance find from the western half of the hillfort which also includes a Claudian Roman fort (Brailsford 1962: p. vii; Spratling 1972: 386). The Hunsbury terret is also a chance find and, given the relative lack of Roman material from the site (R. Jackson 1985: 175), probably dates to the site's main phase of occupation from the second to first centuries BC (D. Jackson 1993–4: 18). Occupation of the western 'village' at Meare probably commenced in, or around, the third century BC and was abandoned in, or around, the first to second centuries AD (Coles 1987: 246–7); more precise dating of the Meare Group II terrets on stratigraphic grounds is problematic (Orme *et al.* 1981: 68; Coles 1987: 243). The Mill Plain example was recovered during excavation of an Iron Age settlement, although its precise context is unrecorded (Spratling 1972: 388). The Group II terret probably from north-west Suffolk is a chance find, whilst the example from Bishop Wilton is recorded as coming from Calais Wold Farm, although its precise context is unknown. None of the Group II terrets can be closely dated with certainty and on current evidence it is not possible to ascertain whether the type had a long or short vogue. They probably date to some period within a range from the third century BC to the first or second century AD. It is notable that, in comparison with the Group I terrets (see above), none of the Group II terrets have been recovered from Roman military sites and, although certainty is not possible with such a small sample of known examples, this observation suggests that it is unlikely that the floruit of the type extended far beyond the mid first century AD.

There are three terrets for which it is not possible to determine whether they belong to Group I or Group II because they are too fragmentary. They are the examples from Bench Cave, Devon (MacGregor 1976: 60); Birtley, Northumberland (Hall 1880: 360–1; MacGregor 1976: 41, 60, no. 48); and Chesters, Northumberland (Piggott 1950–1: 108; MacGregor 1976: 41, 62, no. 49). In addition, one of the Colchester terrets recorded by MacGregor as a simple type (1976: 62) is probably a knobbed type, albeit now minus its knobs (Hawkes and Hull 1947: 330–1, pl. 99.4; Spratling 1972: 37–9, 416–17, no. 89). Two other pieces classified by MacGregor within her simple loops and terret grouping (1976: 60–2) are probably, although not certainly, harness rings. The example from Bigberry Camp, Kent is a ring decorated with pseudo-stitching (Boyd Dawkins 1902: 216; Jessup 1932: 106; Thompson 1983: 274, no. 54) and the unprovenanced example from Saffron Walden Museum is a plain, cast, ring (diameter 30 mm) possibly associated with two, also unprovenanced, lipped terrets (Spratling 1972: 28–9, 393–4, fig. 8, nos. 40–1). Harness rings are discussed below in the section on the possible example from Llyn Cerrig Bach (No. 9).

The adaptation of Spratling's classificatory scheme, outlined and discussed above, is of limited value in assessing the Llyn Cerrig Bach terrets for three reasons. First, the scheme does not provide a close set of dates for the Group I and II terret types. Secondly, although the Group I and II terrets are of relatively simple form, the variations between individual examples within the groups, particularly Group I, are significant and it is not possible to demonstrate the existence of closely datable and distinctive subtypes. Thirdly, the significance of the typological division between Group I and Group II terrets is itself questionable. For example, the close similarities in decoration between the Group I terret from Hod Hill and the Group II terret from Llyn Cerrig Bach (previously noted by Richmond 1968: 39; and Spratling 1972: 27) suggests that, at least in this respect, the two terrets are more closely related to each other than other examples within their respective typological groups. A common problem in constructing typological schemes is that simple forms of artefact types are often difficult to subdivide meaningfully and they frequently have a longer vogue than more distinctive, complex forms. This is arguably the case with the Group I and II terrets.

Cunliffe's Gussage-Bury Hill tradition

Cunliffe has tried to overcome these problems by defining a Gussage-Bury Hill tradition of copper alloy horse furniture and vehicle fittings (1995). This tradition is based on the stylistic similarities between the Bury Hill assemblage and mould fragments from Gussage All Saints, the larger subtype (or Mill Plain type) of the Group II terrets and a number of other finds principally from Wessex and East Yorkshire (Cunliffe 1995: 33–4, 38). The tradition is typified by decorative motifs such as raised roundels with rosettes of pellets and zig-zag petal decoration and is dated to the first half of the first century BC (Cunliffe 1995: 33–4).

There are, however, two problems with Cunliffe's proposed tradition. First, the dating evidence is not as unequivocal as Cunliffe suggests. Considering both the limited scale of the excavations and the fact that the ceramics used to date the site are not recorded as being directly associated with the metalwork, the first century BC date for the Bury Hill assemblage cannot be considered certain. Indeed, subsequent study of the site suggests that much of the metalwork recovered from Bury Hill might date to the late second century BC (Cunliffe and Poole 2000). Nor can the mould fragments from Pit 209 at Gussage All Saints be confidently dated to the first century BC. Two radiocarbon dates of charcoal samples from Pit 209 have calibrated date ranges (expressed to a single standard deviation) of 355 to 20 BC and 165 BC to AD 80 (Wainwright and Switsur 1976: 39, samples F and G; see also Foster 1980: 7; Stead 1991a: 183). Cunliffe's first century BC date for this material is based on stylistic grounds (Wainwright and Spratling 1973: 122–3; Spratling 1979: 125) which, in the light of subsequent work on the burial evidence from East Yorkshire (Stead 1991a: 183) and the Mill Hill cemetery, Deal, Kent (Stead 1995: 95), is probably overly precise. In addition, the majority of the independently datable pieces suggested as potentially being of the Gussage–Bury Hill tradition (Cunliffe 1995: 38) cannot be independently dated to the first century BC and are probably earlier in date. This includes the material from East Yorkshire which is part of the vehicle burial tradition that probably began as early as the fourth to third centuries BC and apparently ended before the mid first century BC (Stead 1991a: 184; Wait 1995: 499) and the linch-pin from Old Down Farm, Andover, Hampshire, which is part of a so-called hoard dated from the third to the early first century BC (S. M. Davies 1981: 124, fig. 29.16). In addition, two pieces cited by Cunliffe are probably later in date than the first century BC; these are the lipped terret from the Romano-British temple at Springhead, Kent (Penn 1959: 49, fig. 10.3; Spratling 1972: 393, no. 39, fig. 8) which was recovered from a rubble deposit with a *terminus post quem* of the mid fourth century AD (Penn 1959: 11) and the strap-union from Old Down Farm, Hampshire dated stratigraphically to the early first to second century AD (S. M. Davies 1981: 138, fig. 38.41). Finally the provenance and circumstances of discovery for the majority of the pieces is either unknown or insufficiently recorded for the purpose of accurate dating. These undated examples include: the Wigginton Common, Tring, Hertfordshire linch-pin (Ward Perkins 1941: 65, pl. XI; Spratling 1972: 428, no. 115, fig. 42); the Tattershall Thorpe, Lincolnshire linch-pins (Owen 1993); the Hunsbury, Northamptonshire multi-knobbed terret (Fell 1936: 62, pl. II.1; Spratling 1972: 391, no. 33), strap-unions (Fell 1936: 64–5, pl. II.B; Spratling 1972: 465–6, nos. 192–4, fig. 78; Taylor and Brailsford 1985: 250, nos. 12–14, fig. 3) and bridle-bit (Fell 1936: 66, no. 13, pl. VI.a; Palk 1984: 32, no. DJ20, fig. C14); the unprovenanced Group II terret from north-west Suffolk (Spratling 1972: 389, no. 26, fig. 6); the Fairford, Gloucestershire lipped terret (Wylie 1852: 15, pl. V.7; Spratling 1972: 392, no. 35, fig. 8); the unprovenanced strap-union from either south-west Norfolk or north-west Suffolk (Taylor and Brailsford 1985: 253, no. 20, fig. 4); the Hengistbury Head, Hampshire bridle-bit (Cunliffe 1978: 62, fig. 29; Palk 1984: 30–1, no. DJ18, fig. C12, pl. IV; Cunliffe 1987: 151–2, no. 36, fig. 110); the Ulceby-on-Humber, Lincolnshire bridle-bits (Spratling 1972: 450–1, no. 161, fig. 59; Nicholson 1980: 14, no. 3, fig. 1; Palk 1984: 38–9, no. DJ37, fig. C21.1); the Old Windsor, Berkshire bridle-bit (Barber and Megaw 1963; Palk 1984: 36, no. DJ30, fig. C19); the Swanton Morley, Norfolk bridle-bit (B. Green 1962; Palk 1984: 38, no. DJ36, fig. C23); the Silkstead, Hampshire bridle-bit (Palk 1984: 38, no. DJ34, fig. C21.2; Denford 1992: 39–41, fig. 12); and the Llyn Cerrig Bach, Anglesey 'vase-headed' linch-pin (No. 8). Critically reviewed the dating evidence suggests that the first half of the first century BC dating of the Gussage–Bury Hill tradition cannot be maintained. Those examples for which independent dates have been established suggest that the tradition may range from the fourth or third centuries BC to as late as the fourth century AD.

The second problem concerning the Gussage–Bury Hill tradition is the question of how coherent a classificatory group it forms. The mould fragments which Cunliffe emphasizes from Gussage All Saints are not representative of the whole character of that assemblage. In addition, each of the examples of the Mill Plain type of Group II terrets, which partially define the Gussage–Bury Hill tradition, represented by mould fragments from Gussage All Saints was different, some having hatched rather than containing zig-zag petal decoration (which also partially defines the tradition) (Foster 1980: 11). This suggests that hatched decoration should also be considered a defining characteristic of the Gussage–Bury Hill tradition. If this is the case then the tradition must include a far wider group of finds and not just necessarily further examples of horse furniture and vehicle fittings. When critically examined, the stylistic and chronological integrity of the Gussage–Bury Hill tradition breaks down and both the validity of the group and its value in studying Iron Age metalwork becomes questionable. Foster's work at Gussage All Saints and Weelsby Avenue has demonstrated the dangers of trying to define precisely terret classificatory groups or make generalizing statements. At Gussage All Saints mould fragments of six types of terret not represented elsewhere in the archaeological record were recognized and it proved possible to divide Spratling's Group I into ten subtypes (Foster 1980: 9–13; 1991: 608). Similarly, none of the forms of terret connecting bar recognized during the study of the mould fragments from Weelsby Avenue could be paralleled in the archaeological record (Foster 1995: 52). This suggests that the known examples of terrets, despite their being a relatively common artefact type, do not form a wholly representative sample. Consequently, overly ambitious typological approaches are probably of limited value in studying this type.

In the absence of a more useful typological or classificatory scheme the only method for producing meaningful statements about, and closer dating of, the Llyn Cerrig Bach terrets is to assess the significance of other characteristics specific to them. Two criteria are potentially of interest: the tang on one of the Group I terrets (No. 2) and the pseudo-stitch decoration on the Group II terret (No. 3).

Tanged terrets

As noted above, in addition to the example from Llyn Cerrig Bach (No. 2), a definite tang occurs on only one other Group I terret: the example from Wilderspool, Cheshire. The mould fragment of a Group I terret from Gussage All Saints (no. 5878) contained a rectangular cutting which would have produced a tang similar to that on the Llyn Cerrig Bach terret (Foster 1980: 13, fig. 6, pl. 7) and slight protuberances on the connecting bars of the Group I terrets from Ardoch, Corbridge, Maryport and Stanwick have previously been interpreted as 'rudimentary' tangs (cf. MacGregor 1976: no. 54). 'Rudimentary' tangs are too slight to have functioned in the same way as the more definite tangs in fixing terrets on to yokes, but they are presumably related features.

The only other terret type on which definite and 'rudimentary' tangs occur are knobbed terrets (Spratling 1972: 35–9, 411–19, nos. 81–94, figs. 30–4; MacGregor 1976: 45–7, 67–71, nos. 64–109). Examples of knobbed terrets with true tangs include: the example from Kirkby Thore, Westmorland (Smyth 1846: 285; MacGregor 1976: 46, 69, no. 87); two of the terrets from Middlebie, Dumfriesshire (Wilson 1863b: 157, fig. 139; Anon. 1893–4: 237; Childe 1935: 230, pl. XV; MacGregor 1976: nos. 90–1); and two of the terrets from Muircleugh, Berwickshire (Anon. 1920–1: 17–19, fig. 4; MacGregor 1976: 69, nos. 96–7). Examples of knobbed terrets with 'rudimentary' tangs include: one from Chesters, Northumberland (Philipson 1885: 209, pl. XIX.31; MacGregor 1976: 45, 67, no. 67); one from Chesterholm, Northumberland (MacGregor 1976: 69, no. 81); one from Fremington Hagg, North Yorkshire (Spratling 1972: 39; MacGregor 1976: 67, no. 68); three from Middlebie, Dumfriesshire (Wilson 1863b: 157, fig. 139; Anon. 1893–4: 237; Childe 1935: 230, pl. XV; MacGregor 1976: nos. 72, 88–9); one from Nether Denton, Cumberland (Budge 1903: 408, no. 184; MacGregor 1976: no. 98); one from Saham Toney, Norfolk (Harrod 1855: 455; Allen 1896: 327; Clinch 1901: 273; Henry 1933: 100, fig. 19.4; Leeds 1933a: 125; Clarke 1939: 70, 100–1; Spratling 1972: no. 92; Hutcheson 2004: no. 125); one from Stowting, Kent (Brent 1867: 414, pl. XIX.V; Spratling 1972: no. 86); and one from Traprain Law, East Lothian (A. O. Curle 1919–20: fig. 11.1; Burley 1955–6: 194, no. 350, pl. XIV; MacGregor 1976: no. 106).

With the exceptions of the Llyn Cerrig Bach, Stowting and Saham Toney examples, and the Gussage All Saints mould fragment, the terrets with definite and 'rudimentary' tangs have a northern British distribution. As previously noted, the Group I terrets from Ardoch, Corbridge and Maryport are either definitely, or presumably, associated with Roman forts of Flavian to Antonine date, the Wilderspool Group I terret is from either a first century AD fort or later industrial site, and the Gussage All Saints mould fragment is dated by radiocarbon dating of Pit 209 to the first two centuries BC (Wainwright and Switsur 1976: 39, samples F and G; see also Foster 1980: 7; Stead 1991a: 183). The knobbed terrets generally have similar provenances. The specific associations of the Kirkby Thore terret are unrecorded, however, it was found during the demolition of a bridge on the site of a Roman fort (Smyth 1846: 281–2; MacGregor 1976: no. 87). The Middlebie terrets are part of a so-called hoard dated to the second half of the first century AD (MacGregor 1976: 179–80; but see Hunter 1997: 109). The Muircleugh terrets are recorded as being found close to the Girthgate on the farm of Muircleugh (Anon. 1920–1: 17); no more detailed account of their discovery is known. The Chesters terret was found during excavations in 1885 on the site of the Roman fort and, although its specific associations are unrecorded, it was probably deposited in the Hadrianic period or possibly later (MacGregor 1976: no. 67). The Fremington Hagg terret was found before 1833, possibly as part of a larger assemblage of Roman harness mounts, although doubts have been raised about the validity of this association (G. Webster 1971: 107–8; Spratling 1972: 39; Hunter 1997: 113). The Nether Denton terret was found during building work on the site of the Stanegate fort with associations suggestive of a Trajanic date (Budge 1903: 408, no. 184; MacGregor 1976: no. 98). The Saham Toney terret was part of a hoard of copper alloy horse harness found by chance in 1838 near the 'High Banks' rectilinear earthwork enclosure at Ovington, Saham Toney (Harrod 1855: 327; Clarke 1939: 100; Spratling 1972: 417–18). Hutcheson has argued that the Ovington, Saham Toney hoard is unlikely to date before the late first century AD (Hutcheson 2004: 33). The Stowting terret was recovered from a pagan Saxon multiple-burial (Brent 1867: 413–14; Spratling 1972: 413); it had presumably been either residually deposited or collected from elsewhere and interred in the grave as an already ancient artefact. The Traprain Law terret was recovered during the 1919 excavation from a level which supposedly produced either late second century (Burley 1955–6: 122, 194, no. 350; MacGregor 1976: no. 106) or late third century AD coinage (A. O. Curle 1919–20: 86–7).

Although there are both possibly earlier and later examples, the evidence for tanged terrets suggests that they are principally a phenomenon of the late first and early second century AD in northern Britain which are frequently, but not invariably, associated with military sites. The majority of tanged terrets are also knobbed terrets; a type which ranges in date from the mid first century AD to the third, if not fourth century (MacGregor 1976: 46). The validity, however, of comparing the tanged Group I terret from Llyn Cerrig Bach (No. 2) with the tanged knobbed terrets is questionable. At present, it is not possible to evaluate how, if at all, the tanged Group I terret from Llyn Cerrig Bach is related to the knobbed terret type. Although the Ardoch, Corbridge, Maryport and Wilderspool tanged Group I terrets are all probably associated with northern Roman fort sites, only the Wilderspool terret has a definite, as opposed to a 'rudimentary', tang which can be closely paralleled to the Llyn Cerrig Bach example. The only other evidence for a definitely tanged, Group I terret is the mould fragment from Gussage All Saints. In addition, the only knobbed terret with a definite tang which is associated with a Roman fort site is the Kirkby Thore terret; all of the other knobbed terrets from fort sites have 'rudimentary' tangs. Consequently, although tanged terrets are in general a Romano-British phenomenon with military associations, the definitely tanged Group I terret from Llyn Cerrig Bach (No. 2) cannot necessarily be considered to be either of this date or association.

Pseudo-stitch decoration.

As well as the Group II terret (No. 3), two of the copper alloy plated three-link bridle-bits (Nos. 14 and 15) from the Llyn Cerrig Bach assemblage are embellished with pseudo-stitch decoration. The bridle-bits are discussed in Chapter 3, but pseudo-stitch decoration is reviewed here in order to assess its chronological significance.

Pseudo-stitch decoration is the term applied to a small repertoire of skeumorphic met-alworking motifs which imitate leatherwork. Two motifs are typical: a sinuous, frequently raised, line often set within a groove; and a line of punched dots adjacent to a continuous line. Both motifs are present on the terret (No. 3) and the raised, sinuous line occurs on the bridle-bits (Nos. 14 and 15). Fox included the sinuous, raised line motif within his grammar of British, early Celtic ornament (1958: 148–50, fig. 83.87), although he did not recognize its skeumorphic character. Instead he incorrectly considered it to have devel-oped from the necessity of joining copper alloy sheaths around the iron cores of objects such as the terret (No. 3) and the three-link bridle-bits (Nos. 14 and 15) from Llyn Cerrig Bach (Fox 1947a: 28, 37, 80). In fact, none of the artefacts are sheathed in copper alloy sheeting; the terret is a solid copper alloy casting and the iron bridle-bits are plated in copper alloy. The term pseudo-stitching was first coined by MacGregor who used it to define the sinuous line motif within her own grammar of ornament (1976: p. xviii). The stylistic relationship, if any, between this sinuous line motif and the zig-zag petal decora-tion which occurs on the Group II terrets of the Mill Plain type (Spratling 1972: 26–7, 388–9, nos. 25–6, fig. 6; 1979: 134; Cunliffe 1995: 33) and the wider, repoussé wavy ridge motif defined by Fox from the upper and lower roundels of the River Witham shield mount (1958: 150, fig. 83.88) is uncertain. Pseudo-stitch decoration occurs on a range of artefacts distributed throughout Britain and not just on types, such as harness gear, which would have been associated with stitched leatherwork when in use. Its skeumorphic character is arguably paralleled in artistic intent by chagrinage decoration, which occurs on both insular and Continental La Tène swords and scabbards, and which is assumed to represent a copy in metal of the surface of a leather scabbard (De Navarro 1972: 104–5; Stead 1984: 49).

A selection of examples of metalwork decorated with pseudo-stitch decoration is listed in Table 3. It occurs in association with pieces decorated in both Stead's Style IV (e.g. the River Witham shield mount) and Style V (e.g. the Mill Hill, Deal, scabbard plate) of insular La Tène art (the insular art sequence is discussed in Chapter 5). The dating evi-dence for these examples suggests that pseudo-stitch decoration remained in vogue from the fourth or third century BC until, at least, the middle of the first century AD. The demonstrably earliest example is the copper alloy openwork sheath of one of the daggers recovered from the River Thames at Hammersmith, London, which is an example of a La Tène I type dated to either the fourth or early third century BC (Jope 2000: 232). The one surviving iron twin suspension loop (Jope 2000: 21, pl. 25.d) indicates the Hammersmith sheath is an insular piece. The Mill Hill, Deal scabbard plate is part of the assemblage of a warrior burial considered to have an early La Tène II date, possibly c. 200 BC (Stead 1995: 64), however, the scabbard plate is associated with a La Tène I sword and to suggest a third-century BC date for the scabbard plate is not unreasonable. Another possibly early example of insular pseudo-stitch decoration is the King's Barrow, Arras bridle-bit, which may be as early as the fourth or third centuries BC (for a discussion of the dating of the East Yorkshire burial tradition see Stead 1991a: 184; Wait 1995: 499). Late examples of pseudo-stitch decoration include the Group I terret from Hod Hill, which is dated by

TABLE 3: A selection of examples of insular La Tène metalwork embellished with pseudo-stitch decoration

Artefact Type	Provenance	References
Terrets	Bury Hill, Hampshire (3)	Cunliffe 1995: 34, 38, fig. 16.3–5; Cunliffe and Poole 2000: 50, nos. 1.3–1.5, fig. 2.29
	Camerton, Somerset	R. Jackson 1990: 33, no. 57, pl. 5
	Hod Hill, Dorset	Richmond 1968: 39, fig. 31; Spratling 1972: 27, 383, no. 7, fig. 2
	Llyn Cerrig Bach, Anglesey	No. 3 (see catalogue entry for full bibliographical references)
Three-link bridle-bits	King's Barrow, Arras, East Yorkshire	Greenwell 1907: 281, fig. 22; Ward Perkins 1939: 179; Stead 1965a: 37, 89, fig. 18; 1979: 47, 98, fig. 15.1; Palk 1984: 25, no. DJ4, fig. C3
	Llyn Cerrig Bach, Anglesey (2)	Nos. 14 and 15 (see catalogue entries for full bibliographical references)
	Ulceby-on-Humber, Lincolnshire	Ward Perkins 1939: 181, fig. 6; Fox 1958: 35–6, fig. 21.b, pl. 24.c; Megaw 1970: 169–70, no. 293; Nicholson 1980: 14, no. 3, fig. 1; Palk 1984: 38–9, no. DJ37, fig. C21
Rein-ring fragment	Glastonbury lake village, Somerset	Bulleid and Gray 1911: 228, no. E194, pl. 44; Palk 1984: fig. C59.2; Coles and Minnitt 1995: 72
Rings	Bigberry Camp, Kent	Boyd Dawkins 1902: 216; Jessup 1932: 106; MacGregor 1976: 60; Thompson 1983: 274, no. 54
	Welwyn, Hertfordshire	Smith 1911–12a: 16–18, fig. 14; Birchall 1965: 305; Stead 1967: 50, 58
	Winchester, Hampshire	Smith 1911–12a: 16, fig. 15
Scabbard plates	Hammersmith, River Thames	Jope 1961a: 338, no. 26, pl. XXIII.C–E; Jope 2000: 232, pl. 25.f
	Mill Hill, Deal, Kent	Stead 1995: 59, fig. 15a, pl. VIII
Shield mount	River Witham, Lincolnshire	Jope 1971; Spratling 1972: 180–1, 538–9, no. 322, pl. 7a; Brailsford 1975b: 10–13, pl. II; Stead 1991b: 29
Bowl	Glastonbury lake village, Somerset	Bulleid and Gray 1911: 179–82, no. E19, fig. 40, pl. I; Spratling 1972: 228–9, 578, no. 401, fig. 182; Coles and Minnitt 1995: 56, 204
Torcs	New Cairnmuir, Peeblesshire	Wilson 1863a: 464, 496–7, fig. 104; Clarke 1954: 64, pl. XVII.1–2; Feachem 1957–8: 115, pl. XI.4; Megaw 1970: 168, no. 290; MacGregor 1976: 94–5, no. 191, pl. I.b
	Needwood Forest, Staffordshire	Ellis 1848–9; Leeds 1933b: 467, pl. XIII.2; Hawkes 1936–7: 64–5; Clarke 1954: 64–5; Fox 1958: 37, pl. 25
	Hoard E, Snettisham, Norfolk	Clarke 1954: 63–6, pls XV and XVI; Fox 1958: 45–8, figs. 33–4; Megaw 1970: 168–9, no. 291; Brailsford 1975b: 55–61, pls V–VII
	Hoard L, Snettisham, Norfolk	Stead 1991c: 454, pl. IX
Decorative mount (?)	Glastonbury lake village, Somerset	Bulleid and Gray 1911: 236, no. E146, pl. 43; Coles and Minnitt 1995: 36
Brooches	Maiden Castle, Dorset	Wheeler 1943: 258, fig. 83.15
	Verulamium, Hertfordshire	Wheeler and Wheeler 1936: 207, fig. 44.20

associated pottery to the first century AD (Richmond 1968: 39), the Camerton terret, which dates to around the mid first century AD (R. Jackson 1990: 18–23), the brooch from Maiden Castle, which was recovered from a level dated *c.* AD 25–70 (Wheeler 1943: 258) and the brooch from Verulamium that was sealed by an occupation layer dated *c.* AD 50–75 (Wheeler and Wheeler 1936: 207). As consequence of its long vogue, pseudo-stitch decoration does not provide a close date for the Llyn Cerrig Bach Group II terret (No. 3), or for any other artefact it occurs on.

Summary

The three terrets in the Llyn Cerrig Bach assemblage are examples of the Group I: simple form (Nos. 1–2) and Group II: thick ringed types (No. 3). The validity of these classificatory types is problematic and they are not closely datable. Parallels suggest that the Group I type possibly dates from the fourth or third century BC to some point during the Roman period, although its floruit cannot be extended beyond the early second century AD with certainty; the vogue of the Group II terrets may also extend from the third century BC to the first or second century AD. Critical examination of Cunliffe's Gussage-Bury Hill tradition of copper alloy horse furniture and vehicle fittings suggests it is of limited stylistic or chronological validity. Analysis of other criteria specific to the Llyn Cerrig Bach terrets, such as the presence of a tang (No. 2) or pseudo-stitch decoration (No. 3), also fails to provide closer dating.

Nave hoops

Nave hoops are bindings set around the wooden naves of vehicles to prevent them from splitting. The nave, or hub, forms the centre of the wheel and accommodates the axle which passes through it. Without a relatively wide nave the wheel of the vehicle would wobble on the axle and fail to remain constantly vertical. Evidence from vehicle burials, in both Yorkshire and on the Continent, suggests that during the late Iron Age each wheel was bound with two nave hoops; one on either side of the spokes (Stead 1965a: 31; 1979: 44; 1981: 15, fig. 1). There are four copper alloy (Nos. 4–7) and seven iron nave hoops, including two unpublished hoops at Oriel Ynys Môn, Llangefni, Anglesey and not known to Fox, in the Llyn Cerrig Bach assemblage (Fox 1947a: 13, 15, 76, 95, nos. 39–40, 125–7, pls IV, XV, XIX; Lynch 1970: 259, fig. 85.39; Savory 1976a: 57, 59, nos. 17.39–40, 18.5–7, figs. 13.5, 16.1–2). The two iron hoops at Oriel Ynys Môn are presumably those noted by Lynch as being found by Mr W. O. Roberts of Rhosneigr between Llyn Cerrig Bach and the sea (1970: 259, fn. 122). Four of the iron hoops are broad, flat bands (Fox 1947a: 15, 76, 95, nos. 40, 125–7, pls IV, XIX; Savory 1976a: 57, 59, nos. 17.40, 18.5–7, figs. 16.1–2) while three, including the two at Oriel Ynys Môn, are narrower and D-shaped in section (Fox 1947a: 13, 76, no. 39, pl. XV; Lynch 1970: 259, fig. 85.39, fn. 122; Savory 1976a: 57, no. 17.39, fig. 13.5). The copper alloy nave hoops are described in the catalogue;

additional comments on their form, manufacture and function are made below. A detailed consideration of the iron hoops falls outside the parameters of the present study, but they are referred to where this is pertinent to the discussion of the copper alloy hoops.

Nave hoops of the British Iron Age

The nave hoops of the British Iron Age are made of either copper alloy or iron. No Irish examples have been recognized (for a discussion of Irish vehicle fittings see Raftery 1984: 57–61; 1994: 104–10), but there is a wide range of Continental La Tène material which matches the British copper alloy and iron nave hoops (Piggott 1983: 223, 225) (for a discussion of the Continental evidence see: Stead 1965a: 9–18, 32, 96–101; 1979: 24–9, 44; Piggott 1983: 213–14).

The British copper alloy hoops can be divided into three types: those which are flat (Group I), those with a single, central cordon (Group II) and those with a double cordon (Group III) (see Table 4). Within these three types the copper alloy hoops are relatively uniform, although important differences do exist between individual examples. The hoops from the King's Barrow, Arras, do not fit into any of the three classificatory groups, being simple sheaths of copper alloy sheet folded round iron bands. Double cordoned hoops are not paralleled on the Continent (contra Piggott 1983: 223), but there are examples from France of the single cordoned type (Spratling 1972: 82). The copper alloy nave hoops from Llyn Cerrig Bach include one example of the single cordoned type (No. 7) and three examples of the double cordoned type (Nos. 4–6). The internal diameters of the copper alloy nave hoops range in size from 114–29 mm (Llyn Cerrig Bach: No. 4) to 140–5 mm (Santon: Spratling 1972: 82, 443, 619, no. 147). Within this range the hoops from Llyn Cerrig Bach are relatively small, however, examples from the King's Barrow and Lady's Barrow, Arras, Read's Cavern and Garton Slack (internal diameters 125–30, 119–32, 124 and 125–30 mm respectively) are of comparable size. There is no significant relationship between the relative size of the hoops and whether they are flat, or have a single or double cordon. The nave hoops from the Lady's and King's Barrows at Arras, East Yorkshire, are composite fittings which consist of a functional iron component covered by a presumably decorative copper alloy band. The four circular or oval sectioned iron hoops from the Lady's Barrow are covered by the single, central cordon of wider, flanged copper alloy bands; while, as noted above, the surviving fragments of two iron hoops of D-shaped section from the King's Barrow are covered by copper alloy sheeting which is simply folded round the inner, iron band.

In addition to those from Llyn Cerrig Bach, the iron nave hoops of the British Iron Age include: a fragmented example of D-shaped section from the Charioteer's Barrow, Arras, East Yorkshire (Greenwell 1907: 282; Stead 1965a: 32, 90, 113; Spratling 1972: 619; Stead 1979: 40, 44, 98, fig. 11.3); three or four badly corroded hoops, of which only two survive, from Beverley, East Yorkshire (Greenwell 1877: 456; 1907: 278; Stead 1965a: 32, 91, 113, fig. 14.4; Spratling 1972: 619; Stead 1979: 40, 44, 98, fig. 11.4); four bands, one in good condition, the other three fragmentary, from burial no. 43 at Danes' Graves, East

TABLE 4: Copper alloy nave hoops

Group	Provenance	References
I	Polden Hill, Somerset	Spratling 1972: 82, 443, 619, no. 144; Brailsford 1975a: 232, no. 11
	Santon, Norfolk (4)	Smith 1909a: 152–3; Fox 1923: 104; Clarke 1939: 69; Fox 1947a: 76; Spratling 1972: 82, 443, 619, no. 147
II	Lady's Barrow, Arras, East Yorkshire (4)	Greenwell 1907: 284–5; Stead 1965a: 91; 1979: 40, fig. 11.1
	Cawthorn Camps, North Yorkshire	Mortimer 1905: 361; Stead 1965a: 32, 92, 113, fig. 14.2; 1979: 40, 44, 99, fig. 11.5
	Garton Slack, East Yorkshire (3)	Brewster 1971: 291, pl. XIII.b; Stead 1979: 41, 44, 102, pl. 3.b
	Kirkburn, East Yorkshire (4)	Stead 1991a: 42, fig. 35.3–4
	Llyn Cerrig Bach, Anglesey	No. 7 (see catalogue entry for full bibliographical references)
	Santon, Norfolk	Smith 1909a: 152–3; Fox 1923: 104; Clarke 1939: 69; Fox 1947a: 76; Spratling 1972: 82, 443, 619, no. 145, fig. 50
	Wetwang (burial 2), East Yorkshire (4)	Dent 1985: 88, fig. 3
III	Llyn Cerrig Bach, Anglesey (3)	Nos. 4–6 (see catalogue entries for full bibliographical references)
	Read's Cavern, Somerset (4)	Palmer 1922: 13–14, pl. IX; Corcoran 1956: 49–50; Fox 1947a: 76–7; Spratling 1972: 82–3, 444, 619, no. 148
	Santon, Norfolk	Smith 1909a: 152–3; Fox 1923: 104; Clarke 1939: 69; Fox 1947a: 76; Spratling 1972: 82, 443, 619, no. 146, fig. 50
Misc.	King's Barrow, Arras, East Yorkshire (2)	Greenwell 1907: 279–80; Stead 1965a: 32, 89, 113, fig. 14.3; Spratling 1972: 619; Stead 1979: 40, 44, 98, fig. 11.2

Yorkshire (Mortimer 1897–9: 123, nos. 14 and 17; 1905: 359, fig. 1021; Greenwell 1907: 277; Stead 1965a: 32, 92–3, 112, fig. 2; Spratling 1972: 619; Stead 1979: 40–1, 44, 100, fig. 11.6–7); one from Garton Slack, East Yorkshire, which is D-shaped in section (Brewster 1971: 291, pl. XIII.b; Stead 1979: 41, 44, 102, pl. 3.b; 1991a: 41); four from Garton Station, East Yorkshire which are D-shaped in section (Stead 1991a: 41, fig. 33); an unrecorded number from Hunmanby, East Yorkshire (Sheppard 1907: 482–3, 485; Stead 1965a: 94; Stead 1979: 44, 102); an unrecorded number from Hunsbury, Northamptonshire (Fell 1936: 67, no. 16, pl. IV.b.5; Spratling 1972: 83–4); a pair of hoops of uncertain form from Newbridge, Mid Lothian (Carter and Hunter 2003: 532); two hoops of slightly curved section from Pexton Moor, North Yorkshire (Stead 1959: 215, pl. XXI.c; 1965a: 32, 96, 112, fig. 14.5; 1979: 41, 44, 103, fig. 11.8); four from cart burial no. 1 at Wetwang, East Yorkshire, which are D-shaped in section (Dent 1985: 88, fig. 2; Stead 1985a: 58, pl. 80; Stead 1991a: 41); two possible examples with a single cordon from Stanwick, North Yorkshire (MacGregor 1962: 33, 52, nos. 138–9, fig. 15); and four from cart burial no. 3 at Wetwang, East Yorkshire which are D-shaped in section (Dent 1985: 90, fig. 4; Stead 1991a: 41).

The copper alloy nave hoops from Llyn Cerrig Bach

All four copper alloy hoops from Llyn Cerrig Bach are badly damaged. It is uncertain how much of this damage is ancient and how much was caused during the process of peat extraction. All four hoops are distorted and contain several lateral and transverse splits. In particular, one of the hoops (No. 6) was badly buckled and has been repaired and strengthened by the application of four modern solder joins. The degree to which the hoops have been reshaped subsequent to their discovery is uncertain. Fox records that two of the hoops (Nos. 6 and 7) were restored in the British Museum laboratory (1947a: 76). Herbert Maryon, who worked at the British Museum Laboratory from 1945 onwards, commented on the decorated flanges of the other two hoops (Nos. 4 and 5) (Fox 1947a: 13) suggesting that they were also restored at the British Museum. Conservation practice during this period was more concerned with restoring artefacts to their past form than with preserving them as found. The copper alloy hoops were apparently 'reshaped' in the British Museum laboratory; presumably this involved annealing and cold working of the hoops. The cordons of two of the hoops are pocked with small dents (Nos. 4 and 5) which were interpreted by Fox as being ancient (1947a: 13). Certainly, these small dents are unlikely to have been caused during peat extraction. If they are ancient, it is not clear whether they resulted through use, as Fox thought (1947a: 13), or were the result of deliberate damage prior to deposition. The only definite example of ancient damage is the small, transverse split in one of the hoops (No. 6) which was repaired in antiquity by a, now incomplete, copper alloy sheet patch (approximately 11 x 7 mm). The patch was placed on the inside of the hoop and fixed across the split by two copper alloy rivets which were hammered flush with the inside of the hoop. The split runs across a small fixing hole, but it is uncertain whether the fixing hole was the cause of the split or an earlier, aborted attempt at repair. If the fixing hole is an original feature then its purpose is not obvious. The patch is closely paralleled by an iron example on one of the Kirkburn hoops which is also riveted, set on the inside of the hoop and across a transverse split (Stead 1991a: 42, fig. 35.4). The cause of these small, transverse splits is uncertain, but they may be associated with the fitting of the hoops on to the nave. Metallurgical analysis of the example from Llyn Cerrig Bach (see Appendix 2) indicates that both the loop (11.92% Sn, 0.05% Zn, 0.64% Fe, and only traces of other elements) and the patch (12.09% Sn, 0.07% Zn, 0.49% Fe, 0.03% Ag and only traces of other elements) were made from the same alloy. This suggests that the patch was made at the same time as the hoop and strengthens the argument that it was required as a result of damage which occurred during the botched fitting of the hoop.

Two of the hoops (Nos. 6 and 7) are slightly tapered across their breadth. The circumference of one hoop (No. 7) is approximately 385–90 mm on one side and approximately 390–5 mm on the other, while the circumference of the other hoop (No. 6) is approximately 395–400 mm on one side and approximately 400–5 mm on the other. It is uncertain whether this tapering is real or simply a result of the damage and distortion suffered by the hoops. If the tapering is genuine then it presumably reflects the shape of the wooden nave on to which the hoops were fitted. Slight tapering across the width has also been recognized on one of the flat, iron hoops from Llyn Cerrig Bach (Fox 1947a: 95, no. 125, pls IV, XIX; Savory 1976a: 59, no. 18.5, fig. 16.1) and the four plain copper alloy hoops from Santon (Smith 1909a: 152; Spratling 1972: 443, no. 147).

Three of the copper alloy hoops from Llyn Cerrig Bach are decorated. The cordon and flanges of the single cordoned hoop (No. 7) are embellished with incised lines; and both the inner and outer flanges of two of the double cordoned hoops (Nos. 4 and 5) are embellished with apparently punched, transverse parallel lines (approximately 1.5 mm in length) which are bordered on the flange edges with a continuous, longitudinal, incised groove. It is not clear whether these transverse parallel lines were applied before or after the longitudinal groove. Herbert Maryon suggested that they may have been knurled with a toothed wheel (Fox 1947a: 13; Savory 1976a: 57), but this is not likely. The spacing between the lines is irregular, suggesting they were applied with a punch. This form of decoration is paralleled on the double cordoned hoop from Santon which has a punched, herring-bone, pattern on the edges of its flanges (Spratling 1972: no. 146, fig. 50). One of the double cordoned hoops (No. 4) also contains regular narrow grooves on the inner sides of its cordons.

X-radiographic examination of one of the double cordoned hoops (No. 6) suggests that an approximately cruciform mark may have been punched on to one of its cordons in antiquity (Pl. 5; National Museum Wales X-Ray No. 1567; S. Stevenson pers. comm.). Although chemical cleaning of the hoop makes identification uncertain, microscopic study suggests that the mark is made up of several small corrosion pits. The frequent occurrence over large parts of the hoop's surface of corrosion pits suggests that the cruciform shape may be purely fortuitous, but any stamping of the hoop with a mark would increase the potential of that part of the hoop to corrode and therefore the apparently fortuitous arrangement of corrosion pits may reflect the presence and form of a deliberate mark made in antiquity (S. Stevenson pers. comm.). If genuine the mark is difficult to interpret; it would have been too small to have formed a meaningful decorative motif suggesting it was either a maker's mark or possibly an apotropaic device.

The similarity between the single cordoned hoop from Llyn Cerrig Bach (No. 7) and the three copper alloy bands around the Pentaun, Cornwall, tankard (Hencken 1932: 110, 166, 292, fig. 30; Corcoran 1952: 86, 90, 92–3, no. 1, pl. IX.1; Spratling 1972: 82–3, 207–8, 212–13, 216–17, 566, no. 370; Penhallurick 1986: 180–1; Earwood 1993: 73, 285) has led to the suggestion that the Llyn Cerrig Bach hoop may be a tankard binding (Corcoran

1956: 49; Spratling 1972: 83). Although it is not possible to resolve this issue with certainty, the hoop is unlikely to be a tankard binding because of its size. The Pentaun tankard is distorted, but its diameter varies between 153 mm and 183 mm (Spratling 1972: 566). There are only two other complete British Iron Age tankards: a cylindrical example, presumed to be from the River Thames at Kew, whose diameter varies from 172 mm to 178 mm (Smith 1917–18: 17–18, 22–3, fig. 23; Corcoran 1952: 86, 90, 93, 98, no. 6, pl. XIII; Spratling 1972: 207, 210, 212–13, 216, 565–6, no. 369; Earwood 1993: 72–3, 175–7, 277, figs. 46.2 and 111) and a waisted example from Trawsfynydd, Merionethshire (Corcoran 1952: 85–8, 92–4, 97–8, no. 5, fig. 1.a–b, pl. XII; Megaw 1970: 171, no. 296; Spratling 1972: 207, 211–13, 568–9, no. 378; Savory 1976a: 41, pl. V.b; Nicholson 1980: 34–5, no. 53, fig. 11; Earwood 1993: 73, 175–6, 289) whose diameter ranges from 162 mm to 185 mm. The diameters of the three tankards are all greater than that of the single cordoned hoop from Llyn Cerrig Bach (No. 7; diameter 120–31 mm). There are several examples of single cordoned copper alloy hoops, such as the Kirkburn, Garton Slack and Lady's Barrow, Arras, examples (internal diameters approximately 130, 125–30 and 119–32 mm respectively), whose context demonstrates that they are nave bindings and whose size is closer to the Llyn Cerrig Bach hoop than the bindings of the Pentaun tankard. This evidence suggests that the Llyn Cerrig Bach hoop is also a nave binding. In addition, it should be noted that Spratling has effectively refuted (1972: 83) Tratman's suggestion (Corcoran 1956: 49–50) that the double cordoned nave hoops from Read's Cavern are also tankard bindings.

The most distinguishing feature of the copper alloy hoops from Llyn Cerrig Bach are the raised cordons, or ridges, which run round their circumference. Three of the hoops (Nos. 4–6) have double cordons and the other (No. 7) has a single cordon. The purpose of these cordons is linked to the questions of whether the hoops were decorative covers or functional nave bands, and how they were manufactured and fitted. Evaluation of these questions is facilitated by comparing the Llyn Cerrig Bach hoops with the other copper alloy nave hoops of the British Iron Age. It has been argued, by analogy with the nave hoops recovered from Arras, that rather than being nave hoops proper, the copper alloy hoops from Llyn Cerrig Bach are decorative covers whose raised cordons fitted over iron bands which acted as true nave bindings (Fox 1947a: 13–14; Corcoran 1956: 50; Lynch 1970: 259; Spratling 1972: 83), the type of iron band concerned being narrow and D-shaped in section. There are three examples of this type from Llyn Cerrig Bach, including the two held at Oriel Ynys Môn (Fox 1947a: 13, 76, no. 39, pl. XV; Lynch 1970: 259, fig. 85.39, fn.122; Savory 1976a: 57, no. 17.39, fig. 13.5). That copper alloy nave hoops need not necessarily be reinforced by iron bands is demonstrated by the Garton Slack and Kirkburn vehicle burials where *in situ* copper alloy hoops have been recovered without associated iron bands (Stead 1979: 44; 1991a: 42). Furthermore, the argument that the Llyn Cerrig Bach copper alloy hoops were only decorative covers fitted over iron nave bands is demonstrably incorrect.

Comparison of the dimensions of the copper alloy and narrow iron hoops of D-shaped section from Llyn Cerrig Bach demonstrates that none of them could have been paired together. It is not possible to measure precisely the diameters of the copper alloy hoops because of their damaged condition, but they range from 114 to 129 mm (No. 4), 120 to 126 mm (No. 5), 120 to 131 mm (No. 7) and 115 to 139 mm (No. 6) in internal diameter. In comparison the internal diameters of the iron, D-shaped sectioned bands are 112 mm (Fox 1947a: 76, no. 39, pl. XV; Lynch 1970: 259, fig. 85.39; Savory 1976a: 57, no. 17.39, fig. 13.5) and 129 and 132 mm for the two hoops at Oriel Ynys Môn. These measurements suggest that the iron band known to Fox (Fox 1947a: 76, no. 39, pl. XV; Lynch 1970: 259, fig. 85.39; Savory 1976a: 57, no. 17.39, fig. 13.5) was too small to be matched with any of the copper alloy hoops, but that the two hoops at Oriel Ynys Môn could have been fitted underneath three of the copper alloy hoops (i.e. Nos. 4, 6 and 7). The two iron bands at Oriel Ynys Môn are, however, too large, projecting outwards 6.5 and 7 mm respectively, to have fitted under the cordons of any of the copper alloy hoops which are variously raised by 5 mm (Nos. 5 and 6), 5.5 mm (No. 7) and 6 mm (No. 4). Although it is demonstrable that the known, copper alloy hoops and D-sectioned iron bands from Llyn Cerrig Bach were not actually paired together in antiquity this does not in itself disprove that the copper alloy hoops were decorative covers for more closely fitting, narrow, D-sectioned, iron bands, but study of how they were manufactured does.

Examination of the copper alloy nave hoops of the British Iron Age suggests two methods were used in their manufacture. They were either cast as loops and then shaped by secondary cold working or they were wrought in sheet form and then fitted round the nave and closed with an overlapped riveted join. The nave hoops from Read's Cavern are now badly damaged (Fox 1947a: 77; Spratling 1972: 444, no. 148), but an early account notes that one had a soldered joint which was interpreted as an ancient repair (Palmer 1922: 14). The published plate (Palmer 1922: pl. IX) apparently shows a soldered joint in one of the hoops while the other hoops contain neither riveted or soldered joins. Unfortunately, the quality of the plate is poor and whether the possible soldered join was a secondary repair or an original feature of the hoop, as well as the character of the remaining hoops, is impossible to assess. The hoops from Cawthorn Camps, Garton Slack, Wetwang, and the King's Barrow, Arras, are either too incomplete or not published in sufficient detail to identify with confidence their method of manufacture. The nave hoops from the Lady's Barrow, Arras, and Kirkburn were shaped from copper alloy sheet and had overlapping joins which were secured by copper alloy nails hammered through the join and into the nave (Greenwell 1907: 284–5, fig. 28; Stead 1979: 40, fig. 11.1; 1991a: 42, fig. 35.3–4). In contrast to this arrangement are the examples from the Polden Hill and Santon hoards which have no observable riveted or brazed joins and are thicker on their outer edges than they are in the centre (Spratling 1972: 443, nos. 144–7). Spratling, not unreasonably, considered these to have been initially cast as narrower and thicker rings which were subsequently cold worked into their finished form, the variations in their thickness being a result of this secondary cold working (1972: 82). The hoops from Llyn Cerrig Bach were manufactured in the same way. X-radiographic examination (National Museum Wales X-Ray nos. 1570–8) indicates that they were cast into their hoop form rather than being wrought and then joined to form a hoop (contra Fox 1947a: 13). The casting of the hoops is an artistic and technical *tour de force*; to either model a hoop in wax, presumably around a core of clay, and then successfully build a mould round them or produce a mould from a wooden pattern would have required considerable technical expertise. Despite being cast into a circular form the Llyn Cerrig Bach hoops would have still required some cold working to finish them. The amount of secondary, cold working that would have been required is uncertain, although it would be technically easier to cast relatively thick, but narrow, hoops and then subject them to a considerable amount of cold working to produce the cordons.

The two types of copper alloy hoop would have been fitted on to the nave using different methods. The wrought and overlapped hoops were presumably cold worked into long, curved strips which were fitted around the nave and hammered closed and into place through the overlapping join formed by both ends of the strip. In the case of the hoops from Lady's Barrow the strip was fixed over an iron band which had previously been fitted on to the wheel. The iron band would have been fitted when hot and then shrunk-on, by cooling, to form a tight fit (for anecdotal accounts of this technique see Sturt 1923: 117–28; Jenkins 1961: 66, 75–7, pl. 16). In contrast, the copper alloy hoops which were first cast and then cold worked into their finished form must have been fitted by pushing them on to the naves until they formed a tight fit. The hoops would have had to have been manufactured to exactly the correct size. Tapering of both hoops and the ends of naves, as Smith suggested (1909a: 152), would have made this operation easier. Only three finished naves are known from the British Iron Age: two from the Glastonbury lake village, Somerset (Bulleid and Gray 1911: 328, 337–40, nos. X43 and X63, figs. 99 and 112; Earwood 1988: 89; Coles and Minnitt 1995: 72, 86, nos. X43 and X63) and one from Holme Pierrepont, Nottinghamshire (MacCormick 1969: 23–4, fig. 5; Musty and MacCormick 1973). The ends of the naves, where the hoops would have been fitted, are straight on the examples from the Glastonbury lake village (Bulleid and Gray 1911: figs. 99 and 112), but slightly tapered on the example from Holme Pierrepont (MacCormick 1969: fig. 5). At least one of the Glastonbury examples had a charred surface, suggesting that it had been fitted with a shrunk-on iron band (Bulleid and Gray 1911: 328, no. X43) and, therefore, that a tapered form to facilitate the fitting of a cast, copper alloy hoop was not necessary. By having slightly tapered nave ends it would have been easier to fit a closed hoop on to the Holme Pierrepont wheel. As previously noted, two of the closed hoops from Llyn Cerrig Bach (Nos. 6 and 7) and four of the closed hoops from Santon (Smith 1909a: 152; Spratling 1972: 443, no. 147) are tapered across their widths, presumably to aid fitting. Fitting closed hoops would have been difficult even if they were tapered. If they were not perfectly circular, or too much force was used in fitting them, then they would split. It is possible that the patched repairs, noted above, on one of the Llyn Cerrig Bach hoops (No. 6) and one of the Kirkburn hoops (Stead 1991a: 42, fig. 35.4) may have been required as a result of a botched fitting.

It would not be possible to force a close-fitting copper alloy hoop over a previously fitted, narrow, iron band of D-shaped section and have it form a tight fit with the nave. If decorative copper alloy hoops were to be fitted over iron bands then it would be necessary for them to be wrought into a cordoned strip, curved around the iron band already fitted on to the nave, and then joined either by riveting or soldering. It is notable that the only cordoned copper alloy nave hoops associated with underlying iron bands, those from the Lady's Barrow, Arras, have overlapping riveted joins, while none of the continuous cast copper alloy hoops, that is, those from the Llyn Cerrig Bach (Nos. 4–7), Santon and Polden Hill assemblages, are associated with underlying iron bands. This suggests that the copper alloy hoops from Llyn Cerrig Bach did not function as decorative covers for iron hoops (contra Fox 1947a: 13–14; Corcoran 1956: 50; Lynch 1970: 259; Spratling 1972: 83) and that their cordons were decorative elements which mimicked the form of wrought copper alloy bands, such as those from the Lady's Barrow, Arras, which were nailed in place over previously fitted iron bands.

Whether the copper alloy nave hoops from Llyn Cerrig Bach were purely decorative or were strong enough to have functioned as nave hoops is uncertain. Certainly, not all of the overlapped copper alloy nave hoops were necessarily non-functional decorative covers fitted over iron bands. For example, there is no evidence of an associated iron band for the examples of the type from Kirkburn (Stead 1991a: 42, fig. 35.3–4). This suggests that copper alloy hoops were used as functional nave hoops (contra Greenwell 1877: 455; Fox 1947a: 14; Lynch 1970: 259), although the fact that one of the copper alloy hoops from Garton Slack had been replaced with an iron band, presumably after it broke (Stead 1979: 44), indicates that, in general, copper alloy hoops were not as strong as iron hoops.

Dating

More than for any other type of horse furniture or vehicle fitting, the dating of the British nave hoops is dominated by the burial evidence from East Yorkshire. As previously noted, the East Yorkshire vehicle burial tradition, which includes the Arras, Beverley, Cawthorn Camps, Danes' Graves, Garton Slack, Garton Station, Hunmanby, Kirkburn, Pexton Moor and Wetwang nave hoops, probably started at some point in the fourth to third centuries BC and apparently ended before the mid first century BC (Stead 1991a: 184; Wait 1995: 499). As noted above, the Polden Hill hoard, which contains three fragments presumably from a single, plain and undecorated copper alloy hoop, is dated on the strength of three brooches to the third quarter of the first century AD (J. Webster pers. comm.). The hoops from Read's Cavern, Burrington, Somerset, were found together in one of the lower chambers of the cave (Palmer 1922: 13). All of the finds from the cave were recovered from either a single layer or its surface (Palmer 1922: 12). This material included pottery similar to that found at the Glastonbury lake village (Palmer 1922: 14; Spratling 1972: 444) suggesting the sites are probably, but not certainly, coeval and that the Read's Cavern hoops probably date from some point between the mid third and the mid first centuries BC. The Santon hoard, which includes six copper alloy nave hoops associated with a range of both Iron Age and Roman types, is dated on the evidence of brooches included in the hoard to the third quarter of the first century AD (Manning 1972: 232; Spratling 1975: 207). The Stanwick hoard, which contains two iron nave hoops, is approximately dated to the mid first century AD (Fitts *et al.* 1999: 48). The Hunsbury nave hoops are chance finds

33

made during the nineteenth century during quarrying of the hillfort and, as noted above, they probably date to the site's main phase of occupation between the second to first centuries BC (D. Jackson 1993–4: 18).

The survey of the archaeological contexts and associations of the nave hoops suggests a range in date from the third, if not fourth, century BC to at least the mid first century AD. That nave hoops would have been used prior to this period is certain and the third or fourth century BC date may reflect a change in ancient depositional practices rather than the inception of the late Iron Age types discussed. At present it is not possible to distinguish narrower date ranges for the various subtypes of copper alloy nave hoops discussed above. The closest parallels to the Llyn Cerrig Bach nave hoops are some of the examples from the Santon hoard and Read's Cavern. They suggest only an imprecise, late Iron Age to early Roman vogue for the Llyn Cerrig Bach hoops.

Summary

Examination of the copper alloy nave hoops from the Llyn Cerrig Bach assemblage, coupled with study of the other nave hoops of the British Iron Age, suggests that they were cast as hoops, finished by secondary, cold working and that they were not fitted over iron bands as has been previously suggested. Therefore, rather than being decorative covers, the Llyn Cerrig Bach hoops probably functioned as practical bindings. Close dating is not possible and only a general date range from the late Iron Age to the early Roman period is suggested for the nave hoops.

'Vase-headed' linch-pin

There are two linch-pins from the assemblage: one an iron, ring-headed example (Fox 1947a: 19–20, 61, 78, no. 43, pls II and XXXVIII; Lynch 1970: 259, fig. 85; Savory 1976a: 57, no. 17.43, fig. 29.2) and the other of the distinctive 'vase-headed' type that has a wrought iron shank and cast, copper alloy terminals (No. 8). The 'vase-headed' linch-pin is discussed below, but consideration of the ring-headed example falls outside the parameters of the present study. Linch-pins function as pegs which keep a vehicle's wheel in place upon its non-rotating axle. During the British Iron Age, they are presumed to have passed vertically through a perforation in the axle which was set adjacent to the nave of the wheel (for various reconstructions see: Fox 1947a: 25–7, fig. 13; Spratling 1972: fig. 41; Stead 1985a: fig. 79; Furger-Gunti 1991: 358; Raftery 1994: 105, fig. 55). British Iron Age linch-pins were first classified by Ward Perkins (1939: 191–2; 1940; 1941) and have subsequently been discussed by Spratling (1972: 55–66, 423–9, 618–20, nos. 106–18, figs. 38–43), MacGregor (1976: 48–50, 73–6, nos. 128–35) and Stead (1965a: 32–5; 1979: 45–7; 1991a: 44–7).

The 'vase-headed' linch-pin (No. 8) is described in the catalogue. A few remarks about the piece and its manufacture are made here before the type is defined and the example from Llyn Cerrig Bach is considered within its wider typological context.

As previously noted (Fox 1947a: 19) there are several wear facets visible on the linch-pin which suggest it was used prior to its deposition. There are two facets on almost diametrically opposed positions around the upper, flat-headed pedestal element of the upper terminal. A smaller facet also occurs in the same plane as one of the two opposed facets towards the base of the upper terminal. The lower terminal contains two, again almost diametrically opposed, facets which are in the same plane and correspond exactly with those on the upper terminal. A possible wear facet also occurs on the curved back of the lower terminal. With the exception of this last possible facet, the wear on the linch-pin was probably caused by the nave rubbing against the terminals as it revolved (see Spratling 1972: fig. 41 for an analogous reconstruction). That the wear facets occur in two distinct and diametrically opposed planes suggest that at some point in its working life the pin was taken out of the axle and then replaced the opposite way round. Similar wear patterns have been recognized on the 'vase-headed' linch-pins from Beechamwell, Owslebury, Weeting and Wigginton Common as well as the unprovenanced example in the Ashmolean Museum (Spratling 1972: no. 116) and the possible example from Traprain Law, East Lothian (for bibliographical references see Table 5). Uniquely, the upper terminal of the unprovenanced example in Saffron Walden Museum was cast with a D-shaped section, presumably to avoid the unnecessary wastage of metal which results from these patterns of wear (Spratling 1972: 59).

The upper terminal of the Llyn Cerrig Bach linch-pin is decorated by three circum-scribing grooves and two shorter grooves which form a simple triangular design on one side of the terminal. Presumably, the side that the design occurs on was originally intended to face outwards. The wear patterns discussed above suggest that at some point in the linch-pin's working life it was turned round, which would have concealed the design. The grooves which make up the design are all apparently cast features. Decorative trian-gular panels, often more elaborate than this example, are a common motif on insular metalwork in general and 'vase-headed' linch-pins in particular; for example, a similar panel, albeit inverted and infilled with hatched decoration and three hemi-spherical beads, is present on the Wigginton Common 'vase-headed' linch-pin (Ward Perkins 1941: 65, pl. XI; Spratling 1972: no. 115, fig. 42) and several mould fragments of upper terminals of 'vase-headed' linch-pins from Gussage All Saints, Dorset, also contained triangular panels of ornament (Wainwright and Spratling 1973: 122).

A series of striations are visible on the curved back of the lower terminal of the Llyn Cerrig Bach linch-pin. These are deliberate decorative features, rather than a wear phe-nomenon, although whether they were cast or incised following casting is unclear. The lower terminal is turned through a right angle to form a shape arguably reminiscent of an upturned horse's hoof and fetlock (Spratling 1972: 427). With the exception of one of the Bigberry Camp (Jessup 1932: 106, pl. I.b.left; Spratling 1972: no. 110; Thompson 1983: no. 38) and the Old Down Farm examples, the lower terminals of the 'vase-headed' linch-pins, where they survive, are all generally of this form and the comparison between them and horses' hooves and fetlocks has been frequently made (for example, Greenwell 1907: 280; Spratling 1972: 58; Owen 1993: 68). It is possible that the striations on the Llyn Cerrig

Bach example are intended to represent the hair on a horse's leg furthering the zoomorphic character of the terminal. The 'fetlock and hoof' interpretation of the usual form of the lower terminals of 'vase-headed' linch-pins is, however, problematic. The lower terminals of several examples of the type are quite distended in comparison with the example from Llyn Cerrig Bach and their resemblance to a horse's hoof and fetlock is slight. Consequently, it is possible that any zoomorphic character may be unintended and simply coincidental.

Manufacture

It is not certain how the 'vase-headed' linch-pin from Llyn Cerrig Bach was manufactured, although the iron shank was wrought and, by analogy with mould fragments of 'vase-headed' linch-pin terminals from Gussage All Saints, Dorset (Wainwright and Spratling 1973: 122; Spratling 1979: 140; Foster 1980: 18, pls 17–18), the copper alloy terminals were cast using the lost-wax, or *cire perdue*, method. To understand fully how the linch-pin was manufactured it is necessary to appreciate how it functioned. With reference to the Kirkburn, East Yorkshire examples, Stead has argued that the square-sectioned iron shank was designed to fit tightly into the perforation through the axle, and that consequently, only one terminal could have been cast directly on to the shank and the other must have been fixed in such a way as to allow it, and by extension the linch-pin and the wheel, to be easily removed (1991a: 46–7). There is no indication in the discussions of the Gussage All Saints mould fragments which, if any, of the linch-pin terminals were cast directly on to the iron shanks (cf. Wainwright and Spratling 1973: 122; Spratling 1979: 140; Foster 1980: 18, pls 17–18). X-radiography of one of the Kirkburn 'vase-headed' linch-pins suggests that the foot of its iron shank, though straight, tapers, suggesting its lower terminal was slotted-on and detachable (Stead 1991a: 47, fig. 38.3–4). X-radiography of the Llyn Cerrig Bach example, however, suggests this arrangement was not necessarily universal for, though tapered, the foot of the iron shank also curves with the shape of the lower terminal and extends close to the end of the terminal rendering it probably unsuitable for slotting-on and detaching in the manner suggested by Stead (Plate 5; National Museum Wales X-Ray nos. 1260, 1261, 1263 and 1579). The X-radiographic evidence is less clear about the relationship between the upper terminal and the iron shank of the Llyn Cerrig Bach linch-pin; it suggests that the shank is split into at least two, if not four, short tangs which curve around the horizontal perforation through the upper terminal. Again, it is not obvious how such an arrangement could be compatible with a requirement for easy removal of the upper terminal. Although Stead's argument that one of the terminals of a 'vase-headed' linch-pin must be detachable is apparently reasonable, it is uncertain that either of the terminals of the Llyn Cerrig Bach example was detachable. If both of the Llyn Cerrig Bach terminals were fixed by being cast directly on to the iron shank, it is difficult to envisage how the linch-pin could have functioned if it was passed through a vertical perforation in the axle. In a recent experimental reconstruction of an Iron Age chariot it has been suggested that, rather than being passed through a vertical perforation in the axle, linch-pins such as the iron ring-headed example in the Llyn Cerrig Bach assemblage which has a curved shank (i.e. Fox 1947a: no. 43; Savory 1976a: no. 17.43) slotted into a recess cut into the side of the axle adjacent to the nave of the wheel (Hill 2002; J. D. Hill pers. comm.). Whether a 'vase-headed' linch-pin with two fixed terminals could have been successfully used in a similar manner is far from certain. The issue of exactly how 'vase-headed' linch-pins functioned, along with the significance of the horizontal perforation through the upper terminal, is returned to in the discussion on the so-called mini-terrets below.

Classification

Ward Perkins classified linch-pins into two groups: the so-called south-eastern type (1940: 366–7, fig. 5) and the so-called Yorkshire type (1940: 365–6, fig. 3). The south-eastern group has been subsequently subdivided into iron crescent-headed linch-pins (MacGregor 1976: 75–6) and more elaborate crescent-headed linch-pins (Spratling 1972: 56–8, nos. 106–8, fig. 38; MacGregor 1976: 75). The iron crescent-headed linch-pins are of Roman date (Spratling 1972: 55), while the more elaborate crescent-headed linch-pins include a number of examples of demonstrably Iron Age as well as Roman date (Spratling 1972: 56). Ward Perkins's so-called Yorkshire type is of more relevance to the present discussion as it is, more or less, equivalent to the 'vase-headed' linch-pin type (Spratling 1972: 58–60, nos. 109–17, figs. 39–43; MacGregor 1976: 49–50, 73, nos. 128–31).

'Vase-headed' linch-pins consist of a rectangular-sectioned iron shank with two cast, copper alloy terminals. The upper terminal normally consists of a waisted casting with a flat top and a horizontal perforation. When inverted the upper terminal is considered to resemble a pedestalled vase, hence the type's name, although its shape is more reminiscent of a poppy seed head. Although variations in the shape of the upper terminal do occur, the horizontal perforation is present in all examples of the type and is one of its defining characteristics. The lower terminal is generally shaped like the upturned hoof and fetlock of a horse, although, as discussed above, whether this apparent zoomorphic character is deliberate is uncertain. Ward Perkins called the group the Yorkshire type because he considered the examples from the King's Barrow, Arras, to be the earliest and that the type was developed, from Continental prototypes, in East Yorkshire by Marnian invaders and then spread in usage throughout eastern and south-eastern England (1940: 359). This idea has been effectively refuted by Spratling (1972: 59–60) and, although the examples from East Yorkshire may still be among the earliest of the group, the more neutral term 'vase-headed', based as it is on the type's form, is preferred here. Spratling's dismissal of the type's supposed Continental parallels, such as the two linch-pins from the chariot burial at Nanterre, Marne (Henry 1933: 75, fig. 4.1; Ward Perkins 1940: 359, 366, fig. 1.3–4; Stead 1965a: 34, fig. 16.5), suggests the type is a wholly British innovation (Spratling 1972: 60).

Ward Perkins considered the cast copper alloy terminals from Colchester, Essex (Ward Perkins 1940: 359, 361, 365; Hawkes and Hull 1947: 332, fig. 60.3, pl. C.5–6; Spratling 1972: 80, 438, nos. 136.A–C, fig. 48; MacGregor 1976: 50, 73), Merlin's Cave, Symonds

Yat, Herefordshire (Phillips 1931: 22, pl. IV.1–2; Ward Perkins 1940: 359, 365; MacGregor 1976: 73), Santon, Norfolk (Smith 1909a: 151, fig. 4; Ward Perkins 1940: 359, 366; Spratling 1972: 439, nos. 138.A–B, fig. 48; MacGregor 1976: 50, 73) and Westhall, Suffolk (Harrod 1885: 456; Clarke 1939: 68–9, 110, pl. XVIII.4; Ward Perkins 1940: 358, 361, 366; Spratling 1972: 440, nos. 139.A–F, fig. 48; MacGregor 1976: 50, 73) to be from linch-pins of his so-called Yorkshire type. This view was maintained by Fox (1947a: 78, fig. 10) and Hawkes and Hull (1947: 332), but as most of these terminals are open at both ends and none have a transverse perforation it has subsequently been rejected (Stead 1965a: 33; Spratling 1972: 58–9, 80; MacGregor 1976: 49–50). The real function of these terminals is uncertain, but they are examples of a recognized type current in the first century AD and termed either baluster ferrules (Spratling 1972: 80–1, nos. 136–9, fig. 48) or vase-headed castings (MacGregor 1976: 49–50, 73). Their frequent association with items of horse furniture and vehicle fittings suggests that they possibly had a related function.

In addition to the baluster ferrules, there are a number of artefacts considered by Ward Perkins (1940: 365–6) and MacGregor (1976: 73) to be examples of the so-called Yorkshire or 'vase-headed' type which are not considered so here. These include the enamelled linch-pin from King's Langley, Hertfordshire (Kendrick 1939–40; Ward Perkins 1940: 358–61, 365, pl. LVI; Brailsford 1953: 62, pl. XI.3; Fox 1958: 121, 127, pl. 52.a; Megaw and Merrifield 1969: 157, fig. 1.c; Spratling 1972: 56–7, no. 108; fig. 38; MacGregor 1976: 75) which is an example of the elaborate crescent-headed type (Spratling 1972: 56; MacGregor 1976: 75) and the copper alloy terminals from Jewry Wall, Leicester (Kenyon 1948: 259, fig. 87.5; MacGregor 1976: 73; Spratling 1989: 54), Wroxeter, Shropshire (Bushe-Fox 1916: 26, pl. XVII.22; MacGregor 1976: 73; Spratling 1972: 61; 1989: 54) and Newstead, Roxburghshire (J. Curle 1911: 315–16, pl. LXXXIV.2; MacGregor 1976: 73, no. 130; Spratling 1989: 54) which are similar in form to the baluster ferrules and presumably had a comparable function. In addition, the elaborate decorative mount from Cairngryfe, Lanarkshire (Childe 1940–1: 218, pl. LII.4), which MacGregor considered possibly to be the upper terminal of a 'vase-headed' linch-pin (1976: 49, 73, no. 128), is an unparalleled form and on these grounds its inclusion in the type is rejected.

Closely related to the 'vase-headed' linch-pins are the four linch-pins of the so-called vase-ring combination type (MacGregor 1976: 73) from Middleton on the Wolds, East Yorkshire (Mortimer 1905: 360, fig. 1022; MacGregor 1976: 73, no. 135; Stead 1979: 45, fig. 14.2) and the Stanwick hoard, North Yorkshire (MacGregor 1962: 25, 46, nos. 70–1, 79, figs. 10–11; 1976: 73, fig. 2.8; Stead 1979: 45). Like 'vase-headed' linch-pins examples of the so-called vase-ring combination type have wrought, rectangular-sectioned, iron shanks and cast, copper alloy terminals, the upper of which contains a horizontal perforation and the lower of which, where it survives, is shaped like the upturned hoof and fetlock of a horse. These similarities prompted Ward Perkins to consider one of the Stanwick examples to be of his so-called Yorkshire type (1940: 361, 366, fig. 2), however, the upper terminals of the vase-ring combination type are crowned with terret-like loops which suggest they are probably better considered to be a distinctive subtype of the 'vase-headed' linch-pins. The function of the terret-like ring on the upper terminal is uncertain, but it may be related to that of the so-called mini-terrets which are associated with 'vase-headed' linch-pins (see below).

There are at least fifty-six 'vase-headed' linch-pins, or linch-pin terminals, known from Britain (Table 5). Their distribution is mainly restricted to southern Britain and Yorkshire, although there are two possible outliers in Scotland. In addition, an example of the type, undoubtedly an export from Britain, is known from Blicquy in Belgium (Demarez and Leman-Delerive 2001), a small number of 'vase-headed' linch-pin mould fragments were recovered from Pit 209, Gussage All Saints, Dorset (Wainwright and Spratling 1973: 122; Spratling 1979: 140, fig. 101.3; Foster 1980: 18, pls 17–18) and two linch-pins, apparently forged from single pieces of iron, which mimic the form of the 'vase-headed' linch-pins, including the perforated upper 'terminals', were recovered from a pit at Bury Hill, Hampshire (Cunliffe and Poole 2000: 56, nos. 2.25–6, fig. 2.32).

The 'vase-headed' linch-pins form a uniform group; only a few minor variations occur between them. Where intact, the upper terminal is of the distinctive, and partly defining,

TABLE 5: 'Vase-headed' linch-pins from Britain

Provenance	References
Akenham, Suffolk	Martin *et al.* 2000: 497, fig. 152.D
Alcester, Warwickshire	Portable Antiquities Recording Scheme Ref. WMID839; A. Bolton pers. comm.
Alderton, Suffolk	Portable Antiquities Recording Scheme Ref. SF-AC9AD2
King's Barrow, Arras, East Yorkshire (2)	Greenwell 1907: 280, fig. 21; Henry 1933: 82, fig. 9.1; Ward Perkins 1939: 191; 1940: 358–9, 361, 365, fig. 1.5; Stead 1965a: 33, 89, 113, fig. 15.1; Spratling 1972: 58; MacGregor 1976: 73; Stead 1979: 45, 98, fig. 14.1; 1985a: 61, pl. 81
Attleborough, Norfolk (2)	Gurney 1993: 515; 1995: 223; Hutcheson 2004: 110, 128, nos. 48–9; N. Hutcheson pers. comm.
Beechamwell, Norfolk	Spratling 1972: 426, 618, 620, no. 109, fig. 39; Gregory 1980: 339–41, fig. 7; Hutcheson 2004: 109–10, 128, no. 46
Bigberry Camp, Harbledown, Kent (3)	Jessup 1932: 106, pl. I.b; Ward Perkins 1939: 191; 1940: 359, 365, fig. 1.1–2; Spratling 1972: 58, 426, 618, nos. 110–11, fig. 39; Thompson 1983: 274, nos. 38–40, pl. XXXVI.a, fig. 17.31–3
Broome, Norfolk	Gurney 1999: 361, fig. 2.B; Hutcheson 2004: 110, 128, no. 47
Bury Hill, Hampshire	Cunliffe 1995: 34, 38, fig. 16.7; Cunliffe and Poole 2000: 50, no. 1.7, fig. 2.29
Cawston, Norfolk	Gurney 1997: 540; Hutcheson 2004: 111, 128, no. 56; K. Hinds pers. comm.
Collfryn, Montgomery	Britnell 1989: 126, fig. 29, pl. 21.a; Spratling 1989; Stead 1991a: 46
Culbin Sands, Morayshire (?)	MacGregor 1976: 73, no. 129

39

Provenance	References
Great Thurlow, Suffolk	Martin *et al.* 1999: 361; H. Geake pers. comm.
Heighington, Lincolnshire	Portable Antiquities Recording Scheme Ref. LIN-313A74
Kingsbury, Warwickshire	Portable Antiquities Recording Scheme Ref. WMID720; A. Bolton pers. comm.
Kingsholm, Gloucestershire	G. Webster 1990: 293, fig. 9.b
Kirkburn, East Yorkshire (2)	Stead 1991a: 44–7, 181–3, 224, figs. 37–8, 99.g, 126–7; 1991d: 588
near Lapworth, Warwickshire	G. Webster 1990: 293, fig. 9.a
near Leigh, Worcestershire	Anon. 2003: 28, fig. 21
Llyn Cerrig Bach, Anglesey	No. 8 (see catalogue entry for full bibliographical references)
Loddiswell, Devon	Anon. 2003: 27, fig. 19; Portable Antiquities Recording Scheme Ref.COOK-527973
Old Down Farm, Andover, Hampshire	S. M. Davies 1981: 124, fig. 29.16
Owslebury, Hampshire	Collis 1968: 31, pl. XII; Spratling 1972: 60, 65–6, 427–8, 618, 620, no. 113, figs. 40–1; MacGregor 1976: 73
near Owslebury, Hampshire	S. Worrell pers. comm.
Quidenham, Norfolk	Hutcheson 2004: 109, no. 45
Raglan, Monmouthshire	Figgis 1999: 50; A. Gwilt pers. comm.
Saham Toney, Norfolk (2)	Gurney 1997: 541, fig. 1.D; Davies 2000: 226, 229, no.7, fig. 7; Hutcheson 2004: 110, 128, no. 52
St Arvans, Monmouthshire	Figgis 1999: 50; A. Gwilt pers. comm.
near Sleaford, Lincolnshire	Portable Antiquities Recording Scheme Ref.LIN-71D7B3
South Elmham St Mary or Homersfield, Suffolk (2)	Martin *et al.* 2000: 507, fig. 152.C; 2001: 77
Stanwick, North Yorkshire (4)	Henry 1933: fig. 9.3; Ward Perkins 1939: 192; 1940: 358, 366; MacGregor 1962: 24–5, 46, nos. 75–8, fig. 11; 1976: 73, fig. 2.7; Spratling 1972: 58
Tacolneston, Norfolk	Hutcheson 2004: 110, no. 53
Tattersett, Norfolk	Gurney 1996: 390, fig. 1.E; Hutcheson 2004: 110–11, 128, no. 55
Tattershall Thorpe, Lincolnshire (2)	Owen 1993
Thanington, Kent	Parfitt 2000
Traprain Law, East Lothian (?)	Burley 1955–6: 196, no. 359a; Spratling 1972: 58; MacGregor 1976: 73, no. 131
Trevelgue, Cornwall	Ward Perkins 1940: 358, 366; Ward Perkins 1941: 64–6, pl. X; Spratling 1972: 428, 618, no. 114, fig. 42
Waltham Chase, Hampshire	S. Worrell pers. comm.
Weeting, Norfolk	Gregory 1980: 338–9, fig. 6; Hutcheson 2004: 110, 128, no. 51

Wigginton, Hertfordshire	Ward Perkins 1941: 65, pl. XI; Spratling 1972: 60, 428, 618, 620, no. 115, fig. 42
Yoxall, Staffordshire	Portable Antiquities Recording Scheme Ref. WMID2407; A. Bolton pers. comm.
Unprovenanced (East Midlands ?)	Hirst 2001: 46–7, fig. 7
Unprovenanced	Anon. 2001: 116, no. 444
Unprovenanced	Henry 1933: fig. 9.2; Ward Perkins 1940: 366; Spratling 1972: 60, 428–9, 618, 620, no. 116, fig. 43
Unprovenanced	Henry 1933: 82, fig. 11.1–2; Ward Perkins 1940: 366; Spratling 1972: 59–60, 65, 429, no. 117, fig. 43

inverted pedestalled vase form in all but seven cases. The variants are the Bigberry Camp, Kent, and Old Down Farm, Hampshire, examples which have upper terminals of a baluster-shaped form, which is not dissimilar to the normal form; the Weeting linch-pin which is surmounted by a decorative hemispherical boss; the unprovenanced example in Saffron Walden Museum which is of the usual form, but D-shaped in section; and the Bury Hill, Hampshire, linch-pin which has a unique waisted and perforated upper terminal of bulb-like form. As noted above, with the exception of one of the Bigberry Camp and the Old Down Farm linch-pins, where they survive the lower terminals are all curved and have a form reminiscent of the upturned hoof and fetlock of a horse. The lower terminals of the Bigberry Camp and Old Down Farm linch-pins are curved, but end in hemispherical knobs rather than the normal flat surface. The lower terminal from near Sleaford has an integrally cast attachment fitting which may have originally terminated in a loop. The terminals of one of the Saham Toney linch-pins (Gurney 1997: 541, fig. 1.D) and the examples from near Owslebury, Waltham Chase and Weeting are unusual in having integrally cast collar-like sockets which are the same size and cross-section as the iron shank. The terminals of the unprovenanced linch-pin in the Ashmolean Museum (Spratling 1972: no. 116) have polygonal-sectioned sockets to accommodate the iron shank. It is notable that the five linch-pins with collar-like sockets were all embellished with enamel decoration; the significance of this correlation is uncertain.

Where measurable the overall lengths of the 'vase-headed' linch-pins vary between 103 mm (for the example from Blicquy cf. Demarez and Leman-Delerive 2001: 392, fig. 2) and 132 mm (for one of the Bigberry Camp examples cf. Jessup 1932: 106, pl. I.b.left; Ward Perkins 1940: 359, 365, fig. 1.1; Spratling 1972: no. 110, fig. 39; Thompson 1983: 274, no. 38, fig. 17.31, pl. XXXVI.a). A more significant measurement is the distance between the two terminals which is equivalent to the maximum possible diameter of the axle through which the linch-pin passed. For the 'vase-headed' linch-pins the greatest distance between the terminals is 63 mm (for one of the Saham Toney linch-pins, cf. Davies 2000: no.7) and the smallest is 41 mm (for the Wigginton example). Within this range the Llyn Cerrig Bach example is relatively large (length 56 mm), despite being small in overall length. Spratling argued, by comparing the lengths between the terminals of the 'vase-headed' linch-pins with the inner diameters of naves from the Glastonbury lake village, Somerset (Bulleid and Gray 1911: 328, 337–40, nos. X43 and X63, figs. 99, 112; Earwood 1988: 89; Coles and Minnitt 1995: 72, 86, nos. X43 and X63), Holme Pierrepont, Nottinghamshire (MacCormick 1969: 23–4, fig. 5; Musty and MacCormick 1973) and several Roman sites and the internal diameters of various Iron Age nave bands, that the 'vase-headed' linch-pins (along with the nave bands) were used on lighter rather than heavier vehicles (Spratling 1972: 63–4, 618–20). Unfortunately, by necessity this analysis was based on only a small number of artefacts and the significance of Spratling's conclusion is questionable. It is not possible to speculate with confidence, as Spratling did (1972: 64), that 'vase-headed' linch-pins were used on chariots rather than light carts or wagons.

Although several of the 'vase-headed' linch-pins are undecorated the copper alloy terminals of the remainder are embellished either with simple decorative motifs or more complex designs equivalent to Stead's Style V of insular La Tène art (the insular La Tène art sequence is discussed in Chapter 5). The undecorated linch-pins include those from Arras, Collfryn, Bigberry Camp, Cawston, Culbin Sands and Traprain Law; those decorated with simple motifs include those from Alcester, Attleborough, Llyn Cerrig Bach, Loddiswell, Old Down Farm, near Owslebury, Quidenham, Raglan, Saham Toney, South Elmham St Mary or Homersfield, near Sleaford, Stanwick and Tattersett; while those embellished with Style V designs include those from Akenham, Alderton, Beechamwell, Blicquy, Broome, Bury Hill, Great Thurlow, Heighington, Kingsbury, Kirkburn, Owslebury, St Arvans, Tattershall Thorpe, Thanington, Waltham Chase, Wigginton and Yoxall, as well as three of the unprovenanced examples (i.e. Anon. 2001: 116, no. 444; Spratling 1972: nos. 116–17). Corrosion prevents a definite identification of the form of the decorative relief design on the upper terminals of the Trevelgue linch-pin. The linch-pins from Alcester, Broome, Kingsholm, near Lapworth, Loddiswell, Waltham Chase and Weeting as well as two of the unprovenanced examples (Spratling 1972: nos. 116–17) were partly decorated with enamel insets. In addition, the lower terminal of the Saham Toney linch-pins and the base of the lower terminal from near Owslebury both have recessed panels which probably provided fields for enamel decoration. At least partly on the basis of their decoration several of the 'vase-headed' linch-pins have been included in the so-called Gussage–Bury Hill tradition (Cunliffe 1995: 38), but since the validity of this grouping is questionable, it is not considered further here (for a discussion of the so-called Gussage–Bury Hill tradition see the section on terrets).

Dating

Dating evidence for the 'vase-headed' linch-pins suggests that despite their uniformity the type was potentially in vogue for a considerable period. One of the Saham Toney linch-pins (Gurney 1997: 541, fig. 1.D) and the examples from Akenham, Alcester, Alderton, Attleborough, Beechamwell, Broome, Cawston, Great Thurlow, Heighington, Kingsbury, near Lapworth, near Leigh, Loddiswell, near Owslebury, Quidenham, Raglan, St Arvans, near Sleaford, South Elmham St Mary or Homersfield, Tacolneston, Tattersett,

Tattershall Thorpe, Thanington, Waltham Chase, Weeting, Wigginton and Yoxall are all unassociated metal detector or chance finds. As noted above, the East Yorkshire vehicle burial tradition, which includes the Arras and Kirkburn 'vase-headed' linch-pins, prob- ably starts at some point in the fourth to third centuries BC and apparently ended before the mid first century BC (Stead 1991a: 184; Wait 1995: 499). The three Bigberry Camp linch-pins are chance finds from the hillfort where occupation apparently began during the fifth to third centuries BC and ended by the mid first century BC (Thompson 1983: 254–6). Presumably the linch-pins date to this period, although the discovery of a shackle with a barb-spring padlock of Roman type from the site suggests some material from Bigberry may date as late as the mid first century AD (Manning 1972: 230; W. H. Manning pers. comm.). The Blicquy linch-pin was recovered from a secondary levelling deposit during excavations of a Roman period sanctuary site (Demarez and Leman-Delerive 2001: 391–2). The three Bury Hill linch-pins were recovered from contexts dated to the late second to early first centuries BC (Cunliffe and Poole 2000: 24, 41, 45, table 2.3). The example from Collfryn was recovered from a superficial, and consequently undated, con- text in the south-west corner of the enclosure (Britnell 1989: 126). The exact circumstances of the discovery of the Culbin Sands linch-pin are not recorded (MacGregor 1976: no.129). The lower terminal from Kingsholm was recovered from the early Roman military site during a watching brief and, although its exact context and associations are unknown, its deposition presumably post-dates the mid first century AD foundation of the site and pre-dates its vacation in the mid 60s AD (McWhirr 1981: 14; Hurst 1985: 122). The Old Down Farm linch-pin is part of a so-called hoard dated from the third to the early first century BC (S. M. Davies 1981: 122, 124). The Owslebury linch- pin was recovered during excavations from a ploughsoil stratigraphically earlier than a trackway which was cut by a pit-complex with late Iron Age associations (Collis 1968: 21–3, 31). This stratigraphic sequence suggests the linch-pin does not post-date the late Iron Age and could be significantly earlier. One of the Saham Toney linch-pins (Davies 2000: 226, 229, no.7, fig. 7; Hutcheson 2004: 110, 128, no. 52) formed part of a hoard (known as 'findspot B'), which included a pair of two-link bridle-bits of probable Polden Hill subtype, two decorative enamelled discs, a set of iron manacles of Roman type, and several iron bars and strips possibly from a large grill or griddle (Davies 2000: 226–30, nos. 7–9, 16, 20–41, figs. 7–8), which has been intepreted as scrap metal associated with a late Iron Age to early Roman metalworking centre whose deposition probably dated to the second half of the first century AD (Bates 2000: 234–5; Hutcheson 2004: 33). The Stanwick linch-pins are part of an assemblage dated approximately to the mid first cen- tury AD (Fitts *et al*. 1999: 48). The Traprain Law linch-pin was found in the quarry in 1939 presumably as a result of a fall from the site of the native oppidum. Interpreting the dating evidence from Traprain Law is difficult; the site was probably occupied either con- tinuously, or near continuously, throughout the late Iron Age and Roman period (Jobey 1976). The Trevelgue linch-pin was concealed in the wall of a hut demolished in the second century AD (Ward Perkins 1941: 65). This date only provides a *terminus ante quem* for the linch-pin's concealment and other material from the hut ranged in date from the

Iron Age to the early second century AD (Ward Perkins 1941: 65). The 'vase-headed' linch-pin terminal mould fragments from Gussage All Saints were recovered from a pit (Spratling 1979: 129–30, fig. 97) dated by two radiocarbon samples (Wainwright and Switsur 1976: 39, samples F and G) which have calibrated date ranges, expressed to one standard deviation, of 355 BC to 20 BC and 165 BC to AD 80. These suggest a date for the mould fragments in the first two centuries BC (see also Wainwright 1979: 21; Foster 1980: 7; Stead 1991a: 183).

The evidence reviewed above for the date of individual 'vase-headed' linch-pins suggests that, potentially, the type was in vogue from the third or fourth centuries BC to the second century AD, however, such a wide date range must be treated with caution. The potentially early dates cannot be considered certain as they may be a result of the imprecise dating of both the East Yorkshire burial evidence and the Bigberry Camp and Owslebury linch-pins. The Saham Toney linch-pin may have been antique by the time of its deposition, apparently as part of a hoard of scrap, during the second half of the first century AD. Similarly, the potentially late date provided by the Trevelgue linch-pin cannot be maintained with any great confidence. The floruit of the 'vase-headed' linch-pins cannot be extended far beyond the mid first century AD with certainty.

Three other factors are of relevance to the dating of 'vase-headed' linch-pins: the common occurrence of Style V motifs on examples of the type; the use of enamel decoration on several other examples; and the types association with the so-called mini-terrets. As noted above, several of the 'vase-headed' linch-pins are decorated with Style V art. Although originally equated to the first century BC (Stead 1985a: 23) recent work on the burial evidence from East Yorkshire (Stead 1991a: 183) and Deal, Kent (Stead 1995: 95) suggests that the use of Style V art may have begun in the third century BC (the insular art sequence is discussed further in Chapter 5). The enamel decoration on the unprovenanced linch-pins in the Ashmolean Museum and Saffron Walden Museum are both examples of the style of decorated harness and vehicle fittings typified by compass work and inlaid enamel ornament, generally dated to the first and possibly second centuries AD (Bateson 1981: 8–10, 114; Raftery 1991: 568–9). The geometric designs of the inlaid enamel on the linch-pin terminals from near Lapworth, Kingsholm and Weeting are difficult to date stylistically, but the use of polychrome enamel on these terminals (Gregory 1980: 338; G. Webster 1990: 293) is not inconsistent with a first century AD or possibly later date (for the dating of polychrome enamel inlay see: Savory 1976a: 43; Megaw and Megaw 1989: 219, 228). Neither the dating of the Style V or enamel decoration which occurs on several of the 'vase-headed' linch-pins refines our dating of the type, however, the type's association with so-called mini-terrets is worth considering in greater detail.

So-called mini-terrets

The so-called mini-terrets are defined in the section on terrets (see above) as terret-like castings which vary from D-shape to near circular in outline, contain a pair of stops at each end of an attachment bar and have loops which variously thicken or thin towards the stops or are of even thickness. Some of the so-called mini-terrets are flat at the back, none are tanged and all are 33 mm or less in width. They are too small to have functioned as terrets, hence their name. There are at least forty-four so-called mini-terrets known from Britain (Table 6).

Spratling arbitrarily differentiated the so-called mini-terrets from his Group I simple form terrets on the basis of whether their widths were below 30 mm. Consequently, two of the Meare examples (widths 30 and 33 mm) (Spratling 1972: nos. 12–13) and the Owmby Cliff piece (width 33 mm) (Spratling 1972: no. 14) were classified as Group I

TABLE 6: So-called miniature terrets

Provenance	References
King's Barrow, Arras, East Yorkshire (2)	Greenwell 1907: 280; Stead 1965a: 44, 90; Spratling 1972: 51; Stead 1979: 52, fig. 17.6–7
Baldock, Hertfordshire	Stead 1986: 136, no. 381, fig. 60
Barking, Suffolk	Suffolk County Council SMR no. BRK089/SF14371; H. Geake pers. comm.
Brantham, Suffolk	Martin *et al.* 2003: 339.
Burgh Castle, Norfolk	Hutcheson 2004: 114, 131, no. 87
Chelmondiston, Suffolk	Portable Antiquities Recording Scheme Ref. SF.A70334
near Christchurch, Cambridgeshire	Portable Antiquities Recording Scheme Ref. NMS154
Collfryn, Montgomery	Britnell 1989: 126, fig. 29, pl. 21.a; Spratling 1989; Stead 1991a: 46
Fring, Norfolk (2)	Gurney 2001: 697; Hutcheson 2004: 113–14, 115, nos. 79–80 and 91; K. Hinds pers. comm.
Hod Hill, Dorset (2)	Brailsford 1962: 18, nos. I.129–30, fig. 14; Spratling 1972: 51, 420, no. 100, fig. 37; MacGregor 1976: 62
Hemingstone, Suffolk	Suffolk County Council SMR no. HMG014/SF16369; H. Geake pers. comm.
Honley hoard, West Yorkshire (2)	Richmond 1925: 14, 115, figs. 2 (top row) and 2.a.10; Allen 1963: 25; Spratling 1972: 51; MacGregor 1976: 62, nos. 52–3
Hunmanby, East Yorkshire	Sheppard 1907: 485, pl. opp. p. 487; Spratling 1972: 51; MacGregor 1976: 41, 62; Stead 1979: 51–2, fig. 17.5
Hunsbury, Northamptonshire	Fell 1936: 63, no. 6, fig. 3.2; Spratling 1972: 421, no. 101, fig. 37
Kenninghall, Norfolk	Gurney 2000: 518; K. Hinds pers. comm.
Kirkburn, East Yorkshire (2)	Stead 1991a: 44–6, 224, nos. K5.9–10, figs. 37.2 and 38.2
Langley Burrell, Wiltshire	Portable Antiquities Recording Scheme Ref. NMGWPA2000/129/2
Little Cornard, Suffolk	Martin *et al.* 2000: 500, fig. 152.E
Loddon, Norfolk	Gurney 1996: 390; Hutcheson 2004: 114, 131, no. 85
Western Meare lake village, Somerset (4)	Gray and Bulleid 1953: 218–19, 221, 231, nos. E1, E69, E102, E167, pl. XLIX; Spratling 1972: 51, 53, 384, 421, nos. 12–13, 102–3, figs. 3, 37; MacGregor 1976: 62

Provenance	References
Methwold, Norfolk	Gurney 1996: 390; Hutcheson 2004: 114, 131, no. 86
Nettlestead, Suffolk	Portable Antiquities Recording Scheme Ref. SF-2FEE03
Owmby Cliff, Lincolnshire	Whitwell 1966: fig. 4.b.17; Spratling 1972: 26, 385, no. 14, fig. 2
Owslebury, Hampshire	Collis 1970: 252; Spratling 1972: 422, no. 104, fig. 37
near Owslebury, Hampshire	Anon. 2000: 30, fig. 34
Piddlehinton, Dorset (2)	Portable Antiquities Recording Scheme Ref. PAL1178–9; C. Hayward Trevarthen pers. comm.
Quidenham, Norfolk	Gurney 1995: 223; Hutcheson 2004: 114, 131, no. 83
Saham Toney, Norfolk	Davies 2000: 226, 229, no. 6, fig. 7
Shotesham, Norfolk	Gurney 1990: 100; Hutcheson 2004: 114, no. 89; K. Hinds pers. comm.
Sporle with Palgrave, Norfolk	Gurney 1998: 186; Hutcheson 2004: 114, 131, no. 82.
Sutton Benger, Wiltshire	Portable Antiquities Recording Scheme Ref. NMGW-554498
Thetford Castle, Norfolk	Gregory 1992: 11, no. 1, fig. 6.1; Hutcheson 2004: 114–15, 131, no. 90
Trevelgue Head, Cornwall	Ward Perkins 1941: 66, fig. 1; Spratling 1972: 422, no. 105, fig. 37; MacGregor 1976: 62
Wainford Mill, Norfolk	Hutcheson 2004: 114, 131, no. 88
Warburton, Lancashire	Portable Antiquities Recording Scheme Ref. LVPL1365; N. Herepath pers. comm.
Wymandham, Norfolk	Hutcheson 2004: 115, 131, no. 94

terrets, although these three do not have wear facets on the upper part of their stops (a feature typical of 'true' terrets). Traces of wear are noted on the inner face of the attachment bar of one of the Meare examples (a feature witnessed on other so-called mini-terrets) (Spratling 1972: 384, no. 13), and the Kirkburn so-called mini-terrets are of comparable size (widths 32 and 33 mm) (Stead 1991a: 44, 46) suggesting, as Spratling speculated (1972: 53), that they are in fact so-called mini-terrets. It is also possible that a notably small (width 22 mm), unprovenanced lipped terret in Saffron Walden Museum (Spratling 1972: 53, 394, no. 41, fig. 8) should also be considered as a so-called mini-terret (Spratling 1972: 53). There is a single Continental example from the cemetery at La Courte, Leval-Trahegnies, Hainaut province, Belgium (Mariën 1961: 49, no. 61, fig. 20) which has La Tène III associations (Mariën 1961: 45–9, nos. 56–9; Spratling 1972: 52). The so-called strap-ring found by a metal detectorist near North Newbald, East Yorkshire, has been identified as a 'mini-terret' (Leahy 1995), but despite the general similarity of its form to the so-called mini-terrets cited above, its knobbed and enamelled decoration suggest that it is probably an example of an unrelated type of ring.

So-called mini-terrets can be typologically subdivided into two groups: those which are rounded on one side but flat on the other resulting in a distinctive D-shaped or plano-convex section, and those which are rounded on both sides like 'true' terrets. There are twenty so-called mini-terrets with flat backs including one from Fring (Gurney 2001: 697), one from Meare (Gray and Bulleid 1953: 231, no. E167; Spratling 1972: 421, no. 103), the example from near Owslebury (Anon. 2000: 30, fig. 34) and those from Arras, Baldock,

Barking, Hod Hill, Hunsbury, Kirkburn, Methwold, Nettlestead, Piddlehinton, Quidenham, Saham Toney, Shotesham, Sutton Benger, Thetford, Trevelgue, Wainford Mill and Warburton. It is not possible from the published details to ascertain what type the Christchurch and Collfryn so-called mini-terrets are, whilst the Chelmondiston and Kenninghall examples are of unusual form, being rounded on both faces with a central groove and flat on both faces with a 'milled' outer rim respectively (K. Hinds pers. comm.). All of the remaining so-called mini-terrets are rounded on both sides. On current dating evidence (see below) it is uncertain whether this typological subdivision is chronologically significant.

The reason for discussing the so-called mini-terrets here is their association with 'vase-headed' linch-pins. The Kirkburn, the Trevelgue and the Collfryn so-called mini-terrets were recovered in close association with 'vase-headed' linch-pins and both so-called mini-terrets and 'vase-headed' linch-pins were found in the King's Barrow at Arras. The Saham Toney 'mini-terret' was recovered from the same field as one of the so-called vase-headed linch-pins from the same site (Davies 2000: 226, 229, no. 7, fig. 7), although they were not apparently associated (Bates 2000: 234). In addition to these associations the La Courte and Hunmanby so-called mini-terrets, along with the Arras and Kirkburn pieces, were recovered from vehicle burials. These associations and the type's similarity in form to 'true' terrets suggest that they were vehicle fittings, however, they are too small to have functioned as rein rings in the manner of 'true' terrets (MacGregor 1976: 39). This is reflected by the absence of wear facets at the top of their stops (a feature typical of terrets) and the presence of wear facets on the attachment bars of some examples (a feature unrecognized on terrets). An explanation for their function which accounts for these wear facets and both the association with 'vase-headed' linch-pins and the perforations through the upper terminals of the 'vase-headed' linch-pins has been proposed. Stead has suggested that the so-called mini-terrets are mounts on which a thong was lashed which passed through the horizontal perforation of the upper terminal of a 'vase-headed' linch-pin and was tied to its detachable, lower terminal (1991a: 46–7, fig. 38). This arrangement would have prevented the linch-pin from dislodging accidentally and also facilitated its removal for the purpose of repairs, although whether the lower terminals of all so-called vase-headed linch-pins were detachable (see above) and exactly how, or where, the mini-terret was mounted is not obvious (Stead 1991a: 47). It is possible that the terret-like loop of the linch-pins of the so-called vase-ring combination type performed a similar function as that suggested by Stead for the mini-terrets. Notably, with the possible exception of the Collfryn example, all of the so-called mini-terrets associated with 'vase-headed' linch-pins have flat backs. Whether this is significant or only coincidental is unknown. An alternative suggestion that at least some so-called mini-terrets may be a form of personal adornment (Spratling 1972: 52) is difficult to support without more compelling evidence.

The dating evidence for the so-called mini-terrets does not provide a narrow range. The Barking, Brantham, Burgh Castle, Chelmondiston, Fring, Hemingstone, Kenninghall, Langley Burrell, Loddon, Methwold, Nettlestead, Owmby Cliff, Piddlehinton,

Quidenham, Shotesham, Sporle with Palgrave, Sutton Benger, Wainford Mill, Warburton and Wymandham examples are unassociated metal detector or chance finds. As previously noted, the East Yorkshire vehicle burial tradition, which includes the Arras, Hunmanby and Kirkburn so-called mini-terrets, probably extended from the fourth or third centuries BC to the mid first century BC (Stead 1991a: 184; Wait 1995: 499). The Baldock mini-terret was an unstratified find from a settlement site where occupation began in the mid first century BC and continued throughout the Roman period (Stead 1986: 136, no. 381; Stead and Rigby 1986: 82–7). The Collfryn 'mini-terret' was recovered from a superficial, and consequently undated, deposit in the south-west corner of the enclosure (Britnell 1989: 126). The Hod Hill examples were chance finds from the western half of the hillfort which includes a Claudian Roman fort (Brailsford 1962: p. vii; Spratling 1972: 420). The Honley so-called mini-terrets are part of a hoard with a *terminus post quem* provided by coin evidence of AD 72–3 (Allen 1963: 33) and, although precise dating of the hoard to the military consolidation of Brigantia immediately after its subjugation (i.e. *c.* AD 74) (Allen 1963: 38) is debatable, the coin evidence combined with that of an associated brooch of a type in vogue in the second half of the first century AD indicates a date for deposition in the last quarter of the first century AD. The Hunsbury example was found by chance during quarrying of the hillfort in the nineteenth century. As noted above, the main phase of occupation at the site dates from second to first centuries BC (D. Jackson 1993–4: 18) and, given the relative paucity of Roman material from the site (R. Jackson 1985: 175), the 'mini-terret' probably dates to this period. As also noted above, occupation of the western 'village' at Meare probably commenced in, or around, the third century BC and was abandoned in, or around, the first to second centuries AD (Coles 1987: 246–7) and more precise dating of the Meare examples on stratigraphic grounds is problematic (Orme *et al.* 1981: 68; Coles 1987: 243). The excavated Owslebury example was recovered from the fill of an early Roman quarry set along the line of a late Iron Age ditch (Collis 1970: 252; Spratling 1972: 422), although the possibility of residual deposition cannot be discounted. As noted above, the site of the Saham Toney mini-terret has been interpreted as a late Iron Age to early Roman Iceni tribal centre associated with metalworking activity (Bates 2000: 235). The Thetford Castle 'mini-terret' was residually deposited in a layer containing early medieval pottery (Gregory 1992: 7, 11). Ceramic evidence suggests that occupation of the Iron Age fort at Thetford Castle dated to the middle Iron Age, however, given the difficulties of recognizing Iron Age ceramics in Norfolk (Percival 1999), occupation at the site may have continued into the late Iron Age (cf. Gregory 1992: 14–15). The Trevelgue Head example was concealed in the wall of a hut demolished in the second century AD, although, as previously noted, this date can only be considered a *terminus ante quem* for the so-called mini-terret's concealment. Other material from the hut ranged in date from the Iron Age to the early second century AD (Ward Perkins 1941: 65), suggesting the mini-terret may have been concealed for a significant period prior to the wall's demolition. This review of the evidence indicates that the so-called mini-terrets possibly originated as early as the fourth or third centuries BC and that their deposition, if not manufacture, continued into at least the second half of the first century AD. Unfortunately, it does not assist in suggesting a narrower date range for the 'vase-headed' linch-pins.

Summary

The 'vase-headed' linch-pin from Llyn Cerrig Bach is of a distinctive, British type which potentially ranges in date from the third or fourth century BC to at least the mid first century AD, although the uniformity of the type suggests its actual vogue may be significantly shorter. Study of the linch-pin itself shows that it was simply decorated, its lower terminal was possibly of zoomorphic character and that it was used prior to deposition, however, the precise method of its manufacture and use remain unknown.

Possible harness ring

The possible harness ring (No. 9) (diameter 47 mm) is fully described in the catalogue. Rings had a multitude of functions and given the simple form of this ring and its lack of definite associations and exact parallels, identification is problematic. On the basis of the parallel with a subcircular ring (diameter 44.5 mm) with an attached strap-end from the Seven Sisters hoard, Glamorgan (Allen 1905: 137, fig. 7; Fox 1958: fig. 78.11; Davies and Spratling 1976: 125, no. 1, fig. 3; Savory 1976a: 63, no. 34.130, fig. 39.11), Fox identified the piece as a possible harness ring (1947a: 35, 96). Other comparable examples of, albeit smaller, cast, copper alloy rings include: one with pseudo-stitch decoration from Bigberry Camp, Kent (Boyd Dawkins 1902: 216; Jessup 1932: 106; Thompson 1983: 274, no. 54); one from the Romano-British settlement of Rushmore, Dorset (diameter 31mm) (Pitt-Rivers 1887: 52, pl. XV.16); an unprovenanced example (diameter 30 mm) in Saffron Walden Museum (Spratling 1972: 393–4; MacGregor 1976: 62) which is possibly associated with two, also unprovenanced, lipped terrets (Spratling 1972: 28–9, 393–4, nos. 40–1, fig. 8; MacGregor 1976: 64); and the ring (diameter 31 mm) decorated with pseudo-stitch decoration from Winchester, Hampshire (Smith 1911–12a: 16, fig. 15). Unfortunately, the lack of associations for the Bigberry Camp, Rushmore, Saffron Walden and Winchester rings prevents their definite identification as harness fittings and by extension the same interpretation being applied to the example from Llyn Cerrig Bach. In addition, the character of the Llyn Cerrig Bach ring differs markedly to the definite harness ring from the Seven Sisters hoard. The Llyn Cerrig Bach ring is worn evenly around its inner edge whilst the inner edge of the Seven Sisters ring is worn in three distinct facets where its strap-ends were fixed (Davies and Spratling 1976: 124). This difference in wear patterns suggests that the two rings served different functions and that the identification of the Llyn Cerrig Bach ring as part of a harness set, while not unreasonable, is not certain.

Given the martial character of the Llyn Cerrig Bach assemblage, the piece may have been a scabbard suspension ring. The exact method by which scabbards were suspended in the British Iron Age is not certain (Stead 1995: 88), but two types of loops were apparently used: so-called baldric rings and paired suspension rings.

The so-called baldric rings form a heterogeneous group; they consist of a ring and some form of protruding hook or stud-like attachment. Several examples of so-called baldric rings are known, including: one possible, decorated example from Mill Hill, Deal, Kent (diameter 45–6 mm) (Parfitt 1990: 204; 1991: 215–16; Stead 1995: 88, fig. 32.5, pl. X); one tinned or silvered example from Owslebury, Hampshire (diameter approximately 40 mm) (Collis 1968: 25, pl. IX.b; 1973: 126–7, figs. 3.4 and 4.5); and one from Whitcombe, Dorset (diameter 58 mm) (Stead 1990: 73, no. 5, fig. 10.5). The type varies in external diameter from 58 mm (Whitcombe) to approximately 40 mm (Owslebury). So-called baldric rings were used to join two leather straps; one strap was permanently secured to the loop while the other was temporarily secured to the protruding stud-like feature by means of an eyed slit (R. Jackson 1990: 38–9). As well as being used for suspending scabbards, these simple fittings would have served a variety of functions; consequently, only those definitely associated with scabbards or swords are considered here. The location of the examples recovered from so-called warrior burials suggest that they were fitted to belts from which a strap which passed through the paired suspension rings commonly associated with scabbards (see below) was also attached. In the burials from Whitcombe and Owslebury the so-called baldric rings were found near the right shoulder, suggesting that the belt may have been a baldric and that the sword scabbards had been suspended over the right shoulder (Collis 1973: 130). In comparison, the possible example from the Mill Hill cemetery was found adjacent to the suspension loop of the scabbard (Parfitt 1990: 204), suggesting it may have been attached to a conventional belt (Stead 1995: 88). Although the Mill Hill and Owslebury examples are of a comparable size to the Llyn Cerrig Bach ring, the absence of a protruding hook or attachment on the Llyn Cerrig Bach ring suggests it is unlikely to be a so-called baldric ring.

The second ring type used for attaching scabbards in the Iron Age are the paired suspension rings. Six sets of paired suspension rings are known: a fragmented single iron ring from Gelliniog Wen, Anglesey (diameter approximately 38 mm) (Hughes 1909: 256); one cast, copper alloy pair from Ham Hill, Somerset (diameter 38 mm) (Walter 1923: 149, no. 3); one cast, copper alloy pair from Owslebury, Hampshire (diameters 46–8 mm) (Collis 1968: 25, pl. IX.b; 1973: 126, figs. 3.3 and 4.3–4); two cast, copper alloy pairs with coral ornament from Wetwang Slack, East Yorkshire (diameters unrecorded) (Dent 1985: 88, 91, figs. 2 and 4; Stead 1985a: pl. 80; 1995: 88); and one iron pair from Whitcombe, Dorset (diameters 50–56 mm) (Stead 1990: 73, fig. 10.3–4). There are two sets of three suspension rings: one from North Grimston, East Yorkshire (diameters 35–40 mm) (Mortimer 1905: 355, fig. 1019; Stead 1979: 62); and the other of iron rings from St Lawrence, Isle of Wight (diameters 57–63 mm) (Jones and Stead 1969: 354, no. 6, fig. 2.6). Pairs of these plain rings set immediately adjoining and either side of scabbards, or scabbard suspension loops, have been recovered from burials at Owslebury, Wetwang and Whitcombe (Stead 1995: 88). Similar rings have also been recovered from disturbed or poorly recorded burials at Gelliniog Wen, North Grimston and St Lawrence. A leather strap presumably

50

passed through the paired rings, and any associated scabbard suspension loop, and was connected to either a belt or a baldric. The paired rings were presumably adjusted to tighten or loosen this strap. The rings are generally plain, made of either iron or copper alloy and vary in diameter from approximately 38 mm (Ham Hill and Gelliniog Wen) to 57–63 mm (St Lawrence). The term 'paired suspension rings' is a slight misnomer for at North Grimston and St Lawrence three rings were recovered, although at North Grimston one of the rings may have been another example of a so-called baldric ring. The closest parallel to the Llyn Cerrig Bach ring is the pair from Owslebury. Although the Owslebury rings are circular rather than lozenge-shaped in section they are similar enough to the Llyn Cerrig Bach ring to prevent dismissal of the possibility that the Llyn Cerrig Bach ring may be one of a pair of scabbard suspension rings.

Summary

It is uncertain whether the Llyn Cerrig Bach ring was a harness loop, one half of a set of paired scabbard suspension rings or another type of fitting altogether. All that can be ascertained about its function is that it was worn evenly on its inner edge suggesting that it revolved freely around any straps that were attached to it. Following Fox (1947a: 35, 96), it is catalogued here as a possible harness ring although this interpretation is problematic. In the absence of a definite identification it is not possible to suggest a date for the piece.

3

The Copper Alloy Bridle-Bits

Introductory Remarks

Bridle-bits are part of the harness equipment used for controlling horses. They consist of a mouthpiece or bar, made up of one or more links, which is joined at both ends to rein-rings which connect the bridle-bit to the rest of the harness and also receive the reins (Palk 1984: figs. 18–19). There are three principal types of British Iron Age bridle-bit: three-link bridle-bits; two-link bridle-bits; and bridle-bits whose form is derived from three-link bridle-bits. There are also some miscellaneous forms which fit none of the main categories. This classificatory division has remained largely unchanged since Ward Perkins revised (1939) Leeds's classification (1933a: 113–18), and most subsequent work has concentrated on refining elements of this four-part classification. Typological subdivision of the main types is problematic because of the wide variation in form of the bridle-bits (Palk 1984: 3). Both a Pexton Moor subtype and a fused subtype of the three-link bridle-bits are recognizable. The fused subtype provides the typological link between the three-link bridle-bits and the derived forms. A Polden Hill subtype of the copper alloy two-link bridle-bits also exists. In addition, the Irish three-link bridle-bits form a group distinct from the British series of three-link bridle-bits.

There are six three-link bridle-bits, one two-link bridle-bit, one three-link bridle-bit of Irish type, and three bridle-bits of miscellaneous form in the Llyn Cerrig Bach assemblage. The assemblage also includes five tubular rein-rings and two probable centre-links, all arguably from bridle-bits of the three-link type. Bridle-bits consist of several components and a variety of materials and methods were used in the manufacture of these separate parts. Consequently, a simple division between iron and copper alloy bridle-bits is frequently not possible. The catalogue and following discussion includes bridle-bits from Llyn Cerrig Bach manufactured exclusively from copper alloy (i.e. Nos. 10–11, 22–3) and iron bridle-bits which have been plated with copper alloy (i.e. Nos. 12–15). Of the Llyn Cerrig Bach material, only the three bridle-bits of miscellaneous form (Fox 1947a: 83, 95, nos. 56, 57, 128, pls. III, XXVII–XXVIII; Savory 1976a: 58–9, nos. 17.56, 17.57, 18.9, fig. 21; Palk 1984: 58, nos. LL1, LL2, fig. C53), and one of the probable centre-links (Fox 1947a: 89, no. 83, pl. XXVIII; Savory 1976a: 59, no. 17.83, fig. 21.2) were apparently manufactured exclusively from iron. A detailed study of the iron pieces falls outside of the limits of the present study although, where pertinent to the discussion of the cast copper alloy and copper alloy plated bridle-bits, they are referred to. An unpublished, iron two-link bridle-bit, donated to Oriel Ynys Môn, Llangefni, Anglesey, by Evelyn Owen, whose father participated in the original collection of the Llyn Cerrig Bach assemblage, may also be part of the assemblage. The perpendicular bars attached to the rein-rings of this bridle-bit resemble a type that dates from the medieval period to the eighteenth century (cf. Ellis 1985: 171, no. 45, fig. 58; Clarke *et al.* 1995: 43–4, fig. 30.C), but it is also vaguely paralleled by a bridle-bit from La Tène (Vouga 1923: 89–90, pl. XXXI.1), suggesting that it is possibly ancient. The question of this bridle-bit's provenance is probably best left open. Fox identified a ring with two attached S-curved links as a possible bridle-bit (1947a: 34, 90, no. 85, pl. XXVIII), but the position of the wear facets on the ring precludes this identification (Lynch 1970: 268, fig. 85; but see Palk 1984: 21, no. R5, fig. C56). Savory has suggested the item may be part of a suspension loop and chain (1976a: no. 17.85, fig. 21.3).

Three-link bridle-bits

Three-link bridle-bits consist of five separate components: two rein-rings, two side-links and a central link. They are the most common type of bridle bit in the British and Irish Iron Age, but are notably rare on the Continent (Ward Perkins 1939: 179; Piggott 1983: 219, 223; Raftery 1984: 16). The perforations in the side-links of British three-link bridle-bits are in opposite planes, an important feature which distinguishes them from the contemporary Irish three-link bridle-bits (Fox 1947a: 33; Jope 1950: 58; Haworth 1971: 27, fig. 1; Spratling 1972: 93). A variety of materials and methods were used in the manufacture of the British three-link bridle-bits: the links can be of cast copper alloy, forged iron plated in copper alloy, or just forged iron; while the rein-rings can be of cast copper alloy, copper alloy tubes, forged iron plated in copper alloy, or just forged iron.

Whether the three-link bridle-bits are an insular innovation or were introduced from the Continent is debatable. Variations in ancient depositional practices in Britain, Ireland and the Continent have resulted in an apparently unrepresentative distribution of known examples, which makes the recognition of prototypes and sources of influence problematic. Leeds considered three-link bridle-bits to be the earliest type represented in the British Iron Age (1933a: 113), but avoided discussing their origins. Ward Perkins's survey of the Continental three-link bridle-bits suggested that they were early in date and that their distribution was restricted to the Marnian region of France (1939: 177–9). This prompted the view that the type was introduced to Britain by Marnian immigrants (Ward Perkins 1939: 179; Fox 1947a: 30; Hawkes 1959: 179–81; Barber and Megaw 1963: 207), however, only one of the Marnian bridle-bits, the example from the La Tène I vehicle burial at Somme-Tourbe, Marne, is closely comparable to the British three-link bridle-bits (Stead 1965a: 41). This three-link bridle-bit, with its fifth century BC associations, has been cited as a prototype for the British three-link bridle-bits (Stead 1965a: 42; 1979: 50), however, the significant chronological hiatus between it and the earliest British examples, coupled with differences in their form, suggests that this may not be the case (Spratling 1972: 91; 1979: 134). In addition to the Somme-Tourbe bridle-bit, Palk has identified several other Continental bridle-bits of the fifth to fourth century BC which have features reminiscent of the British series (1984: 99–100). The bridle-bits she cites from La Tène (i.e. Keller 1866: 254, pl. LXXII.5; Munro 1890: 294, fig. 89.18; Vouga 1923: 99, pl. XXXVI.4) and Almedinilla, Córdoba, southern Spain (Schüle 1969: tafel.80.2), have side-links with a segmented form similar to several of the British three-link bridle-bits, however, the La Tène and Almedinilla bridle-bits are of the two-link type and are significantly earlier than the British three-link bridle-bits, which suggests that they cannot be identified with confidence as Continental prototypes of the British series either.

Attempts at typological subdivision of the British bridle-bits have concentrated upon the three-link type, but have been flawed by the lack of dating evidence for individual examples and a concomitant over-reliance on doubtful Continental prototypes (Spratling 1972: 85–6; Piggott 1983: 222). Fox suggested a typological division based primarily on the method of manufacture and secondarily upon the form of the side-links (1947a: 30–1, fig. 15). This scheme was based on the assumption that the earliest British examples were manufactured during a period when copper alloy was scarce and that bridle-bits whose side-links were made partly or wholly of iron, such as the Arras examples, pre-dated those cast in copper alloy (Fox 1947a: 30–1). Within this two-fold division Fox argued that the shape of the side-links developed from a 'stream-lined' into a 'knobby', segmented form (1947a: 30, fig. 15). Clarke elaborated this scheme, suggesting that median grooves were earlier than rolls on the central mouldings of the centre-link (1951: 219). The scheme was based upon the assumption that three-link bridle-bits were first introduced to Britain by Marnian invaders and that the bridle-bits from Yorkshire are the earliest examples of the type, however, as noted above, the validity of a Marnian prototype is questionable. Fox's scheme is further undermined by examples of copper alloy plated iron side-links of 'knobby', segmented form (Fox 1947a: 31); cast, copper alloy side-links of stream-lined form (Stead 1965a: 41); and an absence of cast, copper alloy side-links of 'knobby', segmented form.

The shortcomings of Fox's scheme were discussed by Stead who proposed a new classification of the three-link bridle-bits based on the East Yorkshire burial evidence (1965a: 37–42). Stead identified four subtypes: the first had central-links of double-ring form (1965a: 37); the side-links of the second type were cast in one piece with the rein-rings (1965a: 38); the third had central-links of a simple ring form (1965a: 38); and the fourth group was of uncertain form, but arguably different from the other three types (1965a: 38–9). Stead also reversed Fox's sequence of side-link development and suggested that the 'stream-lined' Arras type of side-link with piriform heads developed from side-links of a 'ring-and-muff' or segmented form which had a long British vogue and were ultimately derived from the type represented by the Somme-Tourbe, Marnian example (1965a: 42). As noted above, the validity of identifying the Somme-Tourbe bridle-bit as a prototype for the British series is questionable and the absence of any demonstrably early British bridle-bits with segmented side-links undermines Stead's sequence. In addition, the meaningfulness of separating bridle-bits with different forms of central-link is doubtful as centre-links of simple ring form have frequently been interpreted as replacements for broken, more elaborate originals (for example, Fox 1947a: 81; Barber and Megaw 1963: 211; Savory 1976a: 57). Stead's identification of a subtype of three-link bridle-bit whose side-links are cast in one piece with the rein-rings is, however, of more value.

Barber and Megaw noted that the side-links of some three-link bridle-bits were cast in one piece, or fused, with the rein-rings (1963: 207), but Stead was the first to identify these as a separate subtype (1965a: 38). This form of three-link bridle-bit differed from the related derivative three-link bridle-bits (discussed below) in that its side-links were fused at their heads with the rein-rings (for example, Barber and Megaw 1963: pl. XXIV–XXV), while the side-links of the derivative three-link bridle-bits were fused mid-way along their length with the rein-rings (for example, MacGregor 1962: fig. 3). Stead, not unreasonably, suggested that the derivative three-link bridle-bits developed from the fused three-link bridle-bit subtype (1965a: 42), a view that both he (1979: 50) and others have reiterated (Spratling 1972: 96; MacGregor 1976: 25; Palk 1984: 17) and one which is maintained here. Identification of the subtype can be problematic, however, because it is difficult to ascertain whether the fusing of iron rein-rings and side-links is ancient or the result of post-depositional corrosion.

Another subdivision of the three-link bridle-bits is the Pexton Moor subtype (Stead 1959: 216; 1965a: 38; 1979: 50). This subtype consists of bridle-bits whose side-links are covered by either iron or copper alloy cylindrical sheaths. Three examples are known from: Cawthorn Camps, Danes' Graves and Pexton Moor, all in East Yorkshire (Table 7). The Pexton Moor bridle-bit is also possibly an example of the fused subtype of three-link bridle-bit. The space between the cylindrical cover and side-link in the Cawthorn Camps bridle-bit was packed with wood (Stead 1959: 216; 1965a: 38). The function of the side-link covers is unknown; possibly they protected the side-links in the horse's mouth. Both the small number of examples of the subtype and its restricted distribution suggest that it did not become popular during the Iron Age (Stead 1979: 50).

With the exception of the fused and Pexton Moor subtypes, attempts at subdividing the three-link bridle-bits have been of limited success and most recent authors have avoided attempting further typological subdivision (i.e. Spratling 1972: 85–94; MacGregor 1976: 24–5). Spratling considered variations in the form of three-link bridle-bits to be of regional rather than chronological significance (1972: 86) and suggested an eastern English and a western British tradition (1972: 86–92), but the validity of these traditions is questionable. Bridle-bits of the 'eastern English' tradition were defined as having their side-links cast on to, or in one piece with, their rein-rings and included all of the bridle-bits with double-ridged mouldings on their centre-links and decorated stop-studs on their rein-rings (Spratling 1972: 86–9). The fusing of side-links and rein-rings is the defining characteristic of the fused subtype of three-link bridle-bits noted above, and with the fused example from the River Thames at Old Windsor, Berkshire (Barber and Megaw 1963; Spratling 1972: 449, no. 158, fig. 56; Palk 1984: 36, no. DJ30, fig. C19) the distribution of this subtype extends beyond eastern England. Another problem of this grouping is that the rein-rings of the examples Spratling cites from Ringstead and Swanton Morley in Norfolk (1972: 86–7) actually rotate freely through the sockets of their respective side-links (Palk 1984: 37, 38, nos. DJ32–DJ33 and DJ36). Further undermining the integrity of the 'eastern England' tradition are the examples of unfused three-link bridle-bits with double-ridged mouldings on their centre-links from Hagbourne Hill, Berkshire (Ward Perkins 1939: 177, 180, 189–90, 192, pl. XIX.upper; Spratling 1972: 446, no. 150, fig. 52, pl. I.A; Palk 1984: 28–9, nos. DJ15–DJ16, figs. C9–C10), and the three-link bridle-bits with decorated stop-studs on their rein-rings from the Glastonbury lake village, Somerset (Bulleid and Gray 1911: 228, no. E194, pl. XLIV; Spratling 1972: 446, no. 149, fig. 57; Palk 1984: fig. C59.2) and Hengistbury Head, Hampshire (Spratling 1972: 447, no. 152, fig. 53, pl. 1.B; Cunliffe 1978: 62, fig. 29; Palk 1984: 30–1, no. DJ18, fig. C12, pl. IV; Cunliffe 1987: 151–2, no. 36, fig. 110). Spratling defined the 'western British' tradition as consisting of three-link bridle-bits whose side-links were of Fox's developed, 'knobby' or segmented form (1972: 89–90). Although there are no examples of bridle-bits from eastern Britain with segmented side-links, the occurrence of bridle-bits with side-links of 'stream-lined' form from near Baydon, Berkshire (Cunnington and Goddard 1911: 55, no. 458, pl. XXVIII.5; Fox 1947a: 30, 82; Palk 1984: 25, no. DJ5, fig. C1.2), Glastonbury, Somerset (Bulleid and Gray 1917: 378–9, 390, nos. I36, I78, pl. LXII; Coles and Minnitt 1995: 36, 59), Hayling Island, Hampshire (Downey *et al.* 1980: 293; Piggott 1983: 222; Palk 1984: 29–30, no. DJ17, fig. C11; King and Soffe 1998: 40) and Meare, Somerset (Gray and Bulleid 1953: 243, no. I44, pl. LI; Palk 1984: 35, no. DJ29, fig. C7.4) suggests that Spratling's western British tradition was not universally followed in the west.

The problems of using form to classify the three-link bridle-bits prompted Palk to outline a new classification based on the combinations of metals and techniques used in the manufacture of the bridle-bits (1984: 3). The scheme made no claims to chronological or typological integrity (1984: 2) and is of limited value because not all of the metal combinations can be identified with certainty, copper alloy plating on heavily corroded iron links and rein-rings being particularly difficult to identify. Furthermore, some bridle-bits, do not fit into the classes outlined (for example, the Hunsbury bridle-bit cf. Palk 1984: 32, no. DJ20, fig. C14), and a number of morphological characteristics crossed over several classes, suggesting that they had little, if any, ancient reality or significance.

Several tubular, copper alloy rein-rings, including five from Llyn Cerrig Bach (Nos. 16–20), have been found on their own. They are identified as being from three-link bridle-bits, rather than any other type of bridle-bit, because the only examples of tubular, copper alloy rein-rings still attached to side-links are from three-link bridle-bits; for example, one of the bridle-bits from Hagbourne Hill, Berkshire (Palk 1984: 29, no. DJ16, fig. C10; contra Wainwright and Spratling 1973: 121; Spratling 1979: 138, 142, fig. 106) and two from Llyn Cerrig Bach (Nos. 10–11). In the absence of an example of any other type of bridle-bit with tubular, copper alloy rein-rings, it is not unreasonable to assume that their use was restricted to three-link bridle-bits.

Details of the three-link bridle-bits of the British Iron Age, excluding the examples from Llyn Cerrig Bach, are included in Table 7. In addition to the tabulated bridle-bits, a large number of mould fragments for casting both the links and the stop-studs from the rein-rings of three-link bridle-bits were recovered from Gussage All Saints, Dorset

TABLE 7: Three-link bridle-bits of the British Iron Age (excluding the examples from Llyn Cerrig Bach)

Provenance	Description	References
Botley Copse, near Baydon, Berkshire	iron side-link	Cunnington and Goddard 1911: 55, no. 458, pl. XXVIII.5; Fox 1947a: 30, 82; Palk 1984: 25, no. DJ5, fig. C1.2
Beverley, East Yorkshire (2)	iron bridle-bits	Mortimer 1905: 359; Greenwell 1907: 278; Stead 1965a: 37, 91, 113; 1979: 47, 98
Bigberry Camp, Kent (2)	iron bridle-bits, one of which has copper alloy plated side-links	Boyd Dawkins 1902: 216, pl. III; Jessup 1932: 106; Thompson 1983: 274, nos. 42–3, fig. 17.35–6, pl. XXXVI.b–c,e–f; Palk 1984: 25–6, nos. DJ6–DJ7, figs. C4.1, C5
Bredon Hill, Gloucestershire (2 or 3)	an incomplete iron bridle-bit, a copper alloy plated iron side-link and a possible iron side-link	Hencken 1939: 71–2, nos. 1–3, fig. 5; Ward Perkins 1939: 180; Palk 1984: 26–7, nos. DJ8–DJ10, figs. C6, C7.5, C7.2
City Farm, Hanborough, Oxfordshire	copper alloy plated iron side-link	Case et al. 1966: 36, fig. 35.1; Palk 1984: 27, no. DJ11, fig. C7.3
Garton Slack, East Yorkshire (2)	iron bridle-bits	Brewster 1971: 290–1; 1975: 111; 1980: 388, fig. 249; Palk 1984: 27–8, nos. DJ12–DJ13, fig. C8, pls I–III
Glastonbury lake village, Somerset (6–8)	Fragments of six bridle-bits and a further two possible bridle-bits	Bulleid and Gray 1911: 227–8, nos. E76, E152, E194, pls XLI–XLIV; 1917: 378–9, 389–90, nos. I12a–b, I36, I78, I95, pl. LXII; Coles and Minnitt 1995: 33, 36, 58, 59, 72, 78, 84, fig. 6.11
Gussage All Saints, Dorset	copper alloy plated iron side-link	Wainwright and Spratling 1973: 121; Spratling 1979: 129–30, fig. 97; Palk 1984: 28, 85, no. DJ14, fig. C7.1
Hagbourne Hill, Berkshire (2)	bridle-bits with cast copper alloy links and tubular, copper alloy rein-rings	King 1812: 348–9, no. 1, pl. L; Peake 1931: 65; Ward Perkins 1939: 177, 180, 189–90, 192, pl. XIX.upper; Spratling 1972: 446, no. 150, fig. 52, pl. I.A; Palk 1984: 28–9, nos. DJ15–DJ16, figs. C9–C10
Ham Hill, Somerset	iron side-link	Gray 1924: 114, no. I6, pl. XIII.16; Fox 1947a: 82; Spratling 1979: 129
Harborough Cave, Brassington, Derbyshire	broken iron rein-ring plated or sheathed in a copper alloy sleeve	Smith 1909b: 102, fig. 3; MacGregor 1976: 51; Spratling 1972: 446, no. 151

Provenance	Description	References
Hayling Island, Hampshire	incomplete, cast copper alloy bridle-bit	Downey, King and Soffe 1980: 293; Piggott 1983: 222; Palk 1984: 29–30, no. DJ17, fig. C11; King and Soffe 1998: 40
Hengistbury Head, Hampshire	bridle-bit with cast copper alloy links and iron rein-rings plated or sheathed in copper alloy sleeves	Spratling 1972: 447, no. 152, fig. 53, pl. 1.B; Cunliffe 1978: 62, fig. 29; Palk 1984: 30–1, no. DJ18, fig. C12, pl. IV; Cunliffe 1987: 151–2, no. 36, fig. 110
Hunsbury, Northamptonshire (2)	one complete iron bridle-bit with a copper alloy band on the central link and fragments of another iron bridle-bit	Dryden 1885: 59, pl. VII.8; Fell 1936: 66, no. 13, pl. VI.a; Palk 1984: 32, no. DJ20, fig. C14
western Meare lake 'village', Somerset	part of an iron side-link	Gray and Bulleid 1953: 243, no. I44, pl. I44, pl. LI; Palk 1984: 35, no. DJ29, fig. C7.4
Read's Cavern, Burrington, Somerset	part of a probable tubular, copper alloy rein-ring	Palmer 1922: 13, pl. VIII; Spratling 1972: 444
Ringstead, Norfolk (2)	bridle-bits with cast copper alloy links and iron rein-rings plated or sheathed in copper alloy sleeves	Clarke 1951: 216–19, pls XVI.left, XVII.a; Spratling 1972: 449–50, no. 159; Palk 1984: 37, nos. DJ32–DJ33, fig. C20; Hutcheson 2004: 107, 126, nos. 30–1
Silkstead, Otterbourne, Hampshire	cast copper alloy central link	Palk 1984: 38, no. DJ34, fig. C21.2; Denford 1992: 39–41, fig. 12
River Thames at Strand-on-the-Green, London	iron bridle-bit with copper alloy plated or encased rein-rings	Spratling 1972: 86; Palk 1984: 38, no. DJ35, fig. C22
Swanton Morley, Norfolk	bridle-bit with cast copper alloy links and copper alloy plated or encased iron rein-rings	B. Green 1962; Spratling 1972: 450, no. 160, fig. 58; Palk 1984: 38, no. DJ36, fig. C23; Hutcheson 2004: 106–7, 126, no. 26

Tunstall, Suffolk	incomplete copper alloy bridle-bit; one of the side-links is decorated with an iron terminal boss	Martin *et al.* 2002: 210, fig. 46.A
Ulceby-on-Humber, Lincolnshire (2)	two bridle-bits, of which only an iron rein-ring sheathed in a copper alloy sleeve and part of a cast copper alloy side-link survive	Cuming 1859: 227–8, pl. 22; Leeds 1933b: 466, pl. LXXXI.1; Phillips 1935: 105–7, pl. XXII.a; Ward Perkins 1939: 181, fig. 6; Fox 1958: 35–6, fig. 21.b, pl. 24.c; Megaw 1970: 169–70, no. 293; May 1976: 156, 161–2, figs. 76.1, 78; Nicholson 1980: 14, no. 3, fig. 1; Palk 1984: 38–9, no. DJ37, fig. C21
Walthamstow, Essex	bridle-bit with cast copper alloy links and iron rein-rings sheathed in copper alloy sleeves	Barber and Megaw 1963: 208, 211–13; Spratling 1972: 451, no. 162, fig. 60; Palk 1984: 39, no. DJ38, fig. C24
Dog Holes, Warton Crag, Lancashire	possible iron bridle-bit	J. W. Jackson 1910: 73, pl. II.7; Bulleid and Gray 1917: 379; MacGregor 1976: 53
West Coker, Somerset ? (3)	fragments of three tubular, copper alloy rein-rings	Fox 1952: 109–11, pl. V; Atkinson and Piggott 1955: 228, 234; Fox 1958: 14, fig. 10; Spratling 1972: 452, no. 163, fig. 57
Wetwang Slack, East Yorkshire (2)	two bridle-bits with iron links with cast-on copper alloy terminals and copper alloy plated iron rein-rings	Dent 1985: 90, fig. 3; Stead 1991a: 54
Fused subtype Hunmanby, East Yorkshire	cast copper alloy bridle-bit	Sheppard 1907: 482, 485, pl. opp. 487; Stead 1965a: 38, 42, 94, 113, fig. 18.2; 1979: 47, 50, 102, fig. 15.2; Palk 1984: 31, no. DJ19, fig. C13, pl. V
Kirkburn, East Yorkshire (2)	two bridle-bits with an iron centre-link, iron side-links with cast-on copper alloy terminals and iron rein-rings sheathed in copper alloy sleeves	Stead 1991a: 53–4, fig. 44

Provenance	Description	References
River Thames at Old Windsor, Berkshire	cast copper alloy bridle-bit	Barber and Megaw 1963; Spratling 1972: 449, no. 158, fig. 56; Palk 1984: 36, no. DJ30, fig. C19
Unprovenanced	cast copper alloy bridle-bit	Palk 1984: 39–40, no. DJ39, fig. C25, pl. VII
Probably fused subtype		
King's barrow, Arras, East Yorkshire (2)	two bridle-bits with cast copper alloy links and iron rein-rings either plated or sheathed in copper alloy	Mortimer 1905: 358; Greenwell 1907: 281, fig. 22; Stead 1965a: 37, 42, 89, 113, fig. 18.1; Stead 1979: 47, 49–50, 98, fig. 15.1; Palk 1984: 25, no. DJ4, fig. C3
Charioteer's barrow, Arras, East Yorkshire (2)	two iron bridle-bits, of which only fragments of a rein-ring, side-link and centre-link of one of the bridle-bits survive	Mortimer 1905: 358; Greenwell 1907: 282; Stead 1965a: 38–9, 90, 114; 1979: 47, 50, 98; Palk 1984: 24, no. DJ1, fig. C1.1
Lady's barrow, Arras, East Yorkshire (2)	two bridle-bits with cast copper alloy links and iron rein-rings sheathed in copper alloy sleeves	Greenwell 1877: 455; Mortimer 1905: 359; Greenwell 1907: 285, fig. 29; Stead 1965a: 37, 42, 91, 113; 1979: 47, 49–50, 98, fig. 16; Palk 1984: 24, nos. DJ2–DJ3, fig. C2
Pexton Moor subtype		
Cawthorn Camps, East Yorkshire	fragmented iron bridle-bit with an iron cylindrical side-link cover	Mortimer 1905: 361; Stead 1959: 216; 1965a: 38, 86, 92, 114; 1979: 47, 50, 99
Danes' Graves, Driffield, East Yorkshire	two iron bridle-bits, of which only a rein-ring, side-link and a copper alloy cylindrical side-link cover survive	Mortimer 1897: 3, 9, pl. I; Mortimer 1905: 359, fig. 1021; Stead 1959: 216; 1965a: 38, 86, 93, 114, fig. 2; 1979: 47, 50, 100
Pexton Moor, East Yorkshire	bridle-bit with iron rein-rings sheathed in copper alloy sleeves, iron links and a copper alloy cylindrical side-link cover	Stead 1959: 215, fig. 2; 1965a: 37–8, 40, 42, 86, 95–6, 114, fig. 19; 1979: 47, 50, 103, fig. 15.3; Palk 1984: 36–7, no. DJ31, pl. VI

(Wainwright and Spratling 1973: 121, pl. XXII.1–3; Spratling 1979: 134–40, fig. 104.2–4; Foster 1980: 13–18, 22–4) and a smaller assemblage of mould fragments for three-link bridle-bits was recovered from Weelsby Avenue, Grimsby, Lincolnshire (Foster 1995: 53). A fragment of a mould for casting a bridle-bit with fixed rings is also known from South Cadbury, Somerset (Spratling 1979: 138, fig. 104.1; Barrett *et al.* 2000b: 298).

The archaeological dating evidence for the main group of three-link bridle-bits does not provide a narrow date range. The bridle-bits from Beverley, Cawthorn Camps, Danes' Graves, Garton Slack and Wetwang Slack are all part of the East Yorkshire vehicle burial tradition which probably began at some point in the fourth or third century BC (Stead 1991a: 184; Wait 1995: 499) and apparently ended before the mid first century BC (Stead 1991a: 184). The Botley Copse side-link was recovered from near the site of a Romano-British settlement at Baydon and is associated with an assemblage of typical Romano-British ironwork (Cunnington and Goddard 1911: 55–6, nos. 452–72a), although the recovery of a La Tène I brooch from the site (Fox 1947a: 82) suggests it may have been occupied from as early as the fourth or third century BC. The bridle-bits from Bigberry Camp were chance finds from the hillfort where occupation began during the fifth to third centuries BC and extended to the mid first century BC (Thompson 1983: 254–6; Blockley and Blockley 1989: 245–6; Parfitt 1998: 350). Presumably, the bridle-bit from Bigberry dates to this period, but the discovery of artefacts of Roman type from the site suggests the possibility of later depositional activity at the site (Manning 1972: 230; W. H. Manning pers. comm.). Of the material from Bredon Hill the incomplete iron bridle-bit (Hencken 1939: 71–2, fig. 5.1) and the possible iron side-link (Hencken 1939: 72, fig. 5.3) were recovered from the site's first phase, while the copper alloy plated, iron side-link (Hencken 1939: 72, no. 2, fig. 5.2) was unstratified. Analysis of pottery from the site suggests the initial phase of occupation dates from *c.* 400/300 BC to 100 BC (cf. Cunliffe 1991: 81, fig. A:18). The side-link from City Farm, Hanborough, was recovered from a part of the settlement where occupation was dated from the late third to second century BC (Case *et al.* 1966: 87). The stratified material from the Glastonbury lake village consisted of a tubular, copper alloy rein-ring (Bulleid and Gray 1911: 228, no. E194, pl. XLIV), and two iron side-links (Bulleid and Gray 1917: 378–9, 389, nos. 12a–b, pl. LXII) dated to the late phase (175–80 BC) (Coles and Minnitt 1995: 204) and a possible tubular, copper alloy rein-ring (Bulleid and Gray 1911: 228, no. E152, pl. XLI) dated to the final phase (80–50 BC) (Coles and Minnitt 1995: 206). The remaining finds from Glastonbury were unstratified and could date from any point during the site's occupation from the mid third century to the mid first century BC (Coles and Minnitt 1995: 199–206; Coles and Coles 1996: 94–100; for a critique of the mid third century BC foundation of the Glastonbury lake village see Haselgrove 1997: 60). The side-link, and mould fragments, from Gussage All Saints were recovered from Pit 209 (Spratling 1979: 129–30, fig. 97). Two radiocarbon dates of charcoal samples from Pit 209 (Wainwright and Switsur 1976: 39, samples F and G) have calibrated date ranges, expressed to one standard deviation, of 355 BC to 20 BC and 165 BC to AD 80 which suggests a date range for both the side-link, and the important assemblage of copper alloy working debris from the same pit, to the first two centuries BC (see also Wainwright 1979: 21; Foster 1980: 7; Stead 1991a: 183). The Hagbourne Hill bridle-bits are nineteenth-century finds reportedly recovered from a pit associated with three terrets, a ring-headed pin, coins and a Bronze Age socketed axe and spearhead. Although votive assemblages containing material of both Iron Age and earlier prehistoric date are known, it is possible that the Hagbourne Hill material was found separately and collated into a single collection prior to being recorded (Peake 1931: 65–6; Spratling 1972: 390). Consequently, none of the allegedly associated material can be used with confidence to provide a date for the Hagbourne Hill bridle-bits. The side-link from Ham Hill was found in a small pit associated with pottery apparently of the Glastonbury or South-western Style (Gray 1924: 114–15), which principally dates from the fourth or third centuries BC to the first century BC (Elsdon 1989: 27; Cunliffe 1991: 461). The precise context and associations of the rein-ring from Harborough Cave are unknown (Smith 1909b: 97). Material ranging from the Bronze Age to the medieval period has been recovered from the site and at least two separate focuses of Iron Age and Roman period deposition have been identified (Smith 1909b; Branigan and Dearne 1991: 32); it is probable that the rein-ring was associated with one of these. The incomplete bridle-bit from Hayling Island was a votive deposit associated with the pre-Roman temple phase of the site (Piggott 1983: 222; Downey *et al.* 1980: 293) dated from the early to mid first century BC to the second half of the first century AD (Cunliffe 1991: 512; King and Soffe 1994: 115; 1998: 35). The bridle-bit from Hengistbury Head was recovered in Gray's excavations of 1921, but its precise context is unknown (Spratling 1972: 447). Occupation at Hengistbury Head is continuous throughout the late Iron Age into at least the mid second century AD (Cunliffe 1987: 336–46; but see Haselgrove 1997: 61) and the bridle-bit presumably dates to some point during this period. The Hunsbury bridle-bits are chance finds from the interior of the hillfort (Dryden 1885: 56; George 1917: 3–4; Fell 1936: 57). The main period of occupation at Hunsbury was the second to first centuries BC (D. Jackson 1993–4: 18) and it is during this period that the deposition of the bridle-bits probably occurred. Occupation of the western 'village' at Meare probably commenced in, or around, the third century BC and was abandoned in, or around, the first to second centuries AD (Coles 1987: 246–7). More precise dating of the Meare bridle-bit on stratigraphic grounds is not possible (Orme *et al.* 1981: 68; Coles 1987: 243). The probable tubular, copper alloy rein-ring from Read's Cavern was associated with pottery similar to that from the Glastonbury lake village, Somerset (Palmer 1922: 14; Spratling 1972: 444) suggesting that the sites are probably, but not certainly, coeval. The Ringstead bridle-bits are part of a hoard discovered by chance in 1950 and conventionally dated to the second half of the first century BC (Clarke 1951: 214–15, 224), although Hutcheson has plausibly argued that the hoard may be as early as the second century BC (2004: 33). The circumstances of the discovery of the centre-link from Silkstead are unrecorded (Denford 1992: 29), although the site has speculatively been identified as a temple dating from the Iron Age to the Roman period (Denford 1992: 51–2). The bridle-bit from the River Thames at Strand-on-the-Green, London has no recorded associations (Barber and Megaw 1963: 211, fn. 7). The bridle-bits from Swanton Morley, Tunstall and Ulceby-on-Humber are all chance finds. No details of the discovery or associations of the Walthamstow bridle-bit are known (Ward Perkins 1939: 176; Spratling 1972: 451). The precise context and associations of the possible iron bridle-bit from Dog Holes, Warton Crag are unrecorded (J. W. Jackson 1910: 73); other material recovered from the cave suggests depositional activity occurred at the site from the Iron Age and into the Roman period (Branigan and Dearne 1991: 76–8; 1992: 92–3). There are considerable doubts over the provenance of the three rein-rings possibly from West Coker and, although they may have been recovered from a Roman site, they are best considered as being unprovenanced (Fox 1952: 108). In summary, the archaeological dating evidence for the main group of three-link bridle-bits suggests that the type dates from at least the second century BC, if not the fourth or third century BC, and continues in vogue until at least the second half of the first century BC. Although a number of the bridle-bits may be of Roman date, none of them can be definitely demonstrated to be this late on the basis of either their context of deposition or their associations.

The decorative motifs employed on several of the main group of three-link bridle-bits do not refine the wide chronological span for the type. Bridle-bits from Glastonbury, Hengistbury Head, Ringstead and Ulceby-on-Humber are decorated with pseudo-stitch decoration, which potentially remained in vogue from the fourth or third century BC until at least the middle of the first century AD (see the section on terrets in Chapter 2 for a comprehensive discussion of this decorative style). Partly on the basis of their decoration, several of the main group of three-link bridle-bits have been included in the so-called Gussage–Bury Hill tradition (Cunliffe 1995: 38). The validity of this grouping, and by extension its use for dating purposes, is questionable and it is not considered further here (for a discussion of the so-called Gussage–Bury Hill tradition see the section on terrets in Chapter 2). Bridle-bits from Hengistbury Head, Ringstead, Ulceby-on-Humber and Walthamstow are decorated in Stead's Style V of insular La Tène art. Although formerly dated to the first century BC (Stead 1985a: 23), recent work on burial evidence from East Yorkshire and Deal, Kent (Stead 1991a: 183; 1995: 95) suggests that the use of Style V art began in the third century BC (the insular art sequence is discussed further in Chapter 5). The decoration on the tubular, copper alloy rein-ring possibly from West Coker, Somerset, is probably influenced by the Continental Waldalgesheim Style (Atkinson and Piggott 1955: 228) suggesting that it may be as early as the fourth or third century BC, although it could be significantly later.

The archaeological dating evidence for the fused three-link bridle-bits is also poor, but does suggest a pre-Roman date for the subtype. As noted above, the East Yorkshire vehicle burials, which include the Arras, Hunmanby, Kirkburn and Pexton Moor bridle-bits, probably began as early as the fourth or third century BC and apparently ended before the mid first century BC (Wait 1995: 499; Stead 1991a: 184). Of the remaining fused three-link bridle-bits, both the Old Windsor bridle-bit (Barber and Megaw 1963: 206; Spratling 1972: 449) and the unprovenanced example in the British Museum (Palk 1984: 39–40) have no recorded associations. The precise context of the mould fragment of part of a fused three-link bridle-bit from South Cadbury is unrecorded, but it dates to the Middle

Cadbury phase (Barrett *et al.* 2000b: 298) suggesting a pre-Roman date (see also Alcock 1972: 156; Spratling 1979: 138). As with the main series of three-link bridle-bits (see above), the examples decorated with pseudo-stitch decoration (King's Barrow, Arras) and Stead's Style V art (Old Windsor), as well as the bridle-bits included in the so-called Gussage–Bury Hill tradition (Arras, Hunmanby and Old Windsor), do not narrow the wide date range for the fused three-link bridle-bits.

With the exception of the bridle-bits from East Yorkshire and the possible iron bridle-bit from Dog Holes, Warton Crag, Lancashire, the distribution of three-link bridle-bits is restricted to southern Britain. Contexts of deposition include: the East Yorkshire vehicle burials (Arras, Beverley, Cawthorn Camps, Danes' Graves, Garton Slack, Hunmanby, Kirkburn, Pexton Moor and Wetwang Slack); caves (Harborough Cave and Dog Holes); probable votive deposits buried at the rear of hillfort ramparts (Bredon Hill); pits from settlement sites and hillforts (City Farm, Gussage All Saints, Ham Hill and possibly Hagbourne Hill and Hunsbury); votive deposits buried at temple sites (Hayling Island and possibly Silkstead); the River Thames (Strand-on-the-Green and Old Windsor); and hoard assemblages (Llyn Cerrig Bach, Ringstead and possibly Botley Copse if the recorded association with Romano-British ironwork is valid). Attributing meaning to depositional contexts is difficult, but the majority of those outlined above suggest deliberate ritual deposition rather than casual loss or disposal. A regional pattern of the use of bridle-bits as grave goods in East Yorkshire and as elements of votive deposits in a variety of contexts in southern Britain is observable. This pattern suggests that the known distribution of bridle-bits is more likely to be a product of regional variations in ancient depositional practices, rather than evidence of the limits of their functional use during antiquity. Therefore, the absence of known three-link bridle-bits from large parts of the Midlands, northern Britain and Wales is not necessarily proof that they were not used during antiquity in these areas.

The three-link bridle-bits from Llyn Cerrig Bach include: two complete bridle-bits with tubular, copper alloy rein rings and predominantly cast, copper alloy mouthpieces (Nos. 10–11); four fragments consisting of forged iron rein-rings and attached side-links plated in copper alloy (Nos. 12–15); five tubular, copper alloy rein rings which, for the reasons outlined above, are probably from three-link bridle-bits (Nos. 16–20); and two iron rings which are probably centre-links from three-link bridle-bits, one of which is iron plated with copper alloy (No. 21) and the other of which is apparently just forged from iron (Fox 1947a: 89, no. 83, pl. XXVIII; Savory 1976a: 59, no. 17.83, fig. 21.2). The Irish, cast copper alloy, three-link bridle-bit from Llyn Cerrig Bach (No. 23) is discussed in a subsequent section of this chapter. Two of the fragments consisting of forged iron rein-rings and attached side-links (Nos. 14–15) were previously considered fragments of the same bridle-bit (Fox 1947a: 30–1, 80–1, no. 49, pl. XXII; Spratling 1972: 86, 89–90, 260, 340; Savory 1976a: 57, no. 17.49, fig. 18.1; Palk 1984: 33, no. DJ24, fig. C16.2), but although both fragments are similar it is not certain that they are parts of the same bridle-bit. They could either be an unrelated pair simply manufactured in the same style or, considering the evidence for paired draught in the late Iron Age, fragments from two separate bridle-bits which made up a matching pair. An unaccessioned, modern electrotype in the collections of the National Museum of Wales has previously been mistakenly identified as an ancient bridle-bit which formed a matching pair with the genuine asymmetrical three-link bridle-bit that it is a copy of (i.e. No. 11) (Palk 1984: 35, 92, no. DJ27).

Of the two Llyn Cerrig Bach bridle-bits which contain cast copper alloy components, one has both cast side-links and a cast centre-link (No. 11), while the other has cast side-links but an iron centre-link (No. 10). It is probable that the iron centre-link is a secondary repair and that originally both of these bridle-bits had cast centre-links (Fox 1947a: 28, 81; Spratling 1972: 447; Palk 1984: 32). Other examples of three-link bridle-bits with cast copper alloy mouthpieces include those from Hagbourne Hill, Hayling Island, Hengistbury Head, Ringstead, Swanton Morely, Tunstall and Walthamstow. The careful finishing of these bridle-bits prevents their study being instructive on the methods employed in their manufacture, but the examination of mould fragments of cast bridle-bit mouthpieces from Gussage All Saints, Dorset (Wainwright and Spratling 1973: 121; Spratling 1979: 134–40; Foster 1980: 13–18, 22–4) and Weelsby Avenue, Grimsby, Lincolnshire (Foster 1995) does provide an insight into their production. Although it has been suggested that the casting of copper alloy artefacts was restricted to simple settlement sites during the late Iron Age (Northover 1995: 290), the recovery of a mould fragment of a three-link bridle-bit side-link from the hillfort of South Cadbury, Somerset (Spratling 1979: 138, fig. 104.1; Barrett *et al.* 2000b: 298), suggests that this distribution pattern may be more apparent than real (but see Foster 1995: 57–8). Study of the mould fragments from Gussage All Saints suggests that the links were lost-wax castings and that the mouthpieces were manufactured in two stages; initially the two side-links were separately cast and then the centre-link, joining the two side-links, was cast (Spratling 1979: 138; Foster 1980: 13; contra Palk 1984: 84). This sequence of casting also appears to have been the order followed in the manufacture of Irish three-link bridle-bits (see below). The large number of bridle-bits manufactured at Gussage All Saints suggests the possibility that the wax patterns for the side-links were made in moulds themselves (Foster 1980: 14; see also Tylecote 1962: 123–8). The side-links of both of the bridle-bits with cast copper alloy mouthpieces from Llyn Cerrig Bach are of slightly different length, indicating that this was not the case with their manufacture. If the examples from Llyn Cerrig Bach were manufactured in the same way as the pieces from Gussage All Saints then the most technically difficult part of the manufacturing process would have been the casting of the centre-link. This would have involved the modelling of a wax pattern of the centre-link which articulated with the previously cast side-links and the building of a clay mould round all three of them. Several of the mould fragments from Gussage All Saints demonstrate the relative positions of the side-links during this process (Foster 1980: 16, fig. 11). The space between the articulating sockets of the centre-links and side-links was small and the centre-link mould would have required considerable skill to manufacture. Impressions on the side-link elements of centre-link moulds from Gussage All Saints suggest that fabric may have been wrapped around the side-links to keep them separate from the loops of the centre-link and thereby avoid a miscasting (Foster 1980: 22–3). Despite the slight casting flaw in a side-link of one of the Llyn Cerrig Bach bridle-bits (No. 10) the production of the mouthpieces of these two three-link bridle-bits represents an impressive technical achievement.

The copper alloy plating of iron items of horse harness is not uncommon during the late Iron Age and the four forged iron rein-rings with attached side-links (Nos. 12–15) and one of the probable centre-links (No. 21) from Llyn Cerrig Bach are all copper alloy plated. Metallographic examination of comparable pieces suggests that the plating was achieved by hot-dipping the iron artefacts into molten copper alloy (Northover and Salter 1990: 114–15; Northover 1995: 295). This technique produces a fast reaction which results in a strong and coherent plating being formed (Northover 1995: 295). Plating was probably intended to serve two purposes: first, it would give the treated iron artefacts the appearance of having been cast in copper alloy; and second, it would form a brazed butt-joint between two adjacent pieces of iron (Northover and Slater 1990: 114; Northover 1995: 295). Metallurgical analysis suggests that the side-link from Gussage All Saints had a thin layer of tin plated on it prior to being plated with copper alloy (Palk 1984: 85; Northover and Salter 1990: 114; Fell 1990: 213). The metallurgical advantage of tinning ironwork prior to plating it with copper alloy is not obvious and it is probable that the layer identified as tin on the Gussage All Saints side-link is an incorrectly identified, copper alloy corrosion phenomenon (P. Northover pers. comm.). Metallographic examination of copper alloy plated items of horse harness from Maiden Castle, Dorset and Bury Hill, Hampshire suggests that these items were plated in copper alloy without previously being tinned (Northover and Slater 1990: 114–15; Jones 1992: 35–6).

Producing the appearance of a casting was probably the motivation in plating the iron rein-rings with attached side-links from Llyn Cerrig Bach (Nos. 12–15). The form of the side-links of these pieces is segmented and resembles the cast side-links from Llyn Cerrig Bach (Nos. 10–11). This segmented form would have required considerable additional effort to have forged in iron and serves no purpose other than to imitate a casting. It is not certain whether the bridle-bits were plated so as to avoid the technical difficulties of casting articulating parts, or to overcome a shortage of copper alloy, or even wax, for producing castings. The plating of the iron rein-rings (Nos. 12–15) and centre-link (No. 21) also brazed their butt-joints. This method of forming closed loops would have obviated the need for producing scarf-welded joints, but it would have necessitated that the ironwork was clean prior to plating and required that the gap to be brazed was less than one millimetre in width (Northover and Slater 1980: 115). Although no trace of copper alloy plating remains on either the possible centre-link (Fox 1947a: 89, no. 83, pl. XXVIII; Savory 1976a: 59, no. 17.83, fig. 21.2) or the centre-link of one of the three-link bridle-bits (No. 10) from Llyn Cerrig Bach, the use of butt-joints, rather than scarf welds, to close these iron rings suggests that they too were originally plated. Fox noted traces of copper alloy plating on the centre-link of the bridle-bit (No. 10) (1947a: 28), but these no longer survive.

Study of the copper alloy plated bridle-bits from Llyn Cerrig Bach is hampered by their poor preservation. The rein-rings of the bridle-bits must have been attached to the side-links prior to being plated because this operation would have brazed closed their butt-joints. Consequently, the side-links themselves were probably plated prior to being attached to the rein-rings. Presumably, the rein-rings were plated in more than one operation for they would have been held in tongs preventing their surface being completely coated in one dipping. Two dipping operations would also prevent the socket of the side-link, through which the rein-rings articulated, becoming blocked with excess copper alloy. The need to dip the rein-rings twice would have required that they could be rotated freely through the socket of the side-link until the plating was completed, and therefore the stop-studs must have been inserted following the plating. Microscopic examination of the Llyn Cerrig Bach rein-rings suggests that the rein-rings were indeed plated prior to the insertion of the stop-studs, which had previously been plated themselves. Presumably any evidence of an overlap of copper alloy plating from different dipping operations was polished out during the finishing of the bridle-bits.

Fox incorrectly suggested that two of the plated bridle-bit fragments (Nos. 14–15) were sheathed in copper alloy rather than being plated, because he failed to recognize the non-functional, skeumorphic character of their pseudo-stitch decoration which he considered to be the result of joining a copper alloy sheath round the iron core of the rein-ring (1947a: 28, 80). This decoration consists of a raised line on the outer edge of the rein-rings of both fragments which has been punched alternately on either side to produce a sinuous form. Microscopic examination suggests that the iron rein-ring was forged with a central flange which, when plated, produced the raised copper alloy flange which was subsequently punched to form the sinuous line (for a discussion of pseudo-stitch decoration see the section on terrets in Chapter 2).

Bridle-bits with penannular, tubular, copper alloy rein-rings include the two examples from Llyn Cerrig Bach and one of the Hagbourne Hill, Berkshire, bridle-bits (Palk 1984: 29, no. DJ16, fig. C10; contra Wainwright and Spratling 1973: 121; Spratling 1979: 138, 142, fig. 106). In addition, tubular, copper alloy rein-rings found on their own are known from Glastonbury (Bulleid and Gray 1911: 228, nos. E152 and E194, pls XLI and XLIV; Palk 1984: fig. C59.2), Llyn Cerrig Bach (Nos. 16–20), Read's Cavern and West Coker. Fox considered that one of the tubular rein-rings from Llyn Cerrig Bach (No. 19) was too small to have functioned as a rein-ring and identified it as a bracelet (1947a: 90). Although it is slightly smaller (diameter approximately 70 mm) than the other rein-rings from Llyn Cerrig Bach, it is of a comparable size with examples from Hagbourne Hill (diameter approximately 73–7 mm) and Hengistbury Head (diameter approximately 75 mm) and its identification as a rein-ring is not unreasonable (Lynch 1970: 266; Spratling 1972: 340). Of the parallels for this probable rein-ring quoted by Fox (1947a: 90) the Read's Cavern rein-ring is noted above; the five rings from the vehicle burial at Danes' Grave, East Yorkshire (Mortimer 1897–9: 123, nos. 2–3, 6–7 and 9; Greenwell 1907: 278) have been identified as iron harness rings with penannular copper alloy casings (Stead 1965a: 93; 1979: 51, 100); the ring from Ham Hill, Somerset (Hoare 1827: 42, pl. VI.bottom) although similar in form is probably too small (diameter 43 mm) to have functioned as a rein-ring; and the tubular rein-ring from Birdlip, Gloucestershire is described as closing with a spring (Bellows 1880–81: 139; Smith 1908–9: 332), suggesting that it is probably either a bracelet or an armlet (Spratling 1972: 552).

How these tubular, copper alloy rein-rings were closed and whether they would have been strong enough to function without reinforcement is not certain. Fox suggested that they were fitted with short iron or copper alloy sleeves which were fitted prior to their stop-studs being attached (1947a: 81; 1952: 108). In contrast, Spratling considered them to have only been sleeves themselves, which were originally fitted round iron rings that had preferentially corroded in the burial environment (Spratling 1972: 86; Wainwright and Spratling 1973: 121). Spratling's interpretation was based on analogy with those three-link bridle-bits which do have iron rein-rings with copper alloy sheaths such as the examples from Pexton Moor and Ulceby-on-Humber. Although iron may preferentially corrode in comparison to associated copper alloys (Cronyn 1990: 170) it is unlikely that the tubular rein-rings were fitted around iron cores which have completely corroded away. Corrosion of iron artefacts involves a significant increase in their size as ferrous corrosion products have a greater volume than their parent metal (Watkinson and Neal 1998: 34). Consequently, the preferential corrosion of an iron ring would have resulted in a significant distortion of any surrounding tubular, copper alloy rein-ring. Since the tubular rein-rings from Llyn Cerrig Bach, Hagbourne Hill and West Coker are largely undistorted, the suggestion that they were covers for iron rings can be dismissed. The tubular rein-rings were shaped from rectangular strips of copper alloy which were presumably cold worked around a curved, circular-sectioned, pattern until the penannular ring, with a butt-join round its circumference on its inner edge, was formed. That they would have needed to have been closed to function properly is probable; the method by which this was achieved is less obvious. The rein-rings may have been fitted with sleeves which were fixed into position by stop-studs as Fox suggested (1947a: 81; 1952: 108) or, alternatively, connecting bars between the two ends of the rein-rings may have been inserted and then held in place by rivets.

It is not certain what material the sleeves or connecting bars were manufactured from, although traces of ferrous corrosion in the ends of two of the tubular rein-rings (Nos. 18–19) suggest that, for these two at least, the bars may have been of iron. The occurrence of two sets of diametrically opposed fixing holes on both ends of some of the tubular rein-rings from both Llyn Cerrig Bach (Nos. 10, 17–18) and West Coker (Fox 1952: 110, no. 5, pl. V) suggests that one set may have been used for attaching stop-studs while the other set was used for fixing the connecting sleeve or bar. Other tubular rein-rings from both Llyn Cerrig Bach (Nos. 11, 16, 19–20) and West Coker (Fox 1952: 108, nos. 1–2, fig. 1) only have one set of fixing holes at each end, suggesting that the same rivets were often used for attaching both stop-studs and fixing a connecting sleeve or bar. That the ends of the tubular rein-rings frequently taper suggests that the connecting bars or sleeves were thinner than the rein-rings. Until an example of the type with an intact connecting sleeve or bar is discovered it will remain uncertain how these tubular rings were closed.

Stop-studs are small fittings which are attached to rein-rings either side of the terminal bulb socket of the conjoined side-link. They are designed to prevent the rein-ring from revolving through the side-links (Leeds 1933a: 114; Fox 1947a: 27; Lynch 1970: 266; Spratling 1972: 86; Foster 1980: 18). Their use is restricted to certain examples of both the main group of British three-link bridle-bits and the Irish three-link bridle-bits, although non-functional examples occur on some of the fused subtype of three-link bridle-bit (Spratling 1972: 87). Two types of stop-stud are represented in the Llyn Cerrig Bach assemblage: flattened iron stop-studs plated in copper alloy and attached with iron rivets (Nos. 12–13) and large, hollow, spherical copper alloy studs attached with copper alloy rivets (Nos. 10–11, 16, 20). On the Llyn Cerrig Bach bridle-bits the use of the iron stop-studs is restricted to iron rein-rings and the use of spherical, copper alloy stop-studs is restricted to tubular, copper alloy rein-rings. Examples of spherical copper alloy stop-studs also occur on the bridle-bits from Hagbourne Hill and Harborough Cave, but there are no other known examples of iron stop-studs. A third type of stop-stud was cast in copper alloy with an integral rivet and is variously decorated or plain, and flat or spherical in shape. Examples of this type were manufactured at Gussage All Saints, Dorset (Spratling 1979: 138, fig. 105.1; Foster 1980: 18, pl.16) and occur on three-link bridle-bits, of both the main group and fused subtype, from Ringstead, Old Windsor, Ulceby-on-Humber, Walthamstow as well as both the King's Barrow and Lady's Barrow, Arras. The stop-studs on the fused subtype of three-link bridle-bits were non-functional as the position of their side-links on their rein-rings was fixed. The rein-rings of the unprovenanced fused subtype of three-link bridle-bit (Palk 1984: 39–40, no. DJ39, fig. C25, pl. VII) have stud-like pseudo-terminals which are cast in one with the rein-rings rather than stop-studs. Similar, but functional, stud-like terminals cast in one with the rein-rings occur on many of the Irish three-link bridle-bits, including the example from Llyn Cerrig Bach (No. 23).

Bridle-bits are susceptible to wear and damage where their component parts rub against each other. Although there is some difficulty in distinguishing between wear facets and areas of corrosion, all of the three-link bridle-bits from Llyn Cerrig Bach, with the exception of one of the tubular, copper alloy rein-rings (No. 19), are worn, suggesting that they had been used prior to their deposition. Wear facets on the side-link side of the stop-studs are present on the rein-rings of several of the bridle-bits (Nos. 10–13) and one of the single rein-rings (No. 16). Wear facets around the circumference of the fixing holes through which the stop-studs were riveted to the rein-rings are observable on two of the bridle-bits (No. 10–11) and two of the single rein-rings (No. 17–18). The inner-edge of that part of the rein-ring which accommodated the side-link is also worn on several of the bridle-bits (No. 10–13) and single rein-rings (Nos. 16–17, 20). The remains of the rein-rings of the two bridle-bit fragments which do not appear to have been furnished with stop-studs (No. 14–15) are heavily worn as well. The perforations of the side-links on several of the bridle-bits (Nos. 10–11, 13–14) are worn, and in one case (No. 12) the inner perforation has been completely worn through. It was presumably to compensate for this form of wear that the inner-perforations of four of the bridle-bits' side-links (Nos. 10–11, 14–15) were deliberately placed off-centre. Other evidence of use prior to deposition includes the iron centre-link of one of the bridle-bits (No. 10) which is probably the replacement of a cast copper alloy link which had worn through (Fox 1947a: 28, 81; Spratling 1972: 447; Palk 1984: 32).

One of the three-link bridle-bits from Llyn Cerrig Bach (No. 11) is asymmetrical; one of its side-links contains a separately cast decorative boss mounted on a knob set on the link's terminal bulb socket and fixed by a square headed rivet through its centre. It is not certain whether the boss accommodated a decorative stud (Fox 1947a: 28, 81; Spratling 1972: 448) or was directly inlaid with enamel (Savory 1976a: 32, 58). Its inner surface is roughened in a manner consistent with the application of enamel, however, no trace of inlay survives and the use of enamel remains unproven. This asymmetrical decorative treatment of the bridle-bit has, not unreasonably, been interpreted as evidence that the bridle-bit was used for paired draught (Fox 1947a: 28; Lynch 1970: 265; Spratling 1972: 448; Savory 1976a: 32–3; Palk 1984: 92). A remnant of a presumably similar decorative boss is set on the terminal bulb socket of the side-link of one of the other three-link bridle-bits from Llyn Cerrig Bach (No. 13), but the fragmentary condition of this bridle-bit means that it is not possible to ascertain whether this is also an example of asymmetrical decoration.

The evidence for the use of paired draught in the British Iron Age is considerable and has prompted Spratling to suggest that bridle-bits were always made and used in pairs during this period (1979: 134). Matching pairs of three-link bridle-bits have been recovered from the vehicle burials in East Yorkshire at Beverley, Arras, Kirkburn, Garton Slack and Wetwang Slack. In addition pairs of bridle-bits are known from Ringstead and Hagbourne Hill. As well as the example from Llyn Cerrig Bach noted above (No. 11), three-link bridle-bits with asymmetrical decoration suggestive of paired draught include the examples from Hengistbury Head, Old Windsor and Tunstall. Representational, literary and linguistic evidence also supports the argument for the use of paired draught in the British Iron Age (for a comprehensive discussion of this evidence see Piggott 1983: 209–38), however, bridle-bits have been found singly and it is not possible to rule out either the use of bridle-bits for conventional riding or the drawing of vehicles with a single horse (contra Spratling 1979: 134).

Fox suggested that several of the bridle-bits from Llyn Cerrig Bach had been deliberately damaged prior to their deposition (1947a: 69), but the only demonstrable example of this phenomenon is one of the incomplete three-link bridle-bits (No. 13) whose side-link was apparently forced along the rein-ring beyond the position of its missing stop-stud in antiquity (Fox 1947a: 80). The remaining three-link bridle-bits (Nos. 10–12, 14–15) and tubular, copper alloy, rein-rings (Nos. 16–20), although variously worn, slightly distorted or incomplete, exhibit no definite evidence of having been deliberately damaged. Furthermore, there is no evidence to suggest that the two-link, copper alloy, bridle-bit (No. 22) or the Irish three-link, copper alloy, bridle-bit (No. 23) were deliberately damaged prior to their deposition. Although one of the iron bridle-bits of miscellaneous form is slightly distorted (Fox 1947a: 83, no. 57; Savory 1976a: 58, no. 17.57; Palk 1984: 58, no. LL2), this could equally well be the result of the peat extraction as deliberate ancient damage. It appears that Fox may have exaggerated the degree of deliberate damage inflicted on the bridle-bits from Llyn Cerrig Bach prior to their deposition. Interestingly, he noted that the deliberate damage was only noticed after they had been cleaned at the British Museum laboratory (1947a: 69). At this time conservation work at the British Museum often involved an ethic of restoring artefacts rather than conserving them as they were found. This raises the possibility that while being cleaned/restored, evidence for the deliberate damage during antiquity of the bridle-bits was destroyed and that Fox may not have exaggerated the scale of this phenomenon.

Close dating of the three-link bridle-bits from Llyn Cerrig Bach is difficult; with the exception of the pseudo-stitch decoration on two of the bridle-bits (Nos. 14–15) (see above) none are embellished with datable decoration. The three-link bridle-bits which are most comparable to the examples from Llyn Cerrig Bach include both those with tubular, copper alloy rein-rings and those with side-links of segmented or 'knobby' form. Although the examples of tubular, copper alloy rein-rings from Hagbourne Hill and West Coker (Fox 1952: 109–11, pl. V; Spratling 1972: 452, no. 163, fig. 57) are not closely datable, those from the Glastonbury lake village (Bulleid and Gray 1911: 228, no. E194, pl. XLIV and no. E152, pl. XLI) date respectively to the late (175–80 BC) or final (80–50 BC) phases of the site's occupation (Coles and Minnitt 1995: 204, 206) and the probable example from Read's Cavern (Palmer 1922: 13, pl. VIII; Spratling 1972: 444) is tentatively dated between the third and the mid first century BC (see above). This suggests that the vogue of tubular, copper alloy rein-rings possibly continued no later than the first century BC and may have begun significantly earlier. Relatively closely datable examples of side-links of segmented form, comparable to those from Llyn Cerrig Bach, include: the side-link from Bredon Hill which is dated to the first phase of the site's occupation (c. 100–50 BC) (Hencken 1939: 13); two iron examples from the Glastonbury lake village (Bulleid and Gray 1917: 378–9, 389, nos. 12a–b, pl. LXII) dated to the late phase of the site's occupation (175–80 BC) (Coles and Minnitt 1995: 204); and the example from Gussage All Saints radiocarbon dated to the first two centuries BC (Wainwright and Switsur 1976: 39, samples F and G; see also Foster 1980: 7; Stead 1991a: 183).

The segmented form of the side-links of the three-link bridle-bits from Llyn Cerrig Bach (Nos. 10–11, 14–15) are also similar in form to some of the mirror handles of the British Iron Age (Spratling 1972: 97). In particular, the so-called concave reel moulding used on the side-links of one of the Llyn Cerrig Bach bridle-bits (No. 11) is closely paralleled by some examples of the bar type of mirror handle (Fox 1948: 27–8). A full review of the mirrors of the late Iron Age falls outside the parameters of the present study (for discussions of this find type see: Fox 1948; 1958: 84–105; Spratling 1970a; 1972: 191–206; Fox and Pollard 1973; MacGregor 1976: 140–3, 163; Fitzpatrick 1996: 65–7). The examples of the bar type of mirror handle which parallel the Llyn Cerrig Bach bridle-bits with segmented side-links include the examples from: Ingleton, West Yorkshire (Fox 1948: 26, figs. 1.4, 2–3, pl. II.m; Hawkes 1951: 193, pl. VIII.a; MacGregor 1976: 141, 163, no. 269); Stamford Hill, Plymstock, Devon (Spence Bate 1866: 501–2, pl. XXX.2; Franks 1866; Smith 1908–9: 331; Leeds 1933a: 30–2, 36, fig. 12; Spratling 1972: 193, 559, no. 353, fig. 160); Thetford, Norfolk (Lloyd-Morgan 1991: 132, no. 10, fig. 116); and Carlingwark

Loch, Kirkcudbrightshire (Anon. 1866–8: 8, no. 15, pl. I; Piggott 1952–3: 30, fig. 8, no. C3; MacGregor 1976: 140, 163, no. 268). The circumstances of the discovery of the Ingleton mirror are unknown (MacGregor 1976: no. 269), but the fact that the handle incorporates moulded bovine heads suggests that it does not date before the first century BC and may be two or three centuries later in date (Megaw and Megaw 1989: 220). The Stamford Hill mirror was found in an inhumation burial in a late Iron Age and Roman cemetery; its precise context was not recorded (Spratling 1972: 559). It is an example of the southern English series of mirrors which date from the first century BC to at least the mid first century AD (Stead and Rigby 1989: 103; Fitzpatrick 1996: 67). The Thetford mirror handle is a metal detector find from the site of an Iron Age and early Roman enclosure with probable temple functions (Gregory 1991: 189–201). The Carlingwark Loch deposit, which contains the mirror handle, is conventionally dated to the late first century or early second century AD (Manning 1972: 233). If the parallels between the segmented side-links and the mirror handles are valid then these, combined with the dating evidence for bridle-bits with comparable side-links cited above, suggest a date ranging between the second or first century BC until at least the first century AD for the Llyn Cerrig Bach bridle-bits with this form of side-link.

Summary

As a type the British three-link bridle-bits are not closely datable. The earliest known examples may date to the fourth or third centuries BC and the type was certainly in vogue by the second century BC. Although no individual example can be shown unequivocally to post-date the first century BC, it is possible that their use continued into at least the first century AD. Two features typical of the three-link bridle-bits from Llyn Cerrig Bach, that is, the use of tubular, copper alloy rein-rings and side-links of segmented form, are apparently restricted to the second and first centuries BC. It is within this late Iron Age period that the Llyn Cerrig Bach three-link bridle-bits probably belong. Metallurgical analyses of the Llyn Cerrig Bach bridle-bits indicates that they were manufactured from typical Iron Age copper-tin alloys with arsenic impurities (see Appendix 2). Although far from being conclusive dating evidence, these analytical results are not inconsistent with the suggested date range for the three-link bridle-bits from Llyn Cerrig Bach (for a discussion of the Iron Age and Romano-British copper alloying traditions see Chapter 6).

Two-link bridle-bits

Two-link bridle-bits consist of four separate components: two rein-rings and two side-links. Two-link bridle-bits are relatively rare in the British and Irish Iron Age, but are the most common type found on the Continent (Ward Perkins 1939: 174; Raftery 1984: 16). In two-link bridle-bits the perforations in one of the side-links are in opposite planes, whilst in the other side-link they are in the same plane. In comparison to the three-link bridle-bits, the variety of materials and methods used in the manufacture of two-link bridle-bits are simple: the bridle-bits are either cast entirely in copper alloy or forged from iron. This distinction forms the main criteria for their classification and is also apparently chronologically significant. The two-link bridle-bits of the British Iron Age are predominantly of cast, copper alloy while the later, Romano-British examples of the type are largely forged from iron. A Polden Hill subtype has been recognized for the copper alloy, two-link bridle-bits (Palk 1984: 13, fig. 5.A).

In comparison with the three-link type, there has been relatively little discussion or typological subdivision of the two-link bridle-bits, probably because of the paucity of known examples. The type was first noted by Leeds who identified the Polden Hill hoard as the type site for the whole series (1933a: 114). Although the bridle-bits from the Polden Hill hoard were soon recognized as a distinct subtype of the cast copper alloy two-link bridle-bits (cf. Ward Perkins 1939: 175), the Polden Hill subtype was only explicitly defined much later (Palk 1984: 13). The subtype is based on distinctive flared or 'earred' form of the side-link's terminal bulb socket (Palk 1984: fig. 5.A).

Fox suggested that the iron two-link bridle-bit from La Tène was the ultimate prototype of the British series (Vouga 1923: 99, pl. XXXVI.3; Fox 1947a: 33), however, the Continental examples of the type are so numerous (cf. Stead 1965a: 39–41; 1981: 16, nos. 79–80, pl. 4; Piggott 1983: 219–20; Stead and Rigby 1999: 132, nos. 1370–1, 2330 and 2567, fig. 184) that it is difficult to isolate a specific source. In contrast to the copper alloy British examples, the Continental La Tène two-link bridle-bits are largely forged from iron (Piggott 1983: 219) and this contributes to the difficulties in identifying specific prototypes for the British series. Only three two-link bridle-bits are recorded from Ireland: one from the River Bann, possibly near Coleraine, Co. Derry (Haworth 1971: 46; Raftery 1983: 50, no. 138, fig. 45; 1984: 44, fig. 28.2) and an unprovenanced pair whose authenticity as Irish antiquities is questionable (Wilde 1861: 605, no. 67, fig. 506; Armstrong 1923: pl. III.9–10; Haworth 1971: 46; Raftery 1983: 50, no. 137, fig. 46; 1984: 44, fig. 28.1). The forms of the Irish examples are unlike the British two-link bridle-bits and it is difficult to relate them typologically to either the British or Continental series (Raftery 1984: 44).

The British copper alloy, two-link bridle-bits and those iron two-link bridle-bits that may be Iron Age in date are detailed in Table 8 (for lists of the comparable iron two-link bridle-bits of Roman date see MacGregor 1976: 53–4 and Manning 1985: 67). In addition to the tabulated two-link bridle-bits are a pair from the first vehicle burial discovered at Wetwang Slack, East Yorkshire which are not published in sufficient detail to ascertain their type (Dent 1985: 88, fig. 2). As noted elsewhere (cf. Fox 1947a: 33, fn.2; Spratling 1972: 100), there are no two-link bridle-bits from the Glastonbury lake village, Somerset (contra Ward Perkins 1939: 175). Palk considered the unprovenanced fragment in the Ashmolean Museum, which had been reworked into a spiked loop with an attached ring, to have originally been a two-link bridle-bit (cf. Palk 1984: 47, no. SJ24, fig. C38.3), but it could also have been reworked from a bridle-bit of three-link type. Similarly, the four iron rein-rings with adhering fragments of iron side-links from Maiden Castle, Dorset

(Wheeler 1943: 274–5, pl. XXIX.3–5, 7), which have previously been identified as two-link bridle-bits (MacGregor 1976: 54), could equally be fragments of three-link bridle-bits. A small number of mould fragments for two-link bridle-bits were recovered from first century BC foundry deposits at Weelsby Avenue, Grimsby, Lincolnshire (Foster 1995: 53).

The dating evidence for the pre-Roman, copper alloy, two-link bridle-bits which are not of the Polden Hill type is poor. The Fordington bridle-bit was found in 1840 during building work at the parish church of St George, associated with the burial of a horse. No other material was associated with the horse burial, which is dated solely on the form of the bridle-bit to the Iron Age (RCHME 1970: 574). The Gilsland side-link is an unasso-ciated metal detector find (Richardson 1999: 47). The Lydney side-link was recovered from the 'surface soil' of the 'guest-house' of the Roman temple complex (Wheeler and Wheeler 1932: 83). Presumably, the term 'surface soil' signifies the topsoil overlying the building in which case the side-link is unstratified (Spratling 1972: 454). The temple com-plex itself dates from the second half of the third century AD to the fourth century AD (Casey 1981; Casey and Hoffmann 1999), however, Lydney was also the site of earlier Roman industrial activity and a late Iron Age promontory fort (Wheeler and Wheeler 1932: 11–22) and the side-link could derive from any of these phases of activity. This ambiguity over the dating of the Lydney side-link is unfortunate since the form of its tapering rectangular-sectioned shaft provides the best parallel for the Llyn Cerrig Bach two-link bridle-bit (No. 22). The copper alloy two-link bridle-bit of unusual form from the River Thames is similar to the Polden Hill horse trappings (see below) in that the dec-orative mounts on its rein-rings have central bosses decorated in Style V ornament but are surrounded by geometric insets for enamel. Stylistically, it is an example of the group of embellished horse and vehicle fittings typified by compass work, engraved decoration and inlaid enamel which is conventionally dated to the first and possibly the second centuries AD (Bateson 1981: 8–10, 114; Raftery 1991: 568–9).

Dating evidence suggests a first century AD date for the Polden Hill subtype of copper alloy two-link bridle-bits. The Elvedon, Llanaber, Stratton Strawless and West Acre bridle-bits were all chance finds with no recorded associations. As noted in the previous chapter, the best evidence for dating the deposition of the Polden Hill hoard is provided by three brooches (Brailsford 1975a: 228–9, nos. 1–3, fig. 6.a–c) which are probably Neronian and certainly date to the third quarter of the first century AD (J. Webster pers. comm.). The Santon assemblage is also dated to the third quarter of the first century AD (Manning 1972: 232; Spratling 1975: 207). The Saham Toney bridle-bits were part of a hoard (known as 'findspot B') that has been intepreted as scrap metal, associated with a late Iron Age to early Roman metalworking centre, and which probably dates to the second half of the first century AD (Bates 2000: 234–5; Hutcheson 2004: 33). The prove-nance of the fragment of a side-link socket attributed to Wylye Camp is not certain (Shortt 1947: 26) and consequently it is of limited value for dating.

The first century AD date for the Polden Hill subtype is usually extended to all of the copper alloy two-link bridle-bits in the absence of closer dating evidence for examples which are not of the Polden Hill subtype (i.e. Ward Perkins 1939: 175; Spratling 1972:

TABLE 8: Two-link bridle-bits of the British Iron Age

Provenance	Description	References
Copper alloy two-link bridle-bits		
Fordington, Dorset	incomplete bridle-bit	RCHME 1970: 574, pl. 230; MacGregor 1976: 51; Palk 1984: 41–2, no. SJ4, fig. C27
Gilsland area, Northumberland (?)	part of a side-link	Richardson 1999: 47, no. 218.11, fig. 11
Llyn Cerrig Bach, Anglesey	complete bridle-bit	No. 22 (see catalogue entry for full bibliographical references)
Lydney, Gloucestershire	part of a side-link	Wheeler and Wheeler 1932: 83, no. 59, fig. 18; Spratling 1972: 454, no. 170, fig. 65; Palk 1984: 42, no. SJ6, fig. C37.1
River Thames, presumably near London	bridle-bit of unusual form	Read 1909–11; Leeds 1933a: 116–17; Brailsford 1953: 60, pl. X.4; Spratling 1972: 459, no. 180, fig. 74
Copper alloy two-link bridle-bits of the Polden Hill subtype		
Elvedon, Suffolk	side-link fragment	Ward Perkins 1939: 173, 175; Clarke 1939: 71, 107, pl. XIV.4; Spratling 1972: 453, no. 167, fig. 63; Palk 1984: 41, no. SJ3, fig. C38.2
Llanaber, Merionethshire (2)	two incomplete bridle-bits	Smith 1925: 143; Ward Perkins 1939: 175, fig. 2; Bowen and Gresham 1967: 175, fig. 74; Spratling 1972: 99, 454, no. 168, fig. 64; Palk 1984: 41, nos. SJ1–SJ2, fig. C26
Polden Hill, Somerset (16)	sixteen bridle-bits	Harford 1803: 92, no. 3, pl. XIX.1; Brailsford 1953: 62, pl. XIII.1; Spratling 1972: 455–8, nos. 171–8, figs. 66–73; Brailsford 1975a: 224–7, nos. 1–16, figs. 2–3, pls XX–XXI; Palk 1984: 43–46, nos. SJ7–SJ22, figs. C29–C37
Saham Toney, Norfolk (2)	two bridle-bits	Davies 2000: 226, 230, nos. 10–14, fig. 8; Hutcheson 2004: 108, 126, nos. 33–4
Santon, Norfolk	incomplete bridle-bit	Smith 1909a: 152, fig. 6; Ward Perkins 1939: 175–6; Spratling 1972: 459, no. 179, fig. 63; Palk 1984: 47, no. SJ23, fig. C38.1; Hutcheson 2004: 108, 126, no. 35
Stratton Strawless, Norfolk	side-link	Hutcheson 2004: 107, 126, no. 28
Wylye Camp, Wiltshire (?)	side-link socket fragment	Shortt 1947: 25–6, fig. 5; MacGregor 1976: 53
West Acre, Norfolk	incomplete side-link of unusual form	Gurney 2000: 513; Hutcheson 2004: 107, 126, no. 29; K. Hinds pers. comm.

Provenance	Description	References
Iron two-link bridle-bits of possible Iron Age date		
Blackburn Mill, Cockburnspath, Berwickshire (2)	fragments of two bridle-bits	Piggott 1952–3: 42, nos. B7–B8, fig. 11; MacGregor 1976: 53
Carlingwark Loch, Kirkcudbrightshire (2)	two incomplete bridle-bits	Piggott 1952–3: 30–2, nos. C4–C5, fig. 33; MacGregor 1976: 54; Manning 1985: 67
Ham Hill, Somerset	now lost bridle-bit	Hoare 1827: 42, pl. V; Ward Perkins 1939: 175–6; Fox 1947a: 30–1, 33; Spratling 1972: 100
Hod Hill, Dorset (8)	two complete and six incomplete bridle-bits	Brailsford 1962: 19, nos. K28–K29, pl. XIII; Manning 1985: 66–7, nos. H10–H14, H16–H17; pls 28–9
Hunsbury, Northamptonshire	now lost bridle-bit	Dryden 1885: 59; Fell 1936: 66; Ward Perkins 1939: 176; MacGregor 1976: 54
Newbridge, near Edinburgh, Mid Lothian	complete bridle-bit	Carter and Hunter 2003: 532
Worthy Down, Hampshire	possible side-link	Hooley 1926–30: 190, no. 89, pl. VI

99–100; MacGregor 1976: 30), however, this late and short floruit is based on only two dated assemblages and should be treated cautiously. This point is emphasized by the significantly earlier date of the two-link bridle-bits of uncertain type from a vehicle burial at Wetwang Slack, East Yorkshire (Dent 1985: 88, fig. 2) (for a comprehensive discussion of the East Yorkshire burial evidence see: Stead 1991a: 179–84), the lost iron two-link bridle-bit from Hunsbury, which probably dates to the main phase of the site's occupation, which extended from the second to first centuries BC (D. Jackson 1993–4: 18), and the identification of mould fragments from first century BC deposits at Weelsby Avenue for the casting of side-links similar to those from the Polden Hill assemblage (Foster 1995: 49, 53).

As with the three-link bridle-bits, there is evidence for the use of two-link bridle-bits for paired draft. The bridle-bits from Wetwang Slack (Dent 1985: 88, fig. 2), Llanaber (Spratling 1972: 99, 454) and Saham Toney (Davies 2000: 230) form pairs while the sixteen bridle-bits from the Polden Hill hoard includes seven matching pairs (Spratling 1972: 99; Brailsford 1975a: 224). The iron two-link bridle-bit from Newbridge formed one half of an ill-matched pair (the other had a single-bar mouthpiece) recovered during the excavation of a vehicle burial (Carter and Hunter 2003: 532).

Suggestions that the copper alloy two-link bridle-bits of the Iron Age had a southwestern distribution (Ward Perkins 1939: 114, fig. 1; Fox 1947a: 33) were dismissed by Spratling as being based on the misidentification of bridle-bits from Glastonbury, Meare and Ham Hill, which are all in Somerset (1972: 100). The overall distribution of the type actually extends across southern Britain; the examples of uncertain form from the first vehicle burial at Wetwang Slack, East Yorkshire (Dent 1985: 88, fig. 2) being the only northern outliers of the group. During the early Roman period the use of two-link bridle-bits became more widespread and examples of iron, Romano-British two-link bridle-bits are found throughout Britain (cf. MacGregor 1976: 53–4; Manning 1985: 67). Where identifiable the majority of the contexts of pre-Roman, two-link, bridle-bits suggest deliberate ritual deposition rather than casual loss. They include: vehicle burials (Wetwang Slack); apparent animal burials (Fordington); hoard assemblages (Santon, Llyn Cerrig Bach and Polden Hill); and probably a pit from the interior of a hillfort (Hunsbury). This regional pattern of depositional practice broadly reflects that identified for the three-link bridle-bits (see above) with the use of two-link bridle-bits as grave goods in East Yorkshire and their use as elements of votive deposits in selected parts of southern Britain. The notable exception to this pattern is the poorly recorded horse burial from Fordington, Dorset (RCHME 1970: 574, pl. 230; Palk 1984: 41–2, no. SJ4, fig. C27).

The two-link bridle-bit from Llyn Cerrig Bach (No. 22) is complete and, although there are considerable wear facets visible on the sockets of both of its side-links which suggest that it had been used, there is no evidence that it was deliberately damaged, prior to its deposition. The rein-rings are not furnished with either stop-studs or cast terminals; consequently, they freely rotate through the sockets of the side-links. All four component parts of the bridle-bit are separate lost-wax castings which articulate freely with each other. To manufacture the bridle-bit would have required modelling some of its parts in wax so that they articulated with previously cast adjoining components, and then producing a clay mould around both the wax model and the adjoining casting. The careful finishing of the bridle-bit has removed any evidence which might indicate the order in which its component parts were modelled and cast. Although the gaps between the components of the bridle-bit are not as small as those of the Irish three-link bridle-bit (No. 23), and despite the casting flaws visible on the head of one of the side-links, its manufacture is still an impressive example of craftsmanship.

The two-link bridle-bit (No. 22) is the only piece from the original assemblage whose provenance has been questioned. The finder reported that it was found on a site different from, albeit near to, the area where the peat from Llyn Cerrig Bach was spread (Fox 1947a: 33, 83). The similarity of its side-link to the example from Lydney suggests that there is no reason to question its antiquity. Although the doubt over its provenance raises the intriguing possibility of a second, separate assemblage of metalwork and concomitant focus of ancient deposition in the environs of Llyn Cerrig Bach, Fox's suggestion that the bridle-bit was picked up by a workman from the area where Llyn Cerrig Bach peat was located and then thrown aside is more probable (cf. Fox 1947a: 83).

Dating of the Llyn Cerrig Bach two-link bridle-bit is difficult and it is not possible to suggest a more precise date than the general late Iron Age and early Romano-British floruit for the type as a whole. The bridle-bit is undecorated and, as noted above, the best parallel to it is provided by the unstratified side-link fragment from Lydney, Gloucestershire (Wheeler and Wheeler 1932: 83, no. 59, fig. 18; Spratling 1972: 454, no. 170, fig. 65; Palk 1984: 42, no. SJ6, fig. C37.1). The cylindrical form of the side-link sockets of the Llyn Cerrig Bach bridle-bit, with their projecting bevelled flanges, are unparalleled, which prevents the possibility of dating it by analogy with similar examples.

Derivative three-link bridle-bits and miscellaneous forms

The two types of British Iron Age bridle-bit which are not represented by copper alloy or copper alloy plated iron bridle-bits in the Llyn Cerrig Bach assemblage are those whose form is derived from three-link bridle-bits and those bridle-bits of miscellaneous form. There are, however, three iron bridle-bits from Llyn Cerrig Bach which are examples of miscellaneous form (Fox 1947a: 83, 95, nos. 56, 57, 128, pls III, XXVII–XXVIII; Savory 1976a: 58–9, nos. 17.56, 17.57, 18.9, fig. 21; Palk 1984: 58, nos. LL1, LL2, fig. C53).

Derivative three-link bridle-bits consist of three separate components: an extended centre-link or mouth-bar and two cheek-pieces consisting of a side-link cast-in-one with a rein-ring and frequently decorated with enamel. Derivative three-link bridle-bits are usually manufactured from cast copper alloy, although the example from Lochlee Crannog, Ayrshire is partly made of iron (Palk 1984: 17). The type was first noted by Leeds who defined two subgroups: a Rise type in which the examples were decorated with enamel (1933a: 114–16); and a variant type which was not decorated with enamel (1933a: 116–17). Ward-Perkins unified these in a single classificatory group (1939: 181–3, fig. 6) whose validity has been accepted by subsequent scholars (i.e. Barber and Megaw 1963: 207; Spratling 1972: 94–9, 452–3, nos. 164–6, figs. 61–3; MacGregor 1976: 25–30, 53, nos. 2–10; Stead 1979: 50; Palk 1984: 17–19, 63–5, 82–3, nos. SB1–SB21, figs. C39–C50). As noted above, the fused subtype of three-link bridle-bit provides a typological link between the three-link bridle-bits and the derived type (MacGregor 1976: 25; Palk 1984: 17). The derivative three-link bridle-bits can be distinguished from the fused subtype by the fact that the side-links of the derivative three-link bridle-bits are fused with the rein-rings mid-way along their length (for example, MacGregor 1962: fig. 3), while those of the fused subtype are joined at their heads (for example, Barber and Megaw 1963: pls XXIV–XXV). Suggestions that derivative three-link bridle-bits were non-functional (Barber and Megaw 1963: 209) are invalidated by the numerous examples of the type with wear facets and repairs (Spratling 1972: 95; MacGregor 1976: 25). The distribution of the type is predominantly northerly, although outliers are known as far south as Norfolk and south Wales (Spratling 1972: 94; MacGregor 1976: 25; Palk 1984: 63, fig. 10). The type has a floruit stretching from the late Iron Age into at least the second half of the first century AD (Spratling 1972: 96–8; Palk 1984: 82–3). A bridle-bit from Swanton Morley, Norfolk, which is made up of two cheek-pieces decorated with polychrome enamel that are joined, not by the normal single central link, but by two side-links, forms an unusual variant of the derivative three-link bridle-bit type (cf. Gurney 2001: 698, fig. 2C; Hutcheson 2004: 107, 126, no. 27). It is possible that several of the derivative three-link bridle-bits known only by the type's distinctive cheek-pieces may represent examples of this two side-link varaint.

The miscellaneous bridle-bits are not a coherent or unified type, but a catch-all grouping for those bridle-bits which are not examples of one of the other types. The miscellaneous grouping was first used by Ward-Perkins (1939: 185) and is revived here to classify the three iron bridle-bits from Llyn Cerrig Bach which are not examples of any of the definable Iron Age types (i.e. Fox 1947a: 83, 95, nos. 56, 57, 128, pls III, XXVII–XXVIII; Savory 1976a: 58–9, nos. 17.56, 17.57, 18.9, fig. 21; Palk 1984: 58, nos. LL1, LL2, fig. C53). Although bridle-bits of miscellaneous form are predominantly manufactured from iron, some copper alloy examples are known, for example, the unique two-link bridle-bit from the River Thames in London (Ward Perkins 1939: 185; Spratling 1972: 102, 459, no. 180, fig. 74). For such a diverse group it is inappropriate to discuss the dating of the type as a whole.

The miscellaneous iron bridle-bits from Llyn Cerrig Bach include two loop-linked snaffles (Fox 1947a: 34–5, 83, nos. 56–7, pl. XXVIII; Savory 1976a: 58, nos. 17.56–7, fig. 21.1; Palk 1984: 20, 58, nos. LL1–LL2, fig. C.53) and a plain bit with a mouthpiece consisting of a single bar (Fox 1947a: 34, no. 128, pls III and XXVII; Spratling 1972: 85; Savory 1976a: 59, no. 18.9, fig. 21.4). The loop-link snaffles are paralleled by an example from Ham Hill, Somerset (Fox 1947a: 35, fig. 18). Fox does not record the context of the Ham Hill example, suggesting that it was discovered during nineteenth-century quarrying at the site, and although it may be pre-Roman the quantity of later activity at the site (Burrow 1981: 268–77) means that a Roman date cannot be discounted. Palk's suggestion that the two iron bridle-bits from Madmarston Camp, Oxfordshire, are probably loop-linked snaf-fles (1984: 58, nos. LL3–LL4) cannot be reconciled with their earlier description (Fowler 1960: 43, no. 17). The Llyn Cerrig Bach plain-bit is paralleled by a fragment from Ham Hill, Somerset (Fox 1947a: 34, 95), and complete examples from the Pentyrch hoard, Glamorgan (Savory 1966b: 33, fig. 2.2; 1976a: 64, no. 35.2, fig. 37.2; Palk 1984: no. R4, fig. C56) and the River Churn, near Cricklade, Wiltshire (Manning 1985: 66, no. H9, pl. 28). Again, the specific context of the Ham Hill bridle-bit is unrecorded, suggesting that it may be of either pre-Roman or Roman date. The Pentyrch hoard is conventionally dated to the mid first century AD (Savory 1966b: 40), but could be later in date (Manning 1972: 232). The River Churn bridle-bit is recorded as being associated with, amongst other items, a La Tène III brooch and Claudian coinage (Anon. 1864–7; Manning 1985: 66), which suggests a date in or after the mid first century AD for its deposition. On the strength of the analogous examples the miscellaneous iron bridle-bits from Llyn Cerrig Bach could be of either late Iron Age or early Roman date.

Irish three-link bridle-bits

There is one three-link bridle-bit from Llyn Cerrig Bach of Irish type (No. 23). Irish Iron Age three-link bridle-bits form a group distinct from the contemporary British series. As noted above, the perforations in the side-links of British three-link bridle-bits are in oppo-site planes while the perforations in the side-links of the Irish bridle-bits are in the same plane (Fox 1947a: 33; Jope 1950: 58; Haworth 1971: 27, fig. 1; Spratling 1972: 93; Savory 1976a: 33). Another difference between the Irish and British three-link bridle-bits is that, with only a few exceptions, all of the component parts of the Irish bridle-bits are manu-factured from cast copper alloy, while none of the British three-link bridle-bits consist entirely of cast copper alloy components (Haworth 1971: 34; Raftery 1984: 15–16).

The first typological classification of the Irish three-link bridle-bits was made by J. Raftery who initially proposed a twofold division between the earliest bits of so-called unaltered Hagbourne Hill type (his Group I) and the Attyman type of bridle-bit (Mahr 1937: 411, 427, fig. 29; Ward Perkins 1939: 182, fig. 7; Jope 1950: 57, fig. 1.1–2). Raftery subsequently subdivided the Attyman type into a developed style (his Group II) and a latest type (his Group III) (J. Raftery 1951: 194, figs. 227–9; Jope 1955: 40). Raftery did not explicitly define his three typological groups, but they were based on the form of the side-link (Haworth 1971: 27–8). Jope suggested that stop-studs on the rein-rings of Group II bridle-bits were pegged while those on Group III bridle-bits were cast in one piece with the rein-rings (Jope 1955: 40), however, such a simple distinction is demonstrably invalid (Haworth 1971: 43, fn. 2).

Raftery's classification was revised and expanded by Haworth who still based the typology of the bridle-bits on the form of their side-links, but expanded the scheme to include five groups (labelled A-E) (Haworth 1971: 27–9). Group A bridle-bits have side-links which are not bowed, but rather are symmetrical about a horizontal longitudinal axis and do not have a raised crest at their inner end (Haworth 1971: 28, fig. 2.A; Raftery 1984: 16, fig. 6). Group B bridle-bits have side-links which are slightly bowed, have raised crests at their inner end and generally have undecorated link heads (Haworth 1971: 28, fig. 2B; Raftery 1984: 16–20, figs. 7, 8.1–13, 9). Group C bridle-bits have slight, but bowed, side-links which generally do not have raised crests at their inner ends or any other form of decoration (Haworth 1971: 28, fig. 2C; Raftery 1984: 22–3, figs. 8.14–16, 14). Group D bridle-bits have heavily bowed side-links, which are frequently decorated with either incised or raised scroll work and contain raised transverse crests at their inner ends (Haworth 1971: 28–9, fig. 2D; Raftery 1984: 23, figs. 8.17–24, 15–18). Group E bridle-bits have side-links that are bowed, with outer ends which extend beyond the perforation and inner ends which narrow to a flat disc and are embellished with elaborately decorated, raised transverse crests (Haworth 1971: 29, fig. 2E; Raftery 1984: 23–6, figs. 8.25–30, 19–20). Subsequent authors have used Haworth's scheme with little or no revision (i.e. Raftery 1974: 9; 1983: 11–46, 49; Palk 1984: 100–1; Raftery 1984: 15–30; 1994: 107–8) and its validity is accepted here. Group B bridle-bits equate to Raftery's Group I bridle-bits; Group D bridle-bits equate to Raftery's Group II; and Group E bridle-bits equate to Raftery's Group III. The bridle-bit from Llyn Cerrig Bach (No. 23) is an example of Haworth's Group A (Haworth 1971: 28, 45, fig. 4; Raftery 1983: 11, no. 1, fig. 1; Raftery 1984: 16, fig. 6.1).

Approximately one hundred and forty Irish bridle-bits have been catalogued and discussed by Haworth (1969; 1971) and Raftery (1983: 7–51, figs. 1–46; 1984: 15–44). The author is aware of two additions to Raftery's catalogue: a Group B bridle-bit in the National Museum of Denmark (Eogan 1991: 159, no. 80, fig. 13) and a pair of iron bridle-bits from Co. Dublin (Raftery 1994: 150). Irish Iron Age bridle-bits are predominantly of the three-link type, but other types are recorded from Ireland including: an unprovenanced example of a three-link bridle-bit of British type (Haworth 1971: 46; Raftery 1983: 48, no. 133, fig. 45; 1984: 39–41, fig. 25.2) probably imported from Britain (Raftery 1984: 42); a unique form of three-link bridle-bit associated with a decorated circular mount from Killeevan, Anlore, Co. Monaghan (Jope 1955: 44, pl. II; Raftery 1983: 47–8, no. 132, fig. 44; 1984: 42–4, fig. 26.1, pl. 13; 1994: 108, pl. 34); a two-link bridle-bit from the River Bann, possibly near Coleraine, Co. Derry (Haworth 1971: 46; Raftery 1983: 50, no. 138, fig. 45; 1984: 44, fig. 28.2); and an unprovenanced pair of two-link bridle-bits (Wilde 1861: 605, no. 67, fig. 506; Armstrong 1923: pl. III.9–10; Haworth 1971: 46; Raftery 1983: 50, no. 137, fig. 46; 1984: 44, fig. 28.1). In addition, there is an example of an unprovenanced Type B bridle-bit in which the side-links are apparently deliberately fused to the rein-rings in a manner reminiscent of the fused subtype of the British three-link bridle-bits (Haworth 1971: 41; Raftery 1983: 25, no. 50, fig. 11; 1984: 22, fig. 9.1).

With the exception of a possible iron bridle-bit from an enclosed settlement site at Aughinish, Co. Limerick, radiocarbon dated to the first half of the last millennium BC (Raftery 1994: 32), the absence of Irish bridle-bits of late Bronze Age date suggests that the Irish Iron Age three-link bridle-bits were inspired by contemporary imports rather than being an Irish innovation (Haworth 1971: 31). The Irish three-link bridle-bits have features in common with both the British and Continental three-link bridle-bits, which have both been suggested as sources for the Irish series (Raftery 1974: 9). The mutual occurrence of stop-studs and a superficial similarity between the form of some of the side-links has led some to conclude that the inspiration for the Irish series are the British three-link bridle-bits (Leeds 1933a: 118; Ward Perkins 1939: 182; Piggott 1950: 16; 1983: 224). Indeed, the typologically early position of the Group A bridle-bits within the Irish sequence, and the occurrence of an example of the type at Llyn Cerrig Bach, has suggested to some the possibility that Group A bridle-bits were a British type which was exported to Ireland and provided the inspiration for the Irish series (Haworth 1971: 33; Raftery 1984: 31). However, the absence of any other British three-link bridle-bit manufactured entirely from cast copper alloy components (with the exception of the typologically later Irish bridle-bits allegedly found in Britain and discussed below) and the arrangement of the Group A side-link perforations in the same plane, not only suggest that Group A bridle-bits, including the Llyn Cerrig Bach example, are of Irish origin, but also undermines the suggestion that the British three-link bridle-bits were the only source of inspiration for the Irish series (Haworth 1971: 34; Raftery 1984: 31–2). A second suggested source of inspiration for the Irish bridle-bits is the Marnian region of France where the perforations of side-links recovered from vehicle burials are also in the same plane (Jope 1954: 88; Raftery 1983: 8). Similar problems in identifying the Marnian bridle-bits as prototypes for the British series affect their identification as a source for the Irish series; namely the absence of stop-studs on the Continental examples and the occurrence of copper alloy three-link bridle-bits at only Somme-Tourbe (Raftery 1974: 9). Although both the British and Marnian three-link bridle-bits contain some features which are present in the Irish three-link bridle-bits, the available evidence is not detailed enough to identify with any confidence the source, or more probably sources, which inspired the Irish series (Haworth 1971: 34; Raftery 1984: 32).

The distribution of Iron Age bridle-bits in Ireland is concentrated in two areas: a broad band from Co. Meath to Co. Galway and in the north-east of Ireland (Haworth 1971: 29, fig. 8). Stray examples occur outside these two areas, although relatively few bridle-bits are known from the south of Ireland. Fox argued that, with the exception of the example from Llyn Cerrig Bach, the distribution of Irish Group A bridle-bits was restricted to north-east Ireland and that, therefore, the Llyn Cerrig Bach example was probably imported into Anglesey directly from the coast of either Co. Antrim or Co. Down (Fox 1947a: 34). Of the five other Group A bridle-bits, however, only the example from Ballymagrorty, Co. Donegal (Haworth 1971: 45, no. 14; Raftery 1983: 11, no. 2, fig. 1) is provenanced. Consequently, it cannot be claimed with certainty that the distribution of the type was restricted to north-east Ireland, or that this was the source of the example from Llyn Cerrig Bach. At present, it is not possible to suggest a more precise provenance than Ireland for the Llyn Cerrig Bach bridle-bit.

Dating of the Irish three-link bridle-bits is problematic because many are either unprovenanced or chance finds without associations (Raftery 1983: 7; Palk 1984: 100;

Raftery 1984: 31). It is assumed that Groups A and B are typologically earlier than Groups D and E, although the possibility that typologically earlier forms remained in vogue alongside typologically later forms is acknowledged (Raftery 1974: 9; 1984: 31). The only associated Group A bridle-bit is the example from Llyn Cerrig Bach. The only direct dating evidence for the typologically early bridle-bits is provided by decoration on two unprovenanced Group B bridle-bits. The decorative details on the first of these (Raftery 1974; 1983: 22–3, no. 43, fig. 11; 1984: fig. 11.1) may have both early Continental La Tène and later insular parallels (Raftery 1974: 2–8, figs. 2–3; 1984: 32), while the decoration on the other (Haworth 1971: 46; Raftery 1983: 24–5, no. 49, fig. 5) is possibly of a first century BC to first century AD date (Raftery 1984: 33–4). The recorded associations of Bronze Age material with the Group B bridle-bits from Toomyvana, Co. Tipperary (Haworth 1971: 40, 45; J. Raftery and Ryan 1971: 212, 219) and Ballyblack Moss, Co. Down (Jope 1950: 60) have been rejected for being of doubtful authenticity, and even if they were accurate they would not closely date the bridle-bits (J. Raftery and Ryan 1971: 212; Raftery 1984: 32). Study of the parallels for the decoration on bridle-bits of Groups D and E suggest that the two types are largely coeval and date to the early centuries AD (Jope 1955: 42–4; Palk 1984: 100; Raftery 1984: 37). This dating is supported by the recovery of part of a Group E bridle-bit from excavations at Newgrange, Co. Meath (Haworth 1971: 46, no. 46; Carson and O'Kelly 1977: 52, pl. IX; Raftery 1983: 41–2, no. 107, fig. 39; 1994: 151) in deposits exclusively associated with Roman material of first to fourth century AD date (Carson and O'Kelly 1977: 46; Raftery 1983: 7; 1984: 37), and the discovery of an apparent copy of a Group E bridle-bit in northern Romania (Haworth 1971: 29, 46; Warner 1976: 281; Zirra 1981: 143; Palk 1984: 101) which may have been associated with either the transfer of *Legio II Adiutrix* from Britain, as part of the movement of Legions associated with the Dacian campaigns at the end of the first century AD, or the 'British' auxiliaries serving in Dacia during the second century AD (Warner 1976: 281; Raftery 1984: 39).

Two Type B, four Type D and three Type E Irish three-link bridle-bits have been recovered in association with so-called Y-shaped pendants (Haworth 1971: 39–40, 45; Raftery 1983: 285; 1984: 49–54). Y-shaped pendants are almost certainly items of horse harness, but their precise function is unknown (Haworth 1971: 38–9; Johns 1971: 58–9; Raftery 1983: 7; 1984: 45; 1994: 109). Although several vague Continental parallels and antecedents have been suggested (Jope 1954: 89; Haworth 1971: 39; Raftery 1984: 47–8), the pendants are probably a distinctly Irish type and no definite examples have been found outside Ireland (Haworth 1971: 38; Raftery 1984: 47). Y-shaped pendants form a relatively homogeneous group being predominantly manufactured from cast copper alloy (Haworth 1971: 35), although there is an iron example from Kilberg, Co. Westmeath (Raftery 1983: 79, 286, no. 232, fig. 64; 1984: 53–4; 1994: 108). Haworth identified two types of pendant based on the form of their terminals (Haworth 1971: 35–7, figs. 10–11) and these groups have been subdivided by Raftery (1983: 7, 52–78; 1984: 45–7). The reputed association of Type 1a and Type 2b Y-shaped pendants from Mullingar Co. Westmeath (Haworth 1971: 47; Johns 1971: 60, no. 4, pls XVII.b, XVIII.b; Raftery 1983: 55, 73, 285, nos. 151, 210, fig. 55) suggests that there may not necessarily be a chronological significance to their classification (Raftery 1984: 53). Although just under a hundred examples are known from Ireland the majority are either unassociated chance finds or unprovenanced. A Type 1b pendant from Kishawanny, Co. Kildare (Raftery 1983: 60–1, no. 169, fig. 63) is associated with both a copper alloy bell (Raftery 1983: 222–3, no. 593, figs. 63, 181) with possible first century Romano-British parallels (Raftery 1984: 54) and a copper alloy hook (Raftery 1983: 222, no. 592, figs. 63, 181) which is paralleled by examples in the Carlingwark Loch, Kirkcudbrightshire assemblage (Raftery 1984: 54) suggesting a first to early second century AD date for the pendant if the associations are genuine (Raftery 1984: 54). A Type 1b pendant from Kilberg, Co. Westmeath (Raftery 1983: 61, no. 170, fig. 64), is associated with three iron shafthole axeheads (Raftery 1983: 220, nos. 584a–c, figs. 64, 182) which are difficult to date precisely, but probably belong to the early centuries AD (Raftery 1984: 54). Apart from these two examples of Y-shaped pendants associated with artefact types other than bridle-bits, the only other dating evidence for the pendants consists of decorative motifs on some examples which suggest a date in the early centuries AD (Raftery 1984: 54). Although the dating evidence for the Y-shaped pendants does not refine the dating of the Irish three-link bridle-bits outlined above, it is not inconsistent with it either.

In addition to the example from Llyn Cerrig Bach, four other three-link bridle-bits of Irish type are alleged to have been found in Britain. They include: a Type D bridle-bit recorded as having been recovered from the River Conway, Denbighshire, and now in the Royal Ontario Museum, Canada (Pryor 1980: 19, 59, no. 160; Craddock 1980: 75; Raftery 1983: 49, no. 135, fig. 33.A); a Type D bridle-bit from Tenbury Wells, Worcestershire (Haworth 1969: no. D24; 1971: 29, 46, no. 40; Spratling 1972: 93); a Type E bridle-bit from Devon formerly in the Pitt Rivers Museum, Farnham, Dorset (Jope 1954: 88; A. Fox 1959: 170–1, pls 40–1; Haworth 1971: 29, 46, no. 48; Raftery 1983: 42, no. 111; Brown *et al.* 1987: 115, no. 14.2); and a Type D bridle-bit from Dolgellau, Merionethshire (Raftery 1983: 49, no. 136, fig. 33.A). With the exception of the example from the River Conway, the reliability of the British provenances of these Irish three-link bridle-bits has been questioned (for Tenbury Wells cf. Haworth 1971: 29 and Spratling 1972: 93; for the Devon example, cf. Raftery 1983: 42, no. 111; and for Dolgellau cf. Raftery 1983: 49, no. 136) and as the circumstances of the discovery of the River Conway bridle-bit are unrecorded (H. Easson, pers. comm.) the validity of its provenance cannot be taken for granted either. The only Irish three-link bridle-bit which can be definitely provenanced to Britain is the example from Llyn Cerrig Bach (No. 23). This bridle-bit is also the only part of the Llyn Cerrig Bach assemblage which can be confidently identified as an Irish import. The copper alloy curved-horn fragment (No. 31) has previously been considered an Irish import on the strength of the bias towards Irish examples within the insular distribution of this type (Fox 1947a: 61; Lynch 1970: 271; Raftery 1984: 134; but see Megaw 1970: 147 for a different view), however, for reasons outlined in the section on the curved-horn in Chapter 4, this Irish attribution cannot be accepted as certain.

The Irish bridle-bit from Llyn Cerrig Bach is fully described in the catalogue (No.23), but comments on both its form and method of manufacture are offered here. The buffer-like terminals on the surviving rein-ring protrude further on one side than the other, presumably in imitation of the stop-studs upon which they are based. These buffer-like terminals and the joints between the links of the bridle-bit are designed so as to prevent all but lateral movement. Although one of the rein-rings is missing there is no evidence to suggest that the bridle-bit was deliberately damaged prior to deposition. There are considerably wear facets around all of the surviving joints, suggesting that the bridle-bit was used for a considerable period prior to its deposition. Consequently, it is possible that the narrow neck between the buffer-like terminals of the missing rein-ring, upon which the adjoining side-link articulated, wore through completely, leading to its detachment from the rest of the bridle-bit.

In terms of craftsmanship the production of the Irish bridle-bit from Llyn Cerrig Bach is a technical *tour de force* which is unequalled by any other piece in the assemblage. All four surviving components, and by extension all five original components, are separate lost-wax castings which articulate freely with each other. This would have necessitated the modelling in wax of some parts of the bridle-bit around previously cast adjoining components and then producing a clay mould around both the wax model and the adjoining castings. Even now, after the bridle-bit has been used and its joints have worn considerably, the gaps between the various parts of the bridle-bit are minimal. The skill required to produce the clay mould which incorporated the wax model and adjoining castings and then successfully make a casting from it can scarcely be exaggerated. There is no example of a British three-link bridle-bit in which all five parts are cast and articulate freely, although this form of bridle-bit is the norm for the Irish series. The closest British craftsmen came to emulating this complexity of multiple casting was in pieces like the two-link bridle-bit from Llyn Cerrig Bach (No. 22) which has four articulating, cast components. This apparent inability of British craftsmen to engage in complex, multiple castings was not necessarily due to a lack of skill. Study of the mould fragments from Gussage All Saints, Dorset, has demonstrated that the centre-links of three-link bridle-bits manufactured there were cast around previously cast side-links (Wainwright and Spratling 1973: 122; Spratling 1979: 138; Foster 1980: 13, fig. 11), which would have been an operation as technically demanding as any stage in the manufacture of the Irish three-link bridle-bits. It is possible that the apparent unwillingness of British craftsmen to manufacture bridle-bits with five separately articulating components may have prompted the development of both the fused subtype of three-link bridle-bits and the derivative three-link bridle-bits.

X-radiographic examination of the Irish bridle-bit from Llyn Cerrig Bach (No. 23) indicates that, as previously noted for the Group A bridle-bits (Haworth 1971: 28; Raftery 1983: 11; 1984: 16, fig. 6), the side-links are hollow castings (Pl. 5; National Museum Wales X-Ray Nos. 1646–7). The hollow interior of the side-links extends throughout their length and into the perforated socket which joins them with the adjacent rein-ring. This arrangement suggests that, when cast, the clay which formed the mould of the side-link was integral with the clay core which defined both the outer perforations and the hollow centres of the side-links. This method of producing a hollow casting obviates the need to hold the clay core in place, once the wax had been melted and run off, with protruding copper alloy rods or chaplets (see Hodges 1989: 72). Raftery states that the clay cores of the Llyn Cerrig Bach side-links remain *in situ* (1983: 11, no. 1), but drilling to prepare samples for metallurgical analysis indicates that the side-links are at least partially hollow. To achieve this the clay core would have been raked out through the inside of the outer side-link perforation following casting. The inside of the outer side-link sockets are filled with a concreted greyish residue which is probably a mixture of the original clay core and copper alloy corrosion products, suggesting that the removal of the original clay core was only partially completed.

Assessing the order in which the component parts of the bridle-bit were cast is an interesting problem. The central link has a different colour and patination to the other surviving links and rein-ring, suggesting that it was made from a different alloy type. Similar patination variations have been observed on the Irish bridle-bit allegedly recovered from the River Conway, Denbighshire (Pryor 1980: 19, 59, no. 160; Raftery 1983: 49, no. 135, fig. 33.A) and metallurgical analysis of this bridle-bit has demonstrated that its centre-link is cast from a leaded copper alloy while its other component parts are not cast from leaded alloys (Craddock 1980: 75). Presumably this variation in alloy type is because the centre-link was the final component to be cast and it had to be simultaneously joined to two other parts (Fox 1947a: 29). That this was the case is suggested by the study of both an unfinished, unprovenanced Type E bridle-bit in the National Museum of Ireland (Raftery 1984: 26, fig. 20.1; 1994: 153) and, as noted above, the study of mould fragments of three-link bridle-bits from Gussage All Saints, Dorset (Wainwright and Spratling 1973: 122; Spratling 1979: 138; Foster 1980: 13, fig. 11). The advantage of adding lead to a copper alloy is that it reduces the melting point of the alloy allowing it both to flow more freely during casting and to be successfully cast at a lower temperature which would prevent the partial melting of previously cast, adjacent components during the casting process (Dungworth 1996: 402; 1997a: 5.3.3). The use of leaded copper alloys during the British Iron Age is unusual, although where they do occur it is largely in cast, rather than wrought, artefacts suggesting a sophisticated appreciation of the properties of leaded alloys (Dungworth 1996: 402–3; 1997a: 5.3.3). Whether the use of leaded copper alloys in Iron Age Ireland was common is not certain as little metallurgical work on Irish copper alloy artefacts has been conducted. Metallurgical analysis indicates that the central link of the Llyn Cerrig Bach bridle-bit (No. 23) does have a different composition to the other components of the bridle-bit (see Appendix 2). The centre-link has a lower percentage of tin (7.97%) in comparison to the other surviving components of the bridle-bit (10.64%, 10.98% and 11.29%), although no significant increase in the quantities of lead within its alloy were detected as might have been expected by analogy with the Irish bridle-bit allegedly recovered from the River Conway. Although copper alloys are rarely homogeneous, and lead has a particular tendency to become segregated within a casting, the size and position of the sample should have minimized the chance of this affecting the metallurgical analysis of the central link. Consequently, the use of a different alloy to manufacture the centre-link of thc Irish bridle-bit from Llyn Cerrig Bach does not have an obvious explanation.

Summary

The bridle-bits from the Llyn Cerrig Bach assemblage form an important part of the corpus of known bridle-bits of the British Iron Age. It is not possible to suggest close dates for any of the bridle-bits from Llyn Cerrig Bach, although they are all probably late Iron Age in date. Two of the three principal types of British bridle-bit are represented in the assemblage. The Irish three-link bridle-bit provides the only definite example of an imported piece of metalwork from Llyn Cerrig Bach. There are surprisingly few certain examples of imported metalwork in Iron Age Britain and the majority of that material is derived from the Continent, not Ireland (see Stead 1984 for a comprehensive discussion of this subject). Exotic material elsewhere in Iron Age Anglesey and north Wales is rare, but not unknown; for example, there is the Type D Irish bridle-bit allegedly from the River Conway, Denbighshire (see above), and a Gaulish Celtic coin of the Carnutes from Llanfaes, near Beaumaris, Anglesey (Besly 1995: 47, 62, no. 1). The significance of this imported material in the Llyn Cerrig Bach assemblage is considered in the concluding chapter.

4

The Copper Alloy Artefacts Excluding the Horse Furniture, Vehicle Fittings and Pieces of Artistic Merit

Cauldron fragments

There are three definite (Nos. 24–6), and one possible (No. 32), copper alloy cauldron fragments in the assemblage. The possible fragment is discussed elsewhere in this chapter. The three definite fragments each represent a separate vessel, contrary to the conventional view (i.e. Fox 1947a: 42, 87–8; Lynch 1970: 270; Savory 1976a: 88; Green 1998: 70) based on Fox's mistaken premise that two of the fragments (Nos. 24 and 25), of similar globular form, were from the same vessel (1947a: 42, 87–8). The shoulders, or points of maximum diameter, of both fragments of globular form are distinctively marked by a crease running across their blackened external surfaces. On one (No. 24) the shoulder is set, following the curve of the vessel, 94 mm below the rim, while on the other fragment (No. 25), again following the curve of the vessel, it is set 67 mm below the rim. Such a difference cannot be accounted for by variation within a single vessel. In addition, the character of the polished lines below the rims of both fragments, presumably caused by their reinforcing rims, varies too much for these fragments to have come from the same vessel. Furthermore, metallurgical analysis indicates that the two fragments have different metallurgical compositions (see Appendix 2) suggesting that they represent different vessels.

As noted above, the form of two of the fragments (Nos. 24 and 25) is similar. They both differ markedly from the third (No. 26). Precise reconstruction of the original shape and dimensions of the vessels is difficult because they were deliberately damaged in antiquity prior to their deposition and were also folded during collection (Fox 1947a: 87). Plenderleith's testimony that two of the fragments (Nos. 24 and 25) fell naturally into the forms now seen (Fox 1947a: 87) is doubtful. A similar observation which was used to justify the 'restoration' of one of the decorative coiled copper alloy strips (No. 42) (Fox 1947a: 86) is demonstrably false (see below). Consequently, no estimates of rim diameter or vessel capacity are offered here. Nevertheless, two of the fragments (Nos. 24 and 25) clearly have a distinctive globular form, which curves out from the rim to a point of maximum diameter (i.e. the shoulder). The third fragment (No. 26) was originally probably of hemispherical form as there is no evidence that it had a shoulder and its upper edge, or rim, was apparently the widest part of the vessel. It is not certain whether the hemispherical fragment (No. 26) is from a single piece vessel or a fragment of the basal part of a composite cauldron.

No reinforcing rims or handles survive either attached to the cauldron fragments or as separate artefacts in the assemblage, but study of the cauldron fragments allows some comment to be made on these absent features. Polished, uneven lines (thickness 1–2 mm) run parallel to, and 9–12 mm below, the rim on both the internal and external sides of the two globular fragments (Nos. 24 and 25). The character of the polished lines differs between the two fragments. The polished line on the external side of one of the fragments (No. 24) is 10–11.5 mm below the rim and the line on its internal side is of a similar depth 9–11 mm below the rim. In comparison, the line on the external surface of the other fragment (No. 25) is 10–12 mm below the rim while its internal line is slightly higher at 9–10 mm. On the external surfaces these polished lines demarcate the upper limit of the area of blackening. Presumably, the upper parts of the vessels remained 'unsooted' or unoxidized because they were covered by a reinforcing rim. The form of these rims is unknown, but the polished lines were presumably caused by lateral movement where they were fixed to the vessel body. Although the rims of both globular fragments are pierced by a single rivet hole, this fixing hole probably relates to the attachment of the separate escutcheon features and not the reinforcing rim; the absence of more rivet holes suggests that the rim was either brazed or clamped in place. Ferrous corrosion products visible intermittently on the rim of one of the globular fragments (No. 24) suggests that its reinforcing rim was made of iron. The character of the upper edge, or rim, of the hemispherical fragment (No. 26) was different; the four rivet holes extant along its surviving length of 83 mm suggest that it was attached to either an upper section or a reinforcing rim solely by rivets. One rivet survives and is hammered flush with the internal surface, but extends 1 mm beyond the external surface, indicating that the overlapping upper section or the reinforcing band was external. The edge of the hemispherical fragment's rim is smooth. This contrasts with the ragged and unfinished upper edges of the two globular fragments. There is a slight, ambiguous corrosion differentiation on the external surface of the hemispherical fragment (No. 26) running parallel with the rim, 11–15 mm below it, which presumably relates to either the overlapping upper section or the reinforcing band.

None of the cauldron fragments contain any surviving handles. The two globular fragments (Nos. 24 and 25) both have U-shaped patches of differential corrosion below the rims on their external surfaces, which have not unreasonably been identified as marking the former position of escutcheons associated with handles (Fox 1947a: 42). In a central position above both escutcheons, in the area covered by the reinforcing rim, is a slightly indented rivet hole which may have attached either the handles, the escutcheons, or both the handles and escutcheons to the vessel body. Presumably, even if the rivet hole was used, the escutcheon would also have been partly brazed to the vessel. It has been previously suggested that the escutcheon from one of the globular fragments (No. 24) was partly torn away and repaired with a brazed copper alloy patch in antiquity (Fox 1947a: 42, 87; Savory 1976a: 88; Lynch 1970: 271). This view can no longer be maintained as it is based on a misinterpretation of a fold set across the escutcheon. The fold is a pleat in the original body of the vessel and not a brazed patch. It is uncertain whether this pleat is an accident of manufacture, part of the deliberate destruction of the cauldron prior to its deposition, or a fold sustained during collection.

On the internal surface of one of the globular fragments (No. 24) there is evidence for the attachment of three copper alloy sheet tags or reinforcements set vertically around the area of the escutcheon. The smallest tag is rectangular in shape (dimensions 7 x 15 mm) one end of which is curved and the other possibly torn or incomplete. It is set adjacent to a split in the cauldron. The tag has been fixed to the vessel by a single copper alloy rivet which has been hammered flush with the internal surface. The second tag is now missing, but is represented by a patch of differential corrosion (dimensions approximately 12 x 23 mm) of similar shape to the smaller tag. This patch of differential corrosion is bisected by a vertical split in the cauldron which runs from the rim and through a rivet hole. The setting of the rivet hole and the outline of the tag are similar to the arrangement for the smallest tag. The third tag (dimensions 19 x 53 mm) has an elaborate, slightly asymmetrical, tapering shape which narrows through three consecutive waists. The tag extends from the rim, and includes a band of differential corrosion, set between 7 and 28 mm below the rim, presumably caused by being partly covered by the reinforcing rim and another feature during use. The lower end of this tag is damaged and may be incomplete. Immediately below it half a rivet hole survives on the edge of the vessel fragment. It is uncertain whether this relates to a separate, fourth tag or part of the missing end of the third tag. The function of the three tags is uncertain. The smaller tag and the tag represented by differential corrosion are both set on, or adjacent to, tears in the cauldron and it is possible they are repairs. In size and form they are not dissimilar to the copper alloy patch used to repair a split across one of the copper alloy nave hoops (No. 6). This form of patch, where a narrow copper alloy strip is riveted across a small break, has been termed a splint repair (Raftery 1994: 159), although their small size would suggest such a practical function is unlikely. The larger tag is not situated over a tear, but its purpose is almost certainly not decorative as it is situated on the inside of the cauldron. Differential corrosion along its length suggests it ran underneath the reinforcing rim, indicating that either it was an original feature or the cauldron was dismantled before it was applied and then reassembled. Fox considered this tag to be a strengthening strip designed to support the rivet he assumed held the escutcheon in place (Fox 1947a: 42). The only insular parallel for a tag on the internal surface of a cauldron associated with an escutcheon or handle is that of the Spettisbury Rings, Dorset, vessel which is interpreted as a reinforcing band (Gresham 1939: 120–2, fig. 5; Spratling 1972: 229, 579, no. 404, fig. 184). All three tags on the globular fragment are set around the area covered by the escutcheon. Although they may be decorative features this is difficult to reconcile with their setting on the vessel's internal surface. In the absence of more than one parallel among the insular cauldrons, interpretation of their function remains speculative. The two smaller tags are tentatively interpreted as patches while the larger, elaborate tag is considered a possible reinforcement for supporting the escutcheon.

The blackening of their external surfaces and evidence of patching suggests that all three vessels represented by the fragments were used prior to their deposition. Blackening is visible on the external surface of all of the fragments, particularly the globular vessels (Nos. 24 and 25), and is presumably caused by oxidization from exposure to cooking fires. Interestingly, there are no cauldron chains in the Llyn Cerrig Bach assemblage despite their occurrence elsewhere in the late Iron Age (Manning 1983: 136–42). The blackened surface does not extend above the polished striated line set below the rims of the two globular fragments (Nos. 24 and 25), suggesting that their reinforcing rims remained intact until the end of their functional life and were only removed subsequently. There is a slight difference in colour between the external surface of the hemispherical fragment (No. 26) and both its internal surface and the external area covered by either the upper section or reinforcing rim. This is also possibly related to the preferential oxidization of the vessel's surface. The hemispherical fragment (No. 26) was patched in five places on the internal surface by sub-triangular shaped, copper alloy sheet fragments ranging in size from 11 x 14 mm to 68 x 78 mm. Only four patches remain intact, but differential corrosion indicates the position of the fifth. That one of the patches is superimposed upon another might suggest that they represent at least two episodes of repairs. Metallurgical analysis indicates, however, that the alloy composition of the two overlapping patches is so similar that they were almost certainly manufactured from the same source, suggesting that, despite their superimposition, the patched repairs were probably undertaken at the same time (see Appendix 2: sample nos. 22 and 23). The patches were fixed around their edges by small copper alloy rivets, most of which remain intact. The rivets were hammered flush with the internal surface, but are slightly raised (0.5 mm) on the external surface. None of the patches cover actual holes or tears in the vessel. Presumably, they were applied to strengthen perceived weak points in the vessel body rather than to cover extant perforations. On one of the globular fragments (No. 25) a rivet, set approximately 160 mm below the rim, fixes two square washers to the fragment; it was presumably part of a secondary repair or patch. There are no examples of the so-called paper clip type of patch common on other insular cauldrons (cf. Burns 1969: fig. 2).

Apart from the rivet holes there are no visible tool marks on the cauldron fragments except the sharp straight sides of some of the edges of all three fragments which are consistent with having been deliberately cut in antiquity, presumably as part of a deliberate destructive episode prior to deposition. The lack of tool marks associated with the production of the vessels prevents a significant contribution to previous discussions of vessel manufacture (Maryon 1949: 94–102; Burns 1969: 31; Hodges 1989: 74–5). The vessels were undoubtedly cold worked from single cast ingots and three potential methods of manufacture have been identified; raising, sinking and spinning (Hodges 1989: 74–5). Spinning is a technique whose inception is conventionally dated to the Roman period (Maryon 1949: 97). Although none of the bases are complete enough to include the distinctive hole or chuck-mark where they would have been attached to the lathe, it is doubtful whether they were manufactured by spinning, although it is possible that they may have been finished on a lathe (Tylecote 1962: 150). Of the remaining two techniques,

Maryon has expressed doubt over the suitability of raising a vessel such as a cauldron (1949: 98) and that Iron Age cauldrons were produced by principally using a sinking technique is widely accepted (for example, Burns 1969: 31; Spratling 1971: 111). X-radiographic survey of the fragments does not indicate any stress lines which would be consistent with the cold working of the vessels. Potentially, this is because they were annealed during conservation; a process which would have destroyed any extant stress lines (Hodges 1989: 73). A survey of vessel thickness was undertaken and revealed that the thickness of each fragment varied as follows 0.35–0.75 mm (No. 24), 0.40–0.80 mm (No. 25) and 0.30–0.70 mm (No. 26). The rims, or upper edges, of the vessels were the thickest element, with the vessels becoming generally thinner towards their base. This would be the pattern in vessel thickness anticipated if the cauldrons had been manufactured by a sinking technique, although the measured values may have been influenced by corrosion and aggressive conservation techniques. No evidence of decorative embellishment of the vessels' surfaces is observable on the fragments.

The copper alloy cauldrons of the later British Iron Age have previously been studied and classified by Fox (1947a: 42–4), Hawkes (1951: 179–89), Piggott (1952–3: 12–13), Spratling (1971; 1972: 235–8) and MacGregor (1976: 150–2) (for a detailed review of these typological studies see Macdonald 2000a: 115–17). The paucity of known examples, their frequently fragmentary condition and the inadequate publication of several vessels have hindered the usefulness of these various typological studies. The insular La Tène cauldrons form a relatively heterogeneous artefact type and it is not possible to classify all of the known examples within neatly defined typological groups. Since MacGregor's study the subject has not been re-evaluated, possibly because of a lack of subsequent discoveries of typologically diagnostic cauldrons, although Raftery has usefully surveyed the Irish cauldrons (1980; 1984: 226–36). Of the previous typological studies, Spratling's four-fold classification is the most useful for appreciating the diversity of insular cauldron forms and, with only minor amendments, provides the most detailed context for the evaluation of the Llyn Cerrig Bach fragments.

The integrity of Spratling's Group I, or 'Santon' form, is maintained here. It is defined as consisting of a copper alloy sheet, one-piece, hemispherical base with a projecting belly (resulting in the diagnostic concave-side) attached to either a one-piece or two-piece, copper alloy sheet upper section set vertically or splayed slightly outward with an iron rim and handles attached to the upper section. Examples of the group include vessels from: Ballymoney, Co. Antrim; Bewcastle, Cumberland; the Bog of Allen, Co. Kilkenny; Carlingwark Loch, Kirkcudbrightshire; Santon, Norfolk; an unprovenanced Irish cauldron; and the fragment of a possible example from the Old Croft River at Upwell, Norfolk (Table 9). MacGregor considered that the Silchester, Hampshire (Fox and Hope 1901: 246; MacGregor 1976: 151, 170), and Wormegay, Norfolk (MacGregor 1976: 170), vessels should be added to this group. The absence of published illustrations for these pieces prevents comment on this attribution, although a note on the Silchester vessel (Fox and Hope 1901: 246) indicates that it is made from a single piece of metal, making its inclusion doubtful. MacGregor also considered that the Lound Run, Suffolk, cauldron

TABLE 9: Later Iron Age cauldrons from Britain and Ireland

Group	Provenance	References
I	Ballymoney, Co. Antrim	Armstrong 1923: 25, fig. 13.2; Raftery 1980: 59, no. 4, figs. 7 and 12.1; 1983: 210, no. 558; 1984: 234, 316, pl. 75
	Bewcastle, Cumberland	Feachem 1965: 229, pl. 11.b; Spratling 1971: 111
	Bog of Allen, Co. Kilkenny	McEvoy 1854–5: 131–2; Armstrong 1923: 25, fig. 13.1; Raftery 1980: 59, no. 5, fig. 8; 1983: 210, no. 559, fig. 170; 1984: 234, 316
	Carlingwark Loch, Kirkcudbrightshire	Anon. 1866–6: 7–9, pl. I; Smith 1914–15: 87, 93–4; J. Curle 1931–2: 310–13, fig. 18; Spratling 1971: 111
	Santon, Norfolk	Smith 1909a: 146–8, pl. XV.1; 1914–15: 87–9; Fox 1923: 104; J. Curle 1931–2: 310–11; Clarke 1939: 71–2; Spratling 1972: 235–6, no. 429
	Upwell, Norfolk (?)	Gregory 1978
	Unprovenanced (Ireland)	Raftery 1980: 59–60, no. 6, fig. 9.1; 1983: 211, no. 560, fig. 171
II	Baldock, Hertfordshire	Stead 1971: 251; Stead and Rigby 1986: 55–9, figs. 21, 23
	Ballyedmond, Co. Galway	Rynne 1960: 1–2; J. Raftery 1963: 126, pl. XIII; Raferty 1980: 58, no. 2, figs. 3–4.1 and 11.2; 1983: 208–9, no. 556, fig. 167; 1984: 231–2
	Battersea, London	Smith 1906–07: 328–9, fig. 4; 1914–15: 87–8; Burns 1969: 33; Spratling 1971: 112; 1972: 236, no. 426
	Kincardine Moss, Stirlingshire	Anderson 1884–5: 313, fig. 2; Burns 1969: 32–3; Piggott 1970: 21, no. 106; Raftery 1984: 232, 328; Hunter 1997: 110, 125
	Letchworh, Hertfordshire	Moss-Eccardt 1965; Spratling 1971: 112; 1972: 236–7; Moss-Eccardt 1988: 88–90
	Walthamstow, Essex	Smith 1906–07: 329–30; 1914–15: 87–8; Hatley 1933: 19–20, 29, fig. 14; Spratling 1971: 112; 1972: 236, no. 430
	Spettisbury, Dorset	Gresham 1939: 120–2, fig. 5; Spratling 1972: 229, 579, no. 404, fig. 184
III	Blackburn Mill, Berwickshire (2)	Newton 1852; Smith 1914–15: 87, 93; J. Curle 1931–2: 310, 313–14, fig. 21; MacGregor 1976: 151, 170, nos. 301–2
	Kyleakin, Skye	Anderson 1884–5; Burns 1969: 32–3; MacGregor 1976: 170, no. 306; Raftery 1984: 231
IV	Abercairney, Perthshire	Burns 1969: 31–2; Spratling 1971: 111; MacGregor 1976: 170, no. 300

Group	Provenance	References
	Elvanfoot, Lanarkshire	Burns 1969; Spratling 1971; MacGregor 1976: 151, 170, no. 303
	Whitemills Moss, Dumfriesshire	Anon. 1889–90: 16; MacGregor 1976: 151, 170, no. 307
	Ewartley Shank, Northumberland	Spratling 1971: 112; 1972: 238; MacGregor 1976: 170, no. 304
Misc.	Dirnveagh Bog, Co. Antrim	Anon. 1924: no. 679; MacGregor 1976: 170
	Ipswich, Suffolk	Clarke 1939: 73
	Lound Run, Suffolk	Clarke 1939: 73, pl. XX
	Llyn Cerrig Bach, Anglesey (3)	Nos. 24–6 (see catalogue entries for full bibliographical references)
	Walthanmstow, Essex (?)	Hatley 1933: 19–20, 29, fig. 14; Fox 1947a: 43, 88; Hawkes 1951: 179

belonged to this group (1976: 170), but this attribution is incorrect because the vessel lacks the defining projecting belly and concave-side feature (Clarke 1939: pl. XX). The dating evidence for this group is relatively good (contra MacGregor 1976: 151). In a recent survey their source was plausibly identified as the Continental, late La Tène cauldrons of Emmendingen type dating from the first century BC into the Imperial period (Raftery 1984: 234; see also Fox 1947a: 43, fn.4). Two of the insular examples are datable independently by association. The Carlingwark Loch deposit is conventionally dated to the late first century or early second century AD (Manning 1972: 233) and the Santon assemblage to the third quarter of the first century AD (Manning 1972: 232; Spratling 1975: 207). That the distinctive form continued, albeit associated with differing manufacturing techniques, well into the first millennia AD is demonstrated, with several examples, by Hawkes (1951: 185–8). In general, a date range for the group from the first century BC to at least the second century AD is reasonable.

On the basis of middle to late La Tène Continental parallels Spratling defined his Group II, or Battersea form, as globular composite cauldrons with single piece, copper alloy sheet bases and vertical or inward sloping wrought sheet iron upper sections (Spratling 1971: 112; 1972: 235–6). The Ballyedmond, Co. Galway; Baldock, Hertfordshire; and the Kincardine Moss, Stirlingshire, cauldrons all have surviving two-part upper sections of copper alloy sheet and body shapes of a similar form to Spratling's defining examples from the River Thames at Battersea, London, and Walthamstow, Essex (Table 9). Consequently, the definition of Group II is extended here to include those cauldrons with a single piece, copper alloy sheet base, of hemispherical or slightly globular form, attached to either a copper alloy or iron one-piece or two-piece collar or upper section. The join between the base and the collar is effected by a series of regularly and closely spaced domed rivets. The upper sections are reinforced by either a copper alloy or iron rim and have handles directly attached to them. It should be noted that Spratling did not state how substantial the upper parts, or collars, of Group II cauldrons were, although the Letchworth, Hertfordshire, iron collar was offered as an example (Spratling 1971: 112; 1972: 236–7). Spratling considered the Spettisbury, Dorset vessel to be a bowl on the basis of its similarity to the Glastonbury, Somerset, bowl (Bulleid and Gray 1911: 179–81, fig. 40, pl. I; cf. Spratling 1972: 229, 579, no. 404; Coles and Minnitt 1995: 56), although others have considered the Spettisbury vessel to be a cauldron (i.e. Fox 1947a: 43, 88; Hawkes 1951: 179; MacGregor 1976: 170). The Spettisbury vessel is smaller than the other cauldrons in this group and its classification as either a cauldron or a bowl is somewhat arbitrary. What is significant, however, is the similarity in form and manufacturing technique between the Spettisbury and Glastonbury vessels and the Group II cauldrons. Dating evidence for the group is provided by two vessels: the Baldock cauldron was recovered from a rich, La Tène III burial dated to the first half of the first century BC if not the second century BC (Stead and Rigby 1986: 60–1; Bryant and Niblett 1997: 278), while the Letchworth collar, whose attribution to this group is not certain, is dated by stratified ceramics between the middle of the second and first centuries BC (Moss-Eccardt 1988: 88). The Spettisbury vessel was apparently recovered from the ditch on the north-east side of the Spettisbury Rings hillfort, but unfortunately no record of associated material was made (Donaldson 1856–9: 190; Gresham 1939: 116). Hunter has suggested that the Kincardine Moss vessel is probably pre-Roman in date (1997: 110). Raftery has dated the Ballyedmond cauldron to the early first century AD on the basis of the crescentic form of two of its patches, thought to have been reused bucket mounts, being paralleled by the side-plates of a wooden bucket accompanying the mirror burial at Birdlip, Gloucestershire (1980: 63; 1984: 232). The validity of such a speculative parallel is doubtful. A date ranging from the second century to at least the first century BC is tentatively suggested for this group. Several Continental parallels, and possible antecedents, for this group are discussed by Stead and Rigby (1986: 59).

Group III, or the Blackburn Mill form, of Spratling's typology was defined as globular vessels made from a single sheet of copper alloy and provided with iron rims (1972: 237). Essentially, the type is a revival of Hawkes's one-piece slightly shouldered group (1951: 179). For Spratling the group consisted of the two Blackburn Mill, Berwickshire, vessels, the Kyleakin cauldron from Skye and all three Llyn Cerrig Bach fragments (1972: 237). The validity of including all of the Llyn Cerrig Bach fragments in this group is questionable and a more precise definition of the type is considered appropriate. Group III vessels have a globular, shouldered body made up of a single copper alloy sheet with a narrow rim unperforated by rivet holes. Handles were attached to the upper part of the copper alloy sheet body; it is in this respect that the vessel type differs from Group IV (see below). Both the Blackburn Mill and the Kyleakin cauldrons can be classified as Group III cauldrons by this definition. As the Kyleakin cauldron was a single find divorced from stratigraphic associations, the dating evidence for the group is entirely dependent on the Blackburn Mill vessels. They are part of a deposit conventionally dated to the late first or second century AD (Manning 1972: 232–3). The classification of the Llyn Cerrig Bach fragments is returned to below.

Examples of Spratling's Group IV, or Elvanfoot form, are defined as globular one piece, copper alloy sheet vessels with short upstanding rims with rivet holes pierced through them, at either regular or irregular spacings, which were presumably used for the attachment of iron reinforcing rims. Handles are presumed to have been attached to the rims as no evidence for them is visible on the cauldron body (Spratling 1972: 237–8). Spratling identified four Group IV cauldrons; that is, the vessels from Abercairney, Perthshire; Elvanfoot, Lanarkshire; Whitemills Moss, Dumfriesshire; and Ewartly Shank, Northumberland (Spratling 1972: 238). The rivet holes on the upstanding rims of all four vessels are significantly more widely spaced than those on the Group II cauldrons and it is unlikely that any of them are the bases of misidentified Group II cauldrons. Interestingly the three Scottish vessels are all decorated by the same technique of hammering up circular bosses in relief from the inside of the vessel (Spratling 1972: 238; MacGregor 1976: 151). This decorative technique is not represented on any other cauldrons, emphasizing the typological integrity of the group. Spratling speculated that this bossed ornament style had its origins in poor planishing technique, but conceded that its employment on the Abercairney, Elvanfoot, and Whitehills Moss cauldrons must be intentional (1971: 112). It is possible that the Lound Run, Suffolk, cauldron (Clarke 1939: 73, pl. XX) is another example of this group (see below). Unfortunately, none of the Group IV cauldrons can be dated by either association or context. Burns's overly precise date of the first century AD for the Elvanfoot cauldron (1969: 34) has rightly been dismissed by Spratling for being based on insufficient evidence (1971: 111).

There are several cauldrons which it has not been possible to classify within the amendment of Spratling's scheme outlined above. The vessel recovered from Berner's Street, Ipswich, Suffolk (Clarke 1939: 73), is too fragmented to be typologically diagnostic and the Dirnveagh Bog, Co. Antrim cauldron (Anon. 1924: no. 679; MacGregor 1976: 170) has not been published in sufficient detail to evaluate its form with confidence. There is possibly a second vessel from Walthamstow. Both Fox (1947a: 43, 88) and Hawkes (1951: 179) imply that there are two separate vessels, one a single-piece hemispherical type and the other the Group II vessel noted above, while later commentators have referred to only a single cauldron (Spratling 1972: 236, 588, no. 430; MacGregor 1976: 170). An early account states that two vessels had been recovered from Walthamstow, although only one was illustrated (Hatley 1933: 19–20, 29, fig. 14). The vessel illustrated in this early source has a hemispherical body and a regularly pierced rim and although its handles were missing there is no indication that they were fixed to the body of the vessel. Although these characteristics suggest that it is closest in form to Group IV, definite classification is not possible. It is difficult to place the cauldron from Lound Run, Suffolk (Clarke 1939: 73, pl. XX) within the revision of Spratling's typological scheme. Its hemispherical form and irregularly pierced rim is suggestive of a Group IV assignation, however, its rim diameter (approximately 30 cm) is small in comparison to the other vessels making up this group. It should be noted that, in addition to the Dirnveagh Bog, Co. Antrim vessel (Anon. 1924: no. 679; Raftery 1984: 234), several of the cauldron fragments listed in a 1924 sale catalogue (Anon. 1924: nos. 673–8, 680) may also be of a late Iron Age date, although the illustrated handles (Anon. 1924: no.

673, pl. V) are closely paralleled by the earlier Llyn Fawr, Glamorgan, cauldrons (Crawford and Wheeler 1920–1: 136, pl. XII.1; Fox and Hyde 1939: 372–3, pls LXXII–LXXIV; Savory 1976a: 54–5, nos. 8–9, figs. 2–3, pl. I.b). Raftery has also noted several other possible late Iron Age cauldrons (1980: 60; 1984: 233–4).

Placing the Llyn Cerrig Bach fragments within the typological scheme outlined above is difficult. Two of the fragments (Nos. 24 and 25) have a globular, slightly shouldered form suggestive of Group III. The rims of both of these fragments are pierced by a single rivet hole, discounting the rivets associated with the tags on No. 24, which probably formed part of the attachment of the handle to the reinforcing rim rather than the attachment of the rim to the vessel body. Unlike the Group III vessels, however, the handles on the two globular fragments appear to have been fixed to the reinforcing rim and not the body of the vessel. In this respect they resemble the Group IV vessels. It is uncertain whether the hemispherical fragment (No. 26), which is distorted and artificially flattened, is the lower part of a composite vessel or a fragment of a single piece hemispherical cauldron. Its upper edge, or rim, is pierced by irregularly spaced rivet holes, which are not closely spaced, and there is no evidence of how handles may have been attached to either its body or rim. The rivet holes which pierce its upper edge, or rim, indicate that it is not a Group III cauldron, but they are too irregular and widely spaced for it to be part of a Group I or Group II cauldron either. Discounting its non-globular form this fragment is closest to the vessels of Group IV type. That none of the Llyn Cerrig Bach fragments fit closely into the typological groupings recognized in the study of the other insular cauldrons suggests that they cannot be closely dated on typological grounds. The results of metallurgical analysis of the fragments indicate that the hemispherical fragment (No. 26) and its patched repairs are manufactured from a copper-tin alloy typical of Iron Age alloying traditions, while the two globular fragments (Nos. 24–5) are manufactured from a low arsenic copper-tin alloy more (although not exclusively) typical of Roman alloying traditions (see Appendix 2). Given the occasional occurrence of low arsenic copper-tin alloys in demonstrably Iron Age artefacts, and the absence of Romano-British parallels for the globular cauldron fragments, no chronological significance can confidently be placed upon their metallurgical composition (for a detailed discussion of Iron Age and Romano-British copper alloying traditions and how these affect the interpretation of the Llyn Cerrig Bach assemblage see Chapter 6).

Summary

There are fragments from three (Nos. 24–6), and possibly four (No. 32), cauldrons in the Llyn Cerrig Bach assemblage. Study suggests that the vessels they represent were used and then deliberately damaged prior to their deposition. The fragments are difficult to classify, and by extension date, within the typological scheme for the insular cauldron types, although their general form and character is not inconsistent with their being of late Iron Age date, their metallurgical composition suggests they could also be of Roman date.

Military equipment and weaponry

In addition to the decorated shield-boss mount discussed in Chapter 5 (No. 48), there are three copper alloy objects of a military character from the Llyn Cerrig Bach assemblage. These are the scabbard mouth (No. 27), the probable scabbard or sheath binding (No. 28) and the pommel mount (No. 29). Fox's contention (1947a: 6) that these three pieces form a complete set, or series, is not maintained here.

The scabbard mouth (No. 27) is described in the catalogue. Although previously iden- tified as a sheath fitting for a dagger (Fox 1947a: 6), both the width and flat top of the piece suggest that it was probably a scabbard mouth for a La Tène III sword (Lynch 1970: 252; Savory 1976a: 29). Piggott classified insular examples of this wide, square topped form of sword as part of his Group V or Battersea type (Piggott 1950: 21–2, 28). There are eight La Tène III swords in the Llyn Cerrig Bach assemblage (Fox 1947a: nos. 1–2, 4, 6–7 and 93–5; Savory 1976a: nos.17.1–2, 17.4, 17.6–7, 18.2–3 and 19.1) (G. Darbyshire pers. comm.), although it is not possible to ascertain which, if any, of these the scabbard mouth was originally associated with.

At least twelve examples of copper alloy scabbard mouths from La Tène III swords are known from Britain and Ireland (Table 10), although the Bardney Abbey and Whitcombe examples are perhaps better considered as scabbard bindings set immediately below the tops of scabbards. Not all of the La Tène III swords recovered from Britain have copper alloy scabbard mouths, for example, the scabbard mouth from the warrior burial at St Lawrence, Isle of Wight, is of wrought iron (Jones and Stead 1969: 354, fig. 2.2). The Llyn Cerrig Bach scabbard mouth is plainer than the tabulated parallels. It carries neither elab- orate openwork decoration (unlike the Brough Castle, Chesters, Lambay Island, Normanton le Heath and Orton Meadows examples), incised ornament (unlike the Hod Hill and Stanwick examples) or embossed ornament (unlike the Verulamium example). Its only embellishments are two parallel grooves set below the rim. It is uncertain whether they are cast or were incised after the casting was produced. The closest parallel to the Llyn Cerrig Bach piece is the Stanwick scabbard mouth, which is embellished with a sim- ilar set of grooves, or reeded decoration, around its neck. The Stanwick, Lambay Island and the fragmentary Chesters scabbard mouth also have D-shaped, semi-circular front plates similar to the Llyn Cerrig Bach example. Where measurable, the external widths of the scabbard mouths vary from 54 mm (Brough Castle) to 89 mm (Whitcombe). Again, the closest parallel to the Llyn Cerrig Bach example (external width 56 mm) is the Stanwick piece (external width 57 mm).

As a fitting for a La Tène III sword the Llyn Cerrig Bach scabbard mouth cannot pre- date the appearance of the type which occurred, at least on the Continent and southern Britain, in the first century BC (MacGregor 1976: 84; Stead 1991a: 64). Contextual evi- dence suggests that deposition of the type continued until at least the first century AD. The Bardney Abbey and Battersea scabbards are both unassociated finds from the River Witham and River Thames respectively. The example from Brough Castle was found in 1854, presumably in the vicinity of the Roman fort at which occupation had begun by the

TABLE 10: Cast copper alloy scabbard mouths from La Tène III swords

Provenance	References
Bardney Abbey, Lincolnshire	Kemble 1863: 190, pl. XIV.2; Piggott 1950: 28, pl. II; Spratling 1972: no. 253; Jope 2000: 279, pl. 210.f–g
Battersea, London	Kemble 1863: 193, no. 4, pl. XVIII; Piggott 1950: 28, fig. 10.6; Spratling 1972: no. 254, fig. 106
Brough Castle, Westmorland	Kemble 1863: 194, no.9, pl. XVIII; Smith 1925: 108, fig. 118; Piggott 1950: 22, 28; MacGregor 1976: 84, no.161
Chesters, Northumberland	MacGregor 1976: 84, no. 162
Corfe, Dorset	Unpublished; I. Stead and J. D. Hill pers. comm.
Hod Hill, Dorset	Brailsford 1962: 1, no. A5, fig. 1; MacGregor 1976: 83; Spratling 1972: 160, 498, no. 258, fig. 108
Lambay Island, Co. Dublin	Macalister 1929: 243, no. 24, pl. XXIV.5; J. Raftery 1951: 198, fig. 239; Raferty 1983: 106, no. 277, fig. 106
Llyn Cerrig Bach, Anglesey	No. 27 (see catalogue entry for full bibliographical details)
Normanton le Heath, Leicestershire	Fitzpatrick 1994
Orton Meadows, Cambridgeshire	British Museum acc. no. P1989 3–2 4; I. Stead and J. D. Hill pers. comm.
Stanwick, North Yorkshire	Wheeler 1954: 44–50, pls XXVI, XXVII.a–b, fig. 14; MacGregor 1976: 84–5, no. 172
Verulamium, St Albans, Hertfordshire	Page 1911–12: 132–3, fig. 1; Smith 1911–12b: 136; Piggott 1950: 21, 28, pl. II; Spratling 1972: 160, 510, no. 283
Whitcombe, Dorset	Aitken 1967: 127; Aitken and Aitken 1990: 73, figs. 9, 10.2

Flavian period (MacGregor 1976: no. 161). The Corfe scabbard mouth is an unassociated metal detector find reported to the British Museum. The Hod Hill piece was a chance find from ploughing the interior of the western part of the site, which includes a Claudian Roman fort, in the mid nineteenth century (Brailsford 1962: p. vii). Although the majority of finds recovered from the hillfort in this manner are probably of early Roman date (Manning 1985: 182) the curvilinear decoration on the piece is typical of native ornament (Brailsford 1962: 1) and an earlier date cannot be dismissed. The Normanton le Heath scabbard mouth was recovered from a late Iron Age enclosure ditch (Thorpe and Sharman 1994: 22–3). The Orton Meadows example was associated with a La Tène III sword recovered during gravel working of a relict channel of the River Nene (J. D. Hill pers.comm.). The Verulamium example is also a chance find (Page 1911–12: 132) and its precise date is uncertain. Settlement had begun at the Prae Wood site adjacent to Verulamium by the late first century BC and had extended into the valley of the River Ver by the Claudian Conquest (P. Webster 1984: 6; Bryant and Niblett 1997: 273–4, fig. 27.4); the scabbard mouth could date to either this late Iron Age phase or the subsequent

Roman occupation. The Lambay Island scabbard mouth was recovered from an inhuma-tion burial and is part of a collection dated to the second half of the first century AD (Raftery 1994: 203). The precise provenance of the Chesters piece is unknown, but it is assumed to be from the Roman fort and therefore its deposition is unlikely to pre-date the second quarter of the second century AD (MacGregor 1976: no.162). The Stanwick scab-bard mouth is part of the sword and scabbard excavated in 1951 whose deposition was dated by the excavator to the third quarter of the first century AD (Wheeler 1954: 44). The sword was deposited in a lower silt of a defensive ditch adjacent to an earthwork entrance in a probable votive act (Willis 1999: 100). Wheeler's dating of the sequence at Stanwick was based on only slender archaeological evidence (Haselgrove 1999: 254) and was largely influenced by a desire to place the site within an historical context (cf. Wheeler 1954: 17–26; Haselgrove et al. 1990b: 2). Subsequent work at the site suggests that Wheeler's chronology and sequence can no longer be accepted (Haselgrove 1990; Haselgrove et al. 1990a: 86), but despite the absolute dating evidence remaining slight, a mid first-century AD date for the earthwork phase, and by extension the sword's deposition, is still accepted (Haselgrove 1990: 385; Haselgrove et al. 1990a: 86). The Whitcombe scabbard mouth was recovered from an inhumation dated to the first half of the first century AD (Aitken and Aitken 1990: 75).

Stylistic dating of the decorative designs on the scabbard mouths, whilst being consis-tent with the contextual evidence cited above, does not refine the dating of the type. The openwork decoration on the Battersea scabbard consists of two opposing bird's head motifs which are examples of Stead's Style V of insular La Tène art (1985a: 21–3; 1985b: 27) which potentially dates from the third century BC to at least the first century AD (see Chapter 5). The decoration on both the Brough Castle and Corfe scabbard mouths con-sists of keeled scroll motifs, which are also examples of Stead's Style V. The Hod Hill scabbard mouth has an apparently uncompleted curvilinear decorative device which is dif-ficult to classify, but has certain affinities with Stead's Style V. The openwork decoration on the Normanton le Heath and Orton Meadows scabbard mouths cannot be closely dated on stylistic grounds. The Verulamium example is reminiscent of pieces such as the Elmswell mount dated to the late first century AD (Megaw and Megaw 1989: 230). The openwork of the Lambay Island piece is defined by pelta-shaped voids which has been stylistically dated, perhaps over precisely, to the second half of the first century AD (Rynne 1976: 237). The compass drawn design on the Stanwick scabbard mouth consists of two lentoid panels which both contain a ring and dot motif. Piggott considered the ring and dot motifs to be reminiscent of the studs on earlier insular La Tène II swords as well as the Brough Castle example (Wheeler 1954: 48), however, ring and dot decoration has a long vogue and the close dating of such a ubiquitous motif is questionable. The Chesters example is too fragmented to date stylistically.

The contextual evidence, where it exists, indicates a date range for the deposition of examples of the type, in the first century AD, but it is difficult to draw firm conclusions on the date of the Llyn Cerrig Bach scabbard mouth from only nine parallels. Although the closest parallel is the Stanwick scabbard mouth, which has a mid first century AD depositional date, it is not possible to suggest, with any confidence, a more precise date for the Llyn Cerrig Bach example than either the first century BC or the first century AD.

The probable scabbard or sheath binding (No. 28) is fully described in the catalogue. As Fox noted (1947a: 74), the upper and lower edges of the binding's front are folded over, presumably to prevent them from catching. The rectangular panel on the front of the binding is dented and marked by a linear scratch; this damage is modern (see Fox's illustration of the piece which shows the binding undamaged: 1947a: pl. XVI). The binding has previously been interpreted as a scabbard fitting (Fox 1947a: 6, 74; Spratling 1972: 160, no. 270; Savory 1976a: 29, 57) possibly for a La Tène III sword (Lynch 1970: 252; Savory 1976a: 29). That the binding is from a scabbard is an interpretation accepted here, although the possibility that it could have bound a knife sheath or some other object cannot be dismissed. The only close parallel for the binding is provided by the scabbard mounts on the La Tène III sword from near Thrapston, Northamptonshire (Megaw 1976: 167–9, pl. 2.b–c). The Thrapston sword, which is an unassociated find recovered from a dried-up river bed, is an example of Piggott's Group V sword type whose vogue apparently dates to the first century AD (Piggott 1950: 3, 21–2; Mcgaw 1976: 169), but which, as a La Tène III type, may also date to the first century BC. There are a number of less close parallels for the binding; the nearest is the plain, copper alloy sheet band set above the cast chape on the La Tène III Grimthorpe scabbard (Mortimer 1905: 152, frontpiece; Piggott 1950: fig. 7.1; Stead 1968: 170, figs. 14, 15; 1979: 61, figs. 21.3, 22.2). Other wrought, copper alloy scabbard bindings include examples from the Glastonbury lake village, Somerset (Bulleid and Gray 1911: 239, no. E84, pl. XLIII; Spratling 1972: 160, no. 257, fig. 108; Coles and Minnitt 1995: 59) and Hod Hill, Dorset (Brailsford 1962: 1, no. A7, fig. 1; Spratling 1972: 160, no. 259, fig. 108). Cast copper alloy bindings also occur on the Stanwick, North Yorkshire, scabbard (Wheeler 1954: pls XXXVI and XXVII.a; MacGregor 1976: no. 172). By analogy with the Thrapston scabbard mounts, the Llyn Cerrig Bach binding is interpreted as probably being a La Tène III scabbard fitting which dates from the first century BC to the first century AD.

The third copper alloy example of military equipment is the cast pommel mount which contains the upper part of an iron tang (No. 29). The iron tang was deliberately broken in antiquity. It is uncertain whether the piece is a dagger or sword mount; some have assumed it is from a dagger (Fox 1947a: 6, no.12; Savory 1976a: 29) while others have favoured a sword (Lynch 1970: 252; Spratling 1972: 158, no. 294). The absence of close parallels makes this difficult to resolve, but the fact that the Hod Hill and Cotterdale examples cited below are demonstrably sword pommels strengthens this interpretation for the Llyn Cerrig Bach mount.

Spratling classified the insular sword hilts into two similar groups: a Hod Hill type; and a Bulberry type (1972: 157–9). This classification was based on the more frequently surviving hilt guards rather than pommel mounts and is not directly relevant to a discussion of the Llyn Cerrig Bach mount. The type of mount that the piece is most closely associated with is the cruciform type. There are four other insular examples of cruciform pommel mounts: Hod Hill, Dorset (Brailsford 1962: 1, no. A1, pl. II.A; Spratling 1972:

157, 513–14, no. 289, fig. 120; Manning 1985: 149–52, no. V3, pl. 72); Bradford Peverell, Dorset (Piggott 1950: 28; Spratling 1972: 158, 513, no. 286, fig. 119); South Cadbury, Somerset (Spratling 1972: 158, 516, no. 296, fig. 121; O'Connor *et al.* 2000: 236, fig. 116.1); and Cotterdale, North Yorkshire (Franks 1880; Piggott 1950: 17–20, 27, fig. 9.2D; Spratling 1972: 158–9; MacGregor 1976: 80–1, no. 143). These fittings are all four-armed, curved mounts and, although their character varies, they form a coherent group. All four are rounded, indicating they mounted spherical or pear-shaped pommels. In comparison, the Llyn Cerrig Bach example is closed, implying it was mounted on to a thinner and quite different shape of pommel. This reduces the strength of the parallel and, although the Llyn Cerrig Bach example is similar in design, it must be considered a different, but related, type. The parallels do not provide good dating evidence. The Hod Hill sword was a chance find from the western half of the hillfort which includes a Claudian Roman fort (Brailsford 1962: p. vii). Manning has convincingly argued that, contrary to earlier interpretations (cf. Piggott 1950: 21; MacGregor 1976: 80), the sword is a Roman type which has had native fittings added to it (Manning 1985: 151). The Bradford Peverell hilt was a chance find from Quatre Bras, possibly from a burial (Spratling 1972: 158). The South Cadbury mount was recovered in a residual context (Spratling 1972: 516); activity at the site was more-or-less continuous throughout the Iron Age until some point in the second half of the first century AD (see Alcock 1972: 118–72; Barrett *et al.* 2000a: 169–78). The circumstances of the discovery of the Cotterdale sword are unrecorded (Franks 1880: 251). The Cotterdale mount was apparently set the opposite way up to the others and was probably based upon a Roman pommel type (Franks 1880: 251; Spratling 1972: 158–9), suggesting a late date. Unfortunately, on the strength of this evidence, it is not possible to suggest a specific date for the Llyn Cerrig Bach pommel mount.

The 'Cylinder'

The 'cylinder' (No. 30) is fully described in the catalogue. It is one of the most enigmatic pieces in the assemblage and is without close parallel. It consists of a rolled rectangular sheet of copper alloy (dimensions 62 x 80 mm), which was closed into a tube by two corresponding sets of rivet holes (diameters 1.5 mm) set along its longest edges. None of the rivets survive. It was pierced, on one side, by two sub-rounded holes (diameters 4–7 mm) and on opposite sides by corresponding sub-rectangular perforations (dimensions 16 x 7 mm and 13 x 7 mm). All four of these features are irregular in shape. The 'cylinder' has been damaged, presumably in antiquity. It is opened out and folded along a line of weakness set at a slight diagonal across its back, and its edges are ragged and torn. Presumably it was mounted on either a short cylindrical object or a thin, circular-sectioned rod or pole. The sub-rounded holes possibly contained studs and the sub-rectangular holes may have been joined by a perforation through the object the 'cylinder' was mounted on.

The form of the 'cylinder' is paralleled by a perforated cylinder of horn from Hunsbury, Northamptonshire decorated with incised ring and dot motifs (Dryden 1885: 57, pl. II.12) and it is possible that the 'cylinder' was a decorative sheath or mount for an object of this type. The function of the Hunsbury horn cylinder is uncertain, although it has been compared with the bone, horn and antler toggles of late Iron Age type known from: Borness Cave, Kirkcudbrightshire (Corrie *et al.* 1872–4: 496–7, pl. XXI); Dinorben, Denbighshire (Gardner and Savory 1964: 168–9, nos. 2 and 6, fig. 26; Savory 1976a: 73, no. 110.173 and fig. 33); the Glastonbury lake village, Somerset (Bulleid and Gray 1917: 460–1, nos. H20, H202, H273 and H366, pl. LXVI; Coles and Minnitt 1995: 38, 56, 58 and 63); Ham Hill, Somerset (Bulleid and Gray 1917: 462, fig. 157.A); Maiden Castle, Dorset (Wheeler 1943: 308, no. 15, fig. 105); and the western Meare lake 'village', Somerset (Gray and Cotton 1966: 340, nos. H43, H98, H171 and H219, pl. LIX). These toggles are usually interpreted as dress fasteners (Bulleid and Gray 1917: 460; Gardner and Savory 1964: 168), however, they are not cylindrical, but taper towards each end, suggesting that the analogy with the Hunsbury cylinder and, by extension, the Llyn Cerrig Bach 'cylinder' is problematic. A specific interpretation of the function and date of the Llyn Cerrig Bach 'cylinder' cannot be suggested with confidence.

Curved-horn, or 'trumpet', fragment

A single fragment (No. 31) of a curved-horn, or 'trumpet', is represented in the Llyn Cerrig Bach assemblage (Col. Pl. 1b). The fragment, which consists of a copper alloy sheet tube and a cast copper alloy boss, is fully described in the catalogue. The tube was crumpled and in two pieces when recovered, but was repaired and reshaped by Plenderleith (Fox 1947a: 87). This restoration involved annealing, reshaping and rejoining of the two pieces as well as the application of several solder repairs during the course of which the tube was over-straightened. The torn end of the fragment is too distorted for accurate measurement of its diameter. Consequently, it is not known whether the tube has a uniform diameter or is slightly flared. The boss is only superficially scratched. None of the damage on the fragment is demonstrably ancient and it all could have resulted from the modern extraction and working of the peat.

The hollow biconical boss set at the intact end of the tube is an impressive casting, equal in quality to the so-called horn-cap (No. 49). Its almost perfect circularity suggests that the model the casting was based on was manufactured on a lathe. The flanges at either end of the boss are flush with the main tube and the piece contains no visible casting flaws. The boss has protected the immediately adjacent section of the tubing and kept the joint intact whilst the remainder of the tube was damaged. By analogy with the Loughnashade horn (see below), the boss is interpreted as forming part of the join by which two tubular sections of the horn were originally connected. The boss is fixed in place by a slight raised flange at the end of the tube.

The body of the horn consists of a long, narrow copper alloy sheet rolled over along its length to form a tube. Fixing holes (diameter 2 mm) have been drilled 13 mm apart longitudinally (although this figure occasionally rises to 14.5 mm) and 7 mm apart transversely, on alternate sides of the butt-join, which is situated on the concave side of the horn. Through these fixing holes the join has been riveted to a narrow copper alloy strip (width 16 mm) fixed to the internal surface of the tube. The hammering technique employed during riveting has given the butt-join a sinuous, wavy edge and also caused comparable undulations in the edges of the internal strip. Only the part of the join covered and immediately adjacent to the boss remains closed (length 50 mm). The rivets, of which twenty-five remain, have been filed on both the internal and external surfaces of the tube. The heads of the rivets are larger on the internal surface.

The damaged end of the fragment was ornamented with two separate elements of decoration both set on the concave side of the tube across the butt-join. One element consisted of a (now lost) elongated oval patch (length 51 mm, maximum width 9 mm) decorated with a design of linked ovals filled with chased basket-work pattern (Fox 1947a: pls XII.b and XXXI; Savory 1976a: fig. 23). This patch was fixed by three rivets and partly overlaid the other decorative element. This consists of an engraved pattern set within a, now truncated, rectangular panel (minimum length 20 mm, width 8 mm) which extended across the torn end of the tube. Its original length is unknown and too little of it remains to reconstruct its original composition. It appears to be a wave-like pattern, which is not dissimilar to the design on the patch but is infilled with parallel lines rather than basket-work. The engraved decoration was worked on part of the tube which had been previously brazed, arguably in order to close the butt-join and provide a continuous flat surface to receive the engraving (Fox 1947a: 86; Raftery 1983: 242). Damage and modern repair work prevents ascertaining whether the part of the tube covered by the patch had also been brazed. Fox thought that as the rivet holes on the brazed surface were not distorted this meant that the brazing occurred prior to the riveting, and that therefore both the brazing and the engraved decoration were part of the original design of the horn (Fox 1947a: 87). Examination of the fragment, however, suggests that the brazing, engraved decoration and patch are all secondary additions. Although the rivet hole at this point is undistorted, this does not unequivocally demonstrate that the brazing was conducted prior to riveting, or that the engraved decoration is an original manufacturing feature. Inspection reveals that the hole is not on the same alignment as the other rivet holes, suggesting it was, along with the brazing and engraving, part of a secondary episode of metalworking. The matted patch, because it partly overlaid the engraved decoration, must also be a secondary feature, although whether it is related to the brazing and engraving episode or an unrelated later repair is unknown.

Questions concerning the function, relative dating and origins of the brazing, engraved panel and patch immediately arise. The patch has previously been argued to be a secondary repair required as the result of damaging the horn (Fox 1947a: 86; Raftery 1984: 139), although there is no reason why this secondary repair could not have been required as a result of an accident, or mistake, made during the horn's manufacture and therefore have been carried out in the original workshop. The curving of the tube would have been a technically difficult process and damage to the join might be expected during this phase of manufacture. Metallurgical analysis undertaken by Messrs Minton, Treharne and

Davies Ltd of both the tube and the patch (Savory 1971: 66; see also Appendix 2) indicates that the patch was manufactured from a different alloy to the main horn fragment, but this observation does not indicate whether the patch was applied during the manufacturing process or at a later date. The horn has previously been considered to have been manufactured in Ireland and, as there are no Irish parallels for the matted ornament on the patch (Raftery 1984: 139; but see Savory 1970: 46), the patch has been considered to be a later British repair. This raises the vexed question of whether an Irish origin can be applied to the curved horn artefact type. To address this question it is necessary to place the Llyn Cerrig Bach fragment in a wider insular and Continental context.

There are two definable groups of copper alloy sheet, musical horns recognizable from the archaeological record of the insular Iron Age: the curved-horn and the *carnyx* (for a detailed discussion of the *carnyx* see Hunter 2001). The curved-horns, of which the Llyn Cerrig Bach fragment (No. 31) is an example, are conventionally considered to be large C-shaped instruments that normally consist of two segmented copper alloy sheet tubes that are sealed on their concave edge. The final tubular segment, which terminates in the bell-end or mouth of the instrument, is conical in form, whilst the other tubular segment is uniform in diameter. Although commonly referred to as 'trumpets', because of their conical bore it is musicologically more correct to label them horns (Megaw 1970: 147; Raftery 1983: 239). The *carnyx*, or animal-headed war-trumpet, is a similar instrument which consists of a straight, copper alloy sheet tube which curves into a bell in the form of a, possibly totemic, animal head. The *carnyx* probably had a mouthpiece set at an angle to the tube (Megaw 1968: 350) while the mouthpiece of the curved-horns, for which no evidence survives (Raftery 1983: 241; contra Megaw 1968: 350; 1991: 645), probably continued in the direction of the tube.

Apart from the Llyn Cerrig Bach fragment, three insular examples, all from Ireland, of the copper alloy sheet, curved-horn survive. The complete Loughnashade, Co. Armagh specimen is made up of two tubular sections joined by a biconical, copper alloy sheet boss with a decorated, but acoustically functional, copper alloy disc at the bell-end (Raftery 1983: 239–40, no.781, figs. 201, 202; 1984: 134–9, 143, fig. 77, pls 42–3; 1987: 21–3; O'Dwyer 2004: 67–78). The complete example from Ardbrin, Co. Down (Raftery 1983: 241, no. 782, fig. 203; 1984: 134–5, 143, figs. 72.1, 77, pl. 41; O'Dwyer 2004: 78–83) also consists of two tubular sections, although it is unknown how these were joined. The remaining insular example is an unprovenanced tubular segment in the National Museum of Ireland (Raftery 1983: 241–2, no. 783, fig. 204; 1984: 134–5, figs. 72.2, 77) sometimes recorded as coming from Roscrea, Co. Tipperary (i.e. Kelly 1993: 13). The horn it represents consisted of at least three segments as the surviving element has connecting, cast biconical bosses at both ends (Raftery 1984: 134). Full descriptions and references for these horns are given by Raftery (1983: 239–42). Another six, now lost, copper alloy horns from Ireland are recorded. Three horns, of similar form, were allegedly recovered with the Loughnashade example in the late eighteenth century (Browne 1802; Stuart 1819: 608; Petrie 1833–4; Wilde 1863: 625). The validity of these reports has been questioned (Megaw 1968: 350), but is generally accepted (i.e. Armstrong 1923: 22–3; Raftery 1984:

134; Kelly 1993: 13; Raftery 1994: 184; Lynn 2003: 70–3; O'Dwyer 2004: 68). Another two lost fragments are recorded as originating from Bushmills, Co. Antrim (Petrie 1833–4: 29; Raftery 1984: 134), and there is an unreferenced note recording a possible horn fragment from Loughbrickland, Co. Down (Archaeology Survey of Northern Ireland 1966: 54).

Two Irish, wooden horns of uncertain date but similar form to the insular, copper alloy sheet curved-horns also exist. The first is from Killyfaddy Bog, near Clogher, Co. Tyrone (Wilde 1863: 245; Raftery 1983: 243, no. 785, fig. 205; 1984: 136, fig. 76.1) and consists of four segments. The second, from Diamond Hill, Killeshandra, Co. Cavan, is comparatively short, made from a single length of wood and represents a less convincing parallel (Raftery 1984: 136, fig. 76.2). Two Continental parallels for the insular curved-horns are known (Raftery 1984: 140–3). One from Stenstugan, Sweden (Oldeberg 1947: 76–9) shares a number of technical features with the insular horns, but is not a close parallel. The other, which provides the only close Continental parallel, is an unprovenanced example in the Deutsches Museum, Munich that was reportedly found in Nice (Behn 1954: 143; Megaw 1968: 350; Raftery 1984: 140; 1987: 24). Representations of similar curved-horns are found on the famous statue of the 'Dying Gaul' (Raftery 1984: 139; Mattei 1991) and a small copper alloy anthropomorphic casting from the oppidum site of Hradiště near Stradonice, in the former Czechoslovakia (Megaw 1970: 134, no. 213; Raftery 1984: 140; Megaw 1991: 644–5).

Representations on the Gundestrup cauldron (Piggott 1959: pl. VII.b; Megaw 1991: 646) show that the *carnyx* was held vertically when played. It is less clear how the curved-horns were held when played; a photograph of the two complete Irish examples shows how large and unwieldy the instruments are (Fox 1947a: pl. XII.a). O'Dwyer has demonstrated that the conventional C-shaped arrangement for the instruments' form could present severe technical problems for the individual trying to play it (2004: 70). Although there is representational evidence from Britain of a smaller horn of C-shaped form depicted on an early first century AD coin (Allen and Nash 1980: 148, no. 443, pl. 30), simple interpretation of images from coins is problematic (Megaw 1991: 647), and it is possible that the image concerned, of a centaur blowing a horn, is copied from a Roman source such as an intaglio (Van Arsdell 1989: 421, no. 2089–1, pl. 53). Based partly upon his experience playing reconstructions of the Loughnashade and Ardbrin curved-horns, O'Dwyer has argued that the curved-horns may originally have been sinuous in form rather than C-shaped (2004: 69–72, 116–18). If arranged in an S-shaped form, the curved-horns could have been held vertically over the player's head with the mouthpiece presented to the player's lips and the open bell-end of the instrument pointing forward (O'Dwyer 2004: 71, figs. 43–4). Of the known complete curved-horns, the examples from Ardbrin and Killyfaddy Bog were dismantled into their constituent parts prior to deposition, whilst the early accounts of the Loughnashade horns (i.e. Browne 1802; Stuart 1819: 608; Petrie 1833–4; Wilde 1863: 625) do not explicitly state what the assembled shape of the horns was when they were first discovered (O'Dwyer 2004: 71). At present, the question of the original assembled shape of the curved-horn must remain open.

The Llyn Cerrig Bach fragment is technically similar to the three extant Irish curved-horns, although there are some minor variations between each example. Both the Loughnashade and the unprovenanced fragment have biconical bosses equivalent to the Llyn Cerrig Bach fragment, although the Loughnashade boss is made from copper alloy sheet and is not cast. It is not known how the sections of tubing on the Ardbrin horn were connected, but it is reasonable to suppose that it was through a similar biconical boss. The ends of the tube of the unprovenanced example are folded slightly outwards to fix the bosses in place (Raftery 1983: 241) in an identical manner to the Llyn Cerrig Bach fragment. All three of the Irish horns were sealed on the concave edge with rivets to a narrow internal strip, although part of the Loughnashade horn has a secondary external strip applied over the join. Despite this common method of sealing, none of the Irish examples have a sinuous join comparable with that of the Llyn Cerrig Bach fragment. The spacing and arrangement of the sealing rivets on the unprovenanced example (approximately 10 mm apart) is closest to that of the Llyn Cerrig Bach fragment. The 'horn' attachments of both the Cork and Petrie 'crowns' are sealed by the same method (Raftery 1994: 155). There are a number of secondary repairs to the Loughnashade example, although none of them are directly analogous to the elongated oval patch used on the Llyn Cerrig Bach fragment. Apart from the magnificent decorative disc mounted to the bell-end of the Loughnashade horn, none of the Irish examples are decorated. Because of its fragmentary condition, study of the Llyn Cerrig Bach example can add little to the published discussions of the manufacturing process of the curved-horns (Maryon 1938: 221; Tylecote 1962: 144–5; Raftery 1994: 154–5).

The best evidence for dating the insular curved-horns is provided by the decorative repoussé design on the Loughnashade disc which is mounted on the horn. The disc has been classified as part of the Megaws' first recognizable school of British art (Megaw and Megaw 1986: 23; 1989: 196). With its symmetrical, balanced layout including palmette-like features, the disc approximates closest to Stead's Style IV (itself equivalent to the Megaws' earliest British school), although the trumpet boss terminals of the disc anticipate elements of Stead's Style V (Stead 1985a: 21–3), which may explain the Megaws's wider dating of the piece from the second century BC to the first century BC (1989: 197). Several authors (for example: Megaw 1970: 147; Raftery 1984: 136; Megaw and Megaw 1989: 196) have noted the close parallels with the Torrs Farm, Kirkcudbrightshire pony-cap (Atkinson and Piggott 1955; MacGregor 1976: 23–4, no. 1, pl. I.a). A relatively late date has been suggested on the strength of similarities in the design's layout with the Battersea shield (Megaw 1970: 147; Raftery 1984: 138; see also Lynn 2003: 73), but the parallel is not close and more importantly a definitely late date for the Battersea shield can no longer maintained (Stead 1985b: 47; Kilbride-Jones 1994; Jope 2000: 351).

Other dating evidence has been put forward for the insular curved-horns. The D-shaped patches on the Loughnashade horn have been argued, by analogy with Irish cauldrons with similar patches, to be possibly indicative of a first century AD date (Raftery 1984: 138–9). The D-shaped patch is, however, of dubious chronological significance, and even if a late date is accepted for the Irish cauldrons, it does not follow that all D-shaped patches are datable to the first century AD. The similarity in manufacturing techniques between the curved-horns and the 'horn' elements of the Cork and Petrie 'crowns' (Raftery 1983: 259–61, nos. 820–1, figs. 219–25; 1984: 268–75, figs. 132–5, pl. 84–7) has also been noted (Raftery 1984: 139; Kelly 1993: 13). Raftery has suggested this is also possibly indicative of a late date (1984: 139), but again even if a late date for the Cork and Petrie 'crowns' is accepted the chronological significance of the manufacturing technique remains uncertain (Raftery 1984: 139).

Of the Continental evidence, the date of the unprovenanced horn in the Deutsches Museum is unknown (Raftery 1984: 143; 1987: 24) whilst the Stenstugan horn is dated roughly to the second century AD (Oldeberg 1947: 79; Raftery 1984: 140), but the applicability of applying this date to the insular horns on the strength of one parallel is debatable. Of the representational evidence the anthropomorphic casting from Hradiště is dated to the first century BC (Megaw 1970: 134), but again the appropriateness of the parallel is questionable. The figure of the 'Dying Gaul' is assumed to have been a copy of part of the monument erected at Pergamum after 228 BC (Mattei 1991: 71). Although not overly comparable, the Continental evidence confirms the date range from the second century BC to the first century AD suggested by Raftery for the insular curved-horns (1984: 139).

The origins of the curved-horn are obscure. Megaw has speculated that the insular curved-horns were perhaps a local development from the cast, late Bronze Age, Irish horns (1991: 645). Such assertions are difficult to demonstrate with certainty and the possibility, suggested by the unprovenanced example in the Deutsches Museum and the 'Dying Gaul' figure, that there was a direct contribution from the Continent to the development of the insular curved-horns (Raftery 1984: 143) cannot be discounted. The bias towards Irish horns in the insular distribution of the curved-horns has led to the widespread assumption that they are an Irish artefact type (Fox 1947a: 61; Lynch 1970: 271; Raftery 1984: 134; but see Megaw 1970: 147 for a different view), however, the small number of definite insular examples, combined with the cited Continental parallels, suggests that identifying even such a general provenance for the artefact type is problematic. In an alternative attribution of provenance, the repoussé decoration on the Loughnashade disc has been identified as probably British, rather than Irish, on the strength of parallels with the Torrs pony-cap and the Battersea shield (Megaw and Megaw 1986: 23; 1989: 196; 1991–2: 163; but for an alternative view see Avery 1990: 2). Again, such precise provenancing based on the distribution of only a handful of parallels is problematic; the Loughnashade disc may well have been manufactured in Ireland.

It is possible to make some comments about the context of deposition of two of the Irish curved-horns, although this evidence is not detailed enough to provide close archaeological dating. The Loughnashade horn, and the three other horns reportedly found with it, were recovered from a bog bordering Loughnashade, Co. Armagh (Armstrong 1923: 22–3; Lynn 2003: 70–3). This is the lake adjacent to the important site of Emain Macha, or Navan Fort (Raftery 1994: 74–9; Lynn 1997a; 2003). The deposition of the horns in a watery context, in which human skeletal remains have reportedly also been found (Stuart 1819: 608; Raftery 1987: 21), adjacent to the important early centre is interpreted as a deliberate votive act (Herity and Eogan 1977: 242; Raftery 1994: 184; Lynn 2003: 73). The Ardbrin horn was found in either a lake or a bog (Archaeological Survey of Northern Ireland 1966: 54; Raftery 1994: 154), although a more precise context was not recorded (Armstrong 1923: 23) it is not unreasonable to interpret this as a probable votive deposit as well. While the range of evidence of deposition is not great, the similarity of depositional context of the Loughnashade and Ardbrin examples with that of the Llyn Cerrig Bach fragment is noteworthy.

Summary

The Llyn Cerrig Bach curved-horn fragment has to be considered within its wider insular and Continental context. Although previously assumed to have been made in Ireland, the small number of insular examples of curved-horns and the presence of some Continental parallels reduces the confidence that can be placed in an Irish provenance for its manufacture. If the piece can no longer be considered definitely Irish then Raftery's argument that the elongated-oval patch represents a later repair, because of the absence of Irish parallels for the matted basket-work ornament on the patch, is not necessarily valid. Potentially the patch may have been a repair made, along with the brazing embellished with engraved decoration, in the workshop of origin as the result of a mistake in the manufacturing process. At present, it is not possible to be more precise about the relative date and function of the brazing, engraved decoration and patch. The piece probably dates, by analogy with its insular and Continental parallels, to some point between the second century BC and the first century AD. Although this date is comparable with much of the Llyn Cerrig Bach assemblage the small number of available parallels reduces the confidence which can be placed in it. The curved-horn fragment may be even earlier or later in date.

Small sheet fragments

There are four small, previously unpublished, copper alloy sheet fragments in the Llyn Cerrig Bach assemblage. Metallurgical analysis has revealed that one of them (accession no. 2002.40H/2) is almost pure copper. Undoubtedly, it is modern in date and, consequently, it is not considered further here. The three other fragments (Nos. 32–4) are included in the catalogue. Although the fragments were not detailed in any of the surviving early documentation related to the assemblage, they are noted in the index to the National Museum's Prehistoric Reserve Collection and it is not unreasonable to assume they are part of the assemblage. Fox failed to publish them, presumably because they are so small and fragmented. It is possible that two of the fragments (Nos. 32 and 33) may be detached from one of the known copper alloy sheet objects from the assemblage, such as the three cauldron fragments (Nos. 24–6), but the metallurgical composition (see below) and character of the remaining fragment (No. 34) is sufficiently different from that of any of the other sheet artefacts that it is unlikely to be a fragment from one.

One fragment (No. 32) is marked by an oxidized 'tide-mark' on both sides which separates two areas of differential corrosion. This distinctive feature is paralleled by the marks on the globular cauldron fragments (Nos. 24–5) which were presumably associated with, now lost, reinforcing rim attachments. On the basis of this similarity the fragment is tentatively identified as possibly part of a cauldron. Analysis demonstrates that the fragment's metallurgical composition is close to that of one of the globular fragments (No. 24) (see Appendix 2), although whether it is part of the same vessel or represents a fourth cauldron is uncertain. Interpretation of the remaining fragments is more problematic. The sub-triangular fragment (No. 33) includes a possible fixing hole on one edge and may have been part of a mount. The largest fragment (No. 34) is rectangular in shape and is distinguished by an L-shaped patch riveted into one corner. The L-shaped patch contains a second copper alloy rivet, whilst there is a second rivet hole in the same corner of the main fragment. The fragment is relatively thick for copper alloy sheet from the assemblage (thickness 0.65–0.80 mm) and may have been a reinforcing patch. Metallurgical analysis indicates that it has a notably high zinc content suggesting that it either post-dates the Roman Conquest of southern Britain or is derived from a pre-Conquest import (see Chapter 6).

Coiled decorative strips (or 'ribbons')

The assemblage contains nine copper alloy strips (Nos. 35–43), which are sometimes described as 'ribbons'. These strips are described in the catalogue. Table 11 details the criteria describing the strips. The definitions of those column headings which are not self-explanatory are detailed below. The length of the strips varies between 120 and 490 mm (measurement of strip length is expressed to the nearest 5 mm), their width from 12 to 18 mm, and their thickness from 0.20 to 0.55 mm. Several of the strips are apparently complete, whilst others have been broken, either in antiquity or during the extraction of the peat. Most, if not all, of the strips were originally coiled. One has retained its coiled shape more-or-less intact (No. 37; coil diameter approximately 27 mm), but the majority are too deformed and twisted to reconstruct the original dimensions of their coil (Nos. 35–6, 38, 39–40 and 42). Two are so twisted that it is uncertain whether they were originally coiled (Nos. 41 and 43) although, on analogy with the others, it is reasonable to infer that they were. The assertion that one of the strips (No. 42) retains its original coiled form (Fox 1947a: 46, 86) can no longer be maintained. The strip is divided into a series of panels defined by the modern creases which were caused by a workman folding the strip when it was collected. The majority of these panels are concave, rather than convex as one would suppose, suggesting that when the object was 'restored to its original shape' the coil was mistakenly turned inside out. Hence the current external surface was originally the internal surface of the strip.

Examination of the strips reveals several noteworthy characteristics. First, five of the pieces (Nos. 35–9) are decorated with a single incised line, which runs along their length on the external surface in an approximately central position. These lines were applied with

TABLE 11: Characteristics of the coiled decorative strips

Group	Catalogue no.	Length (mm)	Width (mm)	Weight	Thickness /density	Thickness (mm)	Spiral direction	Edge type	Decoration	Evidence for overlap
I	35	490	12–14	10.6g	17	0.30–0.40	clockwise	smooth	yes	yes
	36	265	12	4.5g	14	0.25–0.35	anti-clockwise	smooth	yes	no
	37	400	13	7.2g	14	0.45–0.50	anti-clockwise	smooth	yes	yes
	38	245	12–12.5	4.1g	14	0.25	?	smooth	yes	no
	39	120	12	1.7g	12	0.25–0.30	anti-clockwise	smooth	yes	yes
II	40	375	16	15.8g	26	0.45–0.55	clockwise	smooth	no	no
	41	415	15–16	14.6g	23	0.45–0.55	?	smooth	no	no
III	42	340	17–18	6.6g	11	0.25–0.30	?	rough	no	no
	43	260	17–18	5.1g	11	0.20–0.30	?	rough	no	no

the aid of a straight-edge, except for a section of one (No. 38) where the line wavers as if applied freehand. Although these lines appear continuous, on two of the strips (Nos. 37–8) misjudged overlaps are visible suggesting that they were, at least in some cases, incised in sections rather than in a single movement. Presumably this decoration was applied before the strips were coiled. Secondly, patches of differential corrosion are observable on the ends of three strips (Nos. 35, 37 and 39). These patches are compatible with the corrosion that would be expected if the ends were overlapped with other copper alloy strips. This observation suggests that at least some of the strips were joined end to end to produce larger composite coils. That these patches of corrosion coincide with nail holes suggests they were joined together by small nails. There is no evidence to suggest they were fixed by soldering. The third characteristic, already alluded to, is the presence of both nail holes and small copper alloy nails (lengths 9–13 mm) on two of the strips (Nos. 36–37). Corrosion products visible in one of the fixing holes of a third strip (No. 43) suggest iron pins were also used. Presumably, the fixing nails were used to attach the strips onto whatever they were mounted, as well as joining coils to each other. These nail holes are set in two different locations: either at the ends of the strips in the centre of their width (Nos. 35–7 and 39), or slightly back from the ends (25–35 mm) on the strips' edges (Nos. 35 and 37). The holes at the ends are interpreted as being for primary fixing nails while those set back from the ends are considered to represent secondary repairs possibly located on the edges to avoid disturbing the central incised decorative lines.

The only previous classificatory work on the strips is that carried out by Fox (1947a). Although Fox did not explicitly classify the strips, he did note that two (Nos. 42–3) had rough edges which distinguished them from the others (Fox 1947a: 86). Fox speculated these two pieces represented workshop waste (1947a: 46).

A tripartite classification is offered here. As noted above, these groupings and the criteria on which they are based, are detailed in Table 11. All but five of the column headings are self-explanatory. 'Thickness/density' is an important classificatory criteria. It is an index of both the thickness and the density of the strips, which was calculated by dividing the weight of each piece (in grams) by its overall surface area (in square millimetres) and multiplying the result by 10,000. Spiral direction is defined by the direction, clockwise or anti-clockwise, in which the strips spiral downwards when viewed from above (this is always the same direction which ever end the coils are viewed from). Edge type is either smooth or rough. The presence of decoration, in the form of the central incised lines, is denoted in the next column. The presence or absence of differential corrosive patterning on the ends of the strips, indicative of the overlapping of strips, is denoted in the last column. These factors, along with width and thickness, form the criteria on which the classification of the strips is based. The principal two criteria used were the index of 'thickness/density' and width. These are plotted against each other for all nine strips (Figure 2). The plot shows three discreet clusters which reflect three classificatory groups. The thickness, spiral direction, decoration, overlap, and edge type are all criteria which confirm and support this classification and allow specific definitions of the groups to be made.

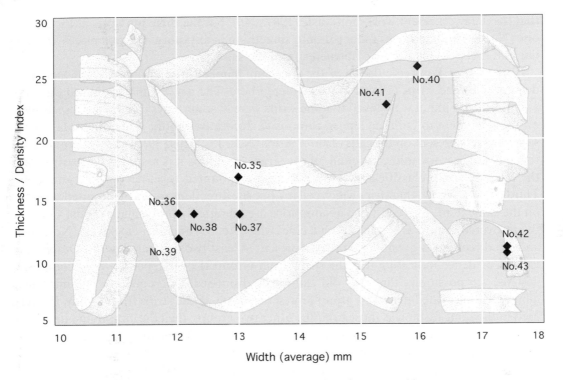

Figure 2: Thickness / density index plotted against width

Group I (Nos. 35–9) is characterized by strips which are 12 to 14 mm in width, decorated with a central incised line, and have smooth edges. Their thickness varies from 0.25 to 0.5 mm. The 'thickness/density' index varies between 12 and 17. Three of these strips (Nos. 35, 37 and 39) show evidence of having been overlapped, indicating that extended decorative designs were built up by applying them in a composite manner. They spiral in both a clockwise (No. 35) and anti-clockwise (Nos. 36–7 and 39) direction. Group II (Nos. 40–1) is characterized by strips which are 15 to 16 mm in width, have smooth edges but no indication of either decoration or having been overlapped into composite designs. Their thickness varies between 0.45 and 0.55 mm and their 'thickness/density' index varies between 23 and 26. Of the two strips in this group one spirals in a clockwise fashion (No. 40) and the other is too damaged for its spiral direction to be ascertained (No. 41). Despite the lack of evidence indicating these strips overlapped to form composite designs it is possible that they did. Group III (Nos. 42–3) is characterized by strips which are 17 to 18 mm in width, have rough edges, no apparent decoration, and show no evidence that they were overlapped. Their thickness varies between 0.20 and 0.30 mm and the 'thickness/density' index for both examples is 11. One of the strips (No. 42) now spirals in an anti-clockwise direction, but it is uncertain whether this was its original spiral direction, and the other (No. 43) is too damaged for its original direction to be ascertained. Fox expressed doubt over whether these two pieces were actually used for decorative purposes and concluded that they may represent workshop waste (1947a: 46), but the three pin holes at the end of one (No. 42) suggest it was mounted onto something in antiquity. The two pieces are similar and it is possible they are fragments from the same strip.

A revision of Fox's calculation of the minimum number of separate objects which were decorated by the strips (1947a: 45–6) is offered here. The new estimate is based on three assumptions. First, it is assumed that the strips were in some cases mounted consecutively on the same item to build up longer, composite, decorative motifs. The differential corrosion products present on the ends of three strips (Nos. 35, 37 and 39) arguably demonstrate this was the case for some, if not all, of the strips. Secondly, it is assumed that strips from the three separate classificatory groups were not mounted together on the same item. Thirdly, it is assumed that strips which coil in opposite directions were not mounted together on the same item. These last two assumptions are admittedly problematic. From Group I the recovered examples spiral in both a clockwise (No. 35) and anti-clockwise (Nos. 36–7 and 39) direction, suggesting that they represent at least two decorated items. Despite the lack of evidence indicating that the strips from Group II overlapped to form composite designs, the possibility that they did cannot be dismissed. Consequently, the minimum number of decorated items this group represents is one. If the strips from Group III were used in the same fashion as those from the other two groups, then the minimum number of decorated objects they represent is one since they could be fragments of the same original strip. Thus the estimated minimum number of separate objects decorated by the strips is three, if the Group III strips are considered workshop waste, and four if they are not.

Study of the strips suggests that several of them were deliberately damaged in antiquity prior to their deposition. Two (Nos. 35 and 38) have creased and folded areas where their nails were set. This suggests that they had been prised from the objects they were mounted upon. Four others (Nos. 39–42) have damaged ends which possibly indicates that they also were torn off the hafts they were fixed to. Although some of this damage may be modern it is probable that much dates to antiquity, suggesting that the objects decorated by the strips were damaged and partly, if not fully, stripped of their fittings prior to deposition.

Although the strips were undoubtedly decorative mounts, any specific identification of the objects they adorned is speculative. The only significant intrinsic evidence is that one of the more complete strips (No. 37) was associated with a fragment of ash wood (Hyde 1947: 98). This led Fox to conclude that their purpose was as decorative elements fixed to an ashen staff used in either a secular or religious ceremonial context (Fox 1947a: 45). This interpretation was supported by analogy with a decorated bronze ribbon found during excavations of a Romano–Celtic temple at Farley Heath, Surrey (Goodchild 1938; see also Goodchild 1946–7; Black 1985). The Farley Heath strip (minimum length 432 mm, width 25 mm) was attached to an iron loop and was decorated by two embossed elements: first, a row of circular dots punched along both of its edges; and secondly, a series of thirteen complex designs representing humans, animals and non-figurative symbols set between the dots. Other analogous spiral copper alloy bindings include: a plain strip in Chedworth Museum whose provenance is unrecorded, but presumably came from either the 'villa' site or temple at Chedworth, Gloucestershire (Lewis 1966: 137; the possibility that the 'villa' site itself might be part of religious complex has been discussed by G. Webster 1983); and the sceptre bindings from the temple site at Wanborough, Surrey (Bird 1989: 316–18, figs. 5–6; O'Connell and Bird 1994: 94–6, 108–15, 121, nos. 16–18, 22, 36–8, figs. 27–9, 32, pls 11, 22–4; A. P. Fitzpatrick pers. comm.). Similar copper alloy strips are known from King Harry Lane, Verulamium, Hertfordshire (Stead and Rigby 1989: 27–8, no. 146, fig. 17) and Lisnacrogher, Co. Antrim (Wakeman 1883–4: 402; Raftery 1983: 279, nos. 865 and 866), but these are not coiled and, although they may be decorative mounts, the parallel with those from Llyn Cerrig Bach is not close.

The spiral bindings from Wanborough provide the closest parallel to the Llyn Cerrig Bach strips and strengthen Fox's interpretation that the bindings were fixed to wooden staffs. They vary in width from 11–12.7 mm (O'Connell and Bird 1994: 108, no. 16) to 32 mm (O'Connell and Bird 1994: 113, no. 18) and are undecorated except for a narrow rib set on one side. The Wanborough strips bound wooden batons, most of which had been broken prior to their deposition, although one (length 93 cm) remained intact (O'Connell and Bird 1994: 95, no. 10). The batons were also embellished with cast copper alloy handle fittings and collars which covered the joins between the spiral bindings. The Wanborough batons have plausibly been interpreted as sceptres that acted as priestly symbols of authority that had been buried, with other items of regalia, in a votive foundation deposit before the temple was built in *c.* AD 160/170 (O'Connell and Bird 1994: 94, 97). Considering both the similarity in form and the evidence of deliberate damage prior to deposition, it is reasonable to suggest that the Llyn Cerrig Bach strips also bound religious wands which may have been deposited in a similar act (A. P. Fitzpatrick pers. comm.).

The analogy with Wanborough, Farley Heath and Chedworth bindings suggests that the Llyn Cerrig Bach strips may also be of Roman date, but dating by analogy with only three parallels is problematic. Recent excavations at Wanborough have revealed an earlier circular temple whose construction dates to the last quarter of the first century AD and which is apparently associated with votively deposited fragments of spiral bindings identical to those found in the earlier excavations (D. Williams 2000a: 3–5; 2000b: 435–7). Although results of these recent excavations suggest that the Wanborough bindings may already have been of some antiquity when they were deposited in *c.* AD 160/170 (S. Lyon pers. comm.) they also confirm the Roman date for their deposition. Supporting evidence for the suggestion on typological grounds of a Roman date for the bindings is supplied by their metallurgical analysis (see Appendix 2). Analyses of the coiled decorative strips demonstrated that all but one of the mounts were manufactured from a low arsenic copper-tin alloy, which is typical of Roman alloying traditions. For a detailed discussion of the chronological implications of the metallurgical analysis of the assemblage see Chapter Six.

Decorative plaques or mounts

In addition to the six examples of so-called casket ornament (Nos. 50–5) and the crescentic plaque (No. 47), discussed in Chapter Five, there are three other copper alloy sheet mounts or plaques from the Llyn Cerrig Bach assemblage: the two bean-shaped plaques (Nos. 44–5) and the curved mount (No. 46).

The two bean-shaped plaques (Nos. 44–5) are almost identical and probably formed either a pair or two parts of a larger set of mounts. Their shape is defined by convex and concave edges arranged to form a distinctive kidney bean-like shape. They are embellished with a central area of repoussé relief which echoes their bean-shaped form and is bordered by a chased line and a level, narrow flange. The plaques were fixed through holes at either corner and at the apex of their convex edge. The corners of one of the plaques (No. 44) are turned up, suggesting it was prised from its backing prior to deposition. The relief decoration on one (No. 44) is dented while the other plaque (No. 45) has a buckled edge and a damaged fixing hole. It is uncertain whether this damage is ancient or modern, although corrosion around the dent on one plaque (No. 44) is suggestive of ancient damage. The corners of both plaques are cut square rather than allowed to continue to the points formed by the extension of their concave and convex edges. These edges are even and apparently a deliberate part of the design rather than secondary damage.

The bean-shaped plaques have previously been interpreted as possible shield mounts (Fox 1947a: 7, 74; Lynch 1970: 257; Spratling 1972: 177–8, fig. 134; Savory 1976a: 30) on the strength of representational evidence of a shield embellished with two lunate mounts from a Gallo-Roman altar found near Nîmes, France (Déchelette 1914: 1174, fig. 496), and dated variously to the late second to first century BC (Savory 1976b: 186, fig. 1) or the first century AD (Lynch 1970: 257). Although the earlier date for the altar is favoured here, the Nîmes parallel is not exact and there are no parallels for the bean-shaped plaques from either the corpus of insular shields (Stead 1991b: 29–31) or insular metalwork in general. Although the plaques may have been mounted on to a shield, all that can be inferred with certainty is that they were decorative mounts, which may have been overlapped to form a composite design. In the absence of a more definite interpretation and, with only a single, problematic parallel, a precise identification and date cannot be suggested.

The third plaque (No. 46) is a decorative mount, or patch, for a curved object. A more specific interpretation is not possible. It has an irregular trapezoidal form (dimensions 23–25 x 32–4 x 0.5–0.75 mm), is curved along its longitudinal axis and would have been fixed through the circular holes (diameter 2 mm) set in each of its corners. The plaque is crumpled and scratched. It is uncertain whether this damage is antique. The outer, convex surface is decorated with a botched incised border and St Andrew's cross design. Fox's assertion (1947a: 58, 60) that the piece was manufactured in north Wales because it was poorly executed and reflected the limitations of native metalworking is not tenable. It is not possible to place either the St Andrew's cross design or the distinctive bean shape of the other two plaques (Nos. 44–5) within the insular La Tène so-called sequence of art. Both are comparatively rare motifs, without direct insular parallels, and are not included within the established grammars of insular ornament (i.e. Fox 1958: 147–8, figs. 82, 83; MacGregor 1976: pp. xvii–xix; Jope 2000: 333–48, pl. I–XII).

5
Artefacts of Artistic Merit

The copper alloy artefacts of artistic merit from Llyn Cerrig Bach include the crescentic decorative mount (No. 47), the mount of a shield boss (No. 48), the so-called horn-cap (No. 49) and six small plaques or examples of 'casket' ornament (Nos. 50–5). Two of these pieces, the crescentic plaque (No. 47) and the shield boss mount (No. 48), are of particular historiographic importance in the study of insular La Tène art. Their discovery encouraged Fox's interest in Iron Age metalwork and led him to publish *Pattern and Purpose: A Survey of Early Celtic Art* (1958). Fox's study of these pieces also resulted in them effectively being used to define one half of the insular La Tène art sequence (Stead 1985a: 21- 2; 1996. 32–4). Considering this historiographical significance, it is appropriate to review the insular La Tène art sequence before considering the manufacture, function, parallels and date of the individual artefacts themselves.

Traditionally, the insular La Tène art sequence is classified into an early period of imported and locally produced material decorated along Continental lines which is only represented by a small number of known examples, followed by a peculiarly insular phase divided into two sequential parts and represented by a relatively large and diverse range of artefacts (Macdonald forthcoming). The most recent articulation of this classification is Stead's revival and expansion of Jacobsthal and de Navarro's stylistic scheme (Stead 1985a: 15–23; 1985b: 27–36; see also de Navarro 1943; 1952). Stead identified three initial styles, or stages, of imported and locally produced material decorated along Continental lines, which he labelled Styles I, II and III. Stead linked these styles with Jacobsthal's 'Early' (Style I), 'Waldalgesheim' (Style II) and 'Sword' and 'Plastic' (Style III) Continental La Tène art styles (Jacobsthal 1944). Stead labelled his two-part division of the subsequent insular phase Style IV and Style V. Stead offered no specific definition of Style IV although, including de Navarro who first proposed the term, several characteristics of the style have been noted. These defining characteristics include the execution of motifs in both linear and plastic form, the frequent embellishment of raised ornament with further linear ornament, the prominent use of palmette and tendril or scroll motifs, the occurrence of bird-headed finials on tendril motifs, the circular rhythm of some designs, the influence of the 'Waldalgesheim' tendril and the importance of the half-palmette to the style (de Navarro 1952: 75; Stead 1985a: 19–21). Stead's Style V was presented as a continuation of the insular sequence into the first century BC and beyond. Again, no specific all-encompassing definition was offered, although Stead noted a number of typical features of Style V. These included tendril designs in elongated fields, fragments of tendrils in minor panels, ambitious designs in both circular and rectangular frames, the use of hatching as background, the frequent interruption of hatching with circles, the use of trumpet motifs to terminate tendrils giving the impression of a 'bird's head', and the importance of voids (especially the so-called Llyn Cerrig Bach or trumpet void composed of a triangle made up of three curves, one convex, one concave and one compound) (Stead 1985a: 22). Stead noted that Style V was also typified by the popular use of repoussé and lost-wax techniques and a willingness to employ a number of different techniques on the same piece (Stead 1985a: 22–3).

Unfortunately, the sequential integrity and chronological significance of Stead's insular La Tène art sequence is suspect. His attempt to validate the sequential character of the scheme with reference to the independent brooch and scabbard typologies (Stead 1985b: 27–32) was only partially successful. Although the typology of the scabbards corresponded closely with the proposed sequence of insular art styles, the brooch typology, especially the La Tène II brooches, provided less of a close fit and Stead conceded that if the brooch typology is considered valid then, at least in some areas, the use of Style II ornament was concurrent with that of Style IV (1985b: 32). The sequential integrity of the traditional stylistic scheme had long been undermined by pieces, such as the torc fragment from Clevedon, Somerset, in which elements of Style V art were juxtaposed with earlier styles of art (Savory 1990: 85). Furthermore, since publishing his revision of the insular La Tène art sequence, Stead's own studies of burial evidence from East Yorkshire and Deal, Kent (Stead 1991a; 1995) have further undermined the chronological integrity of the traditional insular La Tène art sequence. The Kirkburn, East Yorkshire, sword has a La Tène I chape-end and a scabbard decorated with Style V motifs, in particular the trumpet void (Stead 1991a: 66–70, 180–1). Stead's study of the East Yorkshire burial evidence led to his convincing identification of a 'Yorkshire Scabbard Style' of art, which includes the decoration on the Kirkburn sword, and which cannot be dated later than the third century BC (Stead 1991a: 181–3). Evidence for an early date for Style V was also recognized at the Mill Hill cemetery in Deal, Kent. The cemetery included a warrior burial that contained a La Tène I sword and an openwork shield boss mount, which were both decorated with trumpet void motifs that, in the case of the sword, were also associated with Style IV motifs (Stead 1995: 58–72). Stead suggested that this burial dated to the early second century BC on the basis of the sword's chape-end and an associated hinged plate-brooch (1995: 64, 86), but the form of these two items is neither typical of nor easily paralleled with early La Tène II material, and a third century BC date, on the basis of the La Tène I sword, is more likely.

The significance of the burial evidence from East Yorkshire and Deal is that it includes datable assemblages of relatively early decorated metalwork. Prior to Stead's recent studies of this material, the only fixed dates for insular La Tène metalwork assemblages were all relatively late, such as those provided by the mirror burials of southern England. This bias towards late datable assemblages led to the construction of typological sequences for Iron age metalwork which were largely confined to the first century BC simply because the only securely datable material was late (Stead 1991a: 183). Although such 'low-chronologies' have always had their critics, they probably influenced Stead to view Style V as a relatively late development in insular La Tène art. Stead's own recent work has demonstrated that Style V, if it is to be defined by the trumpet void, has a much earlier origin than has previously been recognized.

The recognition that the inception of Style V stretches back to at least the third century BC, combined with the identification of Style IV and V motifs being used on items also decorated in 'earlier' La Tène Styles, suggests that the sequential character of the insular art classification is largely invalid. Recognizing the problems with the sequential character of the insular La Tène art sequence, Stead, in his revision of *Celtic Art in Britain before the Roman Conquest* (1996), conceded that the trumpet void was a motif used in the 'Yorkshire Scabbard Style' (part of his Style IV), but rhetorically sought to justify the sequential relationship between his Style IV and Style V by renaming the different 'styles' as 'stages' and speculatively illustrating how a lobe and cusp design derived from a half-palmette motif could have developed into the trumpet void motif (Stead 1996: 34, fig. 34). The wider implications of the collapse of the sequential dating of the insular La Tène art styles is considered elsewhere (Macdonald forthcoming). With reference to the artefacts decorated in insular La Tène art from Llyn Cerrig Bach, the crescentic plaque (No. 47) and the shield boss mount (No. 48), it means that the relatively close dating previously suggested for these pieces on the general stylistic dating of their art (i.e. Stead 1985a: 23, fig. 28; Megaw and Megaw 1989: 200, pl. 338) can no longer be accepted.

Crescentic decorative mount

The crescentic decorative mount (No. 47) is described in the catalogue. It is a circular plaque perforated by an eccentric circular void, which consequently gives the piece a distinctive crescentic form. The area below the perforation contains an elaborate repoussé triskele design (Col. Pl. 2a).

The edges of the crescentic mount are emphasized by three types of border: the inner border, the upper part of the outer border, and the lower part of the outer border. The upper and lower parts of the outer border meet at the uppermost points of the outrunning lobes of the repoussé design. Both the inner border and the upper part of the outer border were made by scribing lines, approximately 2 mm from the edge, round the reverse side of the plaque. This resulted in the raising of a band with a slight central ridge on the decorated face of the plaque, which was further emphasized by applying a chased line on the decorated face 2–4 mm from the edge. The scribed lines on the reverse side are broken and in places have been applied over the same area several times; they are not decorative features but constructional toolmarks produced creating the ridge on the decorated face of the mount. The chased lines on the decorated surface do not extend across the thinnest part of the plaque. The scribed lines on the outer edge of the reverse side used to raise the border are continuous, although the scribed lines on the reverse side of the inner edge do not continue across the narrowest part of the plaque. The lower part of the outer border consists of a deep engraved line, approximately 2 mm from the edge, on the decorated face. Its application has resulted in a slight ridge being formed on the reverse side of the mount.

The crescentic mount is perforated by eleven fixing holes (numbered i–xi; Figure 3) whose diameters vary between 1.5 and 4 mm (Table 12). All of the holes, except two (nos. vii and ix), have slightly raised ragged rims of metal protruding on the reverse side of the mount which suggest that they were either punched or drilled from the decorated side. Although there is no evidence of ragged rims round the edges of two of the holes (nos. vii and ix) (contra Spratling 1972: 541) it is reasonable to assume that they were also punched or drilled from the decorated side.

TABLE 12: The diameters of the fixing holes
on the decorative crescentic mount (No. 47)

Number	Diameter
i	2 mm
ii	3–4 mm
iii	2 mm
iv	3 mm
v	3.5–4 mm
vi	3 mm
vii	1.5 mm
viii	2.5 mm
ix	3.5 mm
x	1.5 mm
xi	1.5 mm

Circular patterns of differential corrosion (nos. v and vi) and scratches (nos. ii and ix) around the four largest holes on the decorated surface indicate the position of former stud heads with diameters of approximately 10 mm. The circular scratches around two of the fixing holes (nos. ii and ix), whilst incomplete, are clearly not centred directly on the holes suggesting that, at least for these two fixing holes, irregular shaped studs may have been used to fix the mount. The circular impression of differential corrosion previously illustrated on the unperforated trumpet void within the repoussé triskelar roundel (Fox 1947a: pl. XXXII) is not visible. Fox suggested that this impression marked the site of another applied stud (1947a: 46), but the corrosion phenomenon is not visible on an early photographic plate of the mount (Fox 1947a: pl. I) and it is doubtful that it ever existed. Both Fox's interpretation and Waterhouse's illustration (Fox 1947a: pl. XXXII) were presumably informed by their mutual assumption that the arrangement of studs on the mount was regular; this view cannot be maintained. Only four of the fixing holes (nos. ii, v, vi and ix) contained large, presumably decorative, studs. There are only two comparable sized fixing holes (nos. iv and viii) both of which are too close to the outrunning decorative raised lobes to have contained studs of similar shape and size. No circular scratches or patches of differential corrosion are visible around the remaining fixing holes (nos. i, iii, vii, x and xi), which presumably received smaller and less ostentatious nails or studs.

The fixing holes have an asymmetrical layout. That two of the holes (nos. iii and x) do not have counterpoints on the opposite side of the mount suggests that they may be the result of repairs. This explanation for the asymmetrical layout of the fixing holes is not convincing, for none of the holes are so damaged that they would have been unusable if a nail or stud required replacing. Other potential explanations for the asymmetrical arrangement are that the mount may have been fixed on to more than one object prior to its deposition, or that the position of the fixing holes reflects the irregular character of whatever the mount was fixed upon. Although the form of the mount suggests that it was fixed on to a flat surface, that surface may have contained a number of voids or holes which the asymmetrical distribution of the fixing holes reflects. That said, the absence of a hole in the third trumpet void within the repoussé triskelar roundel is an intentional design element, possibly intended as an extension of the asymmetrical properties of the triskele. It is possible that the asymmetrical arrangement of the remaining holes is also an intentional element of the mount's design.

Although in reasonably good condition the mount has been damaged in several minor ways. It is not possible to ascertain whether several particular examples of damage are ancient or modern. The area around the narrowest part of the mount is broken. This break is modern (Fox 1947a: 46) and the adjacent area of polishing is probably associated with cleaning prior to the modern solder repair of this break. A more significant area of damage is the deformation round one of the fixing holes (no. ii). The hole is set in a slight hollow which is consistent with the damage likely to have been caused if the mount had been prised from its backing. Possible evidence for this type of activity prior to deposition has also been identified on one of the coiled decorative strips (No. 35), one of the bean-shaped plaques (No. 44) and the so-called casket ornament plaques (Nos. 50, and 54–5). None of the other fixing holes of the crescentic mount have been damaged in this way, and this explanation for the damaged fixing hole (no. ii) should not be considered certain. It is equally possible that the deformation was caused by fitting a stud too tightly.

The mount has been folded across the two arms either side of the circular void; creased lines across the mount suggest that it was folded backwards, although probably not far. Such a pattern of folding is not consistent with the mount having been prised from its backing. It is not clear how, or when, this folding occurred. A small number of parallel linear scratches (length approximately 10 mm) are visible on the reverse side of the mount just below the line of the fold. These were made in antiquity although their exact significance, cause and the validity of any association between them and the fold is not clear. Several areas of the raised relief have been compressed so that the raised lobes to the right of the triskele have been artificially flattened and widened, slightly distorting the balance of the design. It is not certain how, or when, this damage occurred. There are also a number of small perforations and tears on the edges of the central decorative motif caused by the weakening and thinning of the copper alloy sheet during the application of chased lines and the repoussé decoration.

Tool marks relating to the hammering up of the repoussé design are visible on the reverse of the mount. These consist of punchmark facets, first noted by Spratling (1972:

541), of which two types are observable: elongated facets (length 2–3 mm) and rounded facets (diameter 0.5–1 mm). It is not certain whether the two types were made using separate punches or by using the same tool in two different ways. The application of the different facet types is not strictly separated on the mount, but the smaller central elements of the triskele design were produced using predominantly the rounded facets, while the outer swollen lobes were manufactured largely using the elongated facets. The only other tool marks visible on the mount are the scribed, chased and engraved lines (noted above), which were employed in defining the borders and emphasizing areas of relief.

The precise function of the mount is ambiguous. Previous interpretations are as diverse as they are speculative. The lack of direct parallels, insular or Continental, for the crescentic form of the mount hinders any attempt at explanation. Fox initially considered the mount to have possibly been the frontal of a curved-horn or 'trumpet', despite the eccentricity of its perforation, because its dimensions were similar to that of the disc set on the mouth of the Loughnashade, Co. Armagh curved-horn, but he dismissed the idea because of the inappropriate position of the fixing holes (Fox 1947a: 46). Fox also considered Christie-Stokes's speculation that the mount, with the roundel design uppermost, was nailed to the dash-board of a chariot and that the draught-pole of the vehicle passed through the perforation (1947a: 46–7). He rejected this argument, however, on both technical and aesthetic grounds: first, because it would require a circular-sectioned draught-pole; and secondly because he considered the mount was intended to have been viewed with the perforation uppermost (Fox 1947a: 47). The validity of these objections is questionable. The piece could not have been a neck ornament, such as the early Bronze Age lunula-collar from Dolbenmaen, Caernarvonshire (Hemp 1917–18: 177–8; Savory 1980: 125, pl. V.a), because the break at the top of the mount did not exist in antiquity and without it the hole is too small for it to have passed over even a child's head (Fox 1947a: 46).

Following Stead (1968: 178) and Lynch (1970: 257), Spratling considered that the crescentic mount and the bean-shaped panels (Nos. 44–5) may have been shield fittings (1972: 177). He speculated that these three items along with the shield boss mount (No. 48) may have even been mounted on the same shield because of the similarity between the triskele designs on the shield boss and crescentic mounts (although the similarity is no greater than that shared by the two mounts with a number of Style V pieces) and his disbelief in Fox's assertion that the constructural finality of the fish-tail ends of the shield boss mount's ribs precluded the addition of decorative terminals. A conjectural reconstruction incorporating a second, hypothetical crescentic mount of this 'Llyn Cerrig Bach' shield was offered (Spratling 1972: 793, fig. 134). The bean-shaped panels joined the fish-tail ends of the shield boss mount's ribs to the crescentic mounts at either end of the shield. The reconstruction was completed by the addition of two Moel Hiraddug/Tal-y-Llyn style peltate side plaques. If the piece was a shield mount then its craftsmanship and delicacy, combined with the lack of significant damage it has suffered, suggest that it was fixed to a ritual or parade item rather than a standard shield or shield cover.

Any attempt at a specific functional explanation of the mount remains speculative. If considered in the context of the rest of the hoard, which is dominated by both military gear and vehicle and horse fittings, then it is tempting to forward an interpretation that it is a decorative element on a shield, chariot or wagon. Such speculations are, however, unprovable and, consequently, are not considered further.

The importance of the crescentic mount to the study of insular La Tène art has been recognized since its discovery (Fox 1945a: 35), and it is a defining example of Stead's Style V (Stead 1985a: 21; 1996: 32–4). In the following description of the mount's decorative design the individual elements and motifs of the design are numbered in square brackets and correspond with the labelling of Figure 3. The embossed decoration is situated at the widest part of the mount, beneath the circular void, and consists of a central roundel containing a balanced, but asymmetrical, triskele made up of a series of swollen lobes [1], domed trumpet coils [3] and trumpet voids [4], flanked on either side by two larger swollen lobes [2] which are in turn linked, again on both sides, with a third, outrunning, large swollen lobe [2] echoing the central triskelar design. Although none of the examples of the four design elements are identical, they are all similar in form. The swollen lobes [1] and the larger outer lobes [2] are all of slightly different sizes although, as noted above, some of the variation in form of the outer lobes is due to secondary damage. The domed trumpet coils [3] are the design motif which varies the most in execution. The upper and lower examples double back on themselves and closely resemble petal bosses, while the third occurrence of the motif on the right-hand side of the mount is more open. Although the trumpet voids [4] vary considerably in shape they are similar in form, consisting of a triangle made up of a concave, a convex and a compound curve. The overall design has been executed freehand in repoussé relief which has been further emphasized by the application of several chased lines.

The triskele is a common feature of insular La Tène art and a symbol which was used widely throughout the Classical world. The earliest occurrence of the symbol is as part of the painted decoration on the exterior of a locally produced open bowl from Castellazzo di Palma di Montechiaro in the province of Agrigento in Sicily which dates to c. 600 BC, but it was used extensively throughout the Mediterranean world from the sixth century BC onwards (Wilson 2000: 47–8). The triskele's use as a motif on shields and, from the late fourth century BC onwards, its frequent association with the Medusa head suggest that it had an apotropaic function (Wilson 2000: 39–40). Its similarity to the so-called Lycian symbol suggests it may also have been a solar symbol related to the swastika (Wilson 2000: 50). The symbol's use in European Iron Age art presumably represents a heavily adapted borrowing from the Classical world, although the possibility that it was independently invented by La Tène artists cannot be completely dismissed. That the symbol retained its apotropaic meaning in La Tène art is frequently assumed (e.g. Green 1991: 48–9; Wilson 2000: 52), although, considering how freely adapted the form of the motif became it is perhaps not unreasonable to suggest that its meaning may also have been adapted or changed.

Although there are no parallels for the crescentic form of the Llyn Cerrig Bach mount there are a number of close parallels for the repoussé design executed in both openwork

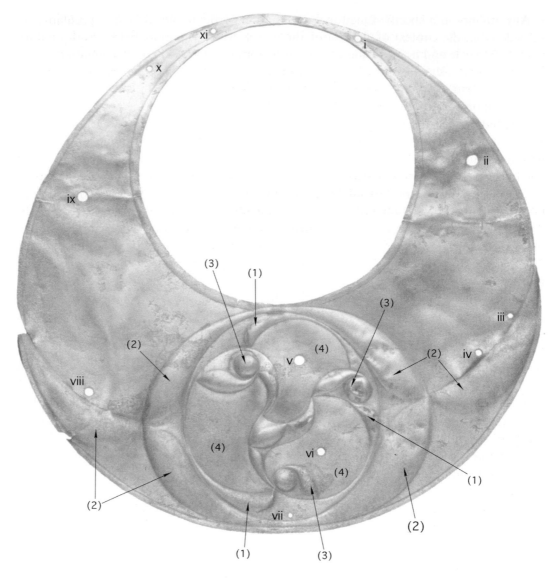

Figure 3: Crescentic decorative plaque (No. 47); fixing holes (i–xi) and design elements (1–4) (scale 3:4)

and raised or plastic art (Figure 4). Fox recognized the similarity of the mount's design with that on the cast copper alloy, spherical, terminal bulb socket of a side-link from one of the bridle-bits from Ulceby-on-Humber, Lincolnshire (Fox 1945b: 204; 1947a: 49; 1958: 35–6, fig. 21a, pl. 24). This piece was recovered with a hoard of other metalwork, including torcs, a bracelet and other bridle-bits, during the excavation of a railway cutting (Cuming 1859: 225–8). Fox also noted the similarity between the outer lobe pattern of the crescentic mount and elements of the copper alloy roundel, possibly a shield mount, from the hillfort at Grimthorpe, East Yorkshire (Fox 1945b: 204; 1947a: 50; 1958: 33–5, fig. 19, pl. 23.b). This roundel, recovered from a burial found in 1868, is associated with copper alloy shield fittings, two copper alloy studs, a sword influenced by La Tène II forms, an iron spearhead and thirteen bone pegs (Mortimer 1869; Stead 1968: 166–70, 179). The two closest parallels for the design are, however, the unprovenanced openwork roundel in the Ashmolean Museum (Fox 1958: 121–3, fig. 75, pl. 69.a) and the design on the diaphragm of the so-called horn-cap from Saxthorpe, Norfolk (Hutcheson 2004: 123, 137, no. 161; I. M. Stead pers. comm.). The designs of both of these pieces are almost perfect copies of the central element of the crescentic mount's design. Illustrations (not to scale) of all three decorative designs have been placed adjacent to each other (Figure 4, for purposes of clarity and to aid comparison the image of the Saxthorpe decoration has been reversed). The terminal of a gold torc, possibly recovered from a field in Bawsey, Norfolk (Jope 2000: 255, pl. 1201), is also decorated with a similar, and possibly incorrectly executed, version of the design on the crescentic mount. Finally, two simplified, more balanced versions of the crescentic mount's design are known. The first is applied

Figure 4: Details of the same design replicated on (a) the crescentic plaque from Llyn Cerrig Bach, Anglesey, (b) the so-called horn-cap from Saxthorpe, Norfolk and (c) an unprovenanced openwork mount from the Ashmolean Museum. Comparable designs on (d) a torc from Bawsey, Norfolk, (e) the 'vase-headed' linch-pin from Kirkburn, East Yorkshire, and (f) an openwork plate from Verulamium, St Albans, Hertfordshire. Images not to scale. For purposes of clarity and to aid comparison the images of the Saxthorpe and Kirkburn motifs have been reversed

to the upper and lower terminals of the 'vase-headed' linch-pin from the vehicle burial at Kirkburn, East Yorkshire, whose deposition probably dates from between either the fourth or third century BC and the mid first century BC (see Stead 1991a: 184; Wait 1995: 499). The second version occurs on an openwork plate from Verulamium, St Albans, Hertfordshire (Wheeler and Wheeler 1936: 70, 216, fig. 48; Kilbride-Jones 1980: 245, fig. 78.2). The Verulamium plate was recovered from the metalled surface of fourth-century AD date, which ran across a causeway immediately outside the north-west gate of the late Roman town (Wheeler and Wheeler 1936: 70). Although the excavators considered the plate to probably be late Roman in date (Wheeler and Wheeler 1936: 216), that the causeway crossed a ditch which probably cut through deposits of late Iron Age and pre-Flavian date recorded elsewhere in the immediate vicinty of the north-west gate (cf. Wheeler and Wheeler 1936: 68–9) suggests the possibility of residual deposition.

The significance of these parallels is difficult to assess. That two of the closest parallels were recovered from Norfolk is not necessarily significant; findspot is not an accurate indication of the place of manufacture of late Iron Age decorated metalwork. Nevertheless, the close similarity of the designs between the crescentic mount, the unprovenanced openwork roundel and the Saxthorpe so-called horn-cap must reflect aspects of the organization of metalworking during this period. Whether this means that all three objects, and possibly the Bawsey torc and Verulamium plate, were produced in the same workshop, that they were manufactured from the same pattern-book (whatever form that may have taken), or that the design had a much wider currency in the British Iron Age than the few surviving examples which have been recovered would suggest, is not possible to ascertain.

The crescentic mount is one of the most frequently discussed and illustrated pieces of Iron Age metalwork from the British Isles, but its dating remains problematic. None of the close parallels for the mount's decorative design provide independent dating evidence which can be extended, by analogy, to the mount. Fox read the design as being an influence on the 'Mirror' style (1947a: 51; Fox 1958: 84–98, fig. 62), but although the two are clearly related, it is no longer possible to view the evolutionary development of Fox's scheme as being chronologically valid (Stead 1996: 58; Stead and Hughes 1997: 17). Although the Megaws have suggested that the crescentic mount should be placed late within their first recognizable British school (largely equivalent to Stead's Style IV) (Megaw and Megaw 1989: 200–2), the presence of trumpet voids, the curvilinear character of the elements making up the overall design which is partly set in a circular frame, the use of repoussé, the employment of trumpet motifs and the absence of engraved embellishment of the areas of relief decoration on the mount are all defining qualities of Stead's Style V (Stead 1985a: 22–3; 1996: 34–5). At present, it is not possible to suggest a narrower date for the crescentic mount than the general floruit for Style V art which extends from the third century BC to at least the first century AD. The Verulamium parallel (i.e. Wheeler and Wheeler 1936: 70, 216, fig. 48; Kilbride-Jones 1980: 245, fig. 78.2) raises the possibilty that the crescentic mount, and the use of trumpet voids, may be significantly later in date than even this broad date range.

Mount of a shield boss

The shield boss mount (No. 48) is made from a single sheet of copper alloy hammered out from an ingot and worked into the shape of the boss (Col. Pl. 3). Following Plenderleith's technical report, Fox suggested that the mount had been raised from the flat (1945b: 199), however, Spratling considered it probable that shield mounts such as the Llyn Cerrig Bach example were partly manufactured by being hammered out over the bosses and spines they were to adorn (1972: 259). His investigation of the decorated bronzes of the southern British Iron Age revealed that a combination of external and internal work was evident on most of the shield boss mounts studied (Spratling 1972: 259). Regrettably, no tool marks are visible on the shield boss mount, presumably owing to careful planishing and polishing of the piece after it was shaped.

The edge of the shield mount is incised with a line, set approximately 1 mm in from the edge. It has been previously noted that this line does not extend round the side flanges (Fox 1945b: 200; Spratling 1972: 530), but traces of a lightly scribed line on these flanges is visible. Previously, this line has been interpreted as a decorative border and its supposed absence on the side flanges perhaps indicating that they were overlapped by further mounts. It is possible, however, that the faintly scribed line on the side flanges is perhaps indicating a manufacturing guide to the trimming of the flange rather than a deliberate act of embellishment or decoration.

The mount is perforated by ten fixing holes; two located at the ends of the spines immediately adjacent to the fish-tail terminals (diameter 2.2 mm), two on both of the side flanges (diameter 2.0 mm), and one above each of the four arches where they begin to merge in to the spines (diameter 2.0 mm). Circular patches of differential corrosion (diameter approximately 8 mm), presumably indicative of the former presence of studs, are visible around the fixing holes set at either end of the widening spines just before the fish-tail terminals. Possible, circular patches of differential corrosion are also situated round the fixing holes set above the arches.

When recovered the shield boss mount was badly damaged and, although the main body of the mount was intact, the junctions with the spines were crumpled and torn (Pl. 6). Fox attributed this to the peat extraction, rather than damage inflicted during antiquity, and the piece was annealed and 'restored to its original form' by Plenderleith (Fox 1945b: 199). Consequently, it is uncertain whether the current angle of the spines reflects the mount's original shape. Whilst being reshaped a solder repair was added to strengthen the piece, resulting in localized colour distortion mainly on the back of the mount.

The upper surface of the mount is decorated in Stead's Style V art with two pairs of conjoined roundels, connected through an S-shaped incised line, set either side of the slight central ridge. All four roundels contain similar asymmetrical triskele designs (for a discussion of the triskele motif see p. 123). This decorative motif has been applied with incised lines and infilled with overlapped tremolo hatching. In the following discussion of the decoration the individual elements and motif variations are numbered in square brackets which corresponds with the labelling of the illustration of the roundel patterns (Figure 5).

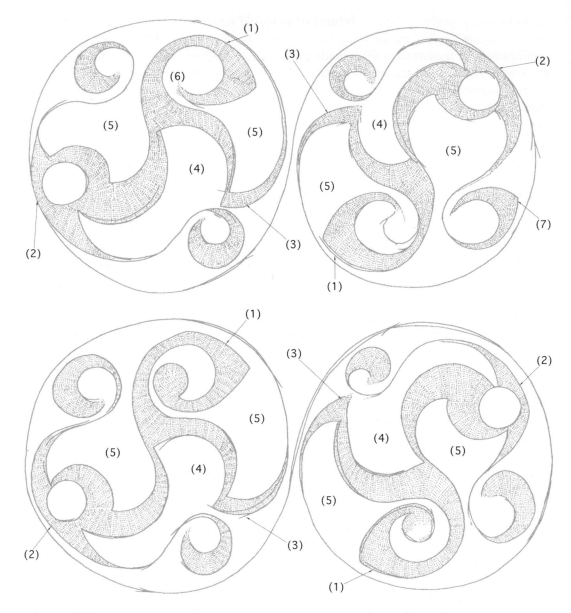

Figure 5: Decorative elements of the shield boss mount (No. 48) (not to scale)

Each roundel contains a similar asymmetrical triskele. Of the three arms extending from the centre; the first extends in to a simple keeled coil with a circular terminal knob [1]. These keeled coils are similar to those employed on the Tal-y-Llyn triskeles which Megaw described as broken backed comma tails (1970: 158) and Lynch as similar to puffin heads (1970: 257). The second arm extends into a curvilinear node perforated by a near-circular void and capped by a tendril scroll which terminates at both ends in a down-wards and outwards simple curved coil [2]. Taken as a whole this second arm is reminiscent of an embellished and asymmetrical lyre loop with flanking coils and is closely paralleled by elements of the design of the Billericay mirror (Fox 1958: 96–7). The third arm forms a double, or 'broken backed', curve which tapers from the break in the curve in an anti-clockwise direction to form a single circumscribing inscribed line which defines the perimeter of the roundel before conjoining with the adjacent triskele through an S-shaped connecting swirl [3]. The anti-clockwise direction in which this third arm spi-rals after the 'broken back' has been previously considered significant (Fox 1947a: 7), because both the other two arms and the more central part of the third arm spiral out-wards in a clockwise direction which arguably lends the motif a sense of clockwise movement (Fox 1945b: 203; 1947a: 7). It has long been recognized that a study of the neg-ative aspects of insular La Tène ornamentation, such as the voids, is potentially as rewarding as studying the positive elements of the design (Fox 1945b: 212; 1947a: 49). One parallel between the designs on the shield boss mount and those of the crescentic plaque (No. 47) recognized by Fox (1945b: 204) is the apparent replication of the common trumpet void motif, which consists of a triangle made up of a compound, a concave, and a convex curve. However, although all three of the voids formed by the arms of the central triskele on the crescentic plaque (No. 47) are true examples of this motif, only one true example occurs on each of the four shield boss triskeles [4], while the other two voids in each triskele [5] are arguably debased forms of the motif (Fox 1945b: 204, fig. 3). Additionally, the examples of the motif on the crescentic mount (No. 47) are closed while the shield boss mount examples are partly open.

It was the broken scroll and the change in direction that the third arm of the triskele [3] encompasses which led Fox to describe the design as having a tense quality, an expression in 'abstract art' of clockwise direction, movement and force being held in place by a taut and rigid broken scroll (Fox 1945b: 203). For Fox the keynote of the design is one of unstable equilibrium, of a balance both precarious and temporary, but Fox's concept of a clockwise movement held in check is perhaps over played. Elements of both arms of the tendril scroll which tops the curvilinear node at the head of the second arm [2] have an anti-clockwise movement and, although this is only a minor part of the overall design, it is enough to dispel any illusion of repressed clockwise movement and replace it with an unstrained static quality.

Although all four roundels contain similar triskele designs there are a number of subtle variations between them. The triskeles all have the same design elements, but their precise size, form and orientation varies. This phenomenon is best witnessed by the fluctuations in the shape of the trumpet voids [4] and [5], but occurs in every design element of the triskeles. More specific variations between the four roundels include the terminal knobs of the large keeled coils on one side of the slight central ridge not being infilled with tremolo hatching or emphasized with outlining incised lines [6]. This is a real phenom-enon, rather than an artificial situation caused by over-zealous stripping during cleaning, as the portions of the mount immediately adjacent to the missing terminal knobs are neither heavily stripped or worn. That the missing knobs were intended initially to be part of the final design is demonstrated by the outline of one traced with a scriber during the initial laying out of the pattern. On the same side of the slight central ridge the curvilinear nodes of the second arm of the triskele [2] directly adjoin the border of the roundel in comparison to the other side where they are only adjacent to it. A third point of difference is the occurrence of a deliberately keeled coil at one of the ends of one of the tendril scrolls [7]. Of the eight instances of this device on the shield boss mount this is the only example which has a distinctive keel or 'broken-back'.

Spratling correctly identified three stages in the application of the decorative motif on the mount (1972: 530). First, the outline of the triskele roundels was lightly sketched out freehand with a scriber, secondly the infilling tremolo hatching was applied, and thirdly the edges of the motif were emphasized by inscribing them with a graver. It is possible to identify this sequence because parts of the hatching go over the lines defined by the scriber, while the final incised lines cut through some areas of hatching. There is frequent variation between the initial line of the scriber and the final incised line. All of the lines and hatching have been applied freehand and at several points the curves of the design are uneven and broken. Presumably the spherical surface of the mount mitigated against the employment of compasses for laying out and executing the design. The infilling of the triskele motifs consists of a series of fine, overlapping, slightly curved tremolo, or zig-zag, lines apparently applied with a rolled round-nosed graver. Some of the edges of the tremolo line have sharp corners as if the graver had an oval cross-section and the pointed edge of the tool had cut further into the boss at this point. The tremolo lines are arranged perpendicularly to the edges of the portion of the triskele design they infill.

Discussion

The La Tène shields and the, presumably votive, miniature shields of the British Isles have most recently been catalogued and classified by Stead (1991b). Although drawing upon long recognized features of the shields, such as the variation between spindle-shaped and round bosses, Stead's catalogue also incorporated a previously unrecognized hide-shaped type of shield. In addition to the full sized shields catalogued by Stead, a possible shield boss has been recovered from the post-Conquest warrior burial at Stanway, near Colchester, Essex (Anon. 1992; 1992–3; Crummy 1993: 495) and a decorated copper alloy boss and spine from Ratcliffe-on-Soar has been recognized in the collection of the Leamington Spa Art Gallery and Museum, Warwickshire (Watkin 1995; Stead 1996: 11, 26, pl. 8; Watkin *et al.* 1996). Stead also excluded several fragmentary copper alloy possible shield mounts from South Cadbury, Somerset, from his catalogue (Spratling 1972: 533, 545, nos. 314–16 and 329, fig. 140; O'Connor *et al.* 2000: 239–41, fig. 117.2–4; Barrett *et al.* 2000c: 365, nos. 2–4). Additional examples of copper alloy miniature shields include one from Woodeaton, Oxfordshire (Bagnall Smith 1999: 151–2, no. 2.2, fig. 1) and one from Barmouth, Merionethshire (Macdonald 2001; acquired by the National Museum of Wales) as well as unpublished examples from Alcester, Warwickshire (A. Bolton pers.

comm.; acquired by Warwickshire Museum) and Middleton, North Yorkshire (recorded under the Portable Antiquities Recording Scheme ref. YORYMB1781).

Of the full-sized shields Stead identified five groups; those made of bronze only (Group A), those completely faced in bronze (Group B), shields with bronze fittings (Group C), those with iron fittings (Group D), and the newly recognized type of bindings from hide-shaped shields (Group E). Groups C and D were further subdivided into fittings from spindle-shaped bosses (Groups Ci and Di) and fittings from round bosses (Groups Cii and Dii). The Llyn Cerrig Bach boss is classified in Group Ci (Stead 1991b: 29–30). This classification is an archaeological construct which, whilst avoiding the difficulties inherent in a typological approach, does not pretend to any Iron Age reality. The fittings of groups C and D could easily have been mounted on to the hide-shaped shields (Group E) which are archaeologically witnessed only by their bindings. Furthermore there are close similarities between a few examples from separate groups and ambiguities over the designation of several individual pieces into any single group. For example, the Ratcliffe-on-Soar shield boss could placed in Group Ci, because it is a copper alloy spindle-shaped boss with extended spines, but one of the rivets still retains a fragment of copper alloy sheet (Watkin 1995: 338), which may have been part of either an adjoining decorative plaque or a complete copper alloy facing of the shield such as the River Witham (Jope 1971) and Battersea (Stead 1985b) shields. This latter interpretation if accepted would place the Ratcliffe-on-Soar boss in Group B. This suggestion is given further plausibility when the close similarity in form between the Ratcliffe-on-Soar and River Witham shields is considered (Watkin 1995: 338; Watkin et al. 1996: 27).

Stead did not take the opportunity of publishing his classification to discuss in depth the dating and typology of the British shields, although the dating evidence of the previously unrecognized hide-shaped shields was reviewed (1991b: 24). Whilst identifying Continental influences on the insular La Tène shields is possible, constructing a meaningful typological sequence for the British shields is problematic. The small number of shields, the over-reliance on the stylistic dating of their art, the lack of close Continental parallels for individual shields and the paucity of securely dated contexts has hampered previous attempts to establish a typological sequence. Perhaps the most significant factors which have undermined past endeavours to construct a typology for the insular La Tène shields are the twin strands of innovation and conservatism within British Iron Age shield design. Consequently, there is no guarantee that typologically 'late' forms are not early, whilst some of the typologically 'early' forms are demonstrably late in date. For example, Savory's suggested third- to second-century BC date for the two Tal-y-Llyn shields (Savory 1964; see also Savory 1971: 67–8 and Kruta et al. 1976: 199), whilst arguably sound on typological grounds, has been undermined by the shields' association with a Romano-British lock-plate (Spratling 1966) and metallurgical analyses which suggest that several of the metallic components of both shields were made from a copper-zinc alloy (brass) whose use is hard to place earlier than the first century AD (P. Northover pers. comm.).

The typical Continental Iron Age shield is oval in shape with an oval, spindle-like boss and sometimes incorporated a longitudinal rib extending from either end of the boss. The boss covered a handle on the reverse of the shield which was arranged perpendicular to the longitudinal axis of the shield. Although this type of shield was known in Italy from at least the seventh century BC (Jope 1971: 61; Spratling 1972: 171), the earliest evidence for its use in northern and western Europe are the engraved figures on the famous Hallstatt scabbard (Jacobsthal 1944: 1–2, 175, no. 96, pls 59–60; Megaw 1970: 54–6, no. 30, fig. 2). The Continental sequence of shields has usefully been discussed by Stead with particular reference to the burial evidence from Champagne (1985b: 36–9). Stead identified several types of Continental shield fitting designed to fit over the spindle-shaped boss, but the most relevant to a discussion of the insular evidence are those covered by a spine cover and two plaques, such as the example from St Rémy-sur-Bussy, Marne, and those covered by an iron band-shaped umbo whose wings were nailed to the body of the shield. The former type has La Tène I origins and continues in use into the early La Tène II phase, whilst the latter type has an early La Tène II origin and continues in use until the end of the first century BC. At the beginning of La Tène III a circular shield boss type appears on the Continent which appears to replace the band-shaped umbo during the La Tène III phase.

Early attempts to identify a Continental prototype for the British shield series identified the La Tène II iron band-shaped umbo as a primary influence. In his discussion of the Moel Hiraddug shield, Hemp suggested that the integral crescentic plaques located either side of the main spindle-shaped boss evolved from the flanged edges of the Continental band-shaped umbo (Hemp 1928: 258). This view was maintained until the mid-1960s (cf. Grimes 1939: 115–17, fig. 39; 1951: 119–21, fig. 39; Lethbridge 1953: 29; Savory 1964: 21, fig. 3), but the considerable typological step between the Continental prototypes and the British shields, combined with the revised dating to late in the insular sequence of shields – such as those from Tal-y-Llyn and Moel Hiraddug, which had previously been considered early – led Stead to reject Hemp's typology (Stead 1968: 173–6).

Following his rejection of Hemp's sequence, Stead proposed that the Continental shields with spindle-shaped bosses covered by a spine cover and two plaques were the likely prototype of the majority of the British shields (Stead 1968: 176) including the Llyn Cerrig Bach mount (No. 48). Stead most fully expressed his view of the typology of British shields and their relationship with the Continental examples in his study of the Battersea shield (1985b: 36–45). Although Stead's convincing identification of the general prototype for the main British shield series is widely accepted (cf. Savory 1971: 69; Spratling 1972: 173; Jope 1976: 185; Savory 1976b: 185; Jope 2000: 53–4), it remains difficult to identify a specific Continental source for the British shields. Although derived from the Continental La Tène I shields, this influence is weak in comparison to the relatively close relationships that exist between the British shields (Stead 1968: 173; 1985b: 40). Although the shape of all but four of the full-sized British shields is unknown, they typically have spindle-shaped bosses which are sometimes augmented by longitudinal ribs and transversely located side mounts. Study of their distinctive bindings, and the miniature shields, suggests that the hide-shaped shields may have been the commonest shield shape (Stead 1991b: 24). One of the distinctive insular traits within the British shield series is the placement of decorative roundels at either end of the longitudinal ribs. Presumably, these longitudinal roundels are the typological source of the upper and lower bosses on the triple bossed shields such as the example from Battersea (see Smith 1905: 93–4; Spratling 1972: 185). One of the earliest examples of the British shield series is the Chertsey shield whose handle has been radiocarbon dated to no later than the beginning of the third century BC (Stead 1991b: 22). The type continues in use in Britain throughout the Iron Age and into the first century AD as indicated by demonstrably late examples such as those from Tal-y-Llyn, Merionethshire (Spratling 1966) and St Lawrence, Isle of Wight (Jones and Stead 1969: 354, fig. 2.4; Stead 1985b: 40). Jope's posthumously published account of the British shields (Jope 2000: 53–72) is apparently an earlier, albeit extended, version of a discussion he published during the mid 1970s (Jope 1976), although the addition of a time-line, several footnotes and catalogue entries in the posthumous account does bring his argument up to date (Jope 2000: pp. xvi, 247–8). Jope follows Stead in identifying the spindle-shaped, La Tène I 'Gaulish' shields as the prototype of the insular sequence, but his emphasis on the significance of Italic influences and identifying the works of individual master craftsmen is less convincing (Megaw and Megaw 2001: 434).

The number of British shields derived from the later Continental shield types is small. The only known examples derived from the Continental iron band-shaped umbo are those recovered from the warrior burial from Owslebury, Hampshire (Collis 1973: 127–9, figs. 3–4), the La Tène III cremation burial from Great Brackstead, Essex (Stead 1985b: 39) and possibly the fragmented boss from the Claudian burial at Stanfordbury, Bedfordshire (Stead 1967: 36, 55; 1985b: 39). The only British shield boss clearly derived from the Continental La Tène III circular boss type is the example from the burial at Snailwell, Cambridgeshire (Lethbridge 1953: 29, 32, pl. V.c; Stead 1967: 36, 54, no. 23).

The Llyn Cerrig Bach mount is an example of the main series of British Iron Age shields. Given the difficulties inherent in constructing a meaningful typological sequence for the British shield series, it is not possible to date the Llyn Cerrig Bach shield boss mount with reference to its relative position within any such sequence. Despite these typological limitations to the dating of the shield boss mount, it has been suggested that it is possible to identify a regional source for its manufacture. Savory has suggested that the Llyn Cerrig Bach mount is a member of a north Wales group of shields which also includes the Tal-y-Llyn and Moel Hiraddug shields (Savory 1964: 28; Savory 1976a: 30).

Savory's notion of a north Wales shield group arose from his critique of the assumption that development of insular La Tène culture in western Britain and Ireland was retarded in comparison to that in southern and eastern England (Savory 1964: 26–8; 1971: 71–3). Although Savory's critique was both timely and valid, the specific arguments on which he based his concept of a formative, western school of insular La Tène metalworking are now far from persuasive. For example, his view that the high zinc content of several of the Tal-y-Llyn shield mounts was a reflection of the use of local copper ores (Savory 1964: 30; 1971: 73; 1976a: 28; 1976b: 194), rather than imported Roman zinc-rich copper alloys, was always questioned (Spratling 1966: 230; Kruta *et al.* 1976: 199) and can no longer be accepted (P. Northover pers. comm.; see also Chapter 6 for a discussion of the metallurgical analysis of insular La Tène copper alloys). Savory's typological and stylistic arguments for an early date for both the Tal-y-Llyn and Moel Hiraddug shields have also been refuted (Spratling 1966; Stead 1968: 173–4; Spratling 1972: 176).

Initially, Savory considered the fact that the only two British shield bosses with pelta-shaped plaques both came from north Wales was confirmation of his theory of a local 'school' being responsible for their manufacture (Savory 1964: 28). He subsequently developed the idea of a north Wales shield group whose never clearly defined characteristics included the tendency of the metal casings of the boss and mid-ribs to form a single unit (Savory 1976b: 187) and the tendency for the sides of the boss mounts to be arcaded (Savory 1976a: 30–1). With the proviso that the total number of known shields from Britain was small, Spratling agreed with the validity of a north Wales regional group of shields noting the similarity in transverse profile of the Llyn Cerrig Bach, Moel Hiraddug and the complete Tal-y-Llyn bosses (Spratling 1972: 174, 176–7). As previously described, Spratling even presented a conjectural reconstruction of a 'Llyn Cerrig Bach' shield in the north Wales shield group style (Spratling 1972: 793, fig. 134). Spratling's reconstruction incorporated two decorative roundels made up of the crescentic mount (No. 47) and a second, hypothetical mount, joined to the longitudinal ribs of the shield boss mount by the bean-shaped plaques (Nos. 44–5). The reconstruction was completed with two Moel Hiraddug/Tal-y-Llyn style peltate side plaques. The argument for Savory's north Wales shield group was strengthened by the recent discovery of a miniature shield from near Barmouth, Merionethshire, which bears an uncanny resemblance to Spratling's 'Llyn Cerrig Bach' shield reconstruction (Macdonald 2001; see Figure 6). The oval miniature shield from near Barmouth has a repoussé elongated oval boss and is decorated with pelta-shaped panels infilled with rocked tracer, incised roundels situated above and below the boss, and incised lines over the boss which recall the radiating embossed lines on the Moel Hiraddug shield boss mount.

Despite the recent discovery of this miniature shield, the validity of a distinctive north Wales shield group remains problematic. The restricted distribution of the pelta-shaped side mounts are perhaps the best evidence for the existence of a distinctive regional tradition of shield design in north Wales. They are present with the Moel Hiraddug and complete Tal-y-Llyn full-sized shields and are also represented on the miniature shield from near Barmouth, but similar oval mounts were also found with the Grimthorpe, East Yorkshire, shield boss (Stead 1968: 168, nos. 2–3, fig. 12). Only two of the north Welsh shield boss mounts, that is, the examples from Llyn Cerrig Bach (No. 48) and Moel Hiraddug, have arcaded sides, but this characteristic feature is also present on the iron shield boss mount recovered from the burial at St Lawrence, Isle of Wight (Jones and Stead 1969: 354, fig. 2.4). Savory argued that, considering the poverty of Yorkshire in fine insular La Tène metalwork before the immediate pre-Conquest period, the Grimthorpe shield boss was an import from north Wales, whilst the iron shield boss mount from St Lawrence, Isle of Wight, was made in southern England in imitation of the north Wales group (Savory 1971: 73). The validity of these arguments is questionable. Furthermore,

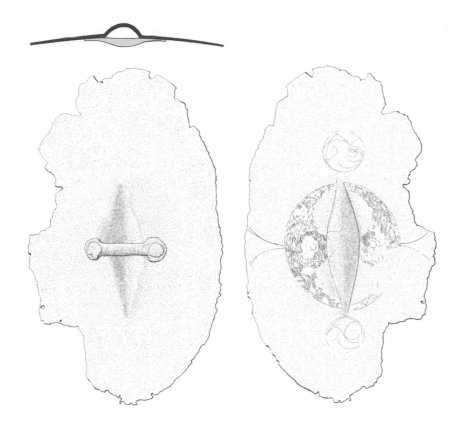

Figure 6: The Barmouth miniature shield (scale 1:1)

although the similarity of the full-sized and miniature shields from north Wales is striking, the small number of British La Tène shields combined with the cited parallels from outside the region suggests the reality of a north Wales shield group should be considered, on present evidence, no more than a probability.

As the only obvious shield fitting recovered from Llyn Cerrig Bach was the shield boss mount (No. 48), it is difficult to identify it as a convincing member of the north Wales shield group. The transverse profile of the mount and its arcaded sides are consistent with more complete examples of the probable regional type, but, as noted above, these features are not exclusive to shield bosses from north Wales. Although no pelta-shaped mounts were recovered from Llyn Cerrig Bach, it is possible that the shield boss mount could have been conjoined to two peltate mounts (Fox 1947a: 10; Lynch 1970: 257, fig. 83; Spratling 1972: 174, 177, fig. 142). Certainly, the observation that the incised border continued round the side flanges does not preclude such an interpretation. Given that no other fittings, apart from the boss mount, are known from Llyn Cerrig Bach then the shield boss mount is best considered a possible member of the probable north Wales shield group.

Regardless of the difficulties inherent in identifying regional traditions and constructing typological schemes for the insular La Tène shields, it is possible to suggest two strands of dating evidence for the Llyn Cerrig Bach mount which are indicative of a relatively late date. First, although the conservative tendency identified in insular La Tène shield design partly undermines the confidence that can be placed on dating by such analogies, the form of the Llyn Cerrig Bach boss is closely paralleled with that of the shield boss from St Lawrence, Isle of Wight (Jones and Stead 1969: 354, fig. 2.4). The St Lawrence shield was associated with a La Tène III sword (Jones and Stead 1969: 354). Second, the Llyn Cerrig Bach shield boss mount is decorated in Stead's Style V art (1985a: 21–3; 1985b: 27). Each of the four engraved roundels consists of a design directly related to the 'Mirror' style, although the style's employment on a raised curvilinear surface is unusual. In particular, the second arm of the triskele of each roundel is closely paralleled by the design on the Billericay mirror found during gravel extraction in 1863 (Cutts 1873: 211; Spratling 1972: 550). This similarity was recognized by Fox who considered the shield boss design an important source-element of the mirror's design (Fox 1958: 97, fig. 61). Although such a direct reading of the stylistic influence, and by extension relative date of the two pieces, is difficult to maintain, they are closely related. Although the general date range for Style V art extends from the third century BC to at least the first century AD, the close parallel with a design on the back of the Billericay mirror does provide an analogy with the southern English series of mirrors which date from the first century BC until at least the mid first century AD (Stead and Rigby 1989: 103; Fitzpatrick 1996: 67). These two strands of evidence combine to suggest that the mount was possibly produced in either the first century BC or early first century AD.

The so-called horn-cap

The so-called horn-cap (No. 49) is an example of a rare, but distinctive, artefact type of the British Iron Age consisting of a circular-sectioned, hollow, copper alloy casting with wide discoidal mouldings at either end and a waisted shaft. The near perfect circularity of the 'horn-cap' suggests that the pattern around which the casting-mould was invested was made from lathe-turned wood (Spratling 1972: 256). One end of the 'horn-cap' was closed with a separately cast copper alloy disc, or diaphragm, while the other remained open, presumably so that the casting could be mounted as a terminal. It is not certain how the diaphragm was fixed on to the casting; presumably it was brazed into place. A deposit of concreted clay and grits inside the lower discoidal moulding of the 'horn-cap' are possibly the remains of a clay core used as part of the casting process. The 'horn-cap' is embellished with a decorative design applied to the disc that closes it at one end.

The separately cast disc, or diaphragm, is set in the centre of the closed end of the 'horn-cap' and contains a decorative device which is defined by its own perimeter (Col. Pl. 2b). The decorative work has been crudely applied using a fine punch to produce lines of dots (approximately 22 dots per 10 mm). There are essentially two elements to the design;

the enclosing circular perimeter and a paddle-arm swastika. The circular perimeter partly disguises the brazed join of the diaphragm and the 'horn-cap', although the punched dots wander out by 0.5 mm in places from the actual edge of the diaphragm. Within the circular perimeter a swastika design has been applied using the same punched-dot technique. The swastika motif is also poorly executed, having obviously been applied freehand; some of the lines contain kinks when the artist's apparent intention was to produce straight lines. Today the decoration is not particularly noticeable, although in antiquity the punch facets may have been blackened while the rest of the piece was polished to produce a striking contrast between the design and the body of the 'horn-cap'. In comparison with the quality of the casting, the craftsmanship employed on the decoration is poor, suggesting that it may have been a secondary addition (Fox 1947a: 19; Peckham 1973: 9). The swastika motif consists of a central 'rectangle' (dimensions 5.5 x 6.5 mm) which is divided into quarters by two diagonal lines of punch-marks. Two of the opposing triangular quarters thus formed are emphasized by dense punch decoration which has been carelessly applied in rows. The remaining two opposed triangular quarters have not been infilled. From each corner of this central rectangular panel a line of punched dots, which extends to the edge of the diaphragm, has been applied. These four lines run at right angles to each other. Further rectangular devices have been added to each of these four arms, producing a flag, or paddle-arm, effect. These four outlying rectangles have also been elaborated by the addition of diagonal lines dividing them into four triangular quarters. These outlying rectangles are slightly smaller (dimensions 4.0 x 5.5 mm) than the central rectangle and none of their internal triangles have been infilled.

The swastika formed by these various elements has a clockwise direction. The only pre-Roman parallel for this design in a British context is the Battersea shield (Stead 1985b) where a similar swastika/flag motif was employed, albeit using a different technique, in an anti-clockwise direction and with the addition of a 'tail' to the flag devices. There has been little discussion of the swastika motif in the British archaeological literature, presumably because of the rarity of its occurrence in insular contexts. The only serious discussion is that of Fox (1947a: 18–19) who, borrowing heavily from Jacobsthal (1944: 76), identified two basic swastika types: a simple form, which at its most basic is just a hooked cross; and a complex form incorporating labyrinthine patterns. As an artistic motif the swastika is a globally distributed mark with no discernible point of origin (Quinn 1994: p. xi). Identifying with certainty the immediate source for the motif's adoption into European Iron Age art is difficult, but it may be derived from seventh century BC contexts in northern Italy from where it was adopted into Hallstatt art and became a common motif (Frey 1991: 91). Both simple and complex forms appear in early Continental La Tène contexts, although the simple form is more common, for example, the Waldalgesheim copper alloy ring (Jacobsthal 1944: 183–4, no. 156f, pl. 99), the Rezi-Rezicseri iron scabbard (Horváth et al. 1987: 123–4), the gold openwork fragment from Dürkheim (Jacobsthal 1944: 168, no.28, pl. 25; Megaw 1970: 68, no. 59), the pot from Alsópél (Megaw 1970: 92–3, no. 115) and the stele from Kermaria at Pont-l'Abbé (Daire 1991: 239). The two British examples are classifiable as complex swastikas because their crosses extend from diagonally opposite corners of a central rectangle. This step-like character has earlier Continental parallels, for example, the Hundersingen girdle (Jacobsthal 1944: 178, no. 133, pl. 73) and the iron spearhead from Lake Neuchâtel (Jacobsthal 1944: 178, no. 129, pls 72–3), although only the Lake Neuchâtel example is a developed form of the motif. The squares on the arms of the British examples have no Continental parallels, suggesting this departure is probably an insular modification of the motif.

Fox considered the device important enough to include it in his grammar of British early Celtic ornament (1958: 148, fig. 83 F44–5; see also Jope 2000: 337, pl. V, nos. 721–2), but placed in a Continental context the swastika is best considered a common Hallstatt motif which only occurs on a few La Tène pieces (Megaw 1970: 45). There are no Irish examples of the motif. The occurrence of the swastika on hut-shaped urns from Latium and Etruria, frequently adjacent to the 'door', suggested to Fox that the symbol had a magico-religious character (1947a: 18); a view subsequently endorsed by Savory (1976a: 33) and Green (1996: 124). Attributing a specific meaning to the Llyn Cerrig Bach swastika is, however, problematic. It is unlikely that any specific symbolic meaning of the device survived both the Hallstatt sixth century BC adoption and the subsequent half millennium intact. Dating of the 'horn-cap' on the basis of the swastika motif is difficult because of the lack of insular parallels. The Battersea shield does provide a comparable example of the motif; however it is a piece whose dating on both stylistic and typological grounds is fraught with difficulties (Leeds 1933a: 23; Stead 1985b: 47; Kilbride-Jones 1994). Even if close dating of the Battersea shield were possible, the swastika motif has a long floruit on the Continent and, although both the Llyn Cerrig Bach and Battersea swastikas are similar developments of the complex Continental form of the motif, it does not follow that they are necessarily contemporary.

The 'horn-cap' suffered several forms of deliberately inflicted damage prior to its deposition. First, the diaphragm has five linear marks (up to 1.5 mm in length), all aligned in the same direction, which appear to have been applied by chopping the point of a blade onto the diaphragm. Secondly, damage is present on the upper rim in the form of several deep cuts or grooves. These cuts occur all around the upper rim and in two perpendicular planes, suggesting that the object was easy to manipulate when damaged. Some of the grooves are deep (up to 1.5 mm) but it is not certain whether they were caused by a 'chopping' blade or a saw. At three, possibly four, points on the outer ridge of the upper rim the damage is so considerable that facets of the rim (up to 8 mm in length) have sheared away. This may be due to the forceful extraction of a blade embedded in the rim. These marks on the upper rim do not correspond with the alignment of those on the diaphragm, suggesting that the two sets of damage are separate, even if they were inflicted in a single extended episode. The stem, or waist, of the 'horn-cap' has also been deliberately cut on almost opposing sides. The direction of this damage is in a third perpendicular plane to that inflicted on the upper rim and diaphragm. These two cuts are substantial (up to 10 mm in length and 1.5 mm deep). The lower rim has also been damaged, but not to such a great extent as other parts of the piece. There are four major cuts, in two different planes of direction, and numerous minor nicks and dents all round the lower rim. There are also a few small cuts on the lip of the socket through which the piece was fixed, although there are no cuts on the socket's internal edge.

This damage was deliberately inflicted in antiquity prior to deposition. If the piece was a vehicle fitting (see below) then it is unlikely that all of this damage could have been inflicted through normal use because the object would have been fixed and the damage has been precisely inflicted through three perpendicular planes. The damage can best be considered a post-use, but pre-deposition phenomenon. The variety of angles from which the damage was inflicted suggests that the piece was easy to manipulate during this process. This would indicate that it had already been removed from, at least the larger part of, whatever it was originally mounted on to.

Fifteen other so-called horn-caps are known in addition to the example from Llyn Cerrig Bach (Table 13). In addition, a 'horn-cap' mould has been recovered, in association with an assemblage of late Iron Age pottery, from excavations in Beckford, Worcestershire (Hurst and Wills 1987: 492–3), and seven 'horn-cap' moulds are also known from Weelsby Avenue, Grimsby, Lincolnshire (Foster 1995: 54–5, table 1).

'Horn-caps' have been detailed in two surveys (Spratling 1972: 67–79; Peckham 1973) both of which included four 'horn-caps' from Ham Hill rather than the two tabulated below. This ambiguity has arisen because it is uncertain whether the two recorded by Hoare (1827), and then subsequently lost, are the same as those from the Norris Collection now in Somerset County Museum, Taunton Castle. Inconsistencies in the nineteenth-century literature are difficult to reconcile with either proposal. Initially Norris apparently possessed only a single 'horn-cap' reputedly found on the site in 1840 and with associated finds similar to those Hoare noted (Norris 1853: 247). Three years later an exhibition catalogue stated there were two 'horn-caps' in the Norris Collection 'precisely similar' to those found by Hoare (Anon. 1856: 294). One of these was illustrated in 1886 (Anon. 1886: pl. I), but they were only explicitly identified as the same 'horn-caps' as noted by Hoare in a 1905 catalogue of the Norris Collection (Gray 1905: 145). Ultimately, resolution of the issue can only be based upon the similarity of Hoare's illustrations with the objects in Somerset County Museum. The minor variations between the drawings and the objects is probably due to inaccurate draughtsmanship. The explanation that Hoare's 'horn-caps' are one and the same with those from the Norris Collection is the most plausible considering the general similarities between both the objects and their recorded provenances.

No examples of 'horn-caps' have yet been recovered from northern Britain and their distribution is apparently a genuine southern British phenomenon, the Llyn Cerrig Bach 'horn-cap' being a north-westerly outlier and the Weelsby Avenue mould fragments being north-easterly outliers. With the exception of the Maiden Castle 'horn-cap' the Llyn Cerrig Bach example is the smallest of the series. The 'Brentford', Horton, Maiden Castle, Putney and one of the Ham Hill 'horn-caps' are notable in having small diametrically opposed fixing holes set in their shafts. The Llyn Cerrig Bach example is one of only four decorated pieces, the other three being the 'Brentford', Putney and Saxthorpe 'horn-caps', however, it is the only example which has been decorated using a punch-dot method. In

TABLE 13: So-called horn-caps

Provenance	References
Bigberry Camp, Kent	Smith 1917–18: 22; Spratling 1972: 431, no. 119, fig. 44; Peckham 1973: 4; Thompson 1983: 274
River Thames at Brentford, London ?	Smith 1917–18: 22, fig. 22; Megaw 1970: 97–8, no. 130; Spratling 1972: 431, no. 120, fig. 44; Peckham 1973: 4–5; Stead 1984: 62–3
Buckland Rings, Hampshire	Hawkes 1937: 153–4, fig. 13; Spratling 1972: 431, no. 121, fig. 44; Peckham 1973: 5
Burwell Fen, Cambridgeshire	Gray 1905: 146; Fox 1923: 108; 1947a: 77, fn. 1; Spratling 1972: 432, no. 122, fig. 45; Peckham 1973: 5
River Thames at Goring, Oxfordshire	Gray 1905: 146; Spratling 1972: 432, no. 123, fig. 45; Peckham 1973: 6
Ham Hill, Somerset (2)	Hoare 1827; Spratling 1972: 432–3, nos. 124–7, fig. 46; Peckham 1973: 6–8, fig. 2
River Thames at Hammersmith, London	Anon. 1903: 12, no. 125; Spratling 1972: 434, no. 128, fig. 45; Peckham 1973: 8
High Cross, Leicestershire ?	Browne 1888: 24, pl. II.2; Spratling 1972: 434, no. 129, fig. 45; Peckham 1973: 8–9
Horton, Dorset	Wheeler 1943: 274; Spratling 1972: 434, no. 130, fig. 45; Peckham 1973: 9; P. J. Woodward pers. comm.
Llyn Cerrig Bach, Anglesey	No. 49 (see catalogue entry for full bibliographical references)
Maiden Castle, Dorset	Wheeler 1943: 124–7; Spratling 1972: 435, no. 132, fig. 47; Peckham 1973: 9
River Thames at Putney, London	Gray 1905: 146; Smith 1925: 147, fig. 170; Spratling 1972: 435, no. 133, fig. 47; Peckham 1973: 10–11
Saxthorpe, Norfolk	Hutcheson 2004: 123, 137, no. 161; I. M. Stead pers. comm.
St Leonards Hill, Windsor, Berkshire	Stukeley 1718: 22; Fox 1947a: 77; Richmond 1950: 23; Spratling 1972: 436, no. 134, fig. 47
Woolley Down, Berkshire	Peake and Padel 1934: 34; Spratling 1972: 436, no. 135, fig. 47

terms of form, the Llyn Cerrig Bach 'horn-cap' is closest to the Maiden Castle example, although the body of the Maiden Castle 'horn-cap' is made from two separately cast pieces.

Four of the 'horn-caps' were reputedly recovered from the River Thames; that is the 'Brentford', Goring, Hammersmith and Putney 'horn-caps'. They are the only examples of the type recorded from river contexts. Study of the earliest sources for the 'Brentford' 'horn-cap' suggest that its provenance was originally considered problematic, and that the subsequent adoption of the Brentford provenance is an unsupportable assumption (Stead 1984). Although its condition is indicative of a riverine deposition (J. Cotton pers. comm.), a firm provenance for the piece cannot be reliably established. Of the other three 'horn-caps' attributed to the River Thames there is no surviving documentation contemporary with their discovery to corroborate the validity of their provenances.

Five of the 'horn-caps' were recovered from hillforts; that is the Bigberry, Buckland Rings, Ham Hill and Maiden Castle examples. The Bigberry 'horn-cap' was a chance find made during quarrying in the nineteenth century (Spratling 1972: 431; Thompson 1983: 274). Occupation began at the site during the fifth to third centuries BC and ended by the mid first century BC (Thompson 1983: 254–6). Presumably the 'horn-cap' from Bigberry dates to within this period, although the discovery of a shackle with a barb-spring padlock of Roman type from the site suggests that some material deposited at Bigberry may date to the mid first century AD (Manning 1972: 230; W. H. Manning pers. comm.). The 'horn-cap' fragment from Buckland Rings was found during excavation of the north-east entrance of the hillfort (Hawkes 1937: 153–4). The fragment was recovered from an apparently redundant post-hole flanking the inner end of the entrance passage. Although the excavator considered it to be a casual loss made during the dismantling of the site's defences (Hawkes 1937: 150, 153–4) its deposition could be interpreted with equal validity as a votive act. There are parallels for deliberate deposition in similar contexts at other southern British hillforts, the latch-lifter deposit at South Cadbury being one example (Alcock 1972: pl. 36; Macdonald 2000b: 123, 126, nos. 24–9, fig. 60). This phase of the hillfort's sequence was not closely dated, although Hawkes favoured an early Roman date for the deposit (1937: 154). The two 'horn-caps' from Ham Hill were reputedly found, by workmen in a gully of the quarry at the site, in association with an iron bridle-bit (see Chapter 3), human bone, iron weapons and several other pieces of harness equipment (Hoare 1827). It is possible that the workmen collected together the assemblage from several disparate groups to form a single artificial deposit. Consequently, the true character of the assemblage cannot be reconstructed with confidence, although if it is genuine it is unlikely to be the result of casual loss. Considering the scale of Roman activity at the site (Burrow 1981: 268–77) the 'horn-cap' cannot even be dated to the Iron Age with confidence. The Maiden Castle 'horn-cap' was found in an 'occupation earth' dated by ceramics to c. AD 25–45 (Wheeler 1943: 124–7). It was associated with five iron rings (probably from horse-bits), a large number of bronze and iron fragments, and the incomplete leg bones of a pony (Wheeler 1943: 274). Although Wheeler's description of the deposit is too scanty to support a reliable interpretation it is unlikely to be a casual or mundane deposit. As with the two Ham Hill examples, the associations of the Maiden Castle 'horn-cap' with bridle-bits, other items of both bronzework and ironwork as well as animal bone, are remarkably similar to those of the Llyn Cerrig Bach 'horn-cap'.

Few of the remaining 'horn-caps' were recovered in ideal conditions and much early documentation relating to their discoveries is now incomplete or missing. The 'horn-cap' from Burwell Fen is a nineteenth-century chance find (Gray 1905: 146; Fox 1923: 108). The reliability of the provenance of the High Cross 'horn-cap' is questionable. It is traditionally considered to be a chance find made in, or before, 1849 from the area of the intersection of the Fosse Way and Watling Street (Spratling 1972: 434). At some point it was equated with the accession number 2212–1849 in the Jewry Wall Museum, Leicester, which is recorded as a 'bronze lamp' in the foundation collection of the Town Museum and also provides the source of the High Cross provenance. During the first half of the nineteenth century 'horn-caps' were thought to have been lamps (Walter 1853: 86). Such a misidentification may have occurred in this case, suggesting the High Cross provenance is valid. That the attribution may, alternatively, be a curatorial error is suggested by the fact that writing in 1888 Browne, the curator of the Town Museum, could not ascertain the date when the 'horn-cap' was presented to the museum (Browne 1888: 24). It is unlikely that he would not know the accession details of the piece if they had existed prior to this date suggesting the confusion over the accession number is probably the result of a post-1888 curatorial error, rather than a misidentification of the 'horn-cap' (R. A. Rutland pers. comm.). The precise context and any associations of the Horton 'horn-cap' are not recorded. The Saxthorpe 'horn-cap', also known as the Corpusty 'horn-cap' (cf. Hutcheson 2004: 123, no. 161), is a metal detector find without context or any associations. The St Leonards Hill, Windsor, 'horn-cap' is recorded as being found by chance under a stone and reportedly associated with a 'Roman' bronze lamp (Stukeley 1718: 22; the lamp is actually medieval and of dubious association, Richmond 1950; Jope 2000: 315). The Woolley Down 'horn-cap' was recovered during the excavation of a round barrow, presumably in a secondary context, about a foot below the modern surface of the barrow and in association with a bent iron spearhead (Peake and Padel 1934: 34). The date of the barrow was placed in the Iron Age by the excavators (Peake and Padel 1934: 37), but it may date to the Bronze Age. The associated spearhead is a typical Iron Age form but closer dating is not possible (G. Darbyshire pers. comm.).

Where it is possible to comment on the character of the deposition of the 'horn-caps' the overriding theme is one of deliberate, and probably votive, deposition. The finds reportedly from the River Thames and the Buckland Rings example all have a number of parallels in terms of ritual deposition and additionally the Maiden Castle, Ham Hill and Woolley Down 'horn-caps' may all have been votive deposits as well. The comparative rarity of these pieces and their repeated occurrence in ritual contexts suggests that they were not mundane items.

Fox attempted to provide a typological classification of the 'horn-caps' by dividing the series into two main groups; those with an open top (series A) and those without an open top (series B) (Fox 1947a: 17). Each group was further subdivided on the following secondary criteria; the form of the upper rim, diaphragm shape, and the number of cast parts used to make up the body of the piece (Fox 1947a: 17). Unfortunately, Fox's work was flawed because of the inaccuracy of his information concerning those examples he had not had the opportunity to study directly (Spratling 1972: 70). None of the 'horn-caps' can be demonstrated to have originally had open tops, thereby invalidating the scheme's primary taxonomical criteria. Nor are the secondary criteria capable of producing discreet and meaningful divisions within the overall series. These flaws led Spratling to dismiss Fox's classification and conclude that the data were not adequate enough to produce a satisfactory scheme (Spratling 1972: 72–4). Peckham speculated that the presence of diametrically opposed pin holes on the shaft might be of typological significance, but concluded that the differences between the 'horn-caps' were not demonstrably significant (1973: 13).

Fox identified several questionable Continental parallels for the British series (1947a: 78). Fox's Continental 'horn-caps' are a different type being longer and having cast ends mounted on swan necked horn-shaped cones. If the British series is related to these Continental pieces, then it is only to the trumpet-shaped end which occurs on the Waldagesheim example (Jacobsthal 1944: 121, 183, no. 156a, pl. 96). The lack of valid Continental parallels suggests that the 'horn-caps' are an insular find type rather than Continental imports, as has formerly been claimed for the so-called Brentford example on artistic grounds (de Navarro 1952: 73; see also Stead 1984: 62–3). This suggestion has been confirmed by the identification of the 'horn-cap' moulds from Beckford, Worcestershire (Hurst and Wills 1987: 492–3) and Weelsby Avenue, Grimsby, Lincolnshire (Foster 1995: 54–5, table 1).

The function of the 'horn-caps' is uncertain, although that they are terminals of some sort is indisputable. Their circular form, open at one end and predominantly closed at the other, makes such an interpretation clear. The occurrence of small diametrically opposed fixing holes set in the shafts of some of the 'horn-caps' confirms this interpretation (Stead 1984: 63). Unfortunately, no 'horn-cap' has yet been recovered directly associated with whatever it was mounted on.

Some evidence relating to their original fixing does exist. One of the Ham Hill examples (Spratling 1972: 433) has a ferrous deposit inside the lower part of its moulding. It is uncertain whether this was part of the object it was mounted on, a by-product of the manufacturing process, a secondary repair (modern or ancient), or an attempt to improve the balance of the piece. Interestingly this provides a vague parallel for the concreted clay and grits situated in a similar position inside the Llyn Cerrig Bach 'horn-cap'. The stump of a heavily corroded iron rod (diameter approximately 12 mm) is lodged inside the 'horn-cap' from the River Thames at Goring (Spratling 1972: 432). Again, it is uncertain whether this was the original fitting the 'horn-cap' was mounted on to or not. Persuasive evidence for the 'horn-caps' being fixed on wooden settings is provided by the Maiden Castle example. When excavated part of the wooden shaft the Maiden Castle 'horn-cap' was mounted on was preserved (Wheeler 1943: 274). It had been fixed to the 'horn-cap' by a pin through two diametrically opposed drilled holes on the waisted shaft of the piece (Spratling 1972: 435). Similar diametrically opposed holes occur on several of the other 'horn-caps' (see above), suggesting that they, and by extension all 'horn-caps', were also fixed onto wooden shafts (Stead 1984: 63). If the 'horn-caps' were fixed to a single piece of wood then, presumably, the wood would have been shaped so that it fitted both the waisted shaft, where the pin holes are located, and the wider opening at their base (Peckham 1973: 17; *pace* Wheeler 1943: 276, fig. 90).

Although interpreted as bronze lamps in the early nineteenth century and then as saddle pommels (Walter 1853: 86), the 'horn-caps' have traditionally been seen as a form of chariot or wagon fitting. Initially they were considered to be hub-caps (Anon. 1903: 12; Gray 1905: 145; Smith 1917–18: 22), but this idea was revised by Fox who proposed that they were the terminals of hand-holds for chariot mounted warriors (1945a: 15). This interpretation was influenced by Jacobsthal who thought the insular 'horn-caps' had a similar function to the Continental series (Fox 1945a: 15), which he considered to be chariot fittings (Jacobsthal 1944: 121). Fox argued that both the Continental and insular series were the terminals of hand-holds on the basis of the shape of the Waldalgesheim example (1945a: 15). This specific interpretation was superseded by the idea that the 'horn-caps' were upturned terminals to yokes, because of the similarity of the Waldalgesheim and La Bouvandeau 'horns' to the carved cupped terminal on the wooden yoke from La Tène (Mariën 1961: 173; Piggott 1969; Lynch 1970: 263–5). Interestingly, the idea was first suggested to Fox by Christie-Stokes in a private letter written during 1945 and held by the National Museum of Wales (accession no. 44.32). Fox rejected the argument because the 'horn-caps' had never turned up in pairs and because he considered that the Continental 'horn-caps' were demonstrably associated with vehicle bodies. If the 'horn-caps' were chariot or wagon fittings then it must be conceded that the small number of recovered examples, in comparison to the numbers of known Iron Age bridle-bits (Palk 1984) and terrets (Spratling 1972: 25–54), suggests that they were not standard fittings but special, non-practical, decorative elements.

The chariot or wagon fitting interpretations are based on a number of questionable assumptions. The validity of the parallel between the insular and Continental series of 'horn-caps' is doubtful. Secondly, as Piggott conceded (1969: 379), the Continental series, as cited by Jacobsthal (1944: 121) and expanded by Fox (1947a: 78), cannot viably be maintained as a single unified find-type serving the same purpose. Furthermore, the association of the Waldalgesheim 'horn-cap' with any specific part of the cart cannot be demonstrated (Stead 1965b: 262) and the excavator of the La Bouvandeau 'horn-cap' clearly states that the position of the piece demonstrated that it was mounted on the end of the draught-pole (Flouest 1885; Stead 1965b: 262). Rejecting the Continental series as an invalid source for a comparative interpretation of the insular 'horn-caps' leaves only the British evidence.

Spratling dismissed the interpretation of the British 'horn-caps' as vehicle fittings on the grounds that none had ever been recovered in direct structural association with any other object, let alone any definite vehicle fittings (1972: 76). Instead he concluded there was no evidence for identifying their original function (Spratling 1972: 79). This view was adopted by Stead (1984: 63) who noted that the traditional interpretations; hub cap, hand-hold and yoke terminal, would have required a pair of 'horn-caps' and that identical pairs had never been recovered (although Fox actually envisaged only a single hand-hold for the warrior cf. 1947a: 27). Arguably of equal validity to the vehicle fitting interpretation is the reprisal of the ceremonial macehead interpretation (Stead 1984: 63; Jope 2000: 157, 315). Until a 'horn-cap' is recovered in direct association with another object their original function will remain unknown.

Precise dating of the floruit of the 'horn-caps' is difficult. The deposition of the Bigberry Camp example is probably of late Iron Age date but possibly of early Roman date, while conversely the Buckland Rings example was probably deposited in the early

Roman period. The Ham Hill examples are also probably of Iron Age date and the Woolley Down 'horn-cap' is associated with an Iron Age spearhead, although closer dating is not possible. The Maiden Castle 'horn-cap' apparently provides the best evidence for a precise date. Wheeler dated its deposition to *c.* AD 25–45 (1943: 274), apparently on the basis of ceramic evidence (1943: 127), but the lack of published stratigraphic justification of the dating of the interior of Maiden Castle has been criticized (Grimes 1945: 7–9; Spratling 1972: 73, 278) and the dating of the later phases revised (Frere 1961: 88–90) or dismissed altogether (Spratling 1972: 73). It must be questioned exactly what Wheeler meant by the term 'occupation earth' in an area almost devoid of contemporary settlement and whether the assemblage containing the 'horn-cap' was from a feature cut through this layer or deposited directly in the layer. Even if Wheeler's date is accepted, this only provides a date for the deposit in which the 'horn-cap' was found and not for its manufacture. The archaeological evidence for the manufacture of 'horn-caps' is of more value. The Beckford mould fragment was associated with late Iron Age pottery (Hurst and Wills 1987: 492–3) and the foundry activity at Weelsby Avenue is dated to the first century BC (Foster 1980: 49). On this, admittedly slim, archaeological evidence there is no reason to suggest that the manufacture of 'horn-caps' continued into the early Roman period, although the possibility that some examples, such as the Buckland Rings fragment, were deposited as late as the mid first century AD cannot be dismissed.

The other possibility for dating the 'horn-caps' is with reference to the art which embellishes the examples from Llyn Cerrig Bach, 'Brentford', Putney and Saxthorpe. As noted above, close dating of the swastika motif employed on the Llyn Cerrig Bach 'horn-cap' is not possible. The diaphragm of the 'Brentford' 'horn-cap' is embellished with an embossed tripartite palmette design which is an insular example of Style II, or Waldalgesheim, La Tène art (Stead 1985a: 18, fig. 20.d; 1996: 25). On stylistic grounds the 'Brentford' 'horn-cap' may be as early as the fourth or third century BC (Duval 1973; Stead 1985a: 18; 1996: 25), but given the problems with stylistic dating of insular La Tène art (see above) the 'horn-cap' may be considerably later in date (Jope 1961b: 78; Megaw 1970: 97–8; Jope 2000: 158, 315–16; but see also Frey and Megaw 1976: 54). The design in partial relief on the small copper alloy domed pin associated with the Putney 'horn-cap' is difficult to classify stylistically, although its unbalanced asymmetrical S-shaped coil and flanking peltate and lobe segments are suggestive of a relatively late date within the insular La Tène sequence. The decorative motif employed on the diaphragm of the Saxthorpe 'horn-cap' is an example of Style V insular La Tène art which, as noted above, provides a remarkably close parallel to the repoussé decoration on the Llyn Cerrig Bach crescentic mount (No. 47) (see Figure 4, for purposes of clarity and to aid comparison the image of the Saxthorpe decoration has been reversed). In terms of date, Style V art may have begun as early as the third century BC and continued in vogue until at least the first century AD.

The review of the dating evidence for the 'horn-caps' suggests that it is not possible to put forward a narrower range within the third century BC to first century AD period for the example from Llyn Cerrig Bach. In fact, a precise date within the late Iron Age cannot be reliably demonstrated for any individual 'horn-cap', let alone the series as a whole. That said, study of both the art and archaeological evidence does suggest that the manufacture of the type does not post-date the late Iron Age and that deposition of the type does not necessarily extend beyond the mid first century AD.

Miscellaneous ornamental plaques

The only remaining pieces of artistic merit to be discussed from the Llyn Cerrig Bach assemblage are the six plaques of so-called casket ornament (Nos. 50–5) (Col. Pl. 4). The somewhat erroneous term 'casket ornament' was first employed by Fox who defined the type as repetitive, curvilinear ornament executed in relief on narrow strips or squares of thin bronze (1958: 105). A subsequent survey recognized a secondary group of mounts, also decorated in relief, but of non-rectangular shape (Spratling 1972: 240). Examples of 'casket' ornament recovered in association with the objects that they were originally mounted onto suggests that the type was used to decorate a variety of fine wooden items, including stave-buckets, boxes and tankards (Jope 2000: 132; see Table 14). The majority of pieces of 'casket' ornament have, like the examples from Llyn Cerrig Bach, been separated from the objects they originally adorned. In such cases, discussion of their original function is speculative. 'Casket' ornament is not a uniform artefact type, although a number of common, if not universal, characteristics have been noted: the mounts were generally fixed to flat surfaces (Spratling 1972: 239), the rectangular and square mounts are frequently bordered by raised ribs of unvarying width (MacGregor 1976: 157), the strips are cut to conform to the pattern shape (MacGregor 1976: 157) and there is a tendency towards decorative repetition (MacGregor 1976: 157). All six of the Llyn Cerrig Bach plaques fulfil these criteria, but they do not conform to other commonly recognized characteristics of 'casket' ornament such as: the use of punched dots to decorate the edges of the strips and the employment of decorative rosette motifs.

In MacGregor's survey of 'casket' ornament, the corpora listed by Fox (1947a: 89) and Spratling (1972: 239–40, 589–98) has been expanded to include related examples of raised copper alloy mounts not previously considered to be examples of the type (MacGregor 1976: 156–9, 173–6). By concentrating on all of the small copper alloy sheet mounts ornamented with raised decoration, including those adorning cauldrons and buckets as well as examples from post-Invasion contexts, MacGregor has effectively redefined the group on technological grounds rather than those of perceived chronology or function. This has resulted in a larger corpus of arguably more representative material with which to compare the Llyn Cerrig Bach plaques (Table 14). These examples of 'casket' ornament form a heterogeneous group derived from both Iron Age and Romano-British contexts.

A useful criteria in the appreciation of 'casket' ornament is manufacturing technique. Fox suggested that the Llyn Cerrig Bach plaques had been mechanically produced using dies or formers (1947a: 21). This technique of creating pseudo-repoussé decoration involves the carving or casting of the decorative device to be produced in reverse on a

TABLE 14: Selection of Iron Age and Romano-British 'casket' ornament

Provenance	References
Aylesford bucket, Kent	Evans 1890: 360–4, fig. 11; Megaw 1970: 119–20, no. 187; Stead 1971: 260–73; Spratling 1972: 580, no. 406; Stead 1984: 61–2, pl. IV; 1985a: 8–9, fig. 6
Baldock bucket, Hertfordshire	Stead 1971: 254–5, fig. 3; Spratling 1972: 580, no. 407
Birdlip bucket mounts, Gloucestershire (2)	C. Green 1949: 189, pl. XXV; Spratling 1972: no. 422, fig. 190
Corbridge hoard, Northumberland (2)	Allason-Jones and Bishop 1988: 78–9, nos. 256–7, figs. 97–8
Elmswell, East Yorkshire	Corder and Hawkes 1940; Megaw 1970: 174, no. 303; MacGregor 1976: no. 336
Elveden tankard, Suffolk	Evans 1890: 358–9, fig. 10; Corcoran 1952: 98, no. 8; Fox 1958: 109, pl. 54.b; Spratling 1972: 564, no. 365, fig. 166
Gayton Thorpe, Norfolk	Spratling 1972: 596–7, no. 451, fig. 197; MacGregor 1976: 175
Great Chesterford bucket, Essex	Fox 1923: 105; Stead 1971: 278–9, pl. XCI; Spratling 1972: 581, no. 408
Ham Hill, Somerset (2)	Gray 1924: 114, no. E8, pl. XIII; 1926: 63–4, no. E24; Spratling 1972: 590–1, nos. 433–4, figs. 192–3
Hod Hill, Dorset (2)	Brailsford 1962: 1, 18, nos. A7 and I.131, figs. 1 and 14, pl. I; Spratling 1972: 591, no. 435, fig. 193
Kettering, Northamptonshire	Bull 1911: 500, fig. 2; Spratling 1972: 591, no. 436, fig. 194
Lambay Island embossed disc, Co. Dublin	Macalister 1929: 243, no. 21, pl. XXIV.1; Leeds 1933a: 59–60, fig. 24.a–b; J. Raftery 1951: fig. 246; Raftery 1983: 249, no. 794, fig. 159; 1984: 282–4, fig. 139.1
Lexden tumulus, Essex	Laver 1926–7: 249; Foster 1986: 75–8, nos. 33–46, figs. 26–7
Dowgate, London	Merrifield 1965: 188, pl. 140; Megaw and Merrifield 1970; Spratling 1972: 590, no. 431
Great Tower Street, London	Corder and Hawkes 1940: 346, pl. LIII.a; Fox and Hull 1948: 128, fig.5.5; Megaw and Merrifield 1969: 158, pl. XVII.a; Spratling 1972: 590, no. 432
Llyn Cerrig Bach, Anglesey (6)	Nos. 50–5 (see catalogue entries for full bibliographical references)
Lydney, Gloucestershire	Wheeler and Wheeler 1932: 83, no. 66, fig.18; MacGregor 1976: 175
Marlborough bucket, Wiltshire	Nylen 1958; Megaw 1970: 120, no. 188, Spratling 1972: 581, no. 410
western Meare lake 'village' mount, Somerset	Gray and Bulleid 1953: 222, 231, no. E113, fig. 64
Moel Hiraddug embossed triskele, Flintshire	Hemp 1928: 255, 260–2, 265, fig. 16; Leeds 1933a: 56–7, fig. 22; Grimes 1951: 225–6, pl. XVII; Fox 1958: 75, pl. 45.b; Spratling 1972: 542, no. 326A, figs. 136 and 149

Provenance	References
Newstead, Roxburghshire (3)	J. Curle 1911: 303, 309, pls LXXV.5, LXXXI.18 and LXXXIV.7; MacGregor 1976: nos. 339–40
Plunton Castle armlet, Kirkcudbrightshire	Evans 1894–7: 192, fig. 14; Leeds 1933a: 110, fig.32.f; Megaw 1970: 172; MacGregor 1976: no. 211
Rhostryfan, Caernarvonshire	H. Williams 1923: 93, fig. 4; Spratling 1972: 616, no. 487, fig. 210
Rodborough Common, Gloucestershire (2)	Smith 1925: 146, fig. 169; Megaw and Merrifield 1969: 156, 157, pl. XVI.B; Spratling 1972: 593, nos. 440–1, fig.195; Megaw and Megaw 1989: 228, fig.386
Santon, Norfolk (3)	Smith 1909a: 153, pl. XVI.1; Fox 1958: 105, 120, pl. 67.c; Megaw 1970: 172, no. 229; Spratling 1972: 594, no. 442
Silchester, Hampshire (2)	Fox 1958: 105, pl. 77.d; Spratling 1972: 594, nos. 443–4, fig. 196
Snailwell, Cambridgeshire (3)	Lethbridge 1953: 29, pl. I; Stead 1967: 50, 54, no. 18; Spratling 1972: 595, no. 445
Stanfordbury, Bedfordshire (2)	Fox 1923: 99–100, pl. XVIII.4; Spratling 1972: 595, no. 446, fig. 196
Stanwick, North Yorkshire (3)	MacGregor 1962: 49, nos. 99–101, fig. 12; MacGregor 1976: 176
Stichill collar, Roxburghshire	Fox 1958: 107, pl. 62.b; Piggott 1970: 26–7, no. 138; MacGregor 1976: no. 210; Megaw and Megaw 1989: 231, fig. 393
Tattershall Ferry carnyx, Lincolnshire	Piggott 1959: 23–4, fig.2.c; White 1979: 5, no. 10
Traprain Law, East Lothian	Burley 1955–6: 187, no. 270, fig. 5; MacGregor 1976: no. 341
Silkstead or Winchester, Hampshire	Fox 1958: 105, pl. 77.A2; Stead 1971: 279

heavy block, placing the sheet to be embossed over this die and hammering the metal into the shape of the void with punches (Maryon 1949: 124; Hodges 1989: 78). This method, related closely to coin striking in principle, facilitates easier production of ornamentation, but arguably results in inferior mechanized forms of decoration (Fox 1958: 105). Few examples of dies or press-moulds, have been recovered. Two copper alloy formers in the Santon assemblage were recognized by Spratling (1970b: 190), a rectangular iron die was recovered from Wroxeter, Shropshire, with a variety of designs cut into two of its flat surfaces (Atkinson 1942: 216–18) and a circular copper alloy die is known from North Creake, Norfolk (Gurney 1990: 100, fig. 4). It has also been suggested that the wooden block with deeply carved designs from Lochlee crannog, Ayrshire and the ceramic mould from North Wraxall, Wiltshire, are also possible die blocks (MacGregor 1976: 157, 159), but these identifications are problematic.

The use of die-stamping has been recognized in a number of examples of 'casket' ornament and related pieces including: elements of the sheeting on the Aylesford bucket (Stead 1971: 272; Megaw and Megaw 1989: 187); the decorative band on the Baldock bucket

(Stead 1971: 254–5); one of the Hod Hill mounts (Spratling 1972: 591); at least one, if not both, of the Ham Hill mounts (Spratling 1972: 590–1); the Llyn Cerrig Bach mounts (i.e. Nos. 50–5 cf. Fox 1947a: 21–2; Lynch 1970: 262); the Moel Hiraddug embossed triskele (Fox 1958: 75); two of the Newstead mounts (MacGregor 1976: nos. 339–40); the two Rodborough Common strips (Megaw and Megaw 1989: 228); all three examples from the Santon hoard (Megaw 1970: 172); possibly the two Silchester mounts (Spratling 1972: 594); the Silkstead pieces (Stead 1971: 279); the Stanfordbury mounts (Spratling 1972: 595); at least one of the Stanwick mounts (MacGregor 1962: 21); and the Stichill collar (Megaw and Megaw 1989: 231). It is possible that more examples of die-stamped copper alloy sheet mounts exist, but distinguishing the use of the technique from conventional repoussé work in ancient metalwork is difficult and the above list, compiled largely as it was from secondary sources, should not be considered exhaustive.

In general, the lack of reliable associated material and contexts for dating purposes of both the die-stamped and repoussé examples of 'casket' ornament and related mounts has resulted in most commentators assigning vague mid first-century AD dates to the pieces they are describing, however, the Megaws have proposed that die-stamping is an insular metalworking technique whose inception post-dates the Roman invasion. They have suggested that art styles like 'casket' ornament have a provincial character compatible with a date, at the earliest, in the second half of the first century AD (Megaw and Megaw 1989: 228). The Megaws identify within this later art the imitation or adoption of Roman forms, such as the 'berried' rosette and the increased use of straight lines, as well as a change in market from decorating aristocratic-martial items to decorating trinkets. This development they label a 'tourist' art (Megaw and Megaw 1989: 230) and it can be considered analogous with the production of military fittings of native style by British craftsmen for elements of the Roman military (Manning 1985: 151; G. Webster 1990: 293). Although previously thought to be late in the insular sequence (for example: Fox 1947a: 21; Megaw 1970: 172; Megaw and Megaw 1986: 55), die-stamped 'casket' ornament had not previously been dated to the post-Invasion period. Subsequently, Jope has suggested that embossed insular La Tène plaques remained current in the civil province until the late first-century AD and that native traditions of repoussé and stamped ornament were maintained into the second and third centuries AD (Jope 2000: 132, 174). If a post-Conquest date is correct, then this has implications for the dating of both the Llyn Cerrig Bach ornamental plaques and the duration of deposition at the site. The standard interpretive view taken by Fox, and one that has been maintained ever since, is that deposition at Llyn Cerrig Bach must have ended at the latest by the mid first century AD, because objects of a 'transitional Celto-Roman cultural character' were excluded from the assemblage (Fox 1947a: 68). If, however, 'casket' ornament, and in particular die-stamped 'casket' ornament, can be dated, at least in part, to the post-Invasion period, then this invalidates Fox's argument and undermines the conventional dating for the duration of deposition at the site.

The only demonstrably Iron Age examples of die-stamped 'casket' ornament are the decorative strips on the Aylesford (Megaw 1970: 119; Stead 1971: 260–73), Baldock (Stead 1971: 251–60) and possibly Marlborough (Nylen 1958) buckets. These three buckets, all probably deposited with Aylesford type cremation burials, are related to the stave buckets of Belgic Gaul (Megaw and Megaw 1989: 184–7). The Aylesford bucket has been dated to the second half of the first century BC (Corcoran 1952: 97; Megaw 1970: 119), the Marlborough bucket probably does not pre-date the middle of the first century BC (Nylen 1958: 114), while ceramic evidence suggests a mid first-century BC date for the Baldock bucket (Stead and Rigby 1986: 60–1; Stead 1991e: 593). Although these vessels may have been imports from Gaul (Megaw and Megaw 1989: 184–7), Stead has suggested that for objects so unusual there is a stronger argument for a local place of manufacture, close to their context of deposition (1971: 274). Regardless of the insular or Continental origin of the Aylesford, Baldock and Marlborough buckets, it is almost certain that die-stamping as a metalworking technique was known in the late Iron Age in Britain. Although not identical, the technique of striking coinage (Van Arsdell 1989: 51), which was being used in the south-east of Britain soon after c.100 BC (Cunliffe 1991: 114; Jope 2000: 164), is comparable enough with the die-stamping technique employed on 'casket' ornament for it to be difficult to envisage an absence of die-stamping in the late Iron Age on technical grounds. The plausibility of the Megaws' argument is their suggestion that 'casket' ornament developed, even if it was not so conceived, as a response to a changing market for decorated metalwork from native aristocratic patrons to a 'tourist' Roman army (1989: 230). Certainly, although the majority are of uncertain date, three of the examples of die-stamped 'casket' ornament demonstrably have a post-Invasion date. The Newstead mounts were recovered from either pits or unstratified contexts associated with the Roman fort dating to the late first century AD (MacGregor 1976: nos. 339–40). The Santon assemblage is conventionally interpreted as a Boudican deposit (Megaw and Merrifield 1969: 158; Spratling 1970b: 190) and contains hinges of the kind that were fitted to *loricae segmentatae* indicating that the deposition of the assemblage post-dates the Conquest (Spratling 1975: 207). The Stanfordbury fragments of 'casket' ornament were recovered from the second Welwyn-type burial vault at Stanfordbury Park Farm (Dryden 1845: 18) which is dated to the Claudian period (Stead 1967: 47).

Although it cannot be demonstrated that die-stamping is a post-Invasion innovation, the case for a late date for the Llyn Cerrig Bach 'casket' ornament is strengthened by three close parallels to one of the rectangular plaques (No. 54) which, whilst not all being demonstrable examples of die-stamping, have either probable, or definite, Roman dates. They include one of the strips from the Corbridge hoard, Northumberland (Allason-Jones and Bishop 1988: 78, no. 256, fig. 97), which was probably deposited on the abandonment of the fort between AD 122 and 138 (Allason-Jones and Bishop 1988: 109); the strip from Lydney, Gloucestershire, which was recovered with late third- and fourth-century AD associations, albeit in a residual context (Wheeler and Wheeler 1932: 83, no. 66, fig. 18; Lynch 1970: 262); and one of the mounts from Newstead, Roxburghshire, whose deposition is Flavian or later in date (J. Curle 1911: 309, pl. LXXXI.18; MacGregor 1976: no. 339).

Summary

Although the adoption of die-stamping techniques probably pre-dates the Roman Conquest in Britain, the Megaws are right to suggest that 'casket' ornament continued into at least the second half of the first century as a form of 'tourist' art. Consequently, the Llyn Cerrig Bach plaques may have a later first century AD date. This possibility is reinforced by the close parallels for one of the plaques (No. 54), which have been recovered from Roman contexts at Lydney, Corbridge and Newstead. These parallels undermine the conventional arguments for the date of the end of deposition at Llyn Cerrig Bach and, combined with the evidence for the potentially late date of other items from the assemblage, such as the coiled decorative strips (Nos. 35–43), suggests that episodes of deposition at the site may have continued into at least the second half of the first century AD, after the invasion of Anglesey under Paulinus in AD 60/61 and the Agricolan pacification of the island in AD 77/78. Support for the suggestion of a possibly early Roman date for the Llyn Cerrig Bach 'casket' ornament is provided by their metallurgical analysis (see Appendix 2). Analytical investigation has demonstrated that all six examples of 'casket' ornament were manufactured from a low arsenic copper-tin alloy that is typical of Roman alloying traditions. The chronological implications of the metallurgical analysis of the copper alloy artefacts from the assemblage are considered in the next chapter.

6

The Source and Date of the Assemblage

Prior to discussing the Llyn Cerrig Bach assemblage within its wider archaeological context, it is appropriate to review both the main points raised by the study of the copper alloy artefacts in the assemblage and summarize the character of the ironwork and animal bone components of the assemblage.

The source, or place of manufacture, of the assemblage

The principal way in which the present study differs from the approach adopted by Fox (1947a) is that little attempt has been made to identify the source, or place of manufacture, of the component parts of the assemblage. Fox argued that the heterogeneity of the main artefact types represented in the assemblage suggested that each group was drawn from one of a number of discrete production centres – located mainly in southern England and to a limited degree in Ireland – rather than representing an ancient creative centre of metalworking in north Wales (1947a: 60). With reference to the findspots of comparable examples of metalwork, Fox identified the location of these production centres in: the north-east of Ireland; East Yorkshire and north Lincolnshire; the south-eastern counties of England; and Gloucestershire and Somerset (Fox 1947a: 61–3, fig. 34). Although Fox conceded that some of the more crude items were probably the products of local craftsmen, he noted that there was no satisfactory evidence to suggest that any of the prestigious metalwork in the assemblage had been manufactured in either northern Britain or any other part of the Highland Zone (1947a: 60–1; for his definition of the Highland Zone see Fox 1932: 25–6; 1943: 29). The remainder of Fox's interpretative account of the assemblage was largely concerned with identifying a mechanism by which high-quality metalwork could have been imported into Anglesey (Fox 1947a: 67–72). Fox interpreted the material from Llyn Cerrig Bach within the geographically determinist framework which was outlined in his study *The Personality of Britain* first published in 1932 and revised in 1943. Although not explicitly stated, the absence of Iron Age pottery from north Wales was probably perceived by Fox as confirming the view that Anglesey was a backward area whose population was only 'superficially Celticized' (cf. Fox 1943: 37–8; 1947a: 66; see also Savory 1973: 27–8). Fox's view of the assemblage was also informed by his reading of the Classical sources which emphasize Anglesey's apparent prestige as a religious centre and suggest a possible influx of refugees from the Roman invasion of southern Britain into the region during the mid first century AD. Both of these factors provided Fox with a historical mechanism for the importation of material from southern Britain, and elsewhere, into Anglesey (Fox 1947a: 69–72; for a later expression of these same ideas see Fox 1958: 60–1, 143).

As has long been recognized, Fox's view that the majority of the Llyn Cerrig Bach assemblage was imported from other parts of southern Britain can no longer be maintained unreservedly (Savory 1968: 20–1; Lynch 1970: 255; Savory 1970: 46; 1976a: 29, 49). Fox's arguments concerning the precise sources of the constituent parts of the assemblage have been exhaustively reviewed and effectively refuted by Spratling (1972: 339–44). There is no need to reiterate Spratling's criticisms in detail here; it is now a widely acknowledged truism of the study of insular La Tène metalwork that findspot is not necessarily an accurate guide to an item's place of manufacture. It is difficult to assess the significance of archaeological distribution maps, particularly when they relate to high-status, portable antiquities and where the total number of examples of a specific type is small (Spratling 1972: 328). Critically, it was this point that was not considered by Fox in either his study of the sources of the Llyn Cerrig Bach assemblage (1947a), or his subsequent survey of insular La Tène art (1958). In addition to variations in ancient exchange mechanisms and depositional practice, modern excavation and research patterns, nineteenth-century river dredging regimes and post-war patterns of agricultural land use have all had a significant effect on the known distribution pattern of insular La Tène metalwork. These activities have tended to favour southern and eastern England as sources of Iron Age metalwork (although the opposite is apparently the case for some types such as currency bars, cf. Allen 1967: 320; Hingley 1990: 105). This bias in the distribution of La Tène metalwork is increased by the relatively large number of metal detector finds of Iron Age date known from East Anglia, largely as a result of the pioneering liaison work undertaken by museum archaeologists in the region with local metal detecting groups since the 1980s (cf. Dobinson and Denison 1995: 20–1; Davies and Williamson 1999b: 9).

Fox's view that quality items of insular La Tène metalwork could not have been produced in Wales has been undermined by subsequent archaeological research and discoveries (J. L. Davies 1995: 686–8). Excavation has revealed evidence for the smelting of iron from local bog ores on a massive scale at Bryn y Castell, Merionethshire (Crew 1984; 1985: 23–4; 1990: 155) and Crawcwellt West, Merionethshire (Crew 1989: 14–16; 1990: 156–7; 1998), while metallurgical work has suggested that at least one of the currency bars from Llyn Cerrig Bach could have been produced in north-west Wales (Crew and Salter 1993; Crew 1998: 34). That these production sites are not unique in north-west Wales is suggested by the discovery of iron smelting slags at other sites in the region (i.e. Griffith and Crew 1998a; 1998b). Evidence for the smithing and forging of iron has been recognized at a number of Welsh Iron Age sites including: Castell Henllys, Pembrokeshire (Mytum 1989: 8); Dinorben, Denbighshire (Gardner and Savory 1964: 108); Llwyn Bryndinas, Denbighshire (Musson et al. 1992: 268–9, 275, 280–2); and Twyn-y-Gaer, Monmouthshire (Probert 1976: 115). Evidence for the extraction of copper and the working of copper alloys is difficult to recognize archaeologically, possibly because of the use of non-slagging processes in the ancient smelting of copper (Craddock and Meeks 1987; Fell 1990: 33). Llanymynech Hill, Shropshire, has been identified as a possible source of copper extraction in the second to first centuries BC (Musson and Northover 1989: 22–4; Musson *et al.* 1992: 279; J. L. Davies 1995: 687) and evidence for the casting and finishing of copper alloy artefacts, usually in the form of crucible fragments, has been recovered from a number of Welsh Iron Age sites including: Caer Cadwgan, Cardiganshire (Austin *et al.* 1990: 44); Castell Henllys, Pembrokeshire (Mytum 1999: 172); Llanmelin, Monmouthshire (Nash-Williams 1933: 308, no. 6, fig. 54.4; Savory 1976a: 38, 70, no. 89.7); Llwyn Bryn-dinas, Denbighshire (Musson *et al.* 1992: 268–9, 272–82); Merthyr Mawr Warren, Glamorgan (Fox 1927: 47–9, 52, figs. 3–4; Savory 1976a: 66, 68, nos. 61.1–4, 71.73, 72.25–7); Old Oswestry, Shropshire (Savory 1976a: 48, 76, no. 127.2, fig. 34.d); Twyn-y-Gaer, Monmouthshire (Probert 1976: 115); Walesland Rath, Pembrokeshire (Wainwright 1971: 90–1, fig. 36; Savory 1976a: 39, 76, no. 124.36); and Worms Head, Rhossili, Glamorgan (Cunnington 1920: 251–4, 256, pls A and B; Savory 1974; 1976a: 26, 66, no. 60.1, fig. 34.C). Given the relative lack of excavation on Iron Age settlement sites in Wales, the evidence noted above suggests that there is no reason to view Wales as a metallurgically backward area during the late Iron Age, and also lends credence to suggestions that a significant proportion of the Llyn Cerrig Bach assemblage could have been manufactured locally (i.e. Savory 1968: 20–1; Spratling 1972: 344–6; Savory 1973: 27–8; J. L. Davies 1995: 688). This impression is strengthened when the evidence from Wales is compared with the relative lack of pre-Roman metalworking debris from an area, such as Norfolk, where a large amount of insular La Tène metalwork has been recovered (cf. Silvester and Northover 1991: 214; Bates 2000: 235).

Attempts to identify the place of manufacture of individual items of insular La Tène metalwork have been inextricably linked with the endeavour to recognize and isolate regional schools of metalwork production in Britain. The discovery of the Llyn Cerrig Bach assemblage prompted Fox, in an arguably over-ambitious typological and stylistic study of insular La Tène metalwork, to identify a number of regional schools (Fox 1958). Such an approach can no longer be considered viable; the known distributions of insular La Tène metalwork types and decorative styles overlap each other and form a complex pattern which, in general, cannot be plausibly reduced to a series of small, discrete regional groupings. Although it is possible that some regional groups and artefact types, such as the possible north Wales shield group (see Chapter 5) and the massive armlets of eastern Scotland (MacGregor 1976: 106–10), can be recognized, the only definite evidence for recognizing production sites of individual artefact types is that provided by metalworking debris such as mould fragments (Fell 1990: 307). That regional schools of metalworking existed in late Iron Age Britain is a possibility that should not be dismissed. The probability, however, that items of insular La Tène metalwork were exchanged over long distances, and the fact that only two significant foundry deposits, those from Gussage All Saints, Dorset (Spratling 1979; Foster 1980), and Weelsby Avenue, Lincolnshire (Foster 1995), have been studied in detail, means that at present it is not possible to identify regional schools.

The suggestion that metallurgical analysis provides a method by which sources of ancient metalwork, and by extension regional schools of metalwork production, can be identified is not supported here. Attempts to provenance copper alloy artefacts through the study of trace elements and their relation to ore sources have been made (for example, Northover 1984; 1987; 1991a; 1991b). The validity of this approach, however, is questionable, assuming as it does that individual ore sources are chemically homogeneous but distinct from one another, and that smelting conditions and recycling of metals have no significant influence on the chemical composition of copper alloys (Tylecote 1970; Craddock 1986; Budd *et al.* 1994: 99; 1996: 168–9; Dungworth 1997a: 2.1; 1997b: 46–7). Northover has identified nine distinct impurity patterns (1991b: 159, table 42) and, although no reliance is placed here upon their supposed source or date of exploitation, they form a useful basis for an empirical study of the diversity of alloy types represented in the Llyn Cerrig Bach assemblage. Of the fifty-seven full analyses of copper alloy artefacts in the assemblage, only twenty-six could be clearly identified as examples of one of Northover's groups (see Appendix 2). Within the twenty-six identified samples all but one of Northover's alloy types is represented (Table 15) suggesting that the copper alloy artefacts in the Llyn Cerrig Bach assemblage were potentially derived from a wide variety of sources.

TABLE 15: Frequency of Northover's copper alloy impurity patterns
in the Llyn Cerrig Bach assemblage

Northover's group	0	1	2	3	4	5	6	7	8
No. of examples identified	4	4	2	2	6	5	2	1	0

Although a precise approach to identifying regional groupings is not possible, a simple tripartite division of insular La Tène metalwork into material from Ireland, southern Britain and northern Britain has, with some validity, been suggested (Spratling 1972: 328–36). The copper alloy Iron Age metalwork of these three regions has been separately considered in a series of important studies by Spratling (1972), MacGregor (1976) and Raftery (1983; 1984). These broad regional groupings cannot be viewed as exclusive: some types of insular La Tène metalwork have a distribution which extends throughout Ireland and Britain; while some types are found in both southern and northern Britain; and only some types are restricted to either Ireland, southern Britain or northern Britain (Spratling 1972: 331–2). Nor should these groupings be perceived of as hard and fast divisions capable of precise definition; the discovery of a few new finds has altered our perceptions about the distributions of individual artefact types in the past, and there is no reason to suggest that this will not happen again in the future (Spratling 1972: 328; James and Rigby 1997: 44). The extent to which these broad regional groupings reflect genuine variations in the use and distribution of ancient artefact types is uncertain. In particular, it is probable that the differences between the southern and northern British groups are largely the result of variations in depositional practice which have both a cultural and chronological dimension. Furthermore, in suggesting a regional difference in insular La Tène metalwork between southern and northern Britain it is not possible to define precisely the geographical division between these two areas. Spratling viewed southern Britain as an area which included the whole of Wales and England south of Lancashire and Yorkshire (1972: 331–2); but this division is not the same as that made by Fox in defining his Lowland and Highland Zones (Fox 1943: 28–32). Spratling's suggestion that the La Tène metalwork from southern Britain could be subdivided into eastern and western groupings (1972: 332–6) can no longer be maintained (see Chapter 3 for a critique of Spratling's division of the southern British three-link bridle-bits into eastern and western groups).

Despite the reservations noted above, Spratling's tripartite division is worth applying to the copper alloy artefacts from Llyn Cerrig Bach. Where artefacts from the assemblage can be identified as examples of known types, it is notable that several are of types found in both southern and northern Britain including the Group I terrets (Nos. 1–2), the nave hoops (Nos. 4–7), the 'vase-headed' linch-pin (No. 8), the three-link bridle-bits (Nos. 10–15) and the so-called casket ornament (Nos. 50–5). Examples of types known either exclusively or largely from southern Britain include the Group II terret (No. 3), the tubular rein-rings (Nos. 16–20), the two-link bridle-bit (No. 22) and the so-called horn-cap (No. 49). Examples of types known almost exclusively from Ireland include: the three-link bridle-bit of Irish type (No. 23) and the curved-horn fragment (No. 31). There are no examples of copper alloy artefact types known either exclusively or largely from northern Britain. Where identifiable, the bulk of the types represented in the Llyn Cerrig Bach assemblage are typical of the southern British regional grouping of insular La Tène metalwork. With the exception of the three-link bridle-bit of Irish type (No. 23) and possibly the curved-horn fragment (No. 31), all of the identifiable items of metalwork in the assemblage are of types current in southern Britain during the Iron Age. This observation does not, in itself, prove that elements of the assemblage were not imported from northern Britain, items like the Group I terrets (Nos. 1–2) are as typical of northern Britain as southern Britain, but it is perhaps significant that none of the artefact types largely exclusive to northern Britain, such as the massive tradition of metalwork or derivative three-link bridle-bits, are represented in the assemblage.

It is not possible to identify a specific source, or place of manufacture, for any single copper alloy artefact from the assemblage. Although there is no reason why a sizeable element of the assemblage could not have been manufactured in north-west Wales, it is not possible to identify any specific piece as the product of a local workshop. The presence of the three-link bridle-bit of Irish type (No. 23) in the assemblage demonstrates that material manufactured some distance from Anglesey was deposited at Llyn Cerrig Bach. It is unlikely that the three-link bridle-bit of Irish type was the only item in the assemblage which was not manufactured locally, but identifying individual artefacts from the assemblage that were imported from outside north-west Wales is difficult. The view that the curved-horn, or trumpet, fragment (No. 31) was manufactured in Ireland (Fox 1947a: 61; Lynch 1970: 271; Raftery 1984: 134) can no longer be considered certain (Spratling 1972: 342; see Chapter 4), while the possibility that one of the sword fragments from Llyn

Cerrig Bach was also of Irish origin (Raftery 1984: 332, fig. 45.1; S. Green 1991: 609) is questionable (G. Darbyshire pers. comm.). Spratling suggested that the two iron gang-chains (Fox 1947a: 37–9, 84–5, nos. 59–60, pls X–XI, XXXVII; Lynch 1970: 275, 276, figs. 90–1; Savory 1976a: 43, 49, 58, nos. 17.59–60, fig. 28, pl. VI) could be identified as definite imports from the south-east of England (Spratling 1972: 341–2), but his certainty can no longer be maintained. The number of Iron Age gang-chains known from Britain is small, and examples comparable to those from Llyn Cerrig Bach are known only from Lords Bridge, Barton, Cambridgeshire (E. D. Clarke 1821: 61, pl. IV, fig. 13; Fox 1923: 100–1; Thompson 1993: 151) and Bigberry Camp, Kent (Boyd Dawkins 1902: 215–16, pl. III, fig. 7; Jessup 1932: 108–10, pl. II; Thompson 1983: 274, nos. 46–8, figs 16, 18, pl. XXXVII; Thompson 1993: 151). With only a small number of examples of the type known it is not possible to identify, with any confidence, the south-east of England as the source for the type.

In summary, the Llyn Cerrig Bach assemblage demonstrably contains copper alloy artefacts from both southern Britain and, to a much lesser extent, Ireland. It contains no objects of exclusively northern British type, however, it is possible that some of the examples in the assemblage were manufactured in northern Britain. The diversity of impurity patterns identified in the metallurgical analysis of the copper alloy artefacts supports the suggestion that the assemblage was derived from a number of different sources. The proportion of material in the assemblage which was manufactured locally, as opposed to imported from outside of north-west Wales, is impossible to assess, but there is no reason why the assemblage should not contain significant proportions of locally manufactured artefacts as well as imports.

Dating of the assemblage

If identifying the source of the copper alloy artefacts in the Llyn Cerrig Bach assemblage has not been a major concern of the present study, then the re-evaluation of their dating has been. This is because the dating of the assemblage provides the best evidence for understanding depositional activity at Llyn Cerrig Bach. The perennial problem of the study of Iron Age metalwork is the lack of associated and independently dated material. This has resulted in the dating of insular La Tène metalwork being a difficult and frequently controversial affair; the reasons for these difficulties are as legion as they are apparently inescapable.

The principal difficulty is that Iron Age metalwork is usually recovered from unassociated or insecure contexts which are divorced from the conventional archaeological record. In particular, the lack of metalwork deposited on settlement sites and the absence of a comprehensive burial record for the period has resulted in a dearth of stratified sequences which incorporate insular La Tène metalwork in association with closely datable material. Consequently, there is little opportunity to apply independent scientific techniques to the dating of insular La Tène metalwork; and even where these can meaningfully be applied through association, the techniques themselves are often imprecise (Stead 1985a: 4). The tendency for metalwork to be deposited at sites which are difficult to recognize archaeologically has led to the majority of known examples being chance finds recovered in less than ideal circumstances, such as river dredging, construction work or metal detecting. This inevitably reduces the chances of meaningful archaeological associations being identified and recorded. A second problem in dating insular La Tène metalwork has been that the majority of independently dated Iron Age contexts belong to the second half of the first century BC or later and this has resulted in a tendency for chronological attributions to gravitate towards the end of the period (Spratling 1972: 303; Fitzpatrick 1984: 182). Prior to Stead's studies of the material from the cemeteries at Garton Station, Kirkburn and Wetwang Slack, all in East Yorkshire (1991a), and Deal, Kent (1995), the only fixed dates for insular La Tène metalwork assemblages were all relatively late. Despite recognizing this bias towards late assemblages in his survey of the copper alloy artefacts from southern Britain, Spratling (1972) still proposed a chronology which was largely confined to the first century BC simply because the only securely datable metalwork was late (Stead 1991a: 183).

Regional and chronological variations in depositional practices have both had an effect on the dating of Iron Age metalwork. In general, insular La Tène metalwork enters the archaeological record by one of two methods: through votive deposition or, to a more limited degree, as an accompaniment to human burial (Megaw and Megaw 1989: 190; Stead and Hughes 1997: 14). The funerary practices of the British Iron Age are poorly understood. An 'archaeologically invisible' mortuary rite, often assumed to be excarnation by exposure or deposition in rivers, appears to have been practised from the late Bronze Age through to the middle Iron Age (Bradley 1990: 161–4; Cunliffe 1997: 209; Carr and Knüsel 1997: 167; Denison 2000) and late Iron Age burial practice is also under represented in the archaeological record. There are only two major burial traditions incorporating metalwork known for the British Iron Age and both have restricted geographical and chronological limits. The first is the East Yorkshire tradition which is traditionally viewed as an expression of the 'Arras Culture' and includes a number of the vehicle fittings and items of harness cited in the present study. It probably begins in the fourth or third century BC and continues until some point in the mid first century BC (Whimster 1980: 75–128; Stead 1991a: 184; 1991d; Wait 1995: 499). The second is the Aylesford–Swarling cremation tradition which is restricted to south-eastern England from the mid first century BC onwards (Stead 1976; Whimster 1980: 147–66; Foster 1986: 178–87, fig. 44; Stead 1991e; Wait 1995: 497–8). Metalwork is also associated with less common burial types, such as the so-called warrior inhumations which date from the third century BC onwards (Whimster 1980: 129–46) and which includes the important example from Mill Hill, Deal, Kent (Parfitt 1990; 1995: 18–20; Stead 1995: 58–95). Although study of the burial record provides some of the best dating evidence, the small number of burials which contain metalwork in association with independently datable artefact types, such as brooches and sword scabbards, limits the value of this source. In addition, the selective inclusion of artefacts in burial rites means that some types, such as the southern

British mirror series, are represented in a number of closely datable contexts, whilst other types, such as cauldrons, are not (Spratling 1972: 304).

The majority of the known examples of insular La Tène metalwork probably entered the archaeological record through acts of deliberate ritual or votive deposition, usually in watery contexts such as rivers, lakes and bogs (Stead and Hughes 1997: 14–15). As a rite, votive deposition in watery contexts had a long vogue from the Neolithic to the early historic period (Merrifield 1987: 23–30, 107–16; Bradley 1990), but its use, and presumably its meaning, was not continuous and during the early and middle Iron Age in Britain there was a significant decline in the amount of metalwork being ritually deposited (Fitzpatrick 1984: 181–2; Wait 1985: 47–9; Merrifield 1987: 26; Bradley 1987: 358; 1990: 160). The use of votively deposited assemblages for dating purposes is problematic because it is frequently not possible to ascertain whether an assemblage was deposited during a single event or represents an accumulation of items deposited in several episodic acts over a potentially long period of time. Consequently, little or no reliance can usually be placed, for the purposes of dating, on the apparent association of one artefact with another within the same assemblage. A related problem in the dating of Iron Age metalwork is the realization that there may be a significant difference between the date of an object's manufacture and the date of its deposition. The recognition that already antique material, or 'heirlooms', was collated and then subsequently included in both burials and other deposits along with more contemporary material also affects the reliability of dating metalwork by association (for specific examples of this practice see Stead and Rigby 1989: 98; Haselgrove 1997: 53). The blank in our knowledge caused by the decline in the deposition of metalwork, in both votive and burial contexts, during the early and middle Iron Age is also significant. The earliest dates for various artefact types are potentially more informed by changes in depositional practice than the true advent of a new form or type (Manning 1995a: 318). This may explain the frequently made observation that insular La Tène art appears fully formed in the archaeological record with few antecedents.

The problems, outlined above, in dating insular La Tène metalwork have, in the past, resulted in the over-reliance of typological schemes constructed from the study of a potentially unrepresentative sample of artefacts with little reference to independent dating evidence. That the range of known examples of insular La Tène metalwork is not necessarily representative of that manufactured in antiquity is suggested by Foster's study of terret mould fragments at Gussage All Saints, Dorset (1980: 9–13; 1991: 608) and Weelsby Avenue, Lincolnshire (1995: 52), where a number of types were recognized that are not represented in the archaeological record by surviving artefacts. Whether this is because there is only a relatively small number of known examples of Iron Age metalwork in comparison to the range of ancient types, or whether it is a reflection of the poorly understood processes of selection in ancient depositional practice is not obvious. Typological schemes have rightly been considered of little value because they are frequently based on a variety of unsupportable assumptions (Spratling 1972: 280–1). This was illustrated by the study of the mould fragments recovered from Gussage All Saints,

Dorset (Foster 1980: 33; Stead 1985a: 10), which necessitated the total rejection of the established typology for three-link bridle-bits (Palk 1984: 77–8). Even where a typological sequence can be confidently constructed, as with the insular brooch typology which is largely derived from that of the Continent, there can be problems reconciling it to other sequences and schemes (for example, Stead 1985b: 31; see also Haselgrove 1997).

A second flaw in earlier approaches to the study and dating of insular La Tène metalwork has been the over reliance on historical events to provide a framework for artefact chronologies. In the study of the British Iron Age there has been a tendency to view changes in the archaeological record as the result of supposedly historically attested events (Spratling 1972: 283–4). Awareness of the difficulties inherent in such an approach has resulted in the criticism, and rejection, of attempts to explain the British archaeological evidence in terms of the supposed Belgic migration (for example, Hodson 1962: 152–4; Clark 1966: 186–7; Stead 1976: 401–12; Bradley 1978: 126–7), the Gallic War and Caesar's incursion into England (for example, Darvill 1987: 166; Haselgrove 1996: 76). What has not been so widely considered, however, is Spratling's criticism that the historically attested Roman Conquest of an area is often implicitly used to provide a *terminus ante quem* for the occurrence of La Tène monuments and artefacts in that region (Spratling 1972: 283). Such an approach is based on the assumption that changes in the control of political power in a society will be reflected by concomitant changes in the material culture of that society. Ethnographic work in the 1970s (Nicklin 1971–2; Rowlands 1971–2: 220–1; Spratling 1972: 283), and more recent archaeological studies incorporating post-colonial theory (Hingley 1997: 85; Häussler 1998; see also J. Webster 1997), suggest that such a simplistic assumption is not necessarily tenable when applied to post-Conquest Britain. There is no reason why the deposition of assemblages of metalwork, such as those from Seven Sisters, Glamorgan (Allen 1905; Davies and Spratling 1976; Savory 1976a: 62–3, nos. 34.125–57, fig. 39), and Tal-y-Llyn, Merionethshire (Savory 1964; 1976a: 47–8, 56–7, nos. 16.1–16.20, fig. 12, pls II.a and III.a), which include both insular La Tène and Romano-British metalwork, could not be significantly later than the mid first century AD date traditionally ascribed to them, often implicitly, on the questionable assumption that insular La Tène metalwork does not circulate after the Roman Conquest.

All of the problems outlined above apply to the dating of the copper alloy artefacts in the Llyn Cerrig Bach assemblage. In the present study, dating of the copper alloy artefacts has largely been achieved by reference to independently dated comparable material and, where appropriate, with recourse to the stylistic dating of decorative and art motifs. Such an approach is not without its limitations (for the problems concerning stylistic dating of insular La Tène art see Macdonald forthcoming). With the exception of the evidence derived from the foundry deposits at Gussage All Saints and Weelsby Avenue, all of the dates provided by the cited parallels are for the deposition of the artefacts and not their manufacture or their use. The difference in date between the manufacture and deposition of any single artefact may be considerable, and the length of time that individual examples of a type were in use also probably varied considerably. As a result the date ranges suggested for individual copper alloy artefacts in the assemblage frequently span several centuries and reflect an ill-defined vogue for the artefact's type, rather than a precise date for its manufacture, use or deposition. These long time spans make the meaningful comparison of the dates of different artefacts within the assemblage problematic. It is difficult to evaluate whether the assemblage is the product of several episodes of deposition, the collection of material manufactured at different dates but deposited in a single event, or a single deposit of material that had a contemporary vogue.

The analysis of the date of the individual copper alloy artefacts from the assemblage (Chapters 2 to 5) suggests that, where the artefacts can be confidently dated, they fall into two groups. The largest group, which includes the terrets (Nos. 1–3), the nave hoops (Nos. 4–7), the 'vase-headed' linch-pin (No. 8), the three-link bridle-bits and tubular rein-rings (Nos. 10–21), the scabbard mouth (No. 27), the curved-horn fragment (No. 31), the crescentic plaque (No. 47), the shield boss mount (No. 48) and the so-called horn-cap (No. 49), dates from between the fourth or third centuries BC to some point in, or before, the mid first century AD. Although some of these artefacts, such as the terrets (Nos. 1–3), the 'vase-headed' linch-pin (No. 8) and the scabbard mouth (No. 27), are examples of types that may have continued in use until the late first or second century AD, there is no compelling evidence to suggest that the examples from Llyn Cerrig Bach are necessarily this late in date. The second, smaller group, which includes the coiled strips (Nos. 35–43) and the 'casket' ornament (Nos. 50–5), are arguably examples of types which date from around the mid first century AD to some point in the late second century AD. The character of the artefacts in these two groups varies: the earlier group consists largely of military equipment, vehicle fittings and items of horse harness, whilst the later material is non-martial in character.

As well as studying the known copper alloy artefacts from Llyn Cerrig Bach it is perhaps useful to consider, from a chronological perspective, what copper alloy artefact types are not represented in the assemblage. It has previously been noted that the absence of inlaid *champlevé* enamel work, similar to that in the Lesser Garth, Glamorgan (Savory 1966b; 1976a: 63–4, nos. 35.1–35.11, fig. 37), Seven Sisters, Glamorgan (Allen 1905; Davies and Spratling 1976; Savory 1976a: 62–3, nos. 34.125–34.157, fig. 39) and Polden Hill, Somerset (Harford 1803; Brailsford 1975a) assemblages, suggests that either deposition at Llyn Cerrig Bach had ceased by the mid first century AD or that there was a hiatus in deposition during this period (Fox 1947a: 66; Lynch 1970: 285; Savory 1976a: 49). Although the decorative boss mounted on to one of the side links of the asymmetrical three-link bridle-bit (No. 11) may have been inlaid with enamel (see Chapter 3), this is an interesting observation. The use of such decorative enamel work on the bowl from Snowdon, Caernarvonshire (Savory 1976a: 43, 62, no. 32, fig. 38.a) demonstrates that metalwork of this type was current in north-west Wales and suggests that its exclusion from the Llyn Cerrig Bach assemblage is potentially significant (F. Lynch pers. comm.). Traditionally, assemblages of insular La Tène metalwork which include items decorated with curvilinear inlaid enamel ornament have been dated to the mid first century AD (i.e. Savory 1966b: 39–44; Brailsford 1975a: 234; Davies and Spratling 1976: 135–8). Such precise dating, however, is not tenable for the use of enamel itself and its vogue is more accurately dated to the first and possibly second centuries AD (Bateson 1981: 8–10, 114; Raftery 1991: 568–9). Consequently, its absence from the Llyn Cerrig Bach assemblage is not necessarily chronologically significant and does not demonstrate either a mid first century AD *terminus ante quem* or hiatus in deposition at the site.

Fox considered the Llyn Cerrig Bach assemblage to have been pre-Roman in date because it contains no artefacts which show direct Roman influence or have a 'transitional Celto-Roman' character (Fox 1947a: 59–60, 68, 70). Fox's interpretation was partly informed by Tacitus's account of the destruction of sacred groves following Paulinus' invasion of Anglesey (*Annals* 14.30). This dating and the reasoning behind it has been widely accepted (Lynch 1970: 285; Savory 1976a: 49; S. Green 1991: 609), but the present study has suggested, on the basis of analogy, that certain elements of the assemblage may date to the late first or early second centuries AD. The cited parallels do not in themselves prove that the comparable examples from Llyn Cerrig Bach are Roman in date, they merely suggest the possibility. The parallels do, however, undermine the standard interpretative view of the assemblage, originated by Fox and maintained ever since, that deposition at Llyn Cerrig Bach must have ended, at the latest, by the mid first century AD, because it did not contain objects of a Roman or 'transitional Celto-Roman' character. If this potentially late dating for some of the artefacts can be demonstrated to be valid then it would have significant implications for both the dating of insular La Tène metalwork and the continuity of ritual practice between Iron Age and Roman Britain. The other sources of evidence which may clarify the dating of the depositional activity at Llyn Cerrig Bach are the metallurgical analysis of the copper alloy artefacts, and study of the ironwork and animal bone components of the assemblage. These sources are discussed below before the related questions of whether the assemblage represents a single deposit or the accumulation of several deposits, and whether elements of the assemblage post-date the Roman invasions of Anglesey are addressed.

Metallurgical studies (with Mary Davis)

A comprehensive programme of metallurgical analysis of the copper alloy artefacts from Llyn Cerrig Bach has been conducted (see Appendix 2). The scale of analytical work on the copper alloy artefacts of the British Iron Age has increased significantly in the last twenty years. Work on artefacts from southern Britain has mostly been conducted on an ad hoc basis, usually as part of programmes to publish excavations, and with relatively little attempt at synthesis (i.e. Barnes 1985; Cowell 1990; Northover 1984; 1987; 1991a; 1991b). In contrast a large amount of material from northern Britain has been analysed as part of a systematic research project (Dungworth 1995; 1996; 1997a; 1997b; 1999). In addition to the studies noted above, a number of large museum collections have also been analysed (i.e. Craddock 1980; 1986).

Two approaches to the interpretation of analytical work conducted on Iron Age copper alloys have been adopted. The first approach is concerned with provenancing artefacts by studying impurity patterns in their alloys and relating these to ore sources. As noted above, the validity of this approach has been questioned and it is not adopted here. Dungworth has advocated a second approach to the interpretation of analytical data which is concerned with studying variations in alloying traditions through time. Dungworth, whose work has concentrated on northern Britain but which nevertheless is relevant to southern Britain, has identified a number of developments in alloying and smelting practices during the Iron Age and Roman period by sampling material recovered from independently dated archaeological contexts. For the Iron Age these consisted of material from various settlement sites and the so-called Arras Culture burials of East Yorkshire, for the Roman period material from a wider variety of sites was analysed. In addition to the samples definitely derived from either demonstrably Iron Age or Roman contexts, Dungworth also analysed a small number of copper alloy artefacts recovered from rural sites which were occupied continuously from the late Iron Age into the Roman period and examples of insular La Tène metalwork which could not be independently closely dated.

The developments in copper alloying traditions identified by Dungworth are difficult to relate to the narrow chronological boundaries traditionally used to define and subdivide the archaeological record. They begin with a gradual change from the use of the leaded copper-tin alloys of the late Bronze Age and early Iron Age to an unleaded copper-tin alloy. This deliberate change, dating to $c.$ 400 BC, coincides with an increase in iron impurity levels which may reflect a change in smelting practices (Dungworth 1996: 400; see also Craddock and Meeks 1987: 189–93). Arsenic is a common impurity in what has been identified as the typical copper-tin alloy of the British Iron Age. The almost exclusive use of this single copper alloy type during the Iron Age contrasts with the Roman period when three different alloy types were exploited. These are a copper-tin alloy (bronze) similar to that of the Iron Age, a copper-zinc alloy (brass) and a copper-tin-zinc alloy (gunmetal). By plotting the levels of tin against zinc for his analysed Roman samples, Dungworth has demonstrated that the two elements were inversely correlated, suggesting that the intermediate alloys (gunmetals) were made by mixing brass with bronze (Dungworth 1996: 408; 1997a: 2.2; see also Craddock 1978: 12, fig. 7). Another contrast between the Iron Age and Roman alloying traditions is that, although many Roman artefacts have low levels of lead, a small proportion have relatively high levels (Dungworth 1997a: 5.3.3). The general level of impurities in Roman copper alloys is lower than those of the Iron Age, presumably reflecting either the use of hotter or more oxidizing smelting conditions, repeated smelting or more rigorous fire-refining purification of the finished metal during the Roman period (Dungworth 1997a: 6.6). Another significant contrast between Iron Age and Roman copper alloy impurities is that arsenic is rarely found in Roman alloys, again suggesting that smelting was generally carried out at a relatively higher temperature during the Roman period (Dungworth 1996: 403, 410; 1997a: 6.6.3; 1997b: 46).

Dungworth was able to identify these long-term trends in copper alloying traditions and smelting practices because he based his study on a large sample of material recovered from securely dated contexts. Unfortunately, these trends cannot be used, with any great confidence, to date individual artefacts not recovered from independently dated contexts, such as the material from Llyn Cerrig Bach, to either the Iron Age or the Roman period. This is partly because there is a significant overlap in the character of the different alloying traditions. For example, the typical unleaded copper-tin alloy of the Iron Age is still widely used during the Roman period despite the introduction of copper-zinc and copper-tin-zinc alloys. Consequently, just because an artefact is manufactured from a typical Iron Age unleaded copper-tin alloy it does not follow that it cannot be Roman in date. Even the more marked variations in impurities between the Iron Age and Roman material, such as the change from arsenic being a common impurity in Iron Age copper alloys and a rare impurity in Roman alloys, cannot be confidently used to date single artefacts, as there are both examples of Iron Age copper alloys without arsenic impurities and examples of Roman copper alloys with arsenic impurities.

These problems are exacerbated because the transitions in alloying and smelting practices identified by Dungworth are apparently long-term processes rather than instantaneous changes which can be closely and conveniently dated to historical events such as the Roman Conquest of southern Britain. For example, closely dating the transition from Dungworth's Iron Age to Roman copper alloying traditions, as defined by the introduction of zinc-rich copper alloys into Britain, is problematic. The cementation process by which Roman brasses were produced was developed during the first century BC, although copper-zinc alloys would not have been widely circulated in western Europe prior to the Augustan coin reforms of 23 BC (Bayley 1990: 7, 9). Although undoubtedly derived from Roman imports, the precise date for the introduction of zinc-rich alloys in Britain is uncertain. Dungworth has suggested that the transition was neither instantaneous or occurred simultaneously throughout Britain and that the use of brasses probably began about the beginning of the first century AD and continued after the Conquest (1996: 410–11; 1997a: 5.7). Although non-imported copper-zinc alloy artefacts, such as Colchester A brooches and some Iron Age coinage, do occur in pre-Roman contexts in southern Britain (Bayley 1990: 17, 21; Clogg and Haselgrove 1995: 50–1, 55–60; Dungworth 1999: 40), there are no known examples of copper-zinc alloys from secure Iron Age contexts in northern Britain and the widespread use of the alloy type prior to the Roman Conquest of southern Britain in AD 43 is doubtful (Dungworth 1996: 403, 410). It is reasonable to assume that the copper-zinc alloy inlay of a stamped mark on a recently analysed La Tène II sword from the Thames at Syon Park, Brentford, Middlesex, is an exceptionally early example of brass from Britain. The sword, and presumably by extension the stamped mark, are of third- or second-century BC date, suggesting an exotic origin for the copper-zinc alloy such as contemporary Anatolian coinage (J. D. Hill pers. comm.). Certainly, the earliest evidence of actual brass production in Britain comes from Claudian contexts (Bayley 1984; 1990: 11–13; Fell 1990: 31), and the widespread use of zinc-rich alloys apparently post-dates the Conquest period. One of the most interesting aspects of Dungworth's research was the realization that a significant quantity of the insular La Tène metalwork from northern Britain which cannot be closely dated is of the copper-zinc alloy type and may be significantly later in date than has hitherto been considered likely on stylistic grounds (Dungworth 1997a: 5.4; 1997b: 48).

Given these problems, how are the results of the metallurgical analyses of the copper alloy artefacts from Llyn Cerrig Bach best considered? As noted above, the two most significant indicators for distinguishing between Iron Age and Roman alloying traditions is the introduction of zinc-rich alloys at some point during the first century AD and the tendency for arsenic, which is a common impurity in Iron Age copper alloys, to occur only rarely in Roman alloys.

Only one of the analysed copper alloy artefacts from the assemblage, a riveted sheet fragment (No. 34), was manufactured from a zinc-rich alloy (26.24% Zn, 0.06% Fe, 0.03% As and only traces of other elements) and therefore cannot be any earlier in date than the first century AD. The level of zinc in the fragment is exceptionally high for an ancient brass; none of those analysed by Dungworth (1996; 1997a; 1997b) had a zinc content higher than 25 per cent and only seven of the 444 Roman copper alloys analysed by Craddock had a zinc content above 25 per cent (Craddock 1978: fig. 7). The cementation method could produce alloys with a maximum zinc content of about 28 per cent (Craddock 1978: 9). Dungworth has suggested that the general absence of ancient brasses with a zinc content approaching this maximum level is due to either the regular use of copper already alloyed with lead or tin in the cementation process, or that following cementation the brasses were melted to form cast artefacts or ingots and that, because of the volatility of zinc, a portion of the element was consequently lost (Dungworth 1997a: 6.3.1, 10.3). The rarity of copper alloys with high zinc levels may, however, simply reflect the widespread practice of recycling in antiquity. The only known ancient British artefact with a high zinc content equivalent to the Llyn Cerrig Bach fragment is a brass sheet recovered from the early Roman industrial site at Sheepen, near Colchester, Essex (26.8% Zn, 0.14% Fe and only traces of other elements, cf. Musty 1975), whose high zinc level is considered to be evidence of primary production by the cementation process (Bayley 1990: 11–13). The comparable zinc content of the Llyn Cerrig Bach fragment (No. 34) suggests that it was also probably manufactured from a primary product of the cementation process. If, as suggested above, brasses were not produced in Britain until after the Claudian invasion then the sheet fragment should be considered to either post-date the Conquest of southern Britain, or be part of a pre-Roman Continental import.

The second chronologically significant change between the Iron Age and Roman copper alloying traditions identified by Dungworth is the tendency for arsenic, which is a common impurity in Iron Age copper alloys, to occur only rarely in Roman alloys. As noted above, the presence or absence of arsenic as an impurity in any single artefact from the assemblage cannot be used to identify whether or not it is an example of either the Iron Age or Roman alloying traditions. If, however, we study all of the individual artefacts which make up a particular typological group represented in the assemblage and they consistently, or nearly consistently, subscribe to one or another of the alloying traditions then we can, with some degree of confidence, assign them to an individual alloying tradition. When those samples which have a percentage of arsenic less than 0.01 per cent are isolated from the results of all of the analyses conducted to date (see Appendix 2) four typological groups are delimited; these are the nave hoops (as represented by Nos. 6–7), the globular cauldron fragments (Nos. 24–5), all but two of the coiled decorative mounts (Nos. 36–40 and 42–3) and all of the examples of so-called casket ornament (Nos. 50–5). It is significant that for two of these artefact types, the coiled decorative mounts and the so-called casket ornament, an early Roman date is independently suggested on the basis of analogous parallels (see Chapters 4 and 5). The lack of close parallels for the globular cauldron fragments (see Chapter 4) and the imprecise late Iron Age to mid first-century AD date suggested for the nave hoops on typological evidence (see Chapter 2) means that less interpretive stress can be placed on their metallurgical composition, but there is nothing inconsistent between the results of their typological and metallurgical analyses. In addition, the probable scabbard or sheath binding (No. 28) and one of the sheet fragments (No. 32) also have low or non-detectable levels of arsenic, but as these are single items within the assemblage, the significance of these results is far less certain. The spectographic analysis of the copper alloy coating on one of the three-link bridle-bits (either No. 14 or No. 15) also indicated only a trace of arsenic, but the accuracy of this result is questionable (cf. Savory 1971: 66).

The ironwork

The Llyn Cerrig Bach assemblage includes several artefacts manufactured from both iron and copper alloy. These composite artefacts, all of which are included in the catalogue of copper alloy artefacts and discussed in the present study, are: one of the Group I terrets (No. 1); the 'vase-headed' linch-pin (No. 8); five of the three-link bridle-bits (Nos. 10, 12, 13, 14 and 15); the possible central-link from a three-link bridle-bit (No. 21); and the dagger or sword pommel (No. 29). In addition to the composite artefacts, 124 iron artefacts are recorded as part of the assemblage, of which four are modern, four are possibly modern and one is possibly medieval in date (see Appendix 1). A detailed assessment of the ironwork from Llyn Cerrig Bach falls outside of the parameters of the present study, however, a short commentary on its date is outlined below.

The dating of the ironwork is largely consistent with that put forward for the copper alloy artefacts. Not all of the ironwork can be closely dated; many artefact types are particularly conservative and in some cases remained essentially unchanged from the Iron Age until the nineteenth century (Manning 1972: 228). These artefacts are never likely to be dated except within the limits of the assemblage as a whole (Fox 1947a: 60). The date range of the more closely datable examples of ironwork, discussed below, extends from the fourth or third centuries BC to the time of the Roman Conquest and includes a small number of items which could have been deposited as late as the second half of the first century AD.

British and Irish Iron Age swords were classified by Piggott who identified several forms including a Group II which was derived from the Continental La Tène II type

(1950: 9–10, 26), and a Group V which was equivalent to the Continental La Tène III series (1950: 10, 22, 28). The swords from Llyn Cerrig Bach include one certain (Fox 1947a: no. 92; Savory 1976a: no. 18.1) and one possible (Fox 1947a: no. 3; Savory 1976a: no. 17.3) example of La Tène II type, and eight examples (Fox 1947a: nos. 1–2, 4, 6–7 and 93–5; Savory 1976a: nos. 17.1–17.2, 17.4, 17.6–17.7, 18.2–18.3 and 19.1) of La Tène III type (Piggott 1950: 26, 28). The two scabbard fragments (Fox 1947a: nos. 8–9; Savory 1976a: nos. 17.8–17.9) are probably of La Tène II type (Piggott 1950: 6). La Tène II swords and scabbards range in date from the third to the second century BC, while La Tène III swords and scabbards range in date from the late second century BC until the early first century AD (James and Rigby 1997: 10; for a detailed discussion of the Continental sword and scabbard sequence see Stead 1983). The comparable examples of the iron nave hoops, which include a large number derived from East Yorkshire vehicle burials and also Hunsbury hillfort, are suggestive of a date range for the type from the fourth or third century BC until at least the first century BC (see Chapter 2). The ring-headed linch-pin (Fox 1947a: no. 43; Savory 1976a: no. 17.43) is an example of a type found from contexts dating from the late Iron Age (Manning 1985: 72, fig. 19) to the middle of the first century AD, including: Bigberry Camp (Jessup 1932: 106, pl. III; Thompson 1983: 274, no. 41, fig. 17.34, pl. XXXVI.a), the Polden Hill hoard (Harford 1803: 93, pl. XX.3, no.18; Brailsford 1975a: 230, fig. 7.d), the Waltham Abbey hoard (Manning 1985: 72, no. H39, pl. 31) and Worthy Down, Hampshire (Hooley 1926–30: 189, fig. 82, pl. VI). In comparison with analogous examples the iron bridle-bits of miscellaneous form from Llyn Cerrig Bach (Fox 1947a: nos. 56–7, 128; Savory 1976a: nos. 17.56–17.57, 18.9; Palk 1984: nos. LL1–LL2) could be either late Iron Age or early Roman in date (see Chapter 3). The two gang-chains (Fox 1947a: nos. 59–60; Savory 1976a: nos. 17.59–17.60) are examples of a type dated, albeit on a small number of comparable examples, from the first century BC to the mid first century AD (Thompson 1993: 74). The currency bars (Fox 1947a: nos. 61–4, 130; Savory 1976a: nos. 17.61–17.64, 19.2) are examples of types that are generally accepted to date from the middle Iron Age to the first century BC (Allen 1967: 321–2; Fell 1990: 13; Hingley 1990: 92), although some examples may have circulated until the mid first century AD (Trow 1988: 37). The pair of long tongs (Fox 1947a: no. 131; Savory 1976a: no. 18.32) are an example of a type which has an extended vogue; Darbyshire has cited several Roman and early medieval parallels (1996: 57) and Lynch noted that tongs of this form were used until relatively recently (1970: 270). Finally, the sickle (Fox 1947a: no. 65; Savory 1976a: no. 17.65) is an example of Rees's Type Iib, which also includes a number of Iron Age and Romano-British examples (Rees 1979: 458; see also Manning 1985: 51).

In summary, the ironwork component of the Llyn Cerrig Bach assemblage includes a number of pieces which can be dated from the fourth or third centuries BC to the mid first century AD, as well as several types with differing and largely exclusive date ranges, such as the La Tène II and La Tène III swords. Although there is no specific example of ironwork from the assemblage which can unequivocally be demonstrated to be Romano-British in date, there are several items which may post-date the Conquest.

The animal bone

Fox records that during his first visit to the airfield he saw a considerable mass of animal bone dredged up with the peat that contained the metalwork, but that only a small sample, not expertly selected, was collected (Fox 1947a: 67). The validity of the presumed association between the animal bone and the metalwork was strengthened by the observation that animal bone was not found in any extracted peat apart from that containing the metalwork (Fox 1947a: 3). The collected sample, which included the remains of ox, horse, pig, sheep (or goat) and dog, was studied by L. F. Cowley, who contributed a report to the original publication of the assemblage (Cowley 1947). Of the sample that Cowley studied, only eight bones remain in the collections of the National Museum of Wales; these are: part of the left-hand side of the frontal bone of a juvenile ox (accession no. 44.32.Z.1); part of the left-hand side frontal bone of an adult ox (accession no. 44.32.Z.2); the right radius of an ox (accession no. 44.32.Z.3); the right metatarsal of an ox (accession no. 44.32.Z.7); the left mandible of a sheep or goat (accession no. 44.32.Z.4); the left radius of a sheep or goat (accession no. 44.32.Z.5); the right metatarsal of a sheep (accession no. 44.32.Z.8) and the left mandible of a canid (dog) (accession no. 44.32.Z.6) (E. Walker pers. comm.). Three of these bones were sampled for radiocarbon dating by the Oxford Radiocarbon Accelerator Unit (Hedges *et al.* 1998: 236) which, when corrected to two standard deviations (95.4% confidence), provides a range of dates from the eighth century BC to the first century AD (Table 16). These radiocarbon dates suggest that deposition of animal bone occurred at Llyn Cerrig Bach from at least the fourth to the second century BC, and possibly later (Hedges *et al.* 1998: 236; contra Green and Howell 2000: 28). This date range is consistent with that outlined above for both the copper alloy and iron artefacts from the assemblage, and suggests that the deposition of animal bone at Llyn Cerrig Bach was broadly contemporary with the deposition of metalwork at the site, however, the possibility of an earlier phase of animal bone deposition, which predates the deposition of metalwork, cannot be dismissed.

Summary

Central to understanding the character of deposition at Llyn Cerrig Bach is the question of whether the assemblage is the product of episodic deposition over some considerable period of time, episodic collation of material over several centuries which was deposited in a single act, or the product of a single act of deposition of material that had a contemporary vogue and was collated in a single episode. By comparing the different strands of dating evidence reviewed above it is possible to address this question.

Study of both the closely datable copper alloy and ironwork types suggests that the metalwork component of the assemblage forms two chronological groups: the largest group potentially ranges in date from as early as the fourth or third centuries BC to some point in, or before, the mid first century AD; while a smaller group, identifiable both

TABLE 16: Radiocarbon dates from the Oxford Radiocarbon Accelerator Unit

Laboratory number	Animal bone type	Accession no.	Uncorrected date	Corrected (95.4% confidence)
OxA-6390	Canid mandible	44.32.Z.6	2075 ± 50 BP	350 BC–AD 60
OxA-6391	Sheep/goat mandible	44.32.Z.4	2245 ± 50 BP	400 BC–180 BC
OxA-6392	Ox frontal bone	44.32.Z.2	2345 ± 50 BP	800 BC–200 BC

typologically and metallurgically, apparently ranges in date from around the mid first century AD to possibly some point in the second century AD. Although this suggests that the assemblage may be a single deposit of mid first-century AD date, there are a number of artefact types in the earlier chronological grouping, such as the three-link bridle-bits, the currency bars and the La Tène II swords and scabbard fragments, which are difficult to reconcile with such a late date. This impression was confirmed by the radiocarbon dating of the animal bone which included two dates (OxA-6391 and OxA-6392) that are, at the latest, of third or second century BC date (Table 16). The combined dating evidence demonstrates that the Llyn Cerrig Bach assemblage is not the product of a single act of deposition of material that shared a contemporary vogue (*pace* Roberts 2002). Whether the assemblage is the product of several episodic acts of deposition carried out over a period of time, or represents material assembled over a period of time but deposited in a single, late act is not so apparent. As noted above, the curation of material for significant periods of time prior to its deposition in the Iron Age is a significant phenomenon and such a practice may have occurred at Llyn Cerrig Bach (Green 1986: 142). Although it is not possible to be certain when assessing the metalwork, the study of the animal bone is more instructive. When the excellent condition of the admittedly small sample of animal bone recovered from the assemblage and radiocarbon dated to the third or second century BC at the latest (OxA-6391 and OxA-6392), is considered, it seems unlikely that these bones were collected and curated until the mid first century AD before being deposited (A. Gwilt pers.comm.). By extension, this suggests that, rather than representing a collection of material assembled over a period of time and deposited in a single act, the Llyn Cerrig Bach assemblage represents material deposited episodically over a period of potentially several centuries. It is notable that this is a conclusion which is not new (cf. Fox 1947a: 70; Lynch 1970: 250; Savory 1976a: 49).

Establishing the precise duration of depositional activity at Llyn Cerrig Bach is problematic. The date ranges for individual artefact types in the assemblage frequently span several centuries and, because of fluctuations in the radiocarbon calibration curve for the Iron Age, precise dating of the animal bone is not possible either. Consequently, it is not possible to be certain when exactly deposition at Llyn Cerrig Bach began and ended. The evidence reviewed above suggests that deposition started at the latest by the end of the third century BC and may have begun significantly earlier. Radiocarbon dating suggests that deposition of animal bone may have begun earlier than the deposition of metalwork. The larger and earlier group of datable metalwork ranges in date from the fourth or third centuries BC until some point in, or before, the mid first century AD. It consists largely of military equipment, vehicle fittings and items of horse harness. The arguably later material, the coiled decorative strips and the 'casket' ornament, forms a smaller group which has a different, essentially non-military, character. Metallurgical analysis confirms the validity of these two chronological groups and suggests that the copper alloy artefacts which make up the later, non-military set of deposits were manufactured from alloys typical of a Roman, rather than Iron Age, alloying tradition. When deposition at the site ended, and whether deposition of the later, non-martial elements of the assemblage post-dates the invasions of Anglesey under Paulinus in AD 60/61 and Agricola in AD 77/78, is impossible to assess with certainty, but it is a possibility that cannot be dismissed when interpreting depositional activity at the site. The argument that deposition continued at Llyn Cerrig Bach after the Roman Conquest of Anglesey is strengthened when the archaeological context of the assemblage is evaluated and the character of deposition at analogous sites is considered.

7

Concluding Remarks

Fox's work on the Llyn Cerrig Bach assemblage marked an important advance in the appreciation of prehistoric depositional practices (Parker Pearson 2000: 10–11). In his discussion of the site Fox, prompted by Ian Richmond and influenced by his reading of several Classical sources, most notably Caesar (*De Bello Gallico* 6.17) and Strabo (*Geography* 4.1.13), suggested that the Llyn Cerrig Bach assemblage had accumulated in a series of votive ritual acts (Fox 1947a: 69–70). Fox considered that the deliberate damage demonstrably inflicted on several of the items in the assemblage prior to their deposition in a watery context was indicative of a religious act which marked Llyn Cerrig Bach out as a perennially sacred site (Fox 1947a: 69–70). Following Fox's report on the Llyn Cerrig Bach assemblage, the deposition of prehistoric metalwork in watery contexts has been generally interpreted as votive in character (for example, Manning 1972; Cunliffe 1974: 297; Bradley 1984: 100–1; Fitzpatrick 1984; Darvill 1987: 118–20; Bradley 1990). Prior to the discovery at Llyn Cerrig Bach, despite the frequent recovery of Iron Age metalwork from watery contexts, the possibility that such finds represented ritual deposits had not been widely considered. Only Arthur Evans, in a largely ignored suggestion, had interpreted the deposition of Iron Age metalwork in watery contexts as votive (Evans 1894–7: 408). Curle had vaguely hinted at a ritual element in the contents of the Carlingwark Loch and Blackburn Mill hoards (J. Curle 1931–2: 310–13; Piggott 1952–3: 4–5) and Fox himself had suggested that part of the Llyn Fawr hoard may have formed an offering (Fox and Hyde 1939: 381). Most earlier accounts of prehistoric metalwork recovered from watery contexts, however, had simply avoided discussion of the circumstances of their deposition (for example, Kemble 1863; Meyrick 1830–1; Crawford and Wheeler 1920–1; Smith 1925: 105–11). That the Llyn Cerrig Bach assemblage was deposited in a votive act is not an interpretation disputed here. The recent suggestion that the assemblage is the result of a first century BC shipwreck can be summarily dismissed on the grounds that the condition of the assemblage is inconsistent with deposition in a maritime burial environment (see Chapter 1) and that the dating evidence demonstrates the assemblage was not the product of a single episode of deposition (see Chapter 6) (*pace* Roberts 2002). The character of the deposition at Llyn Cerrig Bach is discussed below in order to place the votive activity at Llyn Cerrig Bach within a wider cultural and historical context. In comparing the assemblage to other insular and Continental deposits, it is appropriate to consider its chronology, the treatment and range of the artefacts deposited, and the character of the site itself.

The dating evidence for the assemblage suggests three possible phases, each with a distinct character, in the depositional sequence at the site. The first, dating approximately to the middle centuries of the first millennium BC, was, if real, restricted to the deposition of animal bone. The validity of this initial phase is questionable, for its recognition is based upon a small number of imprecise radiocarbon dates of animal bones (Hedges *et al.* 1998: 236). The second, and first definite, phase represents the bulk of metalwork deposition at the site and possibly the beginning, but certainly the continuation, of the deposition of animal bone. The metalwork of this phase largely consists of items of military equipment, vehicle fittings and horse harness and its deposition probably extends from either the fourth or third centuries BC until some point in, or before, the mid first century AD. The final phase of deposition is represented by a smaller number of non-martial items, such as the coiled bindings and the so-called casket ornament that have parallels of mid first-century AD to late second-century AD date and were manufactured from copper alloys typical of the Roman alloying tradition. Whether this third phase of deposition continued beyond the two historically recorded Roman invasions of Anglesey is considered below (for a detailed discussion of the chronology of the Llyn Cerrig Bach assemblage see Chapter 6).

Several of the items deposited at Llyn Cerrig Bach were deliberately damaged prior to their deposition. This not uncommon element of votive activity, sometimes described as the 'ritual killing' of artefacts (for example, Manning 1972: 243, fn. 121; James 1993: 93; Green 1995b: 471; King and Soffe 1998: 42), is generally interpreted as a means of dis-patching objects into the realm of the dead through an act of sympathetic magic or inanimate sacrifice which renders artefacts so treated fit for the Otherworld (G. Webster 1986: 132; Green 1986: 129; Brunaux 1988: 127). As well as being a feature of votive dep-osition, the deliberate damaging of artefacts occasionally occurs in burials during the Iron Age (for example, Green 1986: 124). Identifying artefacts from the assemblage which were deliberately damaged before deposition is complicated by the possibility that damage also may have occurred during the extraction and harrowing of the peat. Despite this diffi-culty, several of the copper alloy artefacts exhibit definite evidence of having been damaged prior to their deposition, including one of the three-link bridle-bits which was found with its side-link forced along the rein-ring beyond the position of its missing stop-stud (No. 13), the three cauldron fragments (Nos. 24–6), the pommel mount (No. 29), and the so-called horn-cap (No. 49). Other copper alloy artefacts exhibit damage which may have been inflicted either before deposition or during the peat extraction. These include the nave hoops (Nos. 4–7), several of the remaining three-link bridle-bits (Nos. 10–12, 14–21), the 'cylinder' (No. 30), the curved-horn or 'trumpet' fragment (No. 31), the coiled decorative strips (Nos. 35–43), three of the decorative plaques or mounts (Nos. 44–6), the crescentic decorative mount (No. 47), the shield boss mount (No. 48) and at least four of the examples of 'casket' ornament (Nos. 50–1, 54–5). Much of the iron-work from Llyn Cerrig Bach was also deliberately damaged in antiquity. Lynch notes that one of the spearheads had been bent (1970: 254), at least one of the swords had also been damaged (Fox 1947a: 69, 90, no. 92; Savory 1976a: 49, 59, no. 18.1) and the broken character of all but one of the wheel tyres suggests that they were also deliberately damaged prior to their deposition (Savory 1976a: 32).

CONCLUDING REMARKS

Several of the copper alloy artefacts also exhibit evidence, such as wear facets and repairs, of having been well used before they were deposited. These include the three terrets (Nos. 1–3), the 'vase-headed' linch-pin (No. 8), the possible harness ring (No. 9), the three-link bridle-bits (Nos. 10–15), four of the tubular rein-rings (Nos. 16–18, 20), the possible centre-link (No. 21), the two-link bridle-bit (No. 22), the three-link bridle-bit of Irish type (No. 23) and the three cauldron fragments (Nos. 24–6). This suggests that at least a significant proportion of the assemblage was not manufactured solely for deposition at Llyn Cerrig Bach.

The assemblage of animal bone from Llyn Cerrig Bach is usually interpreted as representing the remains of sacrificed animals, or possibly the remnants of feasting activity, associated with the votive rites practised at the site (Fox 1947a: 70; Lynch 1970: 251; J. L. Davies 1995: 693). That the surviving animal bones from Llyn Cerrig Bach show no evidence of butchery (E. Walker pers. comm.) suggests they represent sacrifices rather than the remains of feasting. In previous accounts of the assemblage the possibility that, in addition to animal sacrifice, the sacrifice of humans took place at Llyn Cerrig Bach has been dismissed (for example, Fox 1947a: 70; Lynch 1970: 251; Savory 1976a: 49). In his description of the circumstances of the discovery at Llyn Cerrig Bach, Fox records that the resident engineer at RAF Valley first wrote to him in July 1943 stating that animal bones were associated with the metal objects (1947a: 1), however, the content of this letter differs from Fox's account of it. The letter, which is in the archive on the assemblage held by the National Museum of Wales (accession no. 44.32), actually states that the metalwork had been found with human, not animal, bones. This raises the possibility that either human sacrifice or the deliberate deposition of human bone was practised at Llyn Cerrig Bach, alongside the deposition of metalwork and animal bone. The discoveries at Lindow Moss (Brothwell 1986; Stead *et al.* 1986; Turner 1995; Brothwell and Bourke 1995) and recent work on human skulls and other skeletal remains found in parts of the Thames (Bradley 1987: 358; Bradley and Gordon 1988; Bradley 1995; Denison 2000; *pace* Knüsel and Carr 1995) and other southern British rivers (Martin 1999: 72) lend credence to this possibility (*pace* Scott-Fox 2002: 170; see also Parker Pearson 2000: 10–11).

Prior to undertaking the present study relatively little was known about the topographical context of deposition at Llyn Cerrig Bach. The original site of extraction was flooded by the time Fox visited RAF Valley and so his understanding of the assemblage's original context was based solely on the comments of the workmen and engineers employed at the airfield. It is probable that only a proportion of the metalwork which was spread on the airfield, and a tiny fraction of the bone associated with it, was recovered. This was largely because the workmen who collected the assemblage had little opportunity to walk systematically over the spread of finds and collect material before the site became grassed over. No record of the location of the peat on the airfield containing the finds from Llyn Cerrig Bach was made and therefore it is not possible to return to the precise findspot, excavate the site and retrieve the remaining metalwork and bone. Survey work and study of the environs of Llyn Cerrig Bach and RAF Valley was undertaken in order to establish more detail about the character of the site and attempt to locate the spread of peat on the airfield (see Appendix 3). Although the attempt to locate the peat spread was unsuc-cessful, some new insights into the context of deposition at Llyn Cerrig Bach were made. Study of an aerial photograph of RAF Valley taken in November 1942, one month after the original extraction of the peat containing the assemblage, showed both an outcrop of rock and an area of ground which had not been disturbed by the excavation of peat located immediately to the north-east of the estimated original location of the assemblage (Central Register of Air Photography for Wales, Medmenham, NLA/53.1 PRV frame 1004; Pl. 4). Survey work over this outcrop and area of undisturbed ground revealed a hitherto unrecognized landscape feature: a bedrock ridge which extended north-eastwards for some 160 metres and which was about 35 metres wide. This feature would have formed an elongated island of drier ground within the Iron Age lake or bog at Llyn Cerrig Bach. The estimated location of the original find spot lies only slightly to the south of the shortest distance between the island and the rock platform from which Fox considered the assemblage was deposited into the lake. It is not unreasonable to suggest that this island is of great interpretative significance, and that it may have dictated the siting of the dep-osition at Llyn Cerrig Bach. Although conventionally considered to have been deposited into the lake or bog from the adjacent rock platform (Fox 1947a: 69–70; Lynch 1970: 250–1), it is possible that the Llyn Cerrig Bach assemblage was deposited not from the rock platform, but rather from a causeway connecting the rock platform to the island. It is a regrettable consequence of the wartime peat extraction that any archaeological evi-dence for such a structure at Llyn Cerrig Bach will have been destroyed, but parallels for probable votive deposition of large metalwork assemblages from a causeway into a watery context are known from both the Continent and Britain (see below). Another possibility raised by the recognition of the island feature is that it was the island itself that provided the focus for ritual activity at Llyn Cerrig Bach and not the lake. The interpretation of both the assemblage and the significance of the previously unrecognized landscape fea-ture is facilitated by a comparative study of analogous insular, Continental and Scandinavian late prehistoric sites and deposits.

Survey of Comparative Sites

The insular and Continental assemblages comparable to the Llyn Cerrig Bach deposit form two groups: those deposited in watery contexts, and those deposited in terrestrial contexts but whose treatment and composition is similar to that of the Llyn Cerrig Bach assemblage. The following review forms a representative, but inevitably selective, survey of these comparable deposits and their contexts.

Comparable deposits in watery contexts from Britain, Ireland and the Continent

The deliberate deposition of artefacts in watery contexts is an archaeological phenom-enon recognized throughout northern and western Europe, that extends from the

Neolithic to the early medieval period. Perhaps the most famous of these deposits are those from the Lake Neuchâtel area of Switzerland, which include the sites of La Tène, Cornaux and Port Nidau.

The lake site of **La Tène** is located on the northern edge of Lake Neuchâtel, on the ancient course of a tributary of the River Thiellein, and consists of a bridge or jetty constructed in the mid third century BC, which is associated with a large assemblage of metalwork, mainly consisting of martial items, tools and items of personal adornment (Vouga 1923; de Navarro 1972; Brunaux 1988: 42–3; Dunning 1991). Other items recovered from the site include currency bars, a number of wooden artefacts, several coins, fragments of a quern, pottery, fragments of two glass armlets, and both human and animal bones (Dunning 1991: 366; Egloff 1991: 370–1). Many of the items deposited at La Tène were deliberately damaged prior to their deposition (de Navarro 1972: 17). Despite the reluctance of some Continental archaeologists to accept the interpretation, deposition at the site was probably votive (de Navarro 1972: 17–19; see also Bradley 1990: 156–89; Raftery 1994: 183; Pryor 2001: 434–6). Randsborg has suggested that accounts of timber structures around the deposits at La Tène indicate that the site is similar to Continental sanctuaries such as Gournay-sur-Aronde (1995: 202–3; see below). **Cornaux** is also situated on an ancient course of the River Thiellein, only a few miles from the site at La Tène. The site consists of a bridge or jetty, comparable to that at La Tène, whose excavation has produced a metalwork assemblage including weapons and tools, as well as animal and human bones (Egloff 1987: 30; Dunning 1991: 366; Bradley 1990: 157, 164–5). Dendrochronological dating suggests that the bridge or jetty was constructed c. 300 BC and repaired as late as c. 120–116 BC (Parker Pearson 2003: 181). At **Port Nidau** about sixty La Tène D swords, an equal number of spearheads and several other items were recovered from the old riverbed of the Zihl (Müller 1991: 528). The weapons, which are slightly later than the material from La Tène, were apparently damaged prior to their deposition and Müller has speculated that some of these items were associated with, and possibly fixed to, a wooden structure (Müller 1991: 528).

In addition to the Swiss sites, a number of comparable assemblages of military equipment, frequently associated with the remains of boats, have been recovered from bogs in southern Scandinavia. These so-called booty sacrifices have usually been interpreted as the captured belongings of a defeated enemy which were given to the gods in an act of thanksgiving (Fabech 1991: 89; Rieck 1994: 45; Randsborg 1995: 38; Jensen 1998: 114). Unlike the Swiss sites, human bones have never been found associated with these deposits (Jensen 1998: 114). Scandinavian deposition in bogs and watery places begins in the Neolithic and continues throughout the Bronze Age and Iron Age until the mid first millennium AD (Jensen 1998: 86; Fabech 1991: 88–9). Although assemblages in bogs are found throughout Sweden, Denmark and parts of Norway, deposits of military equipment are restricted to Denmark and southern Sweden (Fabech 1991: 90). The best known examples include the deposits at Hjortspring Kobbel, Krogsbølle and Nydam, all in Denmark.

At **Hjortspring Kobbel** a weapon and ship deposit was recovered from the site of a small bog about 3 kilometres from the coast on the island of Als, off southern Jutland

(Rosenberg 1937; Klindt-Jensen 1957: 86–7; Randsborg 1995: 19; Jensen 1998: 86–90). As well as swords, spears, coats of mail, shields and the boat, several items of personal adornment, containers and a number of animal bones were recovered (Rosenberg 1937: 104–11; Rieck 1994; Randsborg 1995: 21–37). Many of the weapons had been deliberately damaged prior to their deposition (Ellis Davidson 1967: 70; Rieck 1994: 45–6; Randsborg 1995: fig. 7). Radiocarbon dating suggest a fourth- or third-century BC date for the main deposit at Hjortspring Kobbel (Randsborg 1995: 20), although there is evidence of earlier episodes of cattle bone deposition in the bog (Rosenberg 1937: 103; Ellis Davidson 1967: 69; Randsborg 1995: 36). At **Krogsbølle**, Fyn a comparable assemblage, again located a few kilometres from the coast and largely made up of swords and spearheads, but also including knives, a cheekpiece, mallet and several probable axles, was associated with a stone built trackway across a brook in a bog (Becker 1948: 168–70, figs. 17–19; Randsborg 1995: 42). The most famous southern Scandinavian assemblage is that from **Nydam** in southern Jutland. Remains of at least three, third to fifth century AD ships have been excavated at Nydam which was an artificially created freshwater lake located close to the coast (Rieke 1994: 49–54; Coles and Coles 1996: 67; Reike 1999). Recent excavations suggest that these ships were deliberately sunk at the lake which also provided the focus for the contemporary, episodic deposition of a large number of weapons, many of which were deliberately damaged, as well as other personal items, a carved wooden head and horse bones (Coles and Coles 1996: 68, 71, 74, fig. 40; Jensen 1998: 116; Klesius 2000: 30). Several of the horse bones show evidence of injuries inflicted with a sword, suggesting that the animals had been sacrificed (Jensen 1998: 116). Deposition at the site extended from c. AD 200 to c. AD 500. The results of recent excavations suggesting that the deliberate damaging of artefacts prior to their deposition was a more important element of the Nydam rites in the earlier part of this period (Coles and Coles 1996: 67–8). Several other similar southern Scandinavian deposits, including Thorsbjerg and Vimose also in Denmark, which date from the first half of the first millennium AD have been noted (Ellis Davidson 1967: 70; Fabech 1991; Jensen 1998: 114–16).

As well as these Continental examples, several assemblages comparable to that from Llyn Cerrig Bach have been recovered from lakes and bogs in Britain and Ireland. At **Lisnacrogher**, Co. Antrim an assemblage of weaponry, items of personal adornment and tools forms the largest complex of La Tène material from Ireland (Munro 1890: 380–6, figs. 123–4; Raftery 1983: 287–8). It was discovered during nineteenth century turf cutting and the site was destroyed without any archaeological supervision (Raftery 1983: 287; 1984: 314). Early accounts refer to upright and horizontal timbers and areas of brushwood (Munro 1890: 379–80) and the site is often referred to as a crannog, but it is not certain whether such a structure, if it existed, was associated with the metalwork (Munro 1890: 380; Raftery 1983: 287; 1984: 314). The possibility that antiquities have been falsely attributed to the assemblage is significant and it is uncertain whether the assemblage represents a single deposit. Several centuries of activity, however, are implied by the range of material (Raftery 1983: 287) and its deposition was probably votive (Raftery 1984: 314;

1994: 184–5). Although the precise find spot of the assemblage is unknown, deposition probably occurred in an area of bog adjacent to a narrow ridge of higher ground which formed an island-like feature that extended into the surrounding bog (I. Armit pers. comm.).

In the vicinity of Emain Macha (Navan Fort), Co. Armagh, are two sites which provided the focus for ancient deposition. At least one, and probably three other, La Tène curved-horns were recovered from a bog bordering **Loughnashade**, Co. Armagh (Petrie 1833–4: 29; Armstrong 1923: 22–3; Lynn 2003: 70–3, for a discussion of the Loughnashade curved-horns see Chapter 4). Human skulls were also reported to have been discovered at the site (Raftery 1994: 184, 185; Lynn 1997b: 217) and the deposition of the curved-horns and human remains in a watery context adjacent to the early centre of Emain Macha is usually interpreted as a deliberate votive act (Herity and Eogan 1977: 242; Raftery 1994: 184; Lynn 1997b: 216–17). An earlier focus of deposition in the vicinity of Emain Macha is provided by the **'King's Stables'**, Co. Armagh, which is the site of a small artificial pool enclosed by a penannular bank (Lynn 1977; 1988; 1997b: 216). A large number of dog bones, red deer antlers and the facial part of a human skull, as well as two objects of worked bone, late Bronze Age pottery and clay moulds, were recovered during excavation at the site (Lynn 1977: 50–3). The construction of the pool has been radiocarbon dated to *c.*1000–800 BC (Lynn 1977: 53–4; 1997b: 216).

Three assemblages recovered from watery contexts in Scotland are all examples of early Roman ironwork hoards (Piggott 1952–3; Manning 1972: 232–4). The **Blackburn Mill** hoard was discovered by labourers in an old lake bed (Newton 1852; Piggott 1952–3: 3). The assemblage was contained within two cauldrons, suggesting that it had been deposited in a single event while the lake was still in existence (Piggott 1952–3: 7; Manning 1972: 232). The **Carlingwark Loch** hoard was also found contained within a cauldron, suggesting that it too was a single deposit, which was dredged from the bottom of the loch (Anon. 1866–8: 7–9; Stuart 1872–4; Manning 1972: 233), although the discovery of a late Bronze Age sword from the loch suggests that it might be a site of long-term votive significance (Hunter 1997: 117). Carlingwark Loch contains a number of islands including more than one crannog, but no association between the hoard and any of the islands is demonstrable (Piggott 1952–3: 3). The **Eckford** assemblage was recovered from the possible dried-up bed of a loch and, although it was not contained within a vessel, its homogeneous character suggests that it was also a single deposit (Piggott 1952–3: 2; Manning 1972: 234). All three assemblages are conventionally dated to the late first or second century AD and are interpreted as votive deposits (Piggott 1952–3: 4–8; Manning 1972: 232–4). Although of different sizes, the Blackburn Mill, Carlingwark Loch and Eckford assemblages have similar compositions consisting, in addition to the cauldrons, of harness and vehicle fittings, domestic equipment, agricultural and craft tools, and structural fittings (Piggott 1952–3: 20–50, nos. E1–E19, C1–C103, B1–B52, figs. 4–13). The only military equipment included in the assemblages are the sword tips and fragments of chain-mail in the Carlingwark Loch assemblage (Piggott 1952–3: 8, 35, 38–40, nos. C26–C33, C74, fig. 9) and the possible shield boss from Blackburn Mill (Piggott 1952–3:

47, no. B30, fig. 12). Several of the artefacts, such as the sword tips from Carlingwark Loch, were deliberately damaged prior to their deposition (Hunter 1997: 116). Although within the depositional tradition of southern Scotland the hoards are anomalous, the view that the deposition of these hoards should be associated with 'Celtic' auxiliaries from either southern Britain or the Continent (Manning 1972: 242–3) has been questioned (Hutcheson 1997; Hunter 1997: 117).

Another find from Scotland provides an example of the deposition of insular La Tène metalwork deposited in a watery context adjacent to an island. The deliberately dismantled head of the *carnyx* from **Deskford**, Banffshire (Piggott and Daniel 1951: 23, no. 61; Piggott 1959: 24–32, fig. 1.B, pls VIII.a–b, IX.a–c; MacGregor 1976: 87–9, no. 188; Hunter 2001: 78–80), was deposited in the base of a pit cut through a peat bog located in a hollow adjacent to an elongated ridge (Hunter 2001: 82, fig. 2). Recent excavations have revealed evidence of a number of adjacent late Iron Age votive deposits of butchered animal bone and later prehistoric pottery as well as a cache of white quartz pebbles. Excavation also revealed a complex of pits, slots and massive post holes, many of which had been deliberately backfilled, on the southern end of the ridge. Although excavation suggested multi-period use of the site, the majority of the features are later prehistoric in date. Provisional interpretation of the excavation results suggests that the site is not domestic in character, but may form part of a wider ritual complex incorporating massive totems or markers (Hunter 2001: 82–4, figs. 2–4).

Rivers

Large assemblages of prehistoric metalwork have also been recovered from certain British and Irish rivers, most notably the Thames, Witham and Bann. Although these rivers may have formed particular foci of deposition in antiquity, it is also possible that the recovery of large numbers of finds from them, in comparison to other rivers, is due to variations in nineteenth-century river dredging regimes and antiquarian interests. The majority of known archaeological finds from rivers were recovered during dredging operations. This suggests that there may be a bias towards the recovery of large metal items and that other material such as pottery, glass, bones and food remains, may be under-represented in the archaeological record (Fitzpatrick 1984: 179). In contrast to Bronze Age metalwork recovered from rivers such as the Thames (York 2002), the Iron Age finds from British and Irish rivers generally do not show evidence of having been deliberately damaged prior to their deposition, although the discoveries of an Iron Age dagger on the foreshore at Putney, which had been bent several times (Cotton and Wood 1996: 24–5, no. 33, fig. 11) and the La Tène III sword from a dried-up river bed near Thrapston, Northamptonshire, which had been bent once (Megaw 1976), suggests that this was not always the case.

Finds of ornate scabbards, spear ferrules, bridle-bits, bowls and a decorative disc from the **River Bann**, Co. Antrim, are concentrated in two areas around Coleraine and Toome (Jope 1954; Raftery 1984: 315; 1994: 183). Although the finds are largely undamaged their deposition is interpreted as probably being ritual (Raftery 1984: 312; 1994: 183). As well as the Bann, a quantity of La Tène metalwork, including martial items and horse trappings, has been recovered from other Irish rivers including the Shannon, mainly as a result of dredging between Loch Ree and Loch Derg, (Bourke 1996), and the Blackwater (Bourke and Crone 1993).

A large number of prehistoric artefacts, including Neolithic axes and Bronze Age metalwork (Ehrenberg 1980; Bradley 1990: 108), have been recovered from the **River Thames**. Fitzpatrick has summarized the La Tène metalwork from the Thames: weaponry predominates, but harness items, vehicle fittings, tools, brooches, coins and currency bars have also been recovered in significant numbers (Fitzpatrick 1984: 179, fig. 12.1). There is a notable concentration of finds in the Greater London area, although some types, such as swords, are more regularly distributed along the river suggesting that the Greater London concentration may be a result of the more intensive dredging work rather than variations in ancient depositional practice (Fitzpatrick 1984: 179, 181; see also Ehrenberg 1980: 5–7). As well as metalwork a number of mid to late Bronze Age human skulls have been recovered from the Thames (Bradley and Gordon 1988; Bradley 1990: 108–9) and recent excavations at Eton, Berkshire, suggest that human bones, radiocarbon dated from 1300 BC to 200 BC, were deposited on sandbank islands in the middle of the river (Denison 2000). The recovery of a large amount of Romano-British metalwork dating to the first two centuries AD, several Saxon weapons and human skulls from the Walbrook suggests that votive deposition in a riverine context continued in this tributary of the Thames into the Roman period and possibly later (Manning 1972: 249, fn. 148; 1985: 183–4; Merrifield 1995). In comparison to the Thames, the number of Iron Age finds recovered from the **River Witham** in Lincolnshire is relatively small (White 1979; Fitzpatrick 1984: 179–80, fig. 12.2). Items of a martial character dominate the Iron Age metalwork recovered from the Witham (White 1979; Fitzpatrick 1984: 180, fig. 12.2; Parker Pearson and Field 2003a: 162–4). Examples of Neolithic axes and Bronze Age metalwork have also been recovered from the river, although their deposition appears to be concentrated in different areas to the Iron Age finds (Parker Pearson and Field 2003a: 150–6). Although usually interpreted as votive, it has been suggested that the La Tène metalwork deposited in rivers may be associated with funerary rites (Jope 1971: 65; Fell 1990: 60–2; see also Denison 2000).

As well as single finds, rivers occasionally provided a focus for the deposition of assemblages of ancient metalwork. An assemblage consisting of twenty-three items of ironwork, including various tools, cart fittings and a sword, was discovered during gravel extraction at **Waltham Abbey**, Essex (Manning 1972: 231; 1977; 1985: 184). The workmen who discovered the hoard believed that the items had lain together, suggesting the assemblage represents a single deposit. Traces of wood noted at the time suggest it may have been deposited in a box. The hoard was probably deposited either in marshy ground or shallow water at the edge of the River Lea (Manning 1977: 87; 1985: 184). Several of the items had been deliberately damaged prior to their deposition. The two most closely datable finds are the ring-headed linch-pin (Manning 1985: 72, no. H39, pl. 31) and sword (Manning 1977: 89; 1985: 148, no. V1, pl. 71) which have late Iron Age parallels, although there is no reason why the hoard could not have been deposited in the early Roman period (Manning 1972: 231; 1985: 184).

Causeways

Causeways in watery settings also provide a particular focus for deposition in Britain. At **Fiskerton**, Lincolnshire, a causeway, located on the north side of the River Witham, at least 160 metres in length, constructed in 457 BC and periodically repaired for the next 167 years, provided the focus for two separate phases of votive deposition in the late Iron Age and Roman period (Field 1986; Parker Pearson and Field 2003b). The causeway may have led to a sandbank within a braided system of channels (Wilkinson 1987). The Iron Age deposition was probably concentrated in a short period of time, during the late fourth to third centuries BC, after the causeway fell into decay; it consisted of a large number of military items and tools. In addition to the metalwork component, deposition of animal bone, pottery, bone 'gouges', and a small number of amber and jet rings and beads also occurred (Field 1983; Parker Pearson and Field 2003b). Many of the tools show signs of having been used prior to their deposition (Fell 1990: 270), although none of the artefacts had been deliberately damaged (Parker Pearson and Field 2003b: 176). Two human bones radiocarbon dated from early fifth to the second centuries BC were also recovered adjacent to the causeway (Chamberlain 2003; Marshall 2003).

At **Flag Fen**, near Peterborough, Cambridgeshire, the episodic deposition of a large number of deliberately damaged, late Bronze Age to middle Iron Age items of metalwork (Coombs 1992: 506–16; Pryor 1994: 184; Coombs and Pryor 1994; Coombs 2001) took place along a timber 'alignment', or causeway, dendrochronologically dated from the first half of the thirteenth century BC until shortly after 924 BC (Pryor 2001: 421). This 'alignment' extended for a kilometre across a Fenland embayment and incorporated along its length a massive wooden platform which formed an artificial island-like feature (Pryor 1992a: 439, fig. 3; 1994; 2001: 426–7). The majority of the deposited metalwork was of late Bronze Age date and martial in character, although a number of later personal ornaments were also recovered (Coombs 2001: 293–4). In addition to the metalwork, other material deposited beside the 'alignment' included animal bone, pottery, quernstones, wooden artefacts and a single human body (Pryor 1992b: 524; 1994: 181–2). Pryor has interpreted the 'alignment' as both a symbolic dam to keep rising waters back and, perhaps less convincingly, a boundary between the worlds of the living and the ancestors along which small-scale acts of deposition formed a focus of stability during a period of increasing social fragmentation and change (Pryor 2001: 430–1). Dendrochronological work suggests that the 'alignment' went out of use *c.* 900 BC and that the later, Iron Age, deposition must have taken place in the absence of a contemporary structure (Pryor 1992b: 520; 1994: 184). Pryor has discussed several other British causeway sites comparable with Flag Fen (Pryor 2001: 432–3).

Comparable deposits of similar composition but not from
watery contexts in Britain and the Continent

As well as the comparable assemblages deposited in watery contexts, there are several Continental and British sites which contain material deposited in terrestrial contexts whose composition and treatment is analogous with the deposition at Llyn Cerrig Bach. The most important of these are the Gaulish sanctuaries of Brunaux's so-called Belgic type (1988: 11). Although most of the known examples of this type of sanctuary are from northern France it is probable that they also occur throughout most parts of Gaul and beyond (Brunaux 1988: 11). Sanctuaries of this type are defined by large deposits of offerings and sacrificial remains, enclosures which delimit a sacred space, and a central construction within the enclosure which has a ritual function (Brunaux 1988: 12; J. Webster 1995: 458). These sanctuaries appear to have been carefully sited, either at the centre or the periphery of territorial areas (Brunaux 1988: 12). The two best known examples are the excavated sites of Gournay-sur-Aronde, Oise and Ribemont-sur-Ancre, Somme.

At **Gournay-sur-Aronde** the sanctuary was located near the border of three tribes and was situated less than 100 metres from a large pool within the oppidum of the Bellovaci (Brunaux 1988: 13–14; James 1993: 92). The sanctuary had a long history from the fourth or third century BC to the mid first century BC, during which time it underwent several changes (Brunaux 1988: 13–16; James 1993: 93). Many animal bones, some human bones, and about 2000 deliberately damaged weapons were episodically deposited in the enclosing ditch (Brunaux 1988: 15). In the earlier phases of the sanctuary the centre of the enclosure contained ten pits which formed receptacles for the temporary deposition of sacrificed animal bones and artefacts (Brunaux 1988: 15, 28–9; 1991: 364; J. Webster 1995: 455). During the late third or early second century BC all of the pits, except the central one, were infilled and a series of structures were constructed in the centre of the enclosure (Brunaux 1988: 15–16). The sanctuary was carefully closed in the mid first century BC by burning the timber features and infilling both the central pit and enclosure ditch (Brunaux 1988: 14; 1991: 365). During the fourth century AD a small Gallo-Roman temple was built precisely at the centre of the earlier enclosure, suggesting a long-term continuity in cult activity at the site (Brunaux 1988: 14–15; Brunaux 1991: 365). An enclosed sanctuary similar to Gournay was excavated at **Ribemont-sur-Ancre** from which weapons, animal bones, and a large quantity of human bones were recovered (James 1993: 94). Remains of a box-like structure, or 'ossuary', constructed of human bones representing at least two hundred individuals, dating to the second century BC and surrounded by a variety of martial equipment, were located in the corner of the enclosure (Brunaux 1988: 17, 21; J. Webster 1995: 458; Randsborg 1995: 135). A second 'ossuary' at the site has also been excavated (J. Webster 1995: 458). As at Gournay, the enclosing ditch at Ribemont was filled with episodically deposited material, such as weapons and bones, and the entire site was deliberately dismantled in a carefully executed act of closure (Brunaux 1988: 17; J. Webster 1995: 458). In addition to the sanctuaries of Gournay-sur-Aronde and

Ribemont-sur-Ancre, Belgic type sanctuaries are known at Estrées-Saint-Denis, Oise; Saint-Maur, Oise; Vendeuil-Caply, Oise; Morviller-Saint-Saturnin, Somme; Chilly, Somme; Mirebeau, Côte-d'Or; Nanteuil-sur-Aisne, Ardennes; and Mouzon, Ardennes (Brunaux 1988: 11, 21–4; J. Webster 1995: 455, fig. 24.2).

Sites similar to the so-called Belgic type of sanctuary are also known from southern Britain (Brunaux 1988: 24). **Hayling Island**, Hampshire was the site of a sanctuary, dating from the early to mid first century BC, and consisting of a central pit, set within a square enclosure, which was itself set within a rectangular outer enclosure (King and Soffe 1998: 36; 2001: 111–13). From either the late first century BC or the early first century AD the inner enclosure was replaced with a circular structure (King and Soffe 1998: 36–9; 2001: 113–15). The sequence and form of the Hayling Island structures and deposits is similar to that from Gournay-sur-Aronde and other northern French sanctuaries (King and Soffe 1998: 44). The enclosed area and the boundary ditch contained a large number of episodically deposited martial items, harness and vehicle fittings, as well as items of personal adornment, currency bars, glass, amphorae, coins, animal bones and a small number of human bones (Downey *et al.* 1980: 290–4; King and Soffe 1998: 39–42; 2001: 115–17). Many of the items had been deliberately damaged prior to their deposition (King and Soffe 1994: 115; 1998: 43–4; 2001: 119). In *c.* AD 60–70 the circular structure at Hayling Island was replaced with a stone temple largely built on the same plan (Downey *et al.* 1980: 296–9; King and Soffe 1994: 115–16). This coincided with a rapid decline in the deposition of metalwork, such as weapons, harness and vehicle fittings, that could be associated with the warrior element in pre-Roman society (Downey *et al.* 1980: 298; King and Soffe 1994: 116). In addition to Hayling Island, excavation has demonstrated that several other southern British temple sites, such as Gosbecks, Essex (Wait 1985: 157, 387), Harlow, Essex (Wheeler 1928; Anon. 1968; France and Gobel 1985; Haselgrove 1989), Heathrow, Middlesex (Grimes 1948; 1961: 25, fig. 7), Lancing Ring, West Sussex (Bedwin 1981) and Uley, Gloucestershire (Woodward and Leach 1993), have several 'Belgic' sanctuary type features (Brunaux 1988: 24; J. Webster 1995: 458). Manning has speculated that the Harrow Hill, West Sussex enclosure may be another southern British sanctuary site analogous to Gournay-sur-Aronde (1995b).

As well as episodic acts of deposition at sanctuary type sites and single acts of deposition in watery contexts dating to the late Iron Age and early Roman period, there are several British hoards of metalwork which were deposited in single acts in non-watery contexts. These include assemblages incorporating late Iron Age and early Roman material, such as the hoards from **Seven Sisters**, Glamorgan (Allen 1905; Davies and Spratling 1976; Savory 1976a: 62–3, nos. 34.125–34.157, fig. 39) and **Tal-y-Llyn**, Merionethshire (Savory 1964; 1976a: 47–8, 56–7, nos. 16.1–16.20, fig. 12, pls I.ia and III.a), which are conventionally dated to a mid first-century AD horizon, but whose deposition may be significantly later. The metalwork incorporated into these types of assemblage is not usually damaged prior to its deposition. Other hoards of Iron Age metalwork are often deposited in the ramparts or entrances of hillforts, such as the assemblage of agricultural implements, craft tools and a currency bar found in a pit at the rear of the rampart at **South**

Cadbury, Somerset (Alcock 1972: 153–4, pls 59–61; Manning 1972: 230; Barrett 2000: 83, fig. 38) and the deposit of latch-lifters and slide keys recovered from the south-west entrance at South Cadbury (Alcock 1972: pl. 36; Macdonald 2000b: 123, 126, fig. 60). The deposition of torcs manufactured from precious metals in unmarked pits is a rite largely restricted to eastern England and is represented by the deposits of great wealth at **Snettisham**, Norfolk (Clarke 1954; Brailsford 1975b: 55–61; Stead 1991c; Fitzpatrick 1992) and **Ipswich**, Suffolk (Brailsford and Stapley 1972; Brailsford 1975b: 44–52; Stead 1985a: 35, fig. 47). Hoards of currency bars form another particular type of British Iron Age deposit; Hingley has demonstrated that they are variously deposited either in close association with hillfort ramparts and the enclosure ditches of settlements, or in a range of natural locations including bogs, rivers, caves and rocky outcrops (Hingley 1990).

Interpreting votive deposition

The parallels to the Llyn Cerrig Bach assemblage cited above, although they can all be plausibly identified as votive or ritual in character, represent a variety of depositional practices which took place at several different types of site. Within the study of prehistoric votive deposition, both regional and chronological trends are recognizable, suggesting that a single explanatory model for the phenomenon is inappropriate. Even where a rite, such as deposition in a watery context, has a long vogue, the meanings associated with that tradition will probably change through time (Merrifield 1987: 115; Bradley 1990: 192–3). In general there is a trend towards the increasing formalisation of both sacred space and votive depositional practices through time (Bradley 1987: 360; 1990: 171–8). Towards the end of the prehistoric period some depositional rites become more structured, sites of deposition are returned to repeatedly and sometimes formalized into special sacred spaces with buildings. In Britain the earliest evidence of this trend is provided by the site of Flag Fen which becomes a formalized focus for repeated deposition by the late Bronze Age. The trend towards the formalization of sacred space and repeated episodic deposition finds its ultimate expression in the creation and use of the so-called Belgic type sanctuaries in the late Iron Age. Spatial structuring of deposits has been recognized at Fiskerton (Parker Pearson and Field 2003b: 174), Flag Fen (Coombs 2001: 295–8, figs. 10.12–10.20; Pryor 2001: 427), Gournay-sur-Aronde (Brunaux 1988: 8–9, 27, 33; James 1993: 93), Ribemont-sur-Ancre (King and Soffe 1998: 41), Hayling Island (King and Soffe 1994: 115; 1998: 42; 2001: 117–19), Harlow (Haselgrove 1989: 74) and in some of the southern Scandinavian 'booty' deposits (Fabech 1991: 91–2). The circumstances in which the Llyn Cerrig Bach assemblage was recovered makes the spatial structuring of deposits at the site impossible to identify. The reason for the trend towards increasing formalization is not obvious; it has been suggested that it may be linked to the influence of the Roman world but it begins too early for this to be the only explanation (Bradley 1990: 182–9). Despite this trend towards formalization, single acts of deposition at sites which have not apparently become formalized as sacred spaces, such as the deposition of the

Waltham Abbey hoard, still continued throughout the Iron Age and into the early Roman period.

Archaeologists have sought to give meanings to these assemblages which extend beyond their identification as votive deposits made during religious rites. Several alternative, but not necessarily contradictory or mutually exclusive, interpretations have been suggested. These interpretations draw heavily upon both a 'contextual' approach to the archaeological evidence and, frequently unacknowledged, historical and ethnographic analogies. They often focus on the great wealth and high status associations represented by the metalwork deposited in hoards, and view its deposition as an act of conspicuous consumption associated with gaining prestige and legitimating social hierarchies. For example, with reference to the southern Scandinavian so-called booty sacrifices, Fabech has suggested that the deposition of weapons reflects a society in which warfare was regarded as a motivating force permeating political, social and religious spheres of life (1991: 94). The emphasis of courage, fighting skills, leadership qualities and other martial traits within votive rituals contributed to the maintenance and reproduction of such a society. Changes in the composition of 'booty' sacrifices both legitimated and reflected the transformation of southern Scandinavian during the first half of the first millennium AD from a kinship-based society to a series of small kingdoms ruled by martial chiefs (Fabech 1991: 94). Fitzpatrick has placed the deposition of La Tène metalwork in the British Iron Age within a similar social context (1984: 184–6). Drawing upon the comments of Diodorus Siculus (5.27.3–4), Caesar (*De Bello Gallico* 6.17.3–5), Strabo (*Geography* 4.1.13) and Suetonius (*Div Iulius* 54), which emphasize the public nature of votive offerings in Gaul, he suggests that the deposition of military equipment in ritual ceremonies helped to both present as natural and stabilise social relations between an elite preoccupied with wealth and warfare, and their clients (Fitzpatrick 1984: 185–6). Barrett has suggested that such ritual deposition may have reflected the character of the agricultural cycle, which potentially provided a metaphor for political authority in the British Iron Age (1989). Fitzpatrick has also noted that metalwork types deposited at sites such as Llyn Cerrig Bach, La Tène, Gournay-sur-Aronde and Hayling Island are invariably associated with male activities, suggesting that deposits of La Tène metalwork should be viewed as male offerings and emphasizing that Iron Age societies were also structured by gender distinctions (1984: 186–7).

A relationship between votive deposition and boundaries, at both a site and a regional level, has also been recognized. Hingley has noted a regional tradition in the Iron Age of central southern England of currency bar hoards being associated with hillfort ramparts and settlement boundary ditches (1990: 98–103), which he interprets as defining the settlement area of individual families and community groups (1990: 106–7). Deposits of currency bars in natural locations, such as lakes, bogs and rivers, may relate to the boundaries of tribes and other large social groups (Hingley 1990: 108). The siting of both some of the Swiss lake deposits and the so-called Belgic sanctuaries on the periphery of territorial areas has also been noted (de Navarro 1972: 325; Brunaux 1988: 12; Bradley 1990: 178). Such locations on tribal boundaries may have had as much political importance as religious significance. James has speculated that the peripheral locations of sanctuaries, and by extension votive deposition, may be connected with the assertion of a community's rights to certain disputed border lands (James 1993: 93). Alternatively, it may have been that areas on the edge of tribal territories formed a politically neutral place where the gods could oversee inter-tribal relations (James 1993: 93). The location of British sanctuary sites and shrines on territorial boundaries has been noted (Wait 1985: 176), and it has also been suggested that the deposition of metalwork in watery contexts like the River Witham, River Thames and the Fen edge may relate to the border zones of tribal groups (Bradley 1987: 359, fig. 4; Haselgrove 1987a: 137; Bradley 1990: 178–9, fig. 39).

As well as the deposition of items of metalwork which have high status and military associations, large quantities of animal bones were also deposited at a number of the sites cited above. This aspect of Iron Age votive deposition has not been studied in as much detail as the metalwork (Fitzpatrick 1984: 187) and is usually interpreted as either the remains of the sacrifice of animals or the remnants of feasting activity associated with the deposition of the metalwork (for example, Green 1992: 92–127). Influenced by a passage in Gregory of Tours's *In Gloria Confessorum* concerning a Gallo-Roman lakeside festival (Piggott 1952–3: 6, fn. 7; 1968: 77), the deposition of faunal assemblages alongside items of metalwork is conventionally interpreted as representing the domestic production, and personal contribution, of the wider population who form the client base of the social elite (Fitzpatrick 1984: 187; Wait 1985: 153; Bradley 1990: 184; J. L. Davies 1995: 693).

Some, if not all, of these interpretations could be validly applied to the Llyn Cerrig Bach deposit. The circumstances in which the Llyn Cerrig Bach assemblage was recovered hinders a fully 'contextual' approach to interpreting the deposit, but by comparing the assemblage to those from other sites it is possible to offer an interpretation of the character of the site.

The character of deposition at Llyn Cerrig Bach

The possible early phase of animal bone deposition and the main phase of deposition of metalwork of martial character at Llyn Cerrig Bach are most obviously paralleled by the comparable examples of deposition in watery contexts noted above. Of these, episodic deposition also occurred at Hjortspring Kobbel, Nydam, Fiskerton and Flag Fen and may have occurred at La Tène, Cornaux, Port Nidau and Lisnacrogher; the deliberate damaging of artefacts prior to their deposition took place at La Tène, Port Nidau, Hjortspring Kobbel, Nydam, Flag Fen, Carlingwark Loch, Blackburn Mill and Waltham Abbey; and the deposition of animal bone occurred at La Tène, Cornaux, Hjortspring Kobbel, Nydam, the 'King's Stables', Fiskerton, Flag Fen, Carlingwark Loch and Blackburn Mill. The comparable sites cited above do not form a uniform phenomenon, but rather represent several distinct regional and chronological traditions of deposition in a watery context. As a site Llyn Cerrig Bach shares some defining characteristics with several of these different groups. For example, Llyn Cerrig Bach is similar to the southern Scandinavian sites of Hjortspring Kobbel, Krogsbølle and Nydam in being sited near to the coast, while it is similar to La Tène, Cornaux, Fiskerton, Flag Fen and possibly Lisnacrogher in being associated with an island or island-like feature. The possible early phase of animal bone deposition at Llyn Cerrig Bach is paralleled by the earlier episodes of cattle bone deposition in the bog at Hjortspring Kobbel. In addition to those assemblages deposited in watery contexts, the treatment and character of the artefactual assemblage from Llyn Cerrig Bach is also comparable to those associated with so-called Belgic sanctuary type sites. At Gournay-sur-Aronde, Ribemont-sur-Ancre and Hayling Island deposition was also episodic, of a martial character, involved the deliberate damaging of artefacts, and was accompanied by the deposition of large numbers of animal and human bone.

Votive deposition in watery contexts associated with either islands or artificial island-like features, which are connected to dryland by causeways, is increasingly being recognized as a phenomenon of ancient depositional practice (M. Parker Pearson pers. comm.). There is evidence from Classical authors to suggest that islands were favoured as cult sites during the Iron Age in western Europe (J. Webster 1995: 451). Deposition at Llyn Cerrig Bach was probably associated with an island, which was possibly connected to dryland by a causeway; this arrangement is arguably paralleled at Flag Fen, Fiskerton, La Tène and Cornaux, and may also be paralleled at Port Nidau, Krogsbølle, Deskford and Lisnnacrogher. King and Soffe suggest that the siting of the Hayling Island sanctuary on an island was significant (1998: 44) and the pre-temple phase of deposition at Harlow, as represented by gold staters and quarter staters, may have occurred when the hillock the site is located on was surrounded by a relict meander of the River Stort which had become an oxbow lake (Haselgrove 1987a: 85). The parallels with Hayling Island and Harlow suggest that Llyn Cerrig Bach, and by extension other sites of deposition in watery contexts associated with islands, can profitably be considered as analogous to sanctuary type sites. The character of the Llyn Cerrig Bach assemblage is similar to the deposits excavated at sanctuaries like Gournay-sur-Aronde, Ribemont-sur-Ancre and Hayling Island. It is the product of several episodic acts of deposition which involved both animal bone and metalwork, the character of the metalwork assemblage is overwhelmingly martial and includes many items that were deliberately damaged prior to their deposition. Brunaux has suggested that lake sites, such as La Tène, are natural sanctuaries without enclosure (Brunaux 1988: 43), however, it may be more accurate to suggest that, for sites like La Tène and Llyn Cerrig Bach, islands formed the sanctuary and that the surrounding lake formed the enclosure (J. Webster has noted that islands are physically bounded by water which conceptually relates them to other forms of enclosure, cf. 1995: 451). The causeways which connect these islands to dryland may be analogous to the entrances of 'Belgic' type sanctuaries and hence form a particular focus for depositional activity.

If identifying Llyn Cerrig Bach as a natural form of sanctuary is problematic, then identifying the character of the religious specialists who practised at the site is even more speculative. In his account of the assemblage, Fox suggested that the wealth represented by the metalwork deposited at Llyn Cerrig Bach was accrued by druids through the provision of magical incantations, interpretation of omens, political advice and prophecy (1947a: 70–1). The structure of Iron Age societies in Britain and Gaul, and the role of the druids within those socio-political structures, is poorly understood. Fox considered the importance and influence of the druidical community of Anglesey to be historically amply attested (1947a: 70), however, the only ancient references to the druids on Anglesey are made by Tacitus (*Annals* 14.30) and he does not state that Anglesey was a particular centre of druidical power (Lynch 1970: 277, fn. 176). Fox's belief in the pre-eminence of the druidical community on Anglesey probably owes more to the Romanticism of Henry Rowlands's *Mona Antiqua Reftaurata* (1723) than the literary evidence (Lynch 1970: 277, fn. 176). There has been a tendency to avoid incorporating the druids into archaeological accounts of late Iron Age society, partly due to the difficulties in relating the literary evidence to the archaeological record (Bradley 1990: 187; J. Webster 1999: 6). The rhetorical paradigms within which Classical authors wrote involved quoting earlier sources as legitimating devices and this has resulted in an artificial conservatism and consistency in descriptions of Iron Age societies (Brunaux 1988: 66; Rankin 1995: 32). Ironically, it is only through the adoption and maintenance of this style of writing that several of the most used sources, such as Posidonius's discussion of the 'Celts', are known, as the original texts are lost and all that survives are the later Classical quotations. This conservatism was reinforced by the Classical philosophical perspective that viewed society as static and therefore essentially timeless (Champion 1985: 16). Most of the important accounts of the druids are arguably based on the now lost writings of Posidonius who travelled in Gaul during the second century BC (Piggott 1968: 96–8; Lynch 1970: 277; but see Nash 1976). The degree to which this apparent dependence on an earlier source means that the surviving accounts of the druids are anachronistic is a point which is as debatable as it is important. Recent studies of the druids have alternatively suggested that their influence in late Iron Age Gaul and Britain was either already waning prior to the Gallic War (Creighton 1995) or that it diminished only as a direct result of the Roman Conquest (J. Webster 1999). These different interpretations largely depend on whether Caesar's account of the druids, which is restricted to an atypical ethnographic section of the sixth book of the *De Bello Gallico* (6.13–14, 6.16.1–3, 6.18.1), is viewed as anachronistic or not. Graham Webster's comment that Tacitus's account of the altars slaked with blood on Anglesey (*Annals* 14.30) has a distinct echo of Lucan's literary account of the civil war (G. Webster 1986: 26; Lucan, *Pharsalia* I.450–8) suggests that both authors may have used 'stock' clichés when writing about barbarian religious practices. Although it is not unreasonable to suggest that druids were amongst the religious specialists practising in late Iron Age Anglesey, that, as is conventionally considered to be the case, they oversaw the rites at Llyn Cerrig Bach is not necessarily the only interpretation supported by the Classical sources. Tacitus's description of the Roman attack on Anglesey records that as well as the conventional male druids calling down curses there were also witch-like women who opposed the Roman army (*Annals* 14.30). Tacitus describes these women as rushing through the ranks of the enemy soldiers in wild disorder, dressed in black with their hair dishevelled, brandishing flaming torches and, in another literary allusion, he compares them, in both their appearance and their rage, to the Furies (*Annals* 14.30). There is evidence from Classical authors to suggest that cult sites associated with islands may have had a specific link with female religious specialists (J. Webster 1995: 451). In a passage quoted by Strabo, Posidonius describes a Gallic temple on a small island off the mouth of the Loire River served by female religious specialists (*Geography* 4.4.6), and Mela refers to virgin priestesses on the island of Sena in Brittany (*De Chorographia* 3.48). With the recognition of the association between the island and deposition at Llyn Cerrig Bach, perhaps it is possible to see a context appearing for where the female religious specialists described by Tacitus may have practised their rites and officiated at ceremonies involving the deposition of animal bone and metalwork.

The wealth represented by just the recovered proportion of the Llyn Cerrig Bach assemblage is considerable, and it is often taken to indicate that the lake had a religious significance which extended throughout large parts of the British Isles during the Iron Age (for example, Lynch 1970: 277; Savory 1976a: 29; Green 1986: 143). Although the exact proportion of items in the assemblage which were imported from outside of north-west Wales is unknown, the number of imported items is likely to be significant (see Chapter 6). The mechanism by which these imported items became available for deposition in Anglesey was a subject which dominated Fox's discussion of the assemblage (1947a: 67–72). The current interpretative emphasis on the deposition of metalwork as an act which legitimated, and presented as natural, social hierarchies favours the view that imported metalwork at Llyn Cerrig Bach was acquired as prestigious items by the local secular or religious elite, through a mechanism of high-status gift exchange, and subsequently sacrificed by them. Such an interpretative view would not necessitate Llyn Cerrig Bach having anything greater than a regional religious significance, despite the presence of imported items in the assemblage. The alternative possibility, that the site at Llyn Cerrig Bach had an importance which drew individuals to it for the purpose of sacrifice from outside north Wales, cannot easily be dismissed. The study of Romano-Gallic religious practice suggests that pilgrimage may have been practised during the pre-Conquest period in Gaul (Aldhouse Green 2000: 17) and this suggests the possibility that imported items, such as the Irish bridle-bit (No. 23), may have been brought directly to Llyn Cerrig Bach by individuals, from the area in which they were manufactured, with the intention that they would sacrifice them personally.

In comparing and contrasting the Blackburn Mill, Carlingwark Loch and Eckford hoards with the Llyn Cerrig Bach assemblage, Piggott noted their largely non-martial character and suggested that this demonstrated that the phrase 'pax Romana' was not an empty one (Piggott 1952–3: 9). The absence of weaponry from Romano-British votive deposits has been noted elsewhere (Haselgrove 1987a: 135; 1989: 84; Bradley 1990: 186) and excavation has demonstrated that the post-Conquest phases of deposition at Hayling Island were also non-military in character (Downey *et al.* 1980: 298; King and Soffe 1994: 116). It is notable that the demonstrably later material in the Llyn Cerrig Bach assemblage, such as the coiled bindings (Nos. 35–43) and the 'casket' ornament (Nos. 50–5), which represents the final phase of deposition at the site is also non-military in character.

CONCLUDING REMARKS

Although it is not possible to demonstrate unequivocally whether this late phase of deposition continued after the two Roman invasions of Anglesey, its non-martial character is consistent with Romano-British votive depositional practices and is paralleled at sites, such as Hayling Island, where deposition continued into the early Roman period. The suggestion that deposition may have continued into the Roman period at Llyn Cerrig Bach contradicts the conventional interpretative gloss placed on the historical account of the destruction of religious sites by Paulinus following the invasion of Anglesey (Tacitus *Annals*, 14.30), however, it is unlikely that the Romans would have had any interest in stopping the native British practice of votive deposition in watery contexts (W. H. Manning pers. comm.). With reference to early post-Conquest Gaul, Haselgrove has suggested that continued investment in religious sanctuaries was permitted, if not sanctioned, by the Romans in order to maintain the stability of indigenous elites and provide a mechanism for the assimilation of native and Roman religious ideologies (Haselgrove 1987b: 115–16). It is not unreasonable to suggest that such a policy may have been followed, if only for a limited period of time, at Llyn Cerrig Bach in post-Conquest Anglesey.

Appendix 1
Tabulated List and Concordance Table for the Llyn Cerrig Bach Assemblage

The known contents of the Llyn Cerrig Bach assemblage are listed here in a table which provides a concordance between the present volume, Fox's report on the assemblage (1947a), Savory's *Guide Catalogue of the Early Iron Age Collections* of the National Museum of Wales (1976a) and the artefacts' accession numbers. The majority of the assemblage forms part of the collections of the National Museum of Wales (NMW). A further four pieces of ironwork, which were retained in private ownership following their discovery, have subsequently been donated to Oriel Ynys Môn, Llangefni, Anglesey. These include a spearhead (Lynch 1969–70; 1991: 379, fn. 33), two unpublished nave hoops and an unpublished bridle-bit. It is possible that other items from the assemblage still remain in private ownership.

Several aspects of the assemblage's curation require explanation. First, in addition to the complete tyre (Fox 1947a: no. 100; Savory 1976a: no. 18.34) and two modern examples (National Museum of Wales accession nos. 44.295.1(B) and 44.295.2(A)), sixty-three tyre fragments were recovered from Llyn Cerrig Bach. Since Fox did not record the dimensions of all of the tyre fragments, and a number of them are no longer labelled or marked, it is not possible to identify thirteen of the fragments. The unidentified tyre fragments are marked in red in the table. Despite these problems, only one of the tyre fragments can actually be considered missing as the National Museum of Wales have twelve unmarked fragments which cannot be matched with Fox's records. These twelve unmarked tyre fragments have been reaccessioned (accession nos. 2002.41/H1–12). Secondly, of the small sample of the animal bone dredged up with the peat that contained the metalwork (Hyde 1947; see Chapter 6), only eight bones now remain in the collections of the National Museum of Wales (accession nos. 44.32.Z.1–8). The location of the remainder of the animal bones studied by Hyde is unknown.

Thirdly, a confusion has entered the literature concerning the number of swords in the assemblage. Two of the sword fragments noted by Savory (1976a: nos. 17.92–17.93) are in fact fragments of one of the other sword blades (Fox 1947a: no. 7; Savory 1976a: no. 17.7) which Savory mistakenly recorded twice (G. Darbyshire pers. comm.). Fourthly, the four previously unpublished copper alloy sheet fragments (Nos. 32-4 and accession no. 2002.40H/2), although not detailed in any of the surviving early documentation relating to the assemblage, are recorded in the current index to the National Museum of Wales's Prehistoric Reserve Collection. Consequently, it is not unreasonable to assume they were collected at the same time as the rest of the assemblage. Presumably, Fox failed to publish them either because they arrived in Cardiff too late to be included in his final report, or because their fragmented character and small size made their identification and interpretation difficult.

Finally, a number of items accessioned as part of the assemblage are either certainly, or possibly, of recent date. These items were largely recovered by workmen towards the end of the war, in some cases three or four years after the assemblage was identified, suggesting that by this date either the integrity of the spread of material on the airfield had become compromised or its precise location had been forgotten. The definitely modern finds are a copper alloy sheet fragment (National Museum of Wales accession no. 2002.40H/2), two complete iron tyres (National Museum of Wales accession nos. 44.295.1B and 44.295.2A), a triangular-shaped iron fitting (Savory 1976a: no. 22.1) and an iron gib-hank (Savory 1976a: no. 22.2). The possibly modern items include an iron socketed spatulate tool of unknown purpose (Fox 1947a: addenda no. 3; Savory 1976a: no. 20.2); two iron strip fragments (Fox 1947a: no. 138; Savory 1976a: nos. 19.7, 22.4); and a riveted iron fitting (Fox 1947a: addenda no. 5; Savory 1976a: no. 20.4). In addition, the unpublished bridle-bit in Oriel Ynys Môn may possibly be medieval or post-medieval in date (see Chapter 3). For the sake of completeness these items have been included in the tabulated list of finds from the assemblage.

TABLE 17: Concordance table of the known contents of the Llyn Cerrig Bach assemblage

Catal. no.	Description	Fox 1947a	Savory 1976a	Material	Location	Accession	Comments
1	Terret	no. 44	no. 17.44	Cu alloy/Fe	NMW	44.32.44	
2	Terret	no. 45	no. 17.45	Cu alloy	NMW	44.32.45	
3	Terret	no. 46	no. 17.46	Cu alloy	NMW	44.32.46	
4	Nave hoop	no. 35	no. 17.35	Cu alloy	NMW	44.32.35	
5	Nave hoop	no. 36	no. 17.36	Cu alloy	NMW	44.32.36	
6	Nave hoop	no. 38	no. 17.38	Cu alloy	NMW	44.32.38	
7	Nave hoop	no. 37	no. 17.37	Cu alloy	NMW	44.32.37	
8	'Vase-headed' linch-pin	no. 42	no. 17.42	Cu alloy/Fe	NMW	44.32.42	
9	Ring	no. 136	no. 18.11	Cu alloy	NMW	44.294.11	
10	Three-link bridle bit	no. 50	no. 17.50	Cu alloy	NMW	44.32.50	
11	Asymmetrical three-link bridle-bit	no. 51	no. 17.51	Cu alloy	NMW	44.32.51	
12	Three-link bridle bit	no. 47	no. 17.47	Cu alloy/Fe	NMW	44.32.47	
13	Three-link bridle bit	no. 48	no. 17.48	Cu alloy/Fe	NMW	44.32.48	
14	Three-link bridle bit	no. 49	no. 17.49	Cu alloy/Fe	NMW	44.32.49i	
15	Three-link bridle bit	no. 49	no. 17.49	Cu alloy/Fe	NMW	44.32.49ii	
16	Rein-ring	no. 52	no. 17.52	Cu alloy	NMW	44.32.52	
17	Rein-ring	no. 53	no. 17.53	Cu alloy	NMW	44.32.53	
18	Rein-ring	no. 54	no. 17.54	Cu alloy	NMW	44.32.54	
19	Rein-ring	no. 86	no. 17.86	Cu alloy	NMW	44.32.86	
20	Rein-ring	no. 129	no. 18.10	Cu alloy	NMW	44.294.10	
21	Ring	no. 84	no. 17.84	Cu alloy/Fe	NMW	44.32.84	
22	Two-link bridle-bit	no. 58	no. 17.58	Cu alloy	NMW	44.32.58	
23	Three-link bridle bit	no. 55	no. 17.55	Cu alloy	NMW	44.32.55	
24	Globular cauldron fragment	no. 76	no. 17.76	Cu alloy	NMW	44.32.76i	
25	Globular cauldron fragment	no. 76	no. 17.76	Cu alloy	NMW	44.32.76ii	
26	Hemispherical cauldron fragment	no. 77	no. 17.77	Cu alloy	NMW	44.32.77	
27	Scabbard mouth	no. 10	no. 17.10	Cu alloy	NMW	44.32.10	
28	Probable scabbard binding	no. 11	no. 17.11	Cu alloy	NMW	44.32.11	
29	Pommel	no. 12	no. 17.12	Cu alloy/Fe	NMW	44.32.12	
30	Cylindrical mount	no. 88	no. 17.88	Cu alloy	NMW	44.32.88	

31	'Trumpet' fragment	no. 74	no. 17.74	Cu alloy	NMW	44.32.74	
32	Sheet fragment	N/A	N/A	Cu alloy	NMW	2002.40H/1	
–	Sheet fragment	N/A	N/A	Cu alloy	NMW	2002.40H/2	Modern
33	Sheet fragment	N/A	N/A	Cu alloy	NMW	2002.40H/3	
34	Sheet fragment	N/A	N/A	Cu alloy	NMW	2002.40H/4	
35	Coiled decorative strip	no. 68	no. 17.68	Cu alloy	NMW	44.32.68	
36	Coiled decorative strip	no. 91	no. 17.91	Cu alloy	NMW	44.32.91	
37	Coiled decorative strip	no. 67	no. 17.67	Cu alloy	NMW	44.32.67	
38	Coiled decorative strip	no. 71	no. 17.71	Cu alloy	NMW	44.32.71	
39	Coiled decorative strip	no. 133	no. 18.34	Cu alloy	NMW	44.294.34	
40	Coiled decorative strip	no. 69	no. 17.69	Cu alloy	NMW	44.32.69	
41	Coiled decorative strip	no. 70	no. 17.70	Cu alloy	NMW	44.32.70	
42	Coiled decorative strip	no. 72	no. 17.72	Cu alloy	NMW	44.32.72	
43	Coiled decorative strip	no. 73	no. 17.73	Cu alloy	NMW	44.32.73	
44	Bean-shaped plaque	no. 17	no. 17.17	Cu alloy	NMW	44.32.17	
45	Bean-shaped plaque	no. 18	no. 17.18	Cu alloy	NMW	44.32.18	
46	Decorated curved plate	no. 87	no. 17.87	Cu alloy	NMW	44.32.87	
47	Crescentic decorative mount	no. 75	no. 17.75	Cu alloy	NMW	44.32.75	
48	Shield boss mount	no. 98	no. 18.31	Cu alloy	NMW	44.294.31	
49	So-called horn-cap	no. 41	no. 17.41	Cu alloy	NMW	44.32.41	
50	'Square' plaque	no. 78	no. 17.78	Cu alloy	NMW	44.32.78	
51	'Square' plaque	no. 79	no. 17.79	Cu alloy	NMW	44.32.79	
52	'Square' plaque	no. 134	no. 18.12	Cu alloy	NMW	44.294.12	
53	Rectangular plaque	no. 80	no. 17.80	Cu alloy	NMW	44.32.80	
54	Rectangular plaque	no. 81	no. 17.81	Cu alloy	NMW	44.32.81	
55	'Tri-disc' plaque	no. 135	no. 18.13	Cu alloy	NMW	44.294.13	
–	Sword	no. 1	no. 17.1	Fe	NMW	44.32.1	
–	Sword	no. 2	no. 17.2	Fe	NMW	44.32.2	
–	Sword	no. 3	no. 17.3	Fe	NMW	44.32.3	
–	Sword	no. 4	no. 17.4	Fe	NMW	44.32.4	
–	Sword	no. 5	no. 17.5	Fe	NMW	44.32.5	
–	Sword	no. 6	no. 17.6	Fe	NMW	44.32.6	
–	Sword	no. 7	no. 17.7	Fe	NMW	44.32.7	Reaccessioned as 44.32.92 and 44.32.93

Catal. no.	Description	Fox 1947a	Savory 1976a	Material	Location	Accession	Comments
–	Sword	no. 92	no. 18.1	Fe	NMW	44.294.1	
–	Sword	no. 93	no. 18.2	Fe	NMW	44.294.2	
–	Sword	no. 94	no. 18.3	Fe	NMW	44.294.3	
–	Sword	no. 95	no. 19.1	Fe	NMW	45.29.1	
–	Scabbard	no. 8	no. 17.8	Fe	NMW	44.32.8	
–	Scabbard	no. 9	no. 17.9	Fe	NMW	44.32.9	
–	Dagger	addenda 1	no. 20.1	Fe	NMW	46.320.1	
–	Spearhead	no. 13	no. 17.13	Fe	NMW	44.32.13	
–	Spearhead	no. 14	no. 17.14	Fe	NMW	44.32.14	
–	Spearhead	no. 15	no. 17.15	Fe	NMW	44.32.15	
–	Spearhead	no. 16	no. 17.16	Fe	NMW	44.32.16	
–	Spearhead	no. 96	no. 18.4	Fe	NMW	44.294.4	
–	Spearhead	addenda 2	no. 21	Fe	NMW	47.19	
–	Spearhead	N/A	N/A	Fe	Oriel Ynys Môn	N/A	Lynch 1969–70; Lynch 1991: 379, fn.33
–	Spearhead	no. 97	no. 19.3	Fe	NMW	45.29.3	
–	Tyre	no. 100	no. 19.5	Fe	NMW	45.29.5	
–	Tyre	N/A	N/A	Fe	NMW	44.295.1(B)	Modern
–	Tyre	N/A	N/A	Fe	NMW	44.295.2(A)	Modern
–	Tyre fragment	no. 19	no. 17.19	Fe	NMW	44.32.19	
–	Tyre fragment	no. 20	no. 17.2	Fe	NMW	44.32.20	
–	Tyre fragment	no. 20A	no. 17.20A	Fe	NMW	44.32.20A	
–	Tyre fragment	no. 21	no. 17.21	Fe	NMW	44.32.21	
–	Tyre fragment	no. 22	no. 17.22	Fe	NMW	44.32.22	
–	Tyre fragment	no. 23	no. 17.23	Fe	NMW	44.32.23	
–	Tyre fragment	no. 24	no. 17.24	Fe	NMW	44.32.24	
–	Tyre fragment	no. 25	no. 17.25	Fe	NMW	44.32.25	
–	Tyre fragment	no. 26	no. 17.26	Fe	NMW	44.32.26	
–	Tyre fragment	no. 27	no. 17.27	Fe	NMW	44.32.27	
–	Tyre fragment	no. 28A	no. 17.28A	Fe	NMW	44.32.28A	
–	Tyre fragment	no. 28B	no. 17.28B	Fe	NMW	44.32.28B	

Tyre fragment	—	no. 29	no. 17.29	Fe	NMW	44.32.29
Tyre fragment	—	no. 30	no. 17.3	Fe	NMW	44.32.30
Tyre fragment	—	no. 31	no. 17.31	Fe	NMW	44.32.31
Tyre fragment	—	no. 32	no. 17.32	Fe	NMW	44.32.32
Tyre fragment	—	no. 33	no. 17.33	Fe	NMW	44.32.33
Tyre fragment	—	no. 34A	no. 17.34A	Fe	NMW	44.32.34A
Tyre fragment	—	no. 34B	no. 17.34B	Fe	NMW	44.32.34B
Tyre fragment	—	no. 34C	no. 17.34C	Fe	NMW	44.32.34C
Tyre fragment	—	no. 90A	no. 17.90A	Fe	NMW	44.32.90A
Tyre fragment	—	no. 90B	no. 17.90B	Fe	NMW	44.32.90B
Tyre fragment	—	no. 90C	no. 17.90C	Fe	NMW	44.32.90C
Tyre fragment	—	no. 90D	no. 17.90D	Fe	NMW	44.32.90D
Tyre fragment	—	no. 90E	no. 17.90E	Fe	NMW	44.32.90E
Tyre fragment	—	no. 90F	no. 17.90F	Fe	NMW	44.32.90F
Tyre fragment	—	no. 90G	no. 17.90G	Fe	NMW	44.32.90G
Tyre fragment	—	no. 90H	no. 17.90H	Fe	NMW	44.32.90H
Tyre fragment	—	no. 90I	no. 17.90I	Fe	NMW	44.32.90I
Tyre fragment	—	no. 90J	no. 17.90J	Fe	NMW	44.32.90J
Tyre fragment	—	no. 90K	no. 17.90K	Fe	NMW	44.32.90K
Tyre fragment	—	no. 90L	no. 17.90L	Fe	NMW	44.32.90L
Tyre fragment	—	no. 90M	no. 17.90M	Fe	NMW	44.32.90M
Tyre fragment	—	no. 123	no. 18.14	Fe	NMW	44.294.14
Tyre fragment	—	no. 108A	no. 18.15A	Fe	NMW	44.294.15A
Tyre fragment	—	no. 108B	no. 18.15B	Fe	NMW	44.294.15B
Tyre fragment	—	no. 122	no. 18.16	Fe	NMW	44.294.16
Tyre fragment	—	no. 112A	no. 18.17A	Fe	NMW	44.294.17A
Tyre fragment	—	no. 112B	no. 18.17B	Fe	NMW	44.294.17B
Tyre fragment	—	no. 112C	no. 18.17C	Fe	NMW	44.294.17C
Tyre fragment	—	no. 109	no. 18.18	Fe	NMW	44.294.18
Tyre fragment	—	no. 113	no. 18.19	Fe	NMW	44.294.19
Tyre fragment	—	no. 101A	no. 18.20A	Fe	NMW	44.294.20A
Tyre fragment	—	no. 101B	no. 18.20B	Fe	NMW	44.294.20B
Tyre fragment	—	no. 101C	no. 18.20C	Fe	NMW	44.294.20C
Tyre fragment	—	no. 110	no. 18.21	Fe	NMW	44.294.21

Catal. no.	Description	Fox 1947a	Savory 1976a	Material	Location	Accession	Comments
–	Tyre fragment	no. 114	no. 18.22	Fe	NMW	44.294.22	
–	Tyre fragment	no. 102	no. 18.23	Fe	NMW	44.294.23	
–	Tyre fragment	no. 103A	no. 18.24A	Fe	NMW	44.294.24A	
–	Tyre fragment	no. 103B	no. 18.24B	Fe	NMW	44.294.24B	
–	Tyre fragment	no. 115	no. 18.25	Fe	NMW	44.294.25	
–	Tyre fragment	no. 104	no. 18.26	Fe	NMW	44.294.26	
–	Tyre fragment	no. 116	no. 18.27	Fe	NMW	44.294.27	
–	Tyre fragment	no. 111	no. 18.28	Fe	NMW	44.294.28	
–	Tyre fragment	no. 105	no. 18.29	Fe	NMW	44.294.29	
–	Tyre fragment	no. 117	no. 18.30A	Fe	NMW	44.294.30A	
–	Tyre fragment	no. 118	no. 18.30B	Fe	NMW	44.294.30B	
–	Tyre fragment	no. 119	no. 18.30C	Fe	NMW	44.294.30C	
–	Tyre fragment	no. 120	no. 18.30D	Fe	NMW	44.294.30D	
–	Tyre fragment	no. 121	no. 18.30E	Fe	NMW	44.294.30E	
–	Tyre fragment	no. 106	no. 18.30F	Fe	NMW	44.294.30F	
–	Tyre fragment	no. 124	no. 18.30G	Fe	NMW	44.294.30G	
–	Tyre fragment	no. 107	no. 19.6	Fe	NMW	45.29.6	
–	Nave hoop	no. 39	no. 17.39	Fe	NMW	44.32.39	
–	Nave hoop	no. 40	no. 17.40	Fe	NMW	44.32.40	
–	Nave hoop	no. 125	no. 18.5	Fe	NMW	44.294.5	
–	Nave hoop	no. 126	no. 18.6	Fe	NMW	44.294.6	
–	Nave hoop	no. 127	no. 18.7	Fe	NMW	44.294.7	
–	Nave hoop	N/A	N/A	Fe	Oriel Ynys Môn	N/A	
–	Nave hoop	N/A	N/A	Fe	Oriel Ynys Môn	N/A	
–	Ring-headed linch-pin	no. 43	no. 17.43	Fe	NMW	44.32.43	
–	Draught pole sheath	no. 99	no. 18.8	Wood/Fe	NMW	44.294.8	
–	Bridle-bit	no. 56	no. 17.56	Fe	NMW	44.32.56	
–	Bridle-bit	no. 57	no. 17.57	Fe	NMW	44.32.57	
–	Bridle bit	no. 128	no. 18.9	Fe	NMW	44.294.9	

196

CONCORDANCE TABLE

	N/A	N/A	Fe	Oriel Ynys Môn	N/A	Possibly medieval
Bridle-bit						
Ring (possible bridle-bit centre link)	no. 83	no. 17.83	Fe	NMW	44.32.83	
Gang-chain	no. 59	no. 17.59	Fe	NMW	44.32.59	
Gang-chain	no. 60	no. 17.60	Fe	NMW	44.32.60	
Currency bar	no. 61	no. 17.61	Fe	NMW	44.32.61	
Currency bar	no. 62	no. 17.62	Fe	NMW	44.32.62	
Currency bar	no. 63	no. 17.63	Fe	NMW	44.32.63	
Currency bar	no. 64	no. 17.64	Fe	NMW	44.32.64	
Currency bar	no. 130	no. 19.2	Fe	NMW	45.29.2	
Tongs	no. 131	no. 18.32	Fe	NMW	44.294.32	
Tongs	no. 132	nos.18.33 and 19.4	Fe	NMW	44.294.33 and 45.29.4	
Sickle	no. 65	no. 17.65	Fe	NMW	44.32.65	
Reaping hook	N/A	no. 22.3	Fe	NMW	47.196.3	
Hook fragment	no. 66	no. 17.66	Fe	NMW	44.32.66	
Iron ring with attached links	no. 85	no. 17.85	Fe	NMW	44.32.85	
Looped fitting	no. 89	no. 17.89	Fe	NMW	44.32.89	
Bar fragment	no. 82	no. 17.82	Fe	NMW	44.32.82	
Bar fragment	no. 137	no. 18.35	Fe	NMW	44.294.35	
Bent and looped bar	addenda 4	no. 20.3	Fe	NMW	46.320.3	
Socketed spatulate tool	addenda 3	no. 20.2	Fe	NMW	46.320.2	Possibly modern
Strip fragment	no. 138	no. 19.7	Fe	NMW	45.29.7	Possibly modern
Strip fragment	N/A	no. 22.4	Fe	NMW	47.196.4	Possibly modern
Riveted fitting	addenda 5	no. 20.4	Fe	NMW	46.320.4	Possibly modern
Triangular-shaped fitting	N/A	no. 22.1	Fe	NMW	47.196.1	Modern
Gib-hank	N/A	no. 22.2	Fe	NMW	47.196.2	Modern
ox or sheep horncore	page 97	N/A	Animal bone	NMW	44.32.Z.1	
ox or sheep horncore	page 97	N/A	Animal bone	NMW	44.32.Z.2	2345 ± 50 BP (800 BC–200 BC)
ox radius (left)	page 97	N/A	Animal bone	NMW	44.32.Z.3	
sheep or goat mandible	page 97	N/A	Animal bone	NMW	44.32.Z.4	2245 ± 50 BP (400 BC–180 BC)

Catal. no.	Description	Fox 1947a	Savory 1976a	Material	Location	Accession	Comments
–	sheep or goat radius	page 97	N/A	Animal bone	NMW	44.32.Z.5	
–	canid mandible	page 97	N/A	Animal bone	NMW	44.32.Z.6	2075 ± 50 BP (350 BC–AD 60)
–	ox metatarsal	page 97	N/A	Animal bone	NMW	44.32.Z.7	
–	sheep or goat metatarsol	page 97	N/A	Animal bone	NMW	44.32.Z.8	

Appendix 2
Metallurgical Analysis of the Copper Alloy Artefacts in the Llyn Cerrig Bach Assemblage

KILIAN ANHEUSER, MARY DAVIS AND PHILIP MACDONALD

As part of the project to re-evaluate the Llyn Cerrig Bach assemblage, chemical analysis of fifty-four samples taken from forty-two of the copper alloy artefacts was conducted. The principal aim of this analytical programme was to assist in the resolution of the chronological problems raised by the typological study of the assemblage. The attempt to provenance individual artefacts from their metallurgical composition was not considered a valid approach to the interpretation of the analytical data, however, consideration was given to an empirical study of the diversity of alloys represented in the assemblage (see Chapter 6).

A total of twenty drill samples were taken from cast objects in the assemblage using a 1 mm drill after removal of corrosion products from the surface in the drilled area (sample nos. 1–20). Most of these samples consisted of fine powder. A proportion of the material from each drilled sample was dissolved in nitric acid for inductively coupled plasma-mass spectrometry (ICPMS) with a Perkin Elmer Elan 5000 ICPMS at the Department of Earth Sciences, Cardiff University. The following twelve elements were analysed: Cu, Sn, Zn, As, Sb, Bi, Fe, Co, Ni, Ag, Au and Pb.

Samples from thirty-four sheet artefacts were taken in the form of small clippings (typical size 1 mm^2, sample nos. 21–54). These were mounted in epoxy resin and a polished cross-section was carbon-coated and analysed using the CamScan MaXim 2040 scanning electron microscope (SEM) with a MicroSpec wavelength-dispersive detector at the School of History and Archaeology, Cardiff University. The following analytical conditions were used: beam energy 20 keV, beam current 20nA, 60s total counting time per element. The following thirteen elements were included in the analysis: S, Fe, Co, Ni, Cu and Zn (Kα lines), As, Ag, Sn and Sb (Lα), Au, Pb and Bi (Mα). Typical detection limits were 0.01–0.02 per cent for S, Fe, Co, Ni, Cu, Zn, Ag, Sn and Sb, and 0.04–0.06 per cent for As, Au, Pb and Bi. For SEM-WD analysis the listed result in each case was the average of three analyses from areas of 4.8 x 6 μm (20000x magnification). Readings below detection level were listed as 'nd' (not detected). If an element was detected only in one or two of the three analyses it was listed as 'tr', meaning that the element was present at trace level near its detection limit. The analyses were carried out on areas of metallic copper, avoiding slag inclusions where present, and therefore representing the content of the copper phase.

In addition to the analysis of the drilled samples using ICPMS, fourteen of these samples were also analysed on the SEM using energy dispersive X-ray analysis. These samples were prepared in a similar manner to the WD samples: mounted in epoxy resin, polished, carbon-coated and analysed using the CamScan MaXim 2040 scanning electron microscope with an Oxford Link Isis energy dispersive X-ray spectrometer (SEM-ED). A beam current of 20 kV was used with a working distance of 35 mm, and each sample was analysed for 200 live seconds. The results were quantified using a ZAF correction program. The listed results in each case are the average of three analyses from as large an area as possible, usually between x5000 and x20000 magnification.

SEM-ED analyses the elements present concurrently rather than sequentially, and there is no need to preselect elements for analysis. The technique also has the advantage of often allowing larger areas to be selected for analysis than is possible with WD; this helps to reduce any distortion of the composition of the sample due to its heterogeneity. However, 'ED has considerably poorer limits of detection (than WD) for all elements, typically by one to two orders of magnitude. The exact figure depends on matrix and counting time, but representative figures for the limits of detection by ED are 0.05–0.26 wt per cent of the element' (Pollard and Heron 1996).

The results of the analytical programme are set out in Table 18, along with those from the two previous sets of analyses conducted on the assemblage. For samples analysed using both the ICPMS and SEM-ED the results have been combined as the SEM will have produced more accurate results for the main alloying elements whilst the ICPMS will have produced more accurate results for the elements that occur as impurities in the alloy. For these combined results the elements measured using the ICPMS are marked in red.

The twenty samples analysed by ICPMS were done prior to the purchase of the SEM at Cardiff University. The percentage totals varied from 93.1 to 100.2. The lower totals were considered unacceptable for assessing the composition of the major elements within the sample. There were several reasons for these poor results, both to do with the analytical method and the limitations of the particular system used at the Department of Earth Sciences at Cardiff University.

The ICPMS is an instrument used mainly for the detection of trace elements, and the particular machine that was used was set up to analyse environmental samples, such as contaminated water, rather than archaeological metalwork. Sample preparation involves dissolution and dilution in acids to an appropriate level. Major elements have to be diluted to a higher level before their solutions can be analysed, which results in an increased risk of error. This problem was compounded in the analysis of the Llyn Cerrig Bach assemblage because many of the original samples were extremely small. As has been previously noted, it would be preferable to restrict the use of ICP-MS to the analysis of trace elements and use a different technique for minor and alloying elements (Young *et al.* 1997). Copper, the main constituent of all the Llyn Cerrig Bach samples, is particularly problematic to analyse as it has a low mass range in relation to the internal standard used. As similar a mass as possible gives the best results; elements heavier than the standard are not affected too much, but lighter elements tend to be more unstable in the machine. The internal standard used for these analyses was rhodium with an atomic mass of 103; copper has an atomic mass of 64. Rhodium was chosen as an internal standard as its presence would not conflict with any of the trace elements being analysed.

The poor overall totals of some of the ICP-MS results are therefore more likely to have affected the results for the major and minor alloying elements but not the trace elements. For this reason, quantitative SEM-ED analysis was carried out on the unused remainder of the samples. Although SEM-ED is arguably less effective in analysing trace elements and in quantifying minor elements, it produced more accurate analyses for copper and tin. These results could therefore be used to show the variations in the main constituents of the alloys being examined.

There have been two previous episodes of metallurgical investigation of the copper alloy artefacts from Llyn Cerrig Bach. The first set of analyses were conducted by Messrs Minton, Treharne and Davies Ltd as part of an investigation into copper alloying traditions of the Iron Age in north Wales prompted by debate over the date of the Tal-y-Llyn hoard and copper-zinc alloys (Savory 1971: 66). Analyses were conducted on four artefacts: the curved-horn, or 'trumpet', fragment (No. 31), the repair strip from the curved-horn fragment (now lost), one of the three-link bridle-bits (probably No. 15, but possibly No. 14) and one of the globular cauldron fragments (either No. 24 or No. 25). The second set of analyses were conducted by Northover (1991a). Nine artefacts were analysed: three three-link bridle-bits (Nos. 10, No. 12, and probably No. 15, but possibly No. 14), two rein-rings (No. 17 and No. 18), one coiled decorative strip (No. 35), two cauldron fragments (No. 26 and either No. 24 or No. 25) and an unaccessioned sheet fragment (possibly either No. 32 or No. 33).[1]

Comparing the results of analyses conducted using different techniques is problematic. Savory does not record any methodological detail about the analyses undertaken by Messrs Minton, Treharne and Davies Ltd using spectrographic analysis (Savory 1971: 66). Their study only recorded a limited range of elements, presumably because it was concerned with identifying broad alloy types rather than detailed impurity patterns. Northover's study was undertaken using electron probe microanalysis and measured the following twelve elements: Cu, Sn, Zn, As, Sb, Bi, Fe, Co, Ni, Ag, Au and Pb. The results of Northover's analyses are directly comparable with those of the current analytical programme. The only difference is Northover's results are normalized to 100 per cent whilst those of the current programme are not (the totals were left as analysed to give an appreciation of the quality of the individual results). Only two of the analyses conducted by Northover were repeated in the current programme of metallurgical investigation. First, Northover sampled one of the globular cauldron fragments (either No. 14 or No. 15), but since his analysis was affected by corrosion (Northover 1991a: 392) it is not possible to compare directly his results with those of the current programme. Secondly, Northover sampled the hemispherical cauldron fragment (No. 26) and, although there is some variation, his results are broadly comparable with those achieved in the current analytical programme.

TABLE 18: Metallurgical analyses of the copper alloy artefacts from the Llyn Cerrig Bach assemblage

Catal. no.	Description	Analysis	Accession	Sample no.	Cu	Sn	Zn
1	Terret main ring	ED/ICPMS	44.32.44	2	85.40	12.11	**tr**
2	Terret connecting bar	ED/ICPMS	44.32.45	1	78.65	11.17	**0.01**
3	Terret connecting bar	ED/ICPMS	44.32.46	3	88.02	9.42	**0.03**
6	Nave hoop	WD	44.32.38	47	85.13	11.92	0.05
6	Nave hoop	WD	44.32.38	48	85.76	12.09	0.07
7	Nave hoop	WD	44.32.37	49	90.76	8.38	0.07
9	Ring	ICPMS	44.294.11	5	87.00	5.60	tr
10	Bridle-bit ring	MP	44.32.50	Northover 338	90.09	9.28	nd
10	Bridle-bit side-link	ED/ICPMS	44.32.50	12	82.49	13.15	**0.05**
10	Bridle-bit side-link	ED/ICPMS	44.32.50	13	90.64	5.72	**0.09**
11	Bridle-bit centre-link	ED/ICPMS	44.32.51	19	84.57	10.20	**0.83**
11	Bridle-bit side-link	ED/ICPMS	44.32.51	18	83.43	10.88	**0.38**
11	Bridle-bit side-link	ED/ICPMS	44.32.51	20	83.73	9.82	**0.80**
12	Bridle-bit plate	MP	44.32.52	Northover 337	89.03	7.96	0.4
14 or 15	Bridle-bit	MP	44.32.49	Northover 331	88.88	9.62	nd
14 or 15	Bridle-bit	SA	44.32.49	(Savory 1971)	91.0	7.0	tr
16	Bridle-bit rein-ring	WD	44.32.52	51	84.87	10.77	0.10
17	Bridle-bit	MP	44.32.53	Northover 332	88.89	10.39	0.02
18	Bridle-bit	MP	44.32.54	Northover 335	88.51	10.51	0.03
19	Bridle-bit rein-ring	WD	44.32.86	50	85.62	11.11	0.07
20	Bridle-bit rein-ring	WD	44.294.10	52	87.16	11.45	0.06
22	Bridle-bit rein ring	ED/ICPMS	44.32.58	11	83.05	12.73	**tr**
22	Bridle-bit rein-ring	ICPMS	44.32.58	8	90.40	8.30	0.01
22	Bridle-bit side-link	ICPMS	44.32.58	9	88.90	8.10	tr
22	Bridle-bit side-link	ED/ICPMS	44.32.58	10	83.79	12.81	**tr**
23	Bridle-bit centre-link	ED/ICPMS	44.32.55	16	87.50	7.97	**0.01**
23	Bridle-bit rein-ring	ED/ICPMS	44.32.55	14	83.87	10.98	**tr**
23	Bridle-bit side-link	ED/ICPMS	44.32.55	15	85.67	11.29	**0.01**
23	Bridle-bit side-link	ED/ICPMS	44.32.55	17	84.39	10.64	**tr**
24 or 25	Cauldron fragment	MP	44.32.76	Northover 334	81.06	18.81	nd
24 or 25	Cauldron fragment	SA	44.32.76	(Savory 1971)	88.5	9.7	–
24	Cauldron fragment i	WD	44.32.76i	46	87.19	10.54	tr
25	Cauldron fragment ii	WD	44.32.76ii	45	83.54	12.44	tr
26	Cauldron fragment	WD	44.32.77	21	88.58	10.48	0.06
26	Cauldron patch	WD	44.32.77	22	83.74	10.73	0.74
26	Cauldron patch	WD	44.32.77	23	85.42	10.78	0.71
26	Cauldron fragment	MP	44.32.77	Northover 333	87.64	11.54	0.01

METALLURGICAL ANALYSIS

As	Sb	Bi	Fe	Co	Ni	Ag	Au	Pb	S	Si	Al	Total
0.08	**0.29**	**tr**	**0.36**	**tr**	**0.22**	**0.27**	**nd**	**0.57**	nd	nd	0.31	100.73
0.03	**0.13**	**tr**	**0.03**	**nd**	**0.25**	**0.14**	**nd**	**1.31**	nd	0.32	nd	92.24
0.32	**0.04**	**tr**	**0.34**	**0.10**	**0.05**	**0.05**	**tr**	**1.11**	nd	nd	0.33	100.54
tr	nd	nd	0.64	nd	tr	tr	nd	tr	tr	–	–	97.73
tr	nd	nd	0.49	tr	tr	0.03	nd	tr	nd	–	–	98.45
tr	tr	nd	nd	tr	tr	tr	nd	nd	tr	–	–	99.21
0.12	0.09	0.05	0.03	nd	0.07	0.07	nd	0.09	–	–	–	93.10
0.23	0.02	nd	0.04	0.08	0.05	0.04	0.02	0.15	–	–	–	
0.41	**0.04**	**tr**	**0.31**	**0.03**	**0.10**	**0.09**	**tr**	**1.71**	nd	nd	0.74	99.63
1.43	**0.14**	**tr**	**0.39**	**0.08**	**0.23**	**0.23**	**0.01**	**1.54**	0.22	nd	0.35	100.23
0.98	**0.10**	**nd**	**0.76**	**0.02**	**0.16**	**0.17**	**nd**	**3.57**	nd	nd	0.37	100.61
0.78	**0.07**	**nd**	**0.28**	**0.01**	**0.15**	**0.14**	**nd**	**7.18**	0.05	0.09	1.02	101.80
1.02	**0.11**	**nd**	**0.34**	**0.02**	**0.18**	**0.16**	**nd**	**7.37**	0.38	nd	0.50	99.48
0.86	0.05	0.03	1.19	0.05	0.13	0.05	nd	0.25	–	–	–	
0.07	nd	nd	0.52	0.48	0.02	0.01	nd	0.4	–	–	–	
tr	tr	–	–	–	<0.1	–	–	0.5	–	–	–	
0.50	0.03	tr	0.09	0.12	0.04	0.06	nd	tr	0.06	–	–	96.87
0.01	0.45	0.04	0.01	0.01	nd	0.1	0.04	0.05	–	–	–	
0.59	0.02	0.01	0.02	0.06	0.09	0.06	nd	0.04	–	–	–	
0.31	nd	nd	0.13	0.07	tr	tr	nd	nd	tr	–	–	97.31
0.70	0.04	nd	nd	0.03	0.10	0.13	nd	nd	tr	–	–	99.68
0.13	**0.13**	**0.02**	**0.37**	**tr**	**0.08**	**0.05**	**nd**	**0.14**	0.53	nd	0.28	100.63
0.10	0.09	0.04	0.02	tr	0.11	0.05	nd	0.08	–	–	–	99.20
0.14	0.33	tr	0.19	tr	0.05	0.23	nd	0.16	–	–	–	98.10
0.94	**0.20**	**0.04**	**0.11**	**tr**	**0.07**	**0.10**	**nd**	**0.14**	0.24	0.17	0.35	100.51
0.08	**0.92**	**nd**	**0.03**	**tr**	**0.27**	**0.38**	**nd**	**0.44**	0.16	nd	0.74	99.41
0.37	**0.76**	**tr**	**0.04**	**tr**	**0.18**	**0.27**	**nd**	**0.53**	0.26	0.07	0.37	98.54
0.10	**0.33**	**tr**	**0.11**	**tr**	**0.31**	**0.45**	**nd**	**0.31**	0.13	0.59	0.12	99.86
0.09	**0.63**	**tr**	**0.15**	**tr**	**0.32**	**0.39**	**nd**	**0.30**	0.28	0.07	0.24	99.85
0.05	nd	nd	0.01	0.01	0.01	0.01	nd	0.05	–	–	–	
–	–	–	0.1	–	0.1	–	–	–	–	–	–	
nd	0.46	tr	tr	tr	nd	0.09	nd	nd	tr	–	–	98.29
nd	0.52	tr	0.04	nd	nd	0.12	nd	nd	tr	–	–	96.66
0.06	nd	tr	0.38	0.41	nd	nd	nd	nd	tr	–	–	99.97
0.99	0.04	nd	1.44	tr	0.17	0.19	nd	tr	tr	–	–	98.04
1.00	tr	nd	0.93	tr	0.18	0.20	tr	tr	tr	–	–	99.22
0.49	0.03	0.03	0.05	0.14	0.04	0.02	nd	0.02	–	–	–	

Catal. no.	Description	Analysis	Accession	Sample no.	Cu	Sn	Zn
27	Scabbard mouth	ICPMS	44.32.10	6	91.70	5.30	0.06
28	Binding	WD	44.32.11	24	85.21	11.20	0.06
29	Pommel	ICPMS	44.32.12	4	89.40	7.40	0.01
30	Cylinder	WD	44.32.88	32	89.07	8.50	0.18
31	'Trumpet'	SA	44.32.74	(Savory 1971)	86.3	11.1	–
31	'Trumpet' repair strip	SA	44.32.74	(Savory 1971)	93.5	5.8	–
32 or 34 ?	Unnumbered sheet	MP		Northover 188	88.78	9.06	0.23
32	Fragment	WD	2002.40H/1	31	87.61	9.74	0.04
N/A	Fragment	WD	2002.40H/2	33	97.14	tr	0.14
33	Fragment	WD	2002.40H/3	34	83.67	11.76	0.45
34	Fragment	WD	2002.40H/4	35	72.84	nd	26.24
35	Coiled mount	MP	44.32.68	Northover 336	89.29	9.97	0.07
36	Coiled mount	WD	44.32.91	44	89.43	10.80	0.07
37	Coiled mount	WD	44.32.67	39	86.30	10.99	0.05
38	Coiled mount	WD	44.32.71	43	82.69	13.25	0.04
39	Coiled mount	WD	44.294.34	37	86.58	11.57	0.04
40	Coiled mount	WD	44.32.69	41	84.77	11.92	0.04
41	Coiled mount	WD	44.32.70	38	87.30	10.85	0.18
42	Coiled mount	WD	44.32.72	40	86.20	12.36	0.05
43	Coiled mount	WD	44.32.73	42	85.70	11.01	0.06
46	Decorative plaque	WD	44.32.87	36	84.86	10.36	0.07
47	Crescentic plaque	WD	44.32.75	53	86.85	11.47	0.05
48	Shield boss mount	WD	44.294.31	54	87.44	12.02	0.07
49	So-called horn-cap	ICPMS	44.32.41	7	65.50	4.70	0.14
50	Casket ornament	WD	44.32.78	27	85.08	11.93	0.07
51	Casket ornament	WD	44.32.79	26	87.46	11.68	0.08
52	Casket ornament	WD	44.294.12	29	86.94	10.27	0.08
53	Casket ornament	WD	44.32.80	25	87.59	9.82	0.05
54	Casket ornament	WD	44.32.81	30	86.59	11.05	0.08
55	Casket ornament	WD	44.294.13	28	86.27	11.39	0.04

METALLURGICAL ANALYSIS

As	Sb	Bi	Fe	Co	Ni	Ag	Au	Pb	S	Si	Al	Total
0.27	0.65	0.02	0.44	tr	0.51	0.46	nd	0.78	–	–	–	100.20
tr	nd	nd	tr	tr	nd	0.04	tr	nd	tr	–	–	96.50
0.20	0.72	0.02	0.16	tr	0.17	0.22	tr	1.36	–	–	–	99.70
0.35	0.05	nd	0.02	tr	0.04	0.18	nd	tr	tr	–	–	98.38
–	–	–	0.15	–	0.06	0.02	–	1.0	–	–	–	98.7
–	–	–	0.1	–	0.09	0.04	–	0.4	–	–	–	99.9
0.35	0.01	nd	0.25	0.02	0.06	0.05	nd	1.2	–	–	–	
nd	0.47	nd	0.03	tr	nd	0.09	nd	nd	tr	–	–	97.99
nd	nd	nd	nd	tr	nd	nd	nd	nd	nd	–	–	97.28
0.06	0.12	tr	0.04	0.02	0.05	0.04	nd	tr	tr	–	–	96.21
0.03	nd	tr	0.06	tr	nd	tr	nd	nd	tr	–	–	99.18
0.29	0.01	0.03	0.09	0.12	0.06	0.07	nd	0.01	–	–	–	
tr	tr	nd	nd	nd	tr	tr	nd	nd	nd	–	–	100.31
tr	0.05	nd	tr	nd	0.06	0.06	nd	nd	nd	–	–	97.51
tr	0.04	nd	nd	nd	0.03	0.06	nd	nd	tr	–	–	96.12
tr	0.03	nd	tr	tr	0.03	0.05	nd	nd	nd	–	–	98.31
tr	0.66	tr	tr	nd	tr	0.32	nd	tr	tr	–	–	97.72
0.08	tr	nd	tr	0.03	nd	0.04	nd	nd	tr	–	–	98.47
tr	0.03	nd	nd	tr	nd	tr	nd	nd	tr	–	–	98.64
tr	0.03	nd	nd	tr	nd	tr	nd	nd	tr	–	–	96.79
0.54	tr	nd	nd	0.15	tr	nd	nd	tr	tr	–	–	95.99
0.81	0.05	tr	nd	0.03	0.09	0.12	nd	nd	nd	–	–	99.47
0.08	0.07	nd	0.18	tr	0.04	0.05	nd	nd	tr	–	–	99.95
1.21	0.09	nd	0.03	0.01	0.27	0.16	nd	30.40	–	–	–	102.40
nd	nd	nd	nd	nd	0.03	tr	nd	nd	nd	–	–	97.12
tr	nd	nd	nd	tr	tr	0.05	nd	nd	tr	–	–	99.26
nd	nd	nd	nd	tr	nd	0.03	nd	nd	nd	–	–	97.32
tr	nd	nd	tr	tr	0.02	0.04	nd	nd	tr	–	–	97.53
nd	nd	nd	tr	tr	0.03	0.06	nd	nd	nd	–	–	97.81
tr	nd	nd	tr	tr	tr	0.04	nd	nd	tr	–	–	97.74

Note to Appendix 2

[1] Identifying three of the artefacts sampled in previous analytical studies is difficult. There are two incomplete three-link bridle-bits which were previously considered to be parts of the same bridle-bit (i.e. No. 14 and No. 15) and so were given the same accession number (no. 44.32.49; see Fox 1947a: 80, no. 49, pl. XXII). Although both fragments are possibly from the same bridle-bit this is not certain and in the present study they have been treated as separate artefacts. One of the fragments has definitely been sampled (No. 15), but there is no evidence to suggest that the other fragment (No. 14) has been. Both Messrs Minton, Treharne and Davies Ltd and Northover record sampling one of the fragments and it is probable that they both analysed the same one (No. 15). Comparing their analyses is difficult because of a typographic error in the publication of the original results (Savory 1971: 66). Although both sets of results are broadly similar, Messrs Minton, Treharne and Davies Ltd recorded traces of antimony and zinc which Northover did not find and the percentage of tin recorded by Messrs Minton, Treharne and Davies Ltd was lower (7.0%) than that recorded by Northover (9.62%). Northover does not comment on the discrepancy between his and the earlier analysis (1991a).

The second problematic identification concerns which of the two globular cauldron fragments (No. 24 or No. 25) was sampled by both Messrs Minton, Treharne and Davies Ltd and Northover. Again these two separate fragments were incorrectly assumed to be from a single vessel (see Fox 1947a: 87-8, no. 76, pl. XXXVIII). No physical evidence of past sampling can be found on either of the fragments. Northover's analysis was affected by corrosion (Northover 1991a: 392), making comparison difficult. Messrs Minton, Treharne and Davies Ltd's analysis is most closely comparable with the results gained from analysing fragment No. 24 in the present study.

The final difficult identification concerns a then unaccessioned sheet analysed by Northover (1991a: 392-3). Prior to the current programme of analysis it was assumed that Northover must have sampled one of the small sheet fragments in the assemblage (Nos. 32-4 and accession no. 2002.40H/2). Since only one of these fragments showed clear evidence of a modern break consistent with having been sampled, it was assumed that it was this fragment (No. 34) which Northover had analysed (Macdonald 2000a: 139). Northover's analysis of the sheet fragment suggested that it was a copper-tin alloy with only a minor trace of zinc as an impurity (Northover 1991a: 392–3), but our analysis of the fragment which appeared to have been sampled (No. 34) indicated that it was a copper-zinc alloy with no detectable trace of tin. Therefore, the sheet fragment which Northover analysed cannot be the fragment it was previously assumed to be (No. 34) and presumably must be either one of the two apparently previously unsampled sheet fragments for which broadly consistent results were obtained (Nos. 32–3) or an otherwise unrecorded and now lost fragment.

Appendix 3
Field Survey at Llyn Cerrig Bach

PHILIP MACDONALD AND TIM YOUNG

Topographic and geophysical survey work was conducted by the authors, with the assistance of Dr Peter Brabham and Dr Amin Barzanji (Cardiff University), in the vicinity of the site of Llyn Cerrig Bach during the summer of 1995. Accounts of both the setting of the site and the circumstances of the recovery of the assemblage are given in Chapter 1. In brief, during the war, peat from local bogs and lake edges was extracted and transported to RAF Valley, where it was cultivated in a successful attempt to consolidate the sand dunes on which the airfield was built. The importance of the assemblage was recognized during the summer of 1943, several months after its extraction in October 1942. The peat containing the assemblage was excavated from the southern margins of Llyn Cerrig Bach. Prior to the extraction of the peat, Llyn Cerrig Bach was a single lake; today, two lakes, formed by the flooding of the partially backfilled basins created by the extraction, exist at the site. The 1995 fieldwork was intended to fill gaps in Fox's account of the setting and retrieval of the assemblage (Fox 1947a: 1–4), and to determine whether intact peat deposits remain at the site which might yield additional artefacts, bone or palaeoenvironmental data.

Primary, Secondary and Tertiary Sites

Three potential sites of interest were identified from Fox's account of the assemblage's recovery (Fox 1947a: 1–4). The first was the primary site within the peat deposits in which the assemblage had been deposited in antiquity. The exact location and extent of this site is unknown, but Fox had located its estimated position using information supplied by the Ministry of War Transport (Fox 1947a: 3, fig. 2; NGR SH30607649). It was not known, prior to the 1995 survey work, whether all of the assemblage had been disturbed during the extraction in October 1942. Fox had noted that there was no evidence that the bog had yielded all its artefacts (Fox 1947a: 66) and had published a section implying that the peat workings only extended approximately 10 m out from the rock face in the area of the find-spot (1947a: fig. 2). This suggested that intact deposits adjacent to the primary site might remain *in situ*.

The secondary site was the rock platform immediately adjacent to the primary site where the extracted peat had been drained before being transported on to the airfield (Fox 1947a: 4). Although the bulk of the peat was removed from the platform, some must have remained as Fox recovered at least one artefact from residual deposits located on the edge of the bog in August 1943 (Fox 1947a: 3). The platform was bisected by the construction of the road which defines the airfield's northern perimeter shortly before March 1945. In addition, part of the platform's southern end had been quarried, probably subsequent to the road building but before August 1945.

The tertiary site was the artefact spread on the airfield where the peat from the primary site was harrowed and from where the assemblage was recognized and principally recovered during the summer of 1943. Given the localized nature of the source of the peat yielding the assemblage, it is likely to have been spread over a restricted area of the airfield. Wartime security considerations prevented Fox from publishing an account of where on the airfield the tertiary site was located. A comprehensive archival search failed to recover any unpublished record of the tertiary site's location and it is doubtful whether any such record survives unrecognized. The recovery of eight items (Fox 1947a: addenda 1, 3–5; Savory 1976a: nos. 20.1–4 and 22.1–4) after the war suggests that, despite the expansion of the airfield between October 1943 and October 1944, the tertiary site remained at least partially accessible until at least 1947. That two of these pieces (Savory 1976a: nos. 22.1–2) and possibly three others (Fox 1947a: addenda 3 and 5; Savory 1976a: nos. 20.2, 20.4 and 22.4) are modern (see Appendix 1), suggests that by 1947 the integrity of the tertiary site may have become compromised. Since 1947 no further items have been recovered from the airfield, presumably because the tertiary site has become grassed over, preventing further surface collection, or it was built upon and the artefact spread was destroyed or rendered inaccessible.

Survey, data processing and desk study

The principal aims of the survey work were to produce a detailed topographic survey of the area around the primary and secondary sites, delimit the extent of the peat extraction within this study area, locate any intact peat deposits or surviving metallic objects within the study area, and improve the understanding of both the ancient and modern topography of the site's environs.

In order to achieve these aims a topographic survey of the site, which was to form the basis for the subsequent geophysical surveys, was conducted (Figure 7). The area of former bog to the south of the airfield's perimeter, in which the primary site was located, was the subject of resistivity and magnetometer surveys. An auger survey, which assisted interpretation of the geophysical surveys, was conducted in both this area and in the area to the north of the perimeter road between the two modern lakes. A metal detector survey of the rock platform was abandoned due to interference caused by modern metallic debris and restricted access due to thick undergrowth; the limited results which were produced were inconclusive. The topographic survey was conducted by the authors using a Topcon EDM, the resistivity survey was conducted with a Campus Imager 25 by Dr Peter Brabham, and the magnetometer survey was conducted with EGG Geometrics G816 magnetometers by Dr Amin Barzanji.

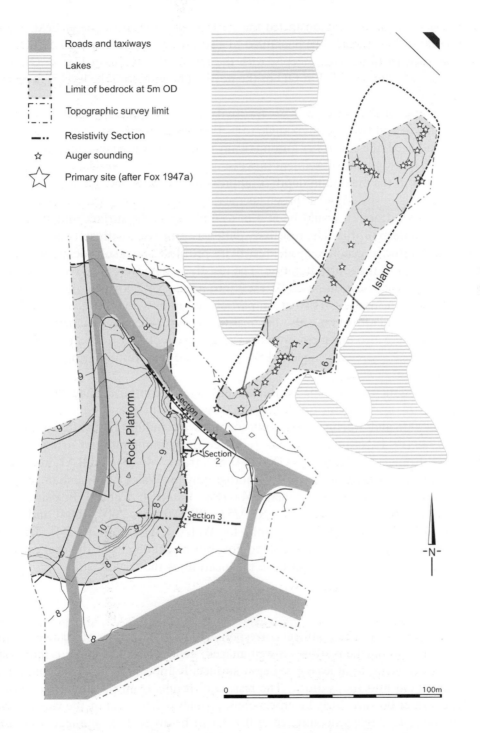

Roads and taxiways

Lakes

Limit of bedrock at 5m OD

Topographic survey limit

Resistivity Section

☆ Auger sounding

Primary site (after Fox 1947a)

Figure 7: Topographic map of the primary site and its immediate environs

The topographic survey demonstrated that, within the bounds of the airfield, the area of former peat workings had been backfilled to a surface at approximately 7.5 m OD. The edge of the rock platform rises steeply, with the top of the platform 11.3 m OD in the south of the study area and 9.3 m OD in the north. The modern lake level is at approximately 5.8 m OD.

Within the area of the former bog, six resistivity lines were taken parallel to the edge of the rock platform and two at a high angle to it. Each line comprised 25 electrodes. In the survey method used, the controller automatically switches between electrode pairs to produce a pseudo-section, and subsequent processing can generate a model of the resistivity within a section to the maximum depth of approximately three and a half times the electrode spacing. A 2 m spacing was chosen, as the documentary evidence suggested that the base of the peat extraction would be at 4 m to 6 m below the surface and so would be imaged in a 7 m deep profile. The resistivity data was processed with software that uses a reiterative technique to generate model resistivity profiles. The results described here are based on products of the fourth iteration. The resistivity data were then recalculated on a spreadsheet from their section-based datasets into a true XYZ format, allowing the construction of contour maps of resistivity at particular depths below surface. The resistivity lines parallel to the platform were also taken as the basis for the magnetometer survey, but additional lines were also taken closer to the edge of the rock face and in the south of the study area, where early results suggested the presence of features requiring more detailed magnetic mapping.

All the survey data was combined within a multi-layered computer image to enable their comparison with various plans (including the c.1840 tithe map and Greenly's geological survey of c.1900) and wartime aerial photographs (including Luftwaffe images from December 1940 (Pl. 1: National Archives and Records Administration, Cartographic and Architectural Branch, USA, RG373 GX-12041 SD, frame 546 23) and RAF images from April 1942 (Pl. 2: Central Register of Air Photography for Wales, Medmenham, H1 4/489 1PRV, frames 46, 47, 48), November 1942 (Pls 3 and 4: Central Register of Air Photography for Wales, Medmenham, NLA/53 1PRV, frames 2004, 1004) and August 1945 (Central Register of Air Photography for Wales, RAF 106BUK655)). The aerial photographs were apparently unavailable to Fox, but reveal details of the peat extraction and spreading operations which constrain the location of the tertiary site.

Results and interpretation

The metagabbros of the rock platform corresponds to resitivity values of 1000–6000 Ωm^{-1} (Figure 8). The edge of the platform is well imaged, generally sharp, and has the form of a buried cliff extending to at least 6 m below surface. It appears to form one margin of a buried channel cut into the bedrock. The resistivity results from the upper metre of the area of the former bog are fairly heterogeneous, probably as a result of the variable intersection of the water table (encountered at 0.9–1.1 m below surface in auger soundings). Below this the values are remarkably low and relatively uniform within the range 40–100

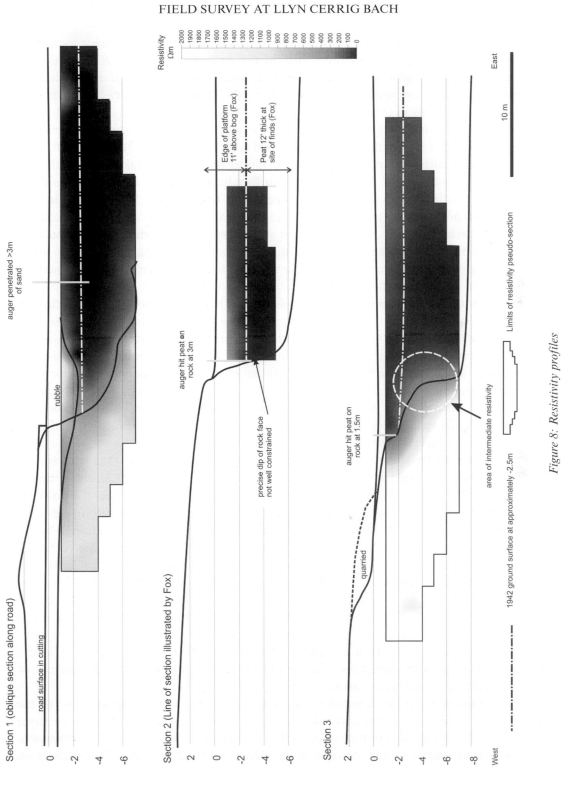

Figure 8: Resistivity profiles

211

Ωm^{-1}. These low values tally with waterlogged unconsolidated sands in auger soundings. The low resistivity layer continues to depths of 6m or 7m (i.e. 0.5–1 m OD) across most of the site. In the absence of control values from known waterlogged peat deposits, it is assumed that all the low resistivity deposits are sands. This low resistivity layer rests on a deposit with resistivity in the range 260–350 Ωm^{-1}. This is interpreted as the 'clay floor' to the peat deposit noted by Fox (1947a: 3, fig. 2). This fact, together with the measured topographic profile on the line of Fox's published section (1947a: fig. 2), indicates that the modern ground surface is approximately 2.5 m higher than the original surface of the bog prior to the peat extraction. This change in surface height was not anticipated and as a consequence the resistivity survey did not penetrate the base of the peat workings as deeply as intended. It also means that any remaining iron artefacts in any peat deposits, which might remain intact, are likely to be at such a depth as to be difficult to detect with the magnetometer, unless they are present in concentrated accumulations. The clay lies at too great a depth to be penetrated by auger soundings, but apparently forms a lower fill of the buried channel identified above.

The steep resistivity gradients seen towards the northern and southern ends of the surveyed portion of the platform suggest that peat extraction took place right to the rock face, as indicated by Fox (1947a: fig. 2). South of the primary findspot, towards the centre of the surveyed area, there are hints of a wider band of material of intermediate resistivity immediately adjacent to the rock platform. These intermediate resistivity deposits could represent remnant peat deposits lying against the face of the buried cliff, but interpretation of this phenomenon is made problematic by the close supposition of the first resistivity line above the steeply dipping rock face. The apparently intermediate resistivity values are more likely to be an artefact of the processing technique.

The magnetometer survey (Figure 9) recorded a background level that rises significantly towards the northern edge of the area surveyed; the significance of this is uncertain, but it is probably related to the presence of the road which defines the northern edge of the airfield. Several discrete magnetic anomalies were located within the study area, most of which are of relatively shallow origin. One large anomaly adjacent to the rock platform in the south of the surveyed area is suggestive of a large piece of buried machinery. An auger sounding on this spot penetrated sand to a depth of at least 3 m, confirming the interpreted deep origin of this anomaly. None of the anomalies can be plausibly associated with archaeologically significant deposits or features. Anecdotal accounts that the USAF disposed of unwanted aircraft in 1946 by burying them in this part of the airfield suggests one possible explanation for these anomalies. A large negative anomaly in the southern part of the area is parallel to the direction of one of the airfield taxiways, and may represent either a remnant block of peat or possibly an approach track to the quarry in the southern part of the rock platform.

Auger soundings were conducted in two areas to a maximum depth of 3 m. To the south of the road, in the area covered by the geophysical surveys, the aim of the auger survey was to provide an interpretive control to the resistivity and magnetometer surveys. Beyond a thin sandy topsoil, only unconsolidated sands were recorded. A few lenses of,

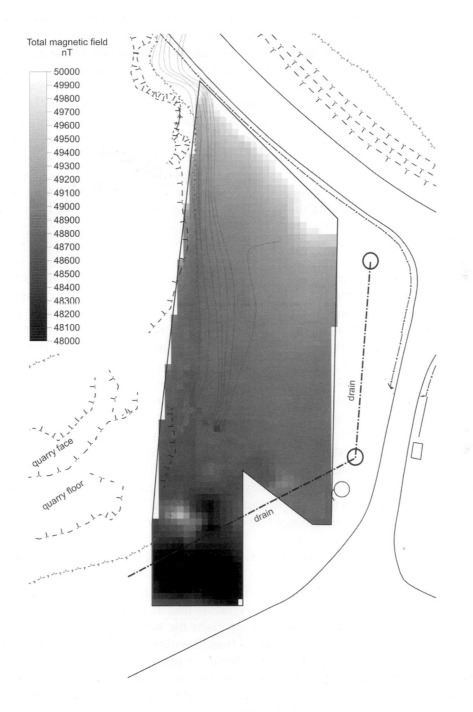

Figure 9: Results of the magnetometry survey

presumably redeposited, peat were recorded within the unconsolidated sand. Fragments of bitumen-impregnated sand and clinker within the sand are consistent with emplacement of the sand during the runway extension, for the substructure of the early runways was produced by bitumen impregnation of the underlying sand, and 'ashes' are recorded as being laid around the runways to prevent aircraft from sinking into loose sand.

To the north of the perimeter road, in the area between the two modern lakes, apparently *in situ* rock outcrops were observed and studies of aerial photographs and pre-war maps suggested that this area was not part of the surrounding bog. This prompted the series of auger soundings which revealed a previously unrecognized landscape feature: a bedrock ridge 160 m long and about 35 m wide, extending northeastwards from about 20 m from the rock platform. This feature is interpreted as having formed an elongated 'island' of drier ground within the ancient lake or bog.

Discussion

Aerial photographs taken during and immediately after extraction indicate that peat working took place within the survey area between April and November 1942 (Plates 2 and 3). Both the geophysical survey and the aerial photographs indicate that there was an almost complete extraction of the peat within the area of the present survey. The section published by Fox implied that the workings only extended approximately 10 m out from the rock face in the area of the findspot (1947a: fig. 2), but this view can no longer be maintained. Within the survey area the peat workings were backfilled with sand, derived from the dune complex, during the expansion of the airfield between October 1943 and October 1944. An access road for the airfield between Llanfair yn Neubwll and Llanfihangel yn Nhowyn, involving the bulldozing of a cutting through the rock platform, had been built by March 1945, and the quarrying of the southern end of the rock platform pre-dates an aerial photograph of August 1945.

The estimated position of the primary findspot lies only slightly to the south of the shortest distance between the rock platform and the island-like feature. This island feature is of great interpretative significance (see Chapter 7 for a more detailed discussion).

Potential for future fieldwork

The geophysical survey results indicate that the prospect that intact peat deposits remain in the immediate vicinity of the primary site is low. It is consequently reasonable to assume that, whatever the rate of recovery from the secondary and tertiary sites, the majority of the assemblage was extracted from its original findspot. Even if any intact peat deposits were to be recognized, the logistical problems of excavating through the thick deposits of overlying unconsolidated waterlogged sand would be considerable. The location of the secondary site on the rock platform, if it was not destroyed by either the road building or the quarrying, is unlikely to be ascertained without a programme of extensive defoliation. The prospect of locating the tertiary site has been enhanced by study

Figure 10: Map of RAF Valley, showing the extent of the area cultivated during 1942 and the area apparently covered by freshly spread peat (13 November 1942), within which the tertiary site probaby lies

of contemporary aerial photographs (Figure 10). The aerial photograph of 13 November 1942 shows the extent of freshly spread peat just one month after the dredging of the primary site (Pl. 3). Although this area is considerably less than the total recorded extent of the peat spreading (2,000,000 square yards/1,672,200 square metres; Anon. 1944) geophysical and metal detector survey of this area would be a major task, particularly so when one bears in mind that it is now adjacent to the three main runways.

The auger survey of the newly discovered island did not reveal any surviving archaeologically significant deposits, although the possibility of rock-cut features remaining intact must be considered. The nearest intact peat sequence suitable for environmental sampling probably lies 80 m to the south-west of the primary site. Future excavation of the island and coring of nearby peat deposits may provide additional information on the context of the assemblage.

Catalogue of the Copper Alloy Artefacts from Llyn Cerrig Bach

1. Terret (accession no. 44.32.44)

Cast copper alloy, plain, oval terret (internal diameter (across) 57 mm (height) 47 mm, external diameter (across) 72 mm (height) 71 mm), circular to oval in cross-section, with moulded collars and a D-shaped, corroded, sub-rectangular sectioned, iron connecting bar, the original form of which is difficult to reconstruct. The terret tapers from both collars towards its top. The collars are made up of two moulded rings separated by a groove. There is no visible decoration. Wear facets above the collars on the internal edges of both sides are visible. One facet is considerably larger than the other. Weight 70.8 g. (Figure 11).

Savory incorrectly states that the tang plate is of copper alloy (Savory 1976a: 57).

Fox 1947a: 35–6, 61, 64, 79, no. 44, pls II and XVI; Spratling 1972: 26, 341, 383, no. 10, fig. 3; Savory 1976a: 33, 57, no. 17.44, fig. 14.5; MacGregor 1976: 62; Jope 2000: 309, pl. 290.n.

2. Terret (accession no. 44.32.45)

Cast copper alloy, plain, oval terret (internal diameter (across) 69.5 mm (height) 62.5 mm, external diameter (across) 85 mm (height with tang) 85 mm), circular to oval in cross-section, with moulded collars and a sub-rectangular-sectioned connecting bar with a short, tapering, rectangular-sectioned chisel-edged tang (length 8 mm, width 8–11 mm). The terret tapers from both collars towards its top. The collars consist of domed oval terminals, with circumscribing grooves on their outer edges. There is no visible decoration. Wear facets above the collar on the inner face on one side and on the inner side of both collars are visible. Weight 102.2 g. (Figure 11).

Savory incorrectly states that the tang plate is of iron (Savory 1976a: 57).

Fox 1947a: 35–6, 60–1, 79, no. 45, pl. XVI; Spratling 1972: 26, 341, 384, no. 11, fig. 3; Savory 1976a: 33, 57, no. 17.45, fig. 14.7; MacGregor 1976: 62; Jope 2000: 309, pl. 290.o.

3. Terret (accession no. 44.32.46)

Small, cast copper alloy terret with horizontal, moulded collars and a curved connecting bar (internal diameter (across) 22 mm (height) 21 mm, external diameter (across) 35 mm (height) 31 mm). The upper part is uniform in size and profile except for a single wear facet on the inner face of one side. The sub-rectangular-sectioned connecting bar tapers from both sides towards its centre. The upper part is decorated by a small cast step-like groove on either side and a sunken ridge at the top. Immediately below both step-like grooves there are borders of post-casting, more-or-less regularly spaced, pseudo-stitching punched dots. The sunken ridge on the top has a raised wavy line of pseudo-stitching made by applying punch-dots on alternate sides. The pseudo-stitching decorative motifs mimic leatherworking. The collars are made up of two moulded rings separated by a groove. Weight 22.0 g. (Figure 11).

Fox 1947a: 36–7, 61, 64–5, 79–80, no. 46, pls IX and XXIX; Spratling 1972: 26–7, 341, 387, no. 22, fig. 5; Savory 1976a: 33, 57, no. 17.46, fig. 22.2; MacGregor 1976: 62; Foster 1980: 10–11.

4. Nave hoop (accession no. 44.32.35)

Cast, copper alloy hoop, originally circular but now distorted and dented (probably in antiquity) (breadth 22–3 mm, internal diameter 114–29 mm (originally 128–9 mm)). Decorated round its circumference by two D-sectioned, repoussé cordons (width 8.5 mm, height 6 mm) flanked by two flanges (width 2.5 mm). The trough between the cordons is at the same level as the flanges. The hoop is further embellished by narrow grooves half way down the inner sides of the cordons and punched transverse lines ('rouletting') on the flanges (approximately 1.5 mm in length, 14–15 per 10 mm) bordered by a continuous incised longitudinal groove. Weight 93.8 g. (Figure 12).

Fox 1947a: 13–15, 61, 65, 76, no. 35, pls VII and XVIII; Spratling 1972: 82–3, 339, 442, 619, no. 140, fig. 49; Savory 1976a: 32, 57, no. 17.35, fig. 15.1.

5. Nave hoop (accession no. 44.32.36)

Cast, copper alloy hoop, originally circular but now distorted and dented (probably in antiquity) (breadth 21–8 mm (originally 25 mm), internal diameter 120–6 mm). Decorated around its circumference by two D-sectioned, repoussé cordons (width 10 mm, height 5 mm) flanked by two flanges (width 2.5 mm). The trough between the cordons is at a higher level than the flanges. The cordons are not decorated, whereas the flanges have punched transverse lines ('rouletting') (approximately 1 mm in length, 12 per 10 mm) bordered by a continuous incised longitudinal groove. Weight 79.8 g. (Figure 12).

Fox 1947a: 13–15, 61, 76, no. 36, pls VII and XVIII; Spratling 1972: 82–3, 339, 442, 619, no. 141, fig. 49; Savory 1976a: 32, 57, no. 17.36, fig. 15.2.

6. Nave hoop (accession no. 44.32.38)

Cast, copper alloy hoop, originally circular but now distorted, torn, locally discoloured, and oval. Conical in section (breadth 32–5 mm, internal diameter 115–39 mm to 118–32 mm) although this could be the result of modern damage. There is an ancient, incomplete patch (11 x 7 mm) neatly fixed by two rivets, with their flat heads on the inner side, across a small transverse split bisecting a small irregular fracture. The hoop has two repoussé cordons (width 13 mm, height 5 mm), the trough between them being on a level with the plain flanges (both width 3 mm).

X-radiographic examination suggests that an approximately cruciform mark may have been punched on one of the cordons in antiquity. Weight 51.2 g (including the weight of modern solder repairs). (Figure 12, Pl. 5).

Fox 1947a: 13–15, 60–1, 76, no. 38, pl. XVIII; Spratling 1972: 82–3, 339, 442, 619, no. 143, fig. 49; Savory 1976a: 32, 57, no. 17.38, fig. 15.4.

7. Nave hoop (accession no. 44.32.37)

Cast, copper alloy hoop, originally circular but due to modern damage torn and slightly oval. Conical in section (breadth 21–5 mm, internal diameter 120–7 mm to 125–31 mm) although this could be the result of modern damage. The hoop has a single repoussé cordon (width 10–12.5 mm, height 5.5 mm) at its centre flanked by two irregular flanges one of which is wider than the other (widths 5–8 mm and 4–5 mm). The edges of the flanges and the top of the cordon are intermittently, due to differential wear and corrosion rather than design, decorated with incised lines. Weight 43.7 g. (Figure 12).

Fox 1947a: 13–15, 61, 76, no. 37, pl. XVIII; Spratling 1972: 82–3, 339, 442, 619, no. 142, fig. 49; Savory 1976a: 32, 57, no. 17.37, fig. 15.3.

8. 'Vase-headed' linch-pin (accession no. 44.32.42)

Rectangular-sectioned, tapering, wrought iron shank with cast copper alloy terminals (length 107 mm). The inverted vase-shaped upper terminal is perforated by a horizontal perforation (diameter 5 mm) and decorated by three grooves, two around the flat-headed pedestal at its top and one round its base, and two shorter grooves which form a decorative triangle whose base is part of the lower groove. The curved, tapering lower terminal ends in a flat base set in the vertical plane. It is decorated with three grooves, two towards its top and a third towards its base and a series of feathered incisions on the convex edge of the terminal. These decorative elements combine to give the lower terminal the modelled appearance of an animal hoof. There are corresponding wear facets on both terminals, set on almost diametrically opposed sides of the pin, but there is no wear on the corresponding, widest point of the upper terminal, suggesting that the wheel was convex in form adjacent to the linch-pin. Weight 101.0 g. (Figure 11, Pl. 5).

Fox 1947a: 19–20, 61, 64, 78, no. 42, pl. XV; Spratling 1972: 339–40, 427, 620, no. 112, fig. 40; Savory 1976a: 32, 57, no. 17.42, fig. 13.3; Jope 2000: 314, pl. 301.a.

9. Ring (accession no. 44.294.11)

Cast, copper alloy ring (external diameter 47 mm) with an asymmetrical lozenge-shaped cross-section (horizontal thickness 6.5 mm, vertical thickness 6 mm) with rounded edges. The internal side of the ring is more rounded presumably due to wear. The surface of the ring is pitted and there is a possible blow-hole on the internal side. Possibly part of a horse harness. Weight 23.9 g. (Figure 11).

Fox 1947a: 35, 96, no. 136, pl. XXVII; Savory 1976a: 59, no. 18.11, fig. 21.5.

10. Three-link bridle-bit (accession no. 44.32.50)

Three-link bridle-bit consisting of two, tubular copper alloy rein-rings, two cast copper alloy side-links, and a forged, iron central link. The two penannular rein-rings are oval in cross-section, vary slightly in size (external diameter 84–6 mm, internal diameter 63–6 mm; and external diameter 89–90 mm, internal diameter 69–71 mm) and are butt-jointed on the inside. Two spherical stop-studs are fixed to each rein-ring by copper alloy rivets which pass from the top of the studs through the rings and are hammered flush with the lower surface of the rings. Adjacent to one is a set of diametrically opposed, unworn, rivet holes, probably the result of a mistake during manufacture.

The side-links are both of a similar segmented form but differ slightly in length. Their terminal bulb sockets have ring-like flanges around the sockets, the link shaft is waisted and the side-link heads are heart shaped with off-centre perforations probably to accommodate wear. The central-link is a circular-sectioned, slightly oval shaped, penannular, forged iron ring and presumably a secondary repair. There is slight wear on the stop-studs, the inner surfaces of the rein-rings, and the perforations of the side-link heads. There is a casting flaw in one of the side-links. Weight 254.3 g. (Figure 13).

Fox 1947a: 28, 31–3, 61, 63, 65–6, 81, no. 50, pls VIII and XXIII; Fox 1958: fig. 64; Spratling 1972: 89–90, 260, 340, 447, no. 153, fig. 54; Savory 1976a: 32, 57, no. 17.50, fig. 19.1; Palk 1984: 32–3, no. DJ22, fig. C15; Northover 1991a: 392; Jope 2000: 302, pl. 273.n.

11. Asymmetrical three-link bridle-bit (accession no. 44.32.51)

Three-link bridle-bit incorporating two copper alloy tubular rein-rings, two cast copper alloy side-links, and a cast copper alloy centre-link. The rein-rings are the same size (external diameter 89–94 mm, internal diameter 68.5–72 mm), penannular, slightly distorted, oval in shape but approximately circular in cross-section (diameter 10.5–11 mm) and butt-jointed on the inside. A spherical stop-stud survives on one of the rings; it is fixed by a copper alloy rivet which passes from the top of the stud through the ring and is hammered flush with the lower surface of the rein-ring and is set adjacent to a set of diametrically opposed rivet holes. There are sets of diametrically opposed rivet holes situated at the other ends of the penannular rein-rings presumably to accommodate the missing stop-studs.

The segmented side-links are similar but differ slightly in form. One contains a separately cast decorative boss (diameter 32 mm) mounted on a knob set on the terminal bulb socket and fixed by a square headed rivet through its centre. The bevelled edge of this setting is decorated with twenty-seven incised, conjoined U-shaped arches further emphasised by punch dot decoration at their tips. The maximum width of these motifs varies between 2.5 and 4.5 mm. Although both side-links have the same design components (i.e. side-link head, link-shaft, and terminal bulb socket) the relative proportions of these vary (Table 19), as first noted by Spratling (1972: 448), but this does not cause a significant variation in the overall lengths of the pieces when the non-functional decorative elements are excluded (contra Palk 1984: 8).

TABLE 19: Lengths of the design components of the side-links (No. 11)

	Decorated side-link (mm)	Undecorated side-link (mm)
side-link head	22	23
link-shaft	17	14
terminal bulb socket	28	29
sub-total	67	66
decorative element	13	N/A
Total	**80**	**66**

The segmented centre-link contains a prominent central-roll which echoes the design of the terminal bulb sockets on the side-links. There are small wear facets on the link side of the stop-stud, on the inside of the ends of the rein-rings, and the perforations of both the side-link heads and the centre-link. Weight 333.3 g. (Figure 13).

Fox 1947a: 28, 31–3, 60–1, 63, 65–6, 81, no. 51, pls IX and XXIV; 1948: 27–8; 1958: 55, 99, fig. 39, 64, pl. 5.b; Savory 1968: fig. 20; Spratling 1972: 89–90, 260, 340, 448, no. 154, fig. 55; Savory 1976a: 32, 57–8, no. 17.51, fig. 19.2; Palk 1984: 34, no. DJ26, fig. C18; Arslan and Vitali 1991: 754, no. 689c; Jope 2000: 153, 302, pl. 273.o–p.

12. Three-link bridle-bit (accession no. 44.32.47)

Iron rein-ring and side-link both plated with copper alloy. The rein-ring is slightly oval (external diameter 77–81 mm, internal diameter 59–63 mm) and circular in cross-section (diameter 9 mm). Two flattened stop-studs (diameter 14 mm, height 8 mm) are fixed through the ring by iron rivets. There are wear facets on the link side of both stop-studs. The portion of the ring which accommodated the side-link is also partially worn through, but this was originally thinner than the main part of the rein-ring. The perforations of the segmented side-link (length 69 mm, width of terminal bulb socket 17 mm) are set in perpendicular planes at right angles to one another. The inner eye of the side-link has worn through. Weight 129.0 g. (Figure 14).

Fox 1947a: 27–8, 30–1, 33, 61, 63, 80, no. 47, pl. XXI; Spratling 1972: 86, 89–90, 260, 340; Savory 1976a: 32, 57, no. 17.47, fig. 17.2; Palk 1984: 35, no. DJ28, fig. C16.3; Northover 1991a: 392–3.

13. Three-link bridle-bit (accession no. 44.32.48)

Iron rein-ring and side-link both plated with copper alloy. The rein-ring is slightly distorted but approximately circular in both shape (external diameter 82–3 mm, internal diameter 64–6 mm) and cross-section (diameter 8–9 mm). A flattened spherical stop-stud (diameter 10.5 mm) survives on the ring and is fixed by an iron rivet. There is a wear facet on the link side of the stop-stud. The portion of the ring which accommodated the side link is partially worn through, but this was originally thinner than the main part of the rein-ring. The perforations of the side-link (length 65 mm) are set in perpendicular planes at right angles to each other and the inner eye of the side-link is worn. The outer face of the socket holding the ring is decorated with two incised parallel lines which run round the back of the socket. In the centre of the bulb socket is the remnant of the neck of a decorative device. Weight 149.0 g. (Figure 14).

Fox 1947a: 27–8, 30–1, 33, 61, 63, 80, no. 48, pl. XXI; Spratling 1972: 86, 89–90, 260, 340; Savory 1976a: 32, 57, no. 17.48, fig. 17.3; Palk 1984: 33, no. DJ23, fig. C16.1.

14. Three-link bridle-bit (accession no. 44.32.49i)

Iron rein-ring and side-link both plated with copper alloy. The rein-ring is thin, distorted and badly worn but approximately circular in shape (external diameter approximately 69 mm, internal diameter approximately 56 mm) and cross-section (diameter 6 mm). Part of a continuous, decorative, wavy pseudo-seam, which mimics leatherworking, survives on the outer edge of the rein-ring. It is not certain whether this was produced by punching up the copper alloy plating or soldering on a wire to the rein-ring; although the punch marks were probably not capable of producing such a feature there is no evidence of solder either. There are no stop-studs. The side-link (length 59 mm) has a segmented shape mimicking the form of cast copper alloy examples. The inner eye of the side-link head is set off-centre probably to compensate for wear, some of which has occurred. Possibly from the same three-link bridle-bit as No. 15. Weight 63.3 g. (Figure 14).

Fox 1947a: 28, 30–1, 33, 61, 63, 65, 80, no. 49, pl. XXII; Spratling 1972: 86, 89–90, 260, 340; Savory 1976a: 32, 57, no. 17.49, fig. 18.1; Palk 1984: 33, no. DJ24, fig. C16.2).

15. Three-link bridle-bit (accession no. 44.32.49ii)

Iron rein-ring and side-link both plated with copper alloy. The majority of the rein-ring is missing and the remainder is thin, worn and corroded, but clearly circular in shape and cross-section (diameter 6 mm). There are no stop-studs. The corroded side-link (length 58 mm) has a segmented shape mimicking the form of cast copper alloy examples. The inner-eye of the side-link head is set off-centre probably to compensate for wear. Possibly from the same three-link bridle-bit as No.14. Weight 40.7 g. (Figure 14).

Fox 1947a: 28, 30–1, 33, 61, 63, 65, 80, no. 49, pl. XXII; Savory 1971: 66; Spratling 1972: 86, 89–90, 260, 340; Savory 1976a: 32, 57, no. 17.49, fig. 18.1; Northover 1991a: 392–3.

16. Rein-ring (accession no. 44.32.52)

Penannular, slightly distorted, copper alloy tubular rein-ring. Oval in shape (external diameter 84–9 mm, internal diameter 63–9 mm) and cross-section (diameter 10–11 mm) with a butt-join on the inner face. Two spherical stop-studs, with wear facets on the sides in contact with the side-link, are set towards either end of the ring and are fixed by copper alloy rivets which pass from the top of the studs through the ring and are hammered almost flush with the lower surface of the rein-ring. Both ends of the ring taper slightly and are worn on the inner face. Weight 56.6 g. (Figure 15).

Fox 1947a: 28, 31, 33, 61, 63, 81, no. 52, pl. XXII; Spratling 1972: 260, 448, no. 155, fig. 51; Savory 1976a: 58, no. 17.52, fig. 18.3.

17. Rein-ring (accession no. 44.32.53)

Penannular, slightly distorted, copper alloy tubular rein-ring. Oval in shape (external diameter 74–7 mm, internal diameter 57–60 mm), circular in cross-section (diameter 8.5 mm) with a butt-join on the inner face. Each end of the rein-ring is pierced by two pairs of diametrically opposed rivet holes (diameter 2 mm) set on the upper and lower sides. The inner pair on one side have wear facets around their perimeter and on the other side the outer pair contains a copper alloy rivet (length 14 mm) which presumably held a lost stop-stud in place. There are also wear facets on the inner face at each end of the ring. Weight 29.1 g. (Figure 15).

Fox 1947a: 28, 31, 33, 61, 63, 81, no. 53, pl. XXVI; Spratling 1972: 260, 449, no. 157, fig. 51; Savory 1976a: 58, no. 17.53, fig. 20.5; Arslan and Vitali 1991: 753, no. 689a; Northover 1991a: 392–3.

18. Rein-ring (accession no. 44.32.54)

Penannular, copper alloy tubular rein-ring, too distorted to reconstruct the original dimensions but curvilinear in shape and circular in cross-section (diameter 8 mm) with a butt-join on the inner face. Each end of the rein-ring is pierced by two pairs of diametrically opposed rivet holes (diameter 2 mm) set on the upper and lower sides. The inner pairs on both sides show considerable wear facets around their circumference, caused by the (now missing) stop-studs, giving the ring a pinched appearance. Wear facets are also observable on the inner face at each end of the ring. Weight 25.9 g. (Figure 15).

Fox 1947a: 28, 31, 33, 61, 63, 81, no. 54, pl. XXVI; Spratling 1972: 260, 449, no. 157,

fig. 51; Savory 1976a: 58, no. 17.54, fig. 20.6; Arslan and Vitali 1991: 753, no. 689a; Northover 1991a: 392.

19. Rein-ring (accession no. 44.32.86)

Penannular, copper alloy, tubular, rein-ring, slightly distorted but circular in shape (external diameter 70 mm, internal diameter 56 mm), circular cross-section (diameter 6.5–7 mm) with a butt-join on the inside. Each end of the ring is pierced by a pair of diametrically opposed holes (diameter 1 mm). There are no wear facets on the ring. Iron corrosion deposits surviving inside the ring at both ends suggest that the connecting 'bridge' or sleeve was iron which has preferentially corroded during deposition. Weight 17.1 g. (Figure 15).

Fox 1947a: 28, 61, 90, no. 86, pl. XXII; Spratling 1972: 340–1; Savory 1976a: 59, no. 17.86, fig. 18.2.

20. Rein-ring (accession no. 44.294.10)

Penannular, copper alloy tubular rein-ring, slightly distorted but oval in shape (external diameter 91–8 mm, internal diameter 70–6 mm), oval cross-section (diameter 10–13 mm) with a butt-join on the inside. The ends of the ring are slightly narrower and at one end the butt-join is slightly overlapped. Each end is also pierced by a pair of diametrically opposed holes (diameter 2 mm), one of which contains a copper alloy spherical stop-stud (diameter approximately 9 mm) fixed by a copper alloy rivet which passes from the top of the stud through the ring and is hammered flush with the lower surface of the ring. The ends of the ring are worn, presumably where they accommodated the side-link. The stop-studs and rivet holes show no signs of wear. Weight 59.8 g. (Figure 15).

Fox 1947a: 28, 61, 63, 95, no. 129, pl. XXIX; Spratling 1972: 260, 448, no. 156, fig. 51; Savory 1976a: 59, no. 18.10, fig. 22.3.

21. Ring (possible centre-link from bridle-bit) (accession no. 44.32.84)

Copper alloy plated iron ring, slightly distorted (external diameter approximately 30 mm), and circular-sectioned (diameter 6 mm). One end is damaged and incomplete, the other is finished with a flat surface, suggesting that the ring was originally penannular or had a butt join. Traces of the copper alloy plating are visible on the flat surface of the undamaged end of the ring, suggesting that if the ring was originally closed then it was not hammer welded but butt-jointed and brazed in the plating process. Possibly a centre-link from a three-link bridle-bit on analogy with the example on No. 10. Weight 8.7 g. (Figure 15).

Fox 1947a: 6, 89, no. 84, pl. XXI; Savory 1976a: 59, no. 17.84, fig. 17.5.

22. Two-link bridle-bit (accession no. 44.32.58)

Two-link bridle-bit consisting of two cast copper alloy rein-rings and two cast copper alloy side-links. One rein-ring is almost circular in shape (external diameter 99–101 mm) and circular in cross-section (diameter 7 mm), the other is also almost circular in shape (external diameter 100–1 mm) but oval in cross-section (diameter 7–8 mm).

Neither have stop-studs or signs of wear. The side-links are of segmented form with rounded terminal bulb sockets flanked by heavy moulded flanges, rectangular-sectioned link shafts with rounded corners, and circular link shaft heads with centrally set perforations. The side-link with both perforations in the same plane is longer than the other (75 mm as opposed to 73 mm) and contains casting flaws in its link-head. There is considerable wear around the link shaft head and terminal bulb socket of both side-links. Weight 315.5 g. (Figure 16).

Fox 1947a: 29, 33, 61, 83, no. 58, pls VIII and XXVI; Spratling 1972: 99–100, 340, 454, no. 169, fig. 65; Savory 1976a: 32, 58, no. 17.58, fig. 20.4; Palk 1984: 42, no. SJ5, fig. C28; Arslan and Vitali 1991: 753–4, 793, no. 689b; Jope 2000: 302, pl. 275.e.

23. Three-link bridle-bit (accession no. 44.32.55)

Cast copper alloy, rein-ring, two side-links, and a centre-link. The rein-ring is circular in shape (external diameter 81 mm, internal diameter 65–7 mm) but slightly oval in cross-section (diameter 7–8 mm). There are no stop-studs, but two buffer-like terminals serve the same function. In between the terminals is a thinner, differentially worn, bar circular in cross-section (diameter 6 mm), on which the side-link plays. The buffer-like terminals protrude more on one side than the other, this asymmetry echoing that of the stop-studs upon which they are presumably based. There are wear facets on the link sides of the terminals.

The two side-links are almost identical (length 70 mm, width of terminal bulb

Colour Plate 1a: Globular cauldron fragment (No. 25) (not to scale)

Colour Plate 1b: 'Trumpet' fragment (No. 31) (not to scale)

*Colour Plate 2: Crescentic plaque (bottom left) and detail of decorative design (top) (No. 47)
(not to scale). Swastika design on so-called horn-cap (bottom right) (No. 49) (not to scale)*

Colour Plate 3: Shield boss mount (No. 48) (not to scale)

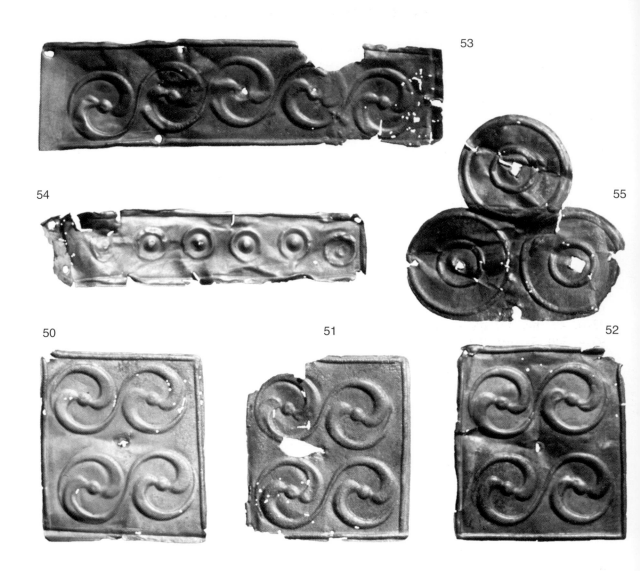

Colour Plate 4: So-called casket ornament (Nos 50–55) (scale 1:1)

socket 18 mm). Unusually the perforations at either end of the side-links are in the same plane. Seen from the side the links are streamlined in shape, and only widen around the perforations in one dimension. There are wear facets around all of the perforations. The prominent central roll of the centre-link is rounded and its perforations, which were originally D-shaped, have a lenticular shape owing to wear. All of the links in this bridle-bit are shaped so the joints are restricted to lateral movement only. Weight 258.4 g. (Figure 16, Pl. 5).

Fox 1947a: 28–9, 33, 61–2, 65, 81, no. 55, pls VIII and XXV; Haworth 1971: 28–9, 33–4, 45, no. 13, fig. 4; Spratling 1972: 93–4, 340; Savory 1976a: 32–3, 35, 58, no. 17.55, fig. 20.1; Raftery 1983: 11, no. 1, fig. 1.1; 1984: 16, 33, fig. 6.1; Palk 1984: 34, no. DJ25, fig. C17; Jope 2000: 153, 304, pl. 280.a.

24. Globular cauldron fragment (accession no. 44.32.76i)

Wrought sheet copper alloy cauldron fragment including rim and shoulder (width approximately 240 mm, height approximately 215 mm, rim length 210 mm), folded during collection (Fox 1947a: 87) and consequently creased with modern tears and folds (including one double-fold adjacent to the elaborate tag which superficially appears to be an antique join or pleat). The shoulder is 94 mm below the rim (following the curve) and is therefore from a different vessel to that represented by No. 25 (contra Fox 1947a: 42, 87–8). The rim is roughly cut; approximately 9–11 mm below it on both the inside and outside are uneven polished lines (about 1–2 mm wide) which run

parallel with the rim and mark where a reinforcing rim was set. Traces of iron corrosion remain on the external side of the rim suggesting that the reinforcing band was made from iron. The external face is blackened apart from the area above the polished line below the rim which has a lighter, mottled character similar to that of the internal surface. This blackening is an oxidization phenomenon presumably owing to use. Three copper alloy tags were riveted to the internal surface below the rim. Two remain: an incomplete tag (7 x 15 mm) fixed by a single rivet and an elaborate tapering, waisted tag (19 x 52 mm) fixed by three rivets. An area of differential corrosion between these indicates the position of the lost, third tag. The two surviving tags show differential corrosion where the reinforcing rim crossed them, and the more elaborate tag is pierced by the rivet which attached the escutcheon to the vessel (see below), suggesting that they are original features and not secondary repairs. Two features of note on the external surface are: the small area of dense horizontal striations below the elaborate tag, whose significance is unknown, and part of a U-shaped patch of differential corrosion below the rim (depth 53 mm) marking the location of a lost escutcheon which, on analogy with fragment No. 25, was attached by a rivet set above it through a recessed fixing hole (diameter 4 mm) on the rim of the fragment. Part of the fragment's edge was deliberately cut in antiquity. Weight 85.9 g. (Figure 17).

Fox 1947a: 42–4, 87–8, no. 76 (fragment I), pl. XXXVIII; Piggott 1952–3: 41; Spratling 1971: 111; Savory 1971: 66; Spratling 1972: 237, 343, 587, no. 427; Savory 1976a: 33, 58, no. 17.76, fig. 29.4 (fragment I); Northover 1991a: 392.

25. Globular cauldron fragment (accession no. 44.32.76ii)

Wrought sheet copper alloy cauldron fragment including rim and shoulder (width approximately 280 mm, height 210 mm, rim length 150 mm), folded during collection (Fox 1947a: 87) and consequently flattened and creased with tears and folds. The shoulder is 67 mm below the rim (following the curve) and is therefore from a different vessel to that represented by No. 24 (contra Fox 1947a: 42, 87–8). The rim is roughly cut; about 9–10 mm below it on the inside and approximately 10–12 mm on the outside are uneven polished lines (1–2 mm wide) which run parallel with the rim and mark where a reinforcing rim was set. Traces of iron corrosion remain on both the internal and external sides of the rim, suggesting that the reinforcing band was made from iron. The external side is blackened apart from the area above the polished line below the rim which has a lighter, mottled character similar to that of the internal surface. This blackening is an oxidization phenomenon presumably due to use. A U-shaped patch of differential corrosion below the rim (width 55 mm, depth 45 mm) marks the location of a lost escutcheon which was fixed to the vessel through a recessed rivet hole (diameter 3 mm) set just below the rim. A rivet fixing two square washers (dimensions 5–6 mm) to the cauldron fragment is set in one corner, presumably it was part of the secondary repair of a hole. Part of the fragment's edge has been deliberately cut in antiquity. Weight 62.6 g. (Figure 18, Col. Pl. 1a).

Fox 1947a: 42–4, 87–8, no. 76 (fragment II), pl. XXXVIII; Piggott 1952–3: 41; Spratling 1971: 111; Savory 1971: 66; Spratling 1972: 237, 343, 587, no. 427; Savory 1976a: 33, 58, no. 17.76, fig. 29.4 (fragment II); Northover 1991a: 392.

26. Hemispherical cauldron fragment (accession no. 44.32.77)

Wrought sheet copper alloy cauldron fragment including rim (width approximately 145 mm, height approximately 275 mm, rim length 83 mm), although now flattened, originally hemispherical in form. The fragment is creased with folds; it is uncertain whether they are ancient or modern. The external surface is darker than the internal surface, presumably as a result of oxidization through use. The rim has a smooth, finished edge below which are pierced four unevenly spaced rivet holes (diameter 2–2.75 mm), one of which retains a copper alloy rivet. The rivet is hammered flush with the internal surface and protrudes approximately 1 mm beyond the external surface, suggesting the rim was reinforced by a thin external band. There is a faint corrosion differential on the external surface of the rim running parallel to the edge about 11–15 mm below it. The internal surface has been repaired, four patches survive and differential corrosion associated with a fifth is observable. The patches were fixed by small rivets and areas of dark blackening around the patch edges suggest that they were possibly brazed in part as well. The superimposition of two of the patches demonstrates that the technique was only partially successful. Part of the fragment's edge was deliberately cut in antiquity. Weight 67.5 g. (Figure 19).

Fox 1947a: 42–4, 88, no. 77, pl. XXXVIII; Piggott 1952–3: 41; Spratling 1971: 111; 1972: 237, 265, 343, 587, no. 428; Savory 1976a: 33, 58, no. 17.77, fig. 29.1; Northover 1991a.

27. Scabbard mouth for a dagger or sword (accession no. 44.32.10)

Cast, copper alloy fitting (dimensions 14.5 x 56 x 24 mm). The flat, elliptically shaped rim (external diameter 56 x 24 mm, internal diameter 52 x 17 mm, depth 3 mm) is decorated with two parallel grooves which are slightly worn at the front. Below this is a flange recessed by 0.5–1.0 mm to accommodate the thin metal of the scabbard. On its outer face the flange extends into a broad D-shaped plate (maximum depth 11.5 mm, width 45.5 mm). Weight 18.8 g. (Figure 20).

Fox 1947a: 6, 73, no. 10, pl. XVI; Piggott 1950: 22, 28; Spratling 1972: 160, 503, no. 269, fig. 113; Savory 1976a: 29, 57, no. 17.10, fig. 14.4.

28. Probable scabbard or sheath binding (accession no. 44.32.11)

Rectangular strip of copper alloy sheet folded over to form a binding of D-shaped section (52 x 11 mm). The back has a convex outward curve and contains the join, a simple lap seam fixed by three rivets, with their flat heads on the inner side, hammered flush with the external surface. The front is decorated with a plain, recessed rectangular panel (44 x 33 mm). The upper and lower edges of the front are folded over to form a flat rim. Weight 15.6 g. (Figure 20).

Fox 1947a: 6, 74, no. 11, pl. XVI; Spratling 1972: 160, 503, no. 270, fig. 113; Savory 1976a: 29, 57, no. 17.11, fig. 14.6.

29. Pommel from a dagger or sword (accession no. 44.32.12)

Cast copper alloy pommel with iron tang. The pommel design consists of three curves arranged to form a pelta shape, or curve sided triangle, consisting of an upper convex curve and two smaller concave curves which meet in a central point set below the outer edges of the upper curve. The sides are flat, 2.5 mm thick, and splay out from the top (width 10–15 mm). The upper part of a deliberately broken, rectangular-sectioned iron tang (length 59 mm) which tapers towards its tip, is slotted through the top of the pommel where it has been worked flush with the surface of the copper alloy. Weight 46.1 g. (Figure 20).

Fox 1947a: 6, 60, 74, no. 12, pl. XV; Spratling 1972: 158, 515, no. 294, fig. 121; Savory 1976a: 29, 57, no. 17.12, fig. 13.6.

30. Cylinder (accession no. 44.32.88)

Short, copper alloy sheet, cylindrical mount (current dimensions 80 x 53 x 0.25 mm, original diameter approximately 19 mm, original length 80 mm), which has been opened out along a line of weakness. Originally fixed through two corresponding sets of four rivet holes (diameter 1.5 mm) situated on opposing edges. The cylinder was pierced by two sub-rectangular holes (dimensions 16 x 7 mm, and 13 x 7 mm respectively) originally situated opposite each other and two sub-rounded holes (diameters 5–7 mm and 4–5 mm respectively) on one side only. The sub-rectangular holes may have accommodated a peg or pin while the sub-rounded holes may have received decorative studs. Presumably a mounting on a pole, the cylinder could have had a variety of uses none of which can be proved. Weight 10.2 g. (Figure 20).

Fox 1947a: 58, 90, no. 88, pl. XVI; Savory 1976a: 59, no. 17.88, fig. 14.3.

31. 'Trumpet' fragment (accession no. 44.32.74)

Fragment of curved copper alloy sheet cylinder (length 357 mm, diameter 26.5 mm, thickness of outer casing 0.50–0.75 mm) broken at one end and terminating in a symmetrical, well cast, hollow biconical boss (length 26 mm, maximum diameter 58.5 mm) fixed by a slight flange to the other end of the cylinder. The tube consists of a narrow sheet of copper alloy rolled to form a cylinder (width/circumference approximately 84 mm) with a butt-join on its concave side. Copper alloy rivets set on alternate sides of the join, 13 mm apart longitudinally and 7 mm apart transversely, fix a narrow strip of copper alloy sheet (width 16 mm) to the internal side of the tube to seal the join. The join has been closed by hammering the rivets, resulting in both the join and internal strip having slightly wavy edges. The rivets (external diameter 2 mm, internal diameter about 4 mm), twenty-five of which survive, have been filed flush with both the internal and external surfaces. Only that part of the join by the boss has remained closed (length approximately 50 mm).

Towards the torn end of the tube a riveted flattened oval-shaped patch (now lost) was decorated with a simple design of linked ovals filled with chased basket-work pattern. Between the patch and the torn end, the join had been brazed and decorated with an engraved pattern set within a rectangular panel (width 8 mm, minimum length 20 mm). Too little survives to identify the pattern. The brazing and both the engraved decoration and patch are arguably secondary additions. Although the rivet hole at this point is perfect, as noted by Plenderleith (Fox 1947a: 87), this does not suggest that the brazing was conducted prior to riveting and that the engraved decoration is a primary element of the trumpet's design, because the hole is not on the same alignment as the other fixing holes, suggesting it was, along with the brazing and engraving, part of a secondary repair. The matted patch, which partly overlaid the engraved decoration, was a later repair.

The fragment was badly crumpled and in two pieces when discovered and was consequently repaired and reshaped, after annealing, by Plenderleith (Fox 1947a: 87) who over straightened it. Weight 227.4 g (including the weight of modern solder repairs). (Figure 21, Col. Pl. 1b).

Fox 1947a: 44–5, 61–2, 86–7, no. 74, pls XII and XXXI; Savory 1968: 20, fig. 14; 1970: 46, fig. 13, pl. VI.a; 1971: 66; Spratling 1972: 342; Savory 1976a: 33, 35, 58, no. 17:74, fig. 23; Raftery 1983: 242, no. 784, fig. 23; 1984: 134–6, 139, fig. 75; Jope 2000: 112, 147, 164, 252, pl. 103.f–h.

32. Sheet (possible cauldron) fragment (accession no. 2002.40H/1)

Rectangular, copper alloy, sheet fragment (dimensions 17.5 x 51 x 0.45–0.55 mm) with an oxidized 'tide-mark', visible on both sides and polished on one, separating two areas of differential corrosion. The 'tide-mark' and character of the fragment are paralleled by one of the cauldron fragments (No. 25) and consequently it is provisionally interpreted as the corrosion pattern caused by a reinforcing band on the rim of a cauldron. Weight 1.9 g. (Figure 20).

33. Sheet fragment (accession no. 2002.40H/3)

Sub-triangular, copper alloy sheet fragment (dimensions 24 x 35 x 0.40–0.45 mm), cracked and fragile. Possible fixing hole on one edge. Weight 0.7 g. (Figure 20).

34. Sheet fragment (accession no. 2002.40H/4)

Distorted, thick, rectangular-shaped copper alloy fragment (dimensions 20 x 81 x 0.65–0.80 mm) with an L-shaped patch riveted onto one corner (thickness 1.15 mm). The other face of the L-shaped patch contains a second copper alloy rivet. There is also a second rivet hole in the same corner of the main fragment. One edge of the fragment is cut. Weight 6.5 g. (Figure 20).

35. Coiled decorative strip (accession no. 44.32.68)

Copper alloy strip fragment (length approximately 490 mm, width 12–14 mm, thickness 0.30–0.40 mm) with smooth lateral edges. One end is torn but the other, although slightly damaged, is original and rounded with a central fixing hole (diameter 2 mm) set 2 mm in from the edge. There is a second fixing hole situated slightly off-

centre about 32 mm from the rounded end. The area round both pin holes is deformed, suggesting that the strip was prised from its backing in antiquity. A linear mark running across the internal side of the rounded end 9 mm from the edge separates a difference in corrosion, possibly indicating the strip was overlapped.

The torn end contains two noteworthy features. First, there are five marks, arranged into two sets, indented into the external surface. The first set is a group of two oval marks about 11 mm from the torn end set on opposing edges of the strip. Both contain a dark turquoise residue. The second set is approximately 79 mm from the torn end, these three marks are shallow and no residue can be observed in them. None of these indentations perforated the strip; they are probably ancient damage. Second, a faint, decorative incised off-centre line extends on the external surface from the edge of the torn end for a distance of about 50–60 mm where it terminates adjacent to some angled scratches. This faint decoration does not visibly continue at any other point. There are also a number of patches of striations (length approximately 10 mm) along the external surface of the strip, which were caused through use in antiquity rather than a crude attempt at decoration or a by-product of manufacture. Weight 10.6 g. (Figure 22).

Fox 1947a: 45–6, 86, no. 68; Savory 1976a: 33, 58, no. 17.68; Northover 1991a: 392.

36. Coiled decorative strip (accession no. 44.32.91)

Copper alloy strip fragment (length approximately 265 mm, width 12 mm, thickness

0.25–0.35 mm) with smooth lateral edges. One end is rounded and pierced by a centrally located fixing hole (diameter 2 mm) set 2 mm from the edge. The other end is cut diagonally at three angles and pierced by a fixing hole, set on the edge, which still retains a small copper alloy nail (length 9 mm) with a rounded head, square-sectioned stem, and a missing tip. The rounded end is original and presumably so is the diagonal end; neither is marked by significant differential patches of corrosion. Decorated by a single, apparently continuous and slightly off-centre, incised line from the edge of the diagonal end to 10 mm from the rounded end. The impression of the incised line is visible on the internal surface. Weight 4.5 g. (Figure 22).

Fox 1947a: 45, 90, no. 91, pl. XVI; Savory 1976a: 33, 59, no. 17.91, fig. 14.1.

37. Coiled decorative strip (accession no. 44.32.67)

Coiled, copper alloy strip with smooth but damaged lateral sides, which spirals downwards anti-clockwise through 3.75 turns (length approximately 400 mm, width 13 mm, thickness 0.45–0.50 mm). One end is square and contains a sub-circular patch of differential corrosion on its external surface while the other end is rounded and contains a rectangular patch of differential corrosion on its internal surface. The coil is pierced by three fixing holes (all diameter 2 mm), two of which are located centrally at either end of the strip 2 mm from the edge. The third is set about 25 mm from the rounded, end adjacent to an edge. A small copper alloy nail (length 13 mm), with a slightly irregular hexagonal-sectioned

upper stem and no head, has become detached from this third hole.

The external surface is decorated by an almost continuous incised line which extends from about 1 mm inside the fixing hole at the square end to the outside of the fixing hole at the rounded end. At one point, approximately 115 mm from the square end of the strip, this decorative incised line is broken. Weight 7.2 g. (Figure 22).

Fox 1947a: 45–6, 86, no. 67, pls IX and XVI; Savory 1976a: 33, 58, no. 17.67, fig. 14.2; Jope 2000: 282, pl. 218.h.

38. Coiled decorative strip (accession no. 44.32.71)

Copper alloy strip (two fragments) (combined length approximately 245 mm, width 12–12.5 mm, thickness 0.25 mm) with smooth lateral edges. One end is original; it tapers evenly on both sides for about 63 mm towards a folded and damaged tip. There are no differential corrosion patches or fixing holes, but this may be because the tip is missing. The other end has an irregular shape, a slightly rough edge and despite a small patch of differential corrosion on its external surface is probably torn. Decorated by a centrally incised line which runs along the external surface from one end to the other. The quality of this decoration is poor; approximately 55 mm from the tapering end there is a misjudged overlap and the decoration from this point towards the tapering end is badly applied. Weight 4.1 g. (Figure 22).

Fox 1947a: 46, 86, no. 71; Savory 1976a: 33, 58, no. 17.71.

39. Coiled decorative strip (accession no. 44.294.34)

Copper alloy strip fragment (length 120 mm, width 12 mm, thickness 0.25–0.30 mm) with smooth lateral edges, and broken at one end. Both ends are square in shape, but the 'true' end is pierced by a centrally placed fixing hole (diameter 2 mm) set 5 mm from the edge, and contains a circular patch of differential corrosion on its external surface. This corrosion is not as obvious as that observed on No. 37. Decorated by a single, apparently continuous and slightly off-centre, incised line which runs from the end without a fixing hole to 9 mm from the edge of the 'true' end. The impression of this line is visible on the internal surface. Weight 1.7 g. (Figure 22).

Fox 1947a: 45, 96, no. 133; Savory 1976a: 33, 59, no. 18.34.

40. Coiled decorative strip (accession no. 44.32.69)

Incomplete, copper alloy strip fragment (length approximately 375 mm, width 16 mm, thickness 0.45–0.55 mm) with smooth lateral edges. Twisted and apparently torn at either end but clearly coiled through at least four complete turns. Both ends although square are damaged enough to have been caused by tearing. There are no fixing holes, decoration or patches of differential corrosion. Weight 15.8 g. (Figure 22).

Fox 1947a: 46, 86, no. 69; Savory 1976a: 33, 58, no. 17.69.

41. Coiled decorative strip (accession no. 44.32.70)

Copper alloy strip fragment (length approximately 415 mm, width 15–16 mm, thickness 0.45–0.55 mm) with smooth lateral edges. Torn and twisted so that it is not apparent whether it was originally coiled or not. Both ends are damaged although one is slightly stepped and tapered and has been cut from above. There are no fixing holes, decoration or significant patches of differential corrosion. Weight 14.6 g. (Figure 22).

Fox 1947a: 46, 86, no. 70; Savory 1976a: 33, 58, no. 17.70.

42. Coiled decorative strip (accession no. 44.32.72)

Copper alloy strip (length approximately 340 mm, width 17–18 mm, thickness 0.25–0.30 mm), although incomplete, it remains in a more or less intact coil which spirals downwards anti-clockwise through 2.75 turns. The strip was folded upon discovery but apparently fell naturally into a coil when examined (Fox 1947a: 86). The lateral edges of the piece are rough and slightly serrated. One end is ragged and was probably torn in antiquity. The other is still intact, square, has a smooth edge and is pierced by three crudely aligned pin holes (diameter 1 mm). Exceptionally, these fixing holes are apparently pierced from the internal surface outwards.

The strip is divided into a series of panels defined by the modern folds. The majority of these panels are concave, rather than convex as one would suppose, suggesting that when the strip was 'restored to its original shape' the coil was mistakenly turned inside out. Hence the current external surface was originally the internal surface of the strip and the three fixing holes were really pierced from the external side. Weight 6.6 g. (Figure 22).

Fox 1947a: 46, 86, no. 72; Savory 1976a: 58, no. 17.72.

43. Coiled decorative strip (accession no. 44.32.73)

Copper alloy strip (length 260 mm, width 17–18 mm, thickness 0.20–0.30 mm); now too folded for it to be certain whether it was originally coiled. The lateral edges are rough and slightly serrated while the ends are smoother but it is still uncertain that they are original. The strip tapers from 17 mm to 14 mm in width over a distance of approximately 95 mm towards one end. The recognition of internal and external sides is based solely on the evidence of a fixing hole, set just off-centre about 61 mm from the wider end, which is assumed to have been pierced from the outside of the strip. The fixing hole is filled with iron corrosion products suggesting that it was fixed by an iron pin now corroded away. No decoration or patches of differential corrosion are visible. Weight 5.1 g. (Figure 22).

Fox 1947a: 46, 86, no. 73; Savory 1976a: 58, no. 17.73.

44. Bean-shaped plaque (accession no. 44.32.17)

Copper alloy bean-shaped panel (length 69 mm, maximum width 35.5 mm), pierced by recessed fixing holes at either corner (diameter 1.5 mm) and an unsunk hole at the apex of the convex edge (diameter 1.0 mm). The corners are turned up, suggesting that the plaque was prised from its backing. The plaque is decorated with a central bean-shaped area of repoussé relief (height 3 mm) further emphasized by a chased line and bordered by a level, narrow flange (width 4–5 mm) for fixing the plaque to a flat surface. The relief decoration is dented near the middle of the concave edge, it is probable that this is antique damage. Almost identical to No. 45. Weight 9.8 g. (Figure 23).

Fox 1947a: 7, 74, no. 17, pl. XXV; Spratling 1972: 177–8, 541, no. 324, fig. 134; Savory 1976a: 30, 57, no. 17.17, fig. 20.2.

45. Bean-shaped plaque (accession no. 44.32.18)

Copper alloy bean-shaped panel (length 70 mm, maximum width 36.5 mm), pierced by recessed fixing holes at either corner (diameter 1.5 mm) and an unsunk hole at the apex of the convex edge (diameter 1.0 mm). The plaque is decorated by a central bean-shaped area of repoussé relief (height 2 mm) further emphasized by a chased line and bordered by a level, narrow flange (width 4–5 mm) for fixing the plaque to a flat surface. The convex edge of the plaque is buckled in two places and one of the fixing holes is damaged; it is uncertain whether this is antique or modern damage. Almost identical to No. 44. Weight 11.2 g. (Figure 23).

Fox 1947a: 7, 74, no. 18, pl. XXV; Spratling 1972: 177–8, 541, no. 324, fig. 134; Savory 1976a: 30, 57, no. 17.18, fig. 20.3.

46. Decorated curved plate (accession no. 44.32.87)

Irregular trapezoidal-shaped, copper alloy plate, curved across its longitudinal axis (dimensions 23–5 x 32–4 x 0.5–0.75 mm). Each corner is rounded and pierced by a circular fixing hole (diameter 2 mm) which is the centre of localized corrosion products. The outer, convex, surface of the plate is decorated by an incised border, which passes outside the fixing holes, and two incised diagonals running from close to the incised border's corners forming a St Andrew's cross design. The execution of the piece is poor and unbalanced, none of the edges are parallel, the application of the incised decoration is unequal, and in one corner the border design is botched. The central portion of the plate has been crumpled and the surface is marked by a series of short, aligned scratches. It is uncertain whether this damage is ancient or not. Weight 3.8 g. (Figure 23).

Fox 1947a: 58, 60, 90, no. 87, pl. XXI; Savory 1976a: 59, no. 17.87, fig. 17.4.

47. Crescentic decorative mount (accession no. 44.32.75)

Circular copper alloy sheet (diameter 183 mm, thickness 0.40–0.85 mm) with an eccentrically set, near circular (diameter 96–8 mm), void. Both the inner and outer edges are emphasized by a border (outer edge 2 mm wide, inner edge 2–3 mm) defined by a single line (chased on the inside and the upper part of the outside, and engraved on the lower part of the outside). The broadest point of the plaque contains a complex repoussé relief and incised design which centres on a roundel containing an asymmetrical triskele. There are eleven fixing holes of varying size (diameters 1.5–4 mm) at least four of which contained now lost decorative studs (two set within the asymmetrical triskele and two set either side of the near circular void). The break at the thinnest point of the plaque is modern. Weight 81.3 g (including the weight of a modern solder repair). For an extended description of the decoration see Chapter 5. (Figure 24, Col. Pl. 2a).

Fox 1947a: 46–53, 55, 59–61, 65, 87, no. 75, pls I, XIII, and XXXII; 1947b: 1–4; 1958: 33, 37, 41, 44, 98, 119, 121–3, 145, figs. 18, 19.2, 25.A,B, 30.A, 31.1, 56.A, 75, pl. 23.a; Savory 1968: 20, fig. 15; Megaw 1970: 151–2, no. 254, fig. 13; Piggott 1970: 12, no. 54; Spratling 1972: 177–8, 342–6, 541, no. 325, fig. 134; Savory 1976a: 30, 35, 40, 58, no. 17.75, pl. IV; Stead 1985a: 22–3, 41, 54, pl. 28; Megaw and Megaw 1989: 200–2, 214–15, 256, fig. 338; Jope 2000: 115, 183, 197, 271, pl. 184.

48. Mount of a shield-boss (accession no. 44.294.31)

Arched, copper alloy sheet mount of domed and elongated form (length 373 mm, breadth 126 mm, height 67 mm) for the spine and boss of a shield and attached through ten fixing holes (diameter 2.0–2.2 mm) set round the edge of the mount. The fixing holes situated at the ends of the spine and above the arches have differential corrosion around them, suggesting that decorative studs were fixed through them. The mount is decorated by an incised line set 1 mm in from its edge, which becomes faint on the two side-flanges where it may just be a manufacturing guide for cutting their shape out, and four similarly incised triskele roundels which are arranged into pairs connected by a single S-shaped incised line. The triskele motifs are infilled with fine, partially overlapping, tremolo hatching produced by rolling a round-nosed graver with an oval cross-section. There are dark, transverse, bands at the end of both spines set adjacent to the fixing holes which suggest that at some point in antiquity organic material was strapped across the mount. The ends of the spines finish in an elaborate fish-tail, or cloven hoof, shapes which are too elaborate for them to have been covered up by an adjoining mount. However, it is possible that the mount was part of a larger design made up of several mounts. Weight 88.4 g (including the weight of a modern solder repair). For an extended description of the decoration see Chapter 5. (Figure 25, Col. Pl. 3).

Fox 1945b; 1947a: 7–11, 53–8, 60–1, 65, 91, no. 98, pl. XXXVI; 1958: 43–4, 56, 97, figs. 28–9, 30C; Savory 1968: 20–1, fig. 17; Spratling 1972: 173–9, 190, 259, 265, 315, 334, 344–6, 530, no. 308, fig. 134; Savory 1976a: 30–1, 35, 59, no. 18.31, fig. 27; Stead 1985a: 22; Jope 2000: 70, 182, 249, pl. 90.

49. So-called horn-cap (accession no. 44.32.41)

Cast, copper alloy, hollow terminal (height 60 mm) circular in cross-section (maximum diameter 53.5 mm, minimum diameter 17.25 mm), with wide discoidal and D-sectioned mouldings at the top and the bottom respectively and a thinner waisted shaft between them. It is open at the lower end and closed at the top by a separately cast disc (diameter 24.5 mm). The disc is decorated with a cir-

cumscribed complex-swastika design crudely executed with a fine punch. The open end forms a socket (diameter 21.5 mm) by which the object was presumably originally fixed to a wooden shaft. Inside the lower moulding there is a residual deposit of core material consisting of concreted clay and grits. The terminal has been deliberately hacked by edged tools or weapons in antiquity on both the discoidal and D-shaped mouldings and the waisted shaft. Weight 138.3 g. (Figure 23, Col. Pl. 2b).

Fox 1947a: 15–19, 27, 61, 65, 77–8, no. 41, pls IX and XV; 1958: 28, 120, fig. 15; Piggott 1969: 379; Spratling 1972: 67–8, 71–5, 256, 339, 435, no. 131, fig. 47; Savory 1976a: 33, 41, 57, no. 17.41, fig. 13.4; Arslan and Vitali 1991: 754, 793, no. 689e; Jope 2000: 316, pl. 302.e.

50. 'Square' plaque (accession no. 44.32.78)

Copper alloy, slightly rhomboid-shaped plaque (43–44 x 49–50 mm, thickness 0.20–0.35 mm) decorated with two similar, if not identical, design elements. Each design element consists of an embossed, wiry, S-shaped scroll which terminates in small raised roundels. Embossed, comma-shaped scrolls, similar in form to the wiry S-shaped scroll, continue the curve from the roundels to give the overall impression of two conjoined circles (overall length of design 36 mm, width 18 mm, minimum distance apart of two design elements 4 mm). Three of the plaque's sides have a repoussé border (width 1.5 mm), the fourth side having a distinct groove running at a slight angle to the edge 1.5–3 mm from the edge, suggesting that it was overlapped at this end by another plaque. There is one small fixing hole in the centre of the plaque (diameter 1 mm) around which is a circular impression (diameter approximately 2.5 mm) presumably caused by the head of a stud. One corner is torn and damaged. Similar to Nos. 51 and 52. Weight 2.0 g. (Figure 26, Col. Pl. 4).

Fox 1947a: 3, 21–3, 60–1, 64–5, 88, no. 78, fig. on p. 58; pl. V.b.E; 1958: 105; Spratling 1972: 239–40, 269, 343–4, 592, no. 437A, fig. 194; Savory 1976a: 33, 49, 58, no. 17.78, fig. 7.3; Jope 2000: 133, 284, pl. 233.f.

51. 'Square' plaque (accession no. 44.32.79)
Copper alloy, slightly rectangular-shaped plaque (43–44 x 49 mm, thickness 0.20–0.30 mm) decorated with two similar, if not identical, design elements. Each design element consists of an embossed, wiry, S-shaped scroll which terminates in small raised roundels. Embossed, comma-shaped scrolls, similar in form to the wiry S-shaped scroll, continue the curve from the roundels to give the overall impression of two conjoined circles (overall length of design 36 mm, width 18 mm, minimum distance apart of design elements 2 mm). Three of the sides have a repoussé border (width 1.5 mm), the fourth being folded back and too damaged to ascertain its original character. The centre of the plaque is also damaged. There are two small fixing holes (diameter 0.5 mm) on the inside of the border on one side. Similar to Nos. 50 and 52. Weight 2.1 g. (Figure 26, Col. Pl. 4).

Fox 1947a: 3, 21–3, 60–1, 64–5, 88, no. 79, fig. on p. 58, pl. V.b.F; 1958: 105; Spratling 1972: 239–40, 269, 343–4, 592, no. 437B, fig. 194; Savory 1976a: 33, 49, 58, no. 17.79, fig. 7.4.

52. 'Square' plaque (accession no. 44.294.12)
Trapezoidal-shaped, copper alloy plaque (45–6 x 51–2 mm, thickness 0.25–0.30 mm) decorated with two similar, if not identical, design elements. Each design element consists of an embossed, wiry, S-shaped scroll which terminates in small raised roundels. Embossed, comma-shaped scrolls, similar in form to the wiry S-shaped scroll, continue the curve from the roundels to give the overall impression of two conjoined circles (overall length of design 36.5 mm, width 18 mm, minimum distance apart of design elements 4 mm). All four sides have a repoussé border (width 1.5 mm). There is a damaged central fixing hole (diameter 1 mm) around which is a faint circular impression (diameter approximately 3–4 mm), presumably caused by the head of a stud, and another, small, fixing hole (diameter 1 mm) set in one of the corners. Another corner is torn and missing. Similar to Nos. 50 and 51. Weight 2.6 g. (Figure 26, Col. Pl. 4).

Fox 1947a: 21–3, 60–1, 64–5, 96, no. 134, fig. on p. 72; 1958: 105; Spratling 1972: 239–40, 269, 343–4, 592, no. 437C, fig. 194; Savory 1976a: 33, 59, no. 18.12, fig. 7.6.

53. Rectangular plaque (accession no. 44.32.80)
Copper alloy, rectangular-shaped plaque (105 x 26–9 mm, thickness 0.20–0.30 mm) with an embossed design consisting of four conjoined, wiry, S-shaped scrolls terminating in raised roundels. Embossed, comma-shaped scrolls, similar in form to the four conjoined, S-shaped scrolls, continue the curve from the outer two roundels to give the overall impression of five conjoined

circles arranged in a slight arc. The S-shaped scrolls and the outer two comma-shaped scrolls are similar, if not identical, to those design elements employed on the 'square' plaques (Nos. 50, 51 and 52). The long sides of the plaque have a repoussé border (width 1 mm) which stops 5–6 mm from one of the short ends in an area which has been deliberately flattened out, while at the other short end the border design is flattened out by an incised line running 2.5–3 mm from the edge, suggesting that the plaque was overlapped at either end by other plaques. The plaque is pierced by six fixing holes, two of which are set in central bosses in the decorative design, and the remainder around the edges or in the corners. Weight 3.5 g (including the weight of a modern solder repair). (Figure 26, Col. Pl. 4).

Fox 1947a: 3, 21–3, 60–1, 89, no. 80, fig. on p. viii, pl. V.b.D; 1958: 105; Spratling 1972: 239, 269, 343–4, 592, no. 438, fig. 194; Savory 1976a: 33, 49, 58–9, no. 17.80, fig. 7.1; Jope 2000: 133, 284, pl. 223.e.

54. Rectangular plaque (accession no. 44.32.81)

Copper alloy, slightly tapering, rectangular plaque (84 x 18–20 mm, thickness 0.35–0.40 mm), folded and slightly torn, decorated with an embossed design consisting of a repeated motif of a central boss surrounded by a raised circular ring (external diameter 9 mm). The motif is repeated seven times and forms an uneven arc. Three sides of the plaque have a repoussé border (width 1.5–2 mm), the other, the thicker of the short sides, is damaged and may be a torn, rather than a true, edge. The border and the decorative design extend to the edge of the damaged end which is pierced by two fixing holes (diameter 2 mm). There were two other fixing holes in the corners of the other end although only one remains (diameter 1.5 mm), the other corner now being torn but complete and perforated in Fox's illustration (1947a: p. viii). Weight 1.7 g. (Figure 26, Col. Pl. 4).

Fox 1947a: 3, 21–3, 60–1, 89, no. 81, fig. on p. viii, pl. V.b.C; 1958: 105; Spratling 1972: 239, 269, 343–4, 592, no. 439, fig. 194; Savory 1976a: 33, 49, 59, no. 17.81, fig. 7.2.

55. 'Tri-disc' plaque (accession no. 44.294.13)

Copper alloy plaque (53 x 57 mm, thickness 0.15–0.20 mm) decorated with three embossed, almost identical, circles (external diameter 27 mm) arranged to form an equilateral triangle. Each circle consists of an inner and outer ring of relief decoration 1.5 mm wide. The external edges of the circles are 2 mm apart from each other at their closest point. The edge of the plaque follows the outline of the circles, leaving a 0.5–1 mm wide flange except at the 'base' where the edge runs straight from the maximum extent of one circle to another, leaving a triangular-shaped void of sheet bronze. The tri-disc is pierced by six fixing holes, one in the centre of each circle and three arranged unevenly around the edge. Several of these holes are torn and appear to have been enlarged. There are two linear folds across the face of the plaque. Weight 1.6 g. (Figure 26, Col. Pl. 4).

Fox 1947a: 21, 23, 96, no. 135, fig. on title-page; Spratling 1972: 597, no. 453, fig. 198; Savory 1976a: 33, 59, no. 18.13, fig. 7.5.

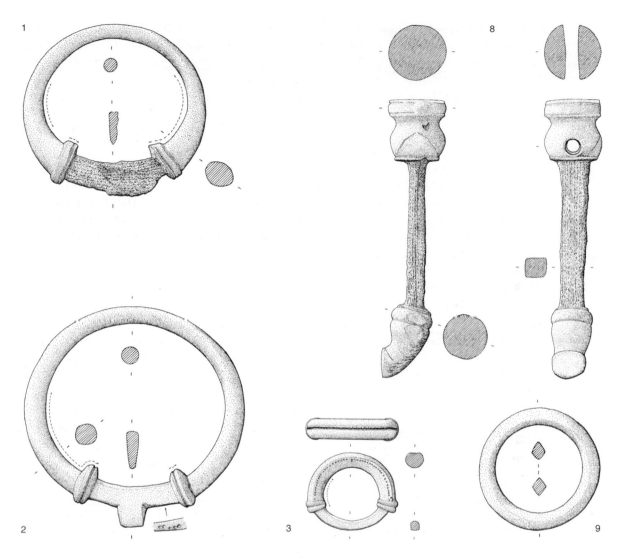

Figure 11: Terrets (Nos. 1–3): the position of the wear facets are indicated by the broken lines; linch-pin (No. 8); ring (No. 9) (scale 2:3)

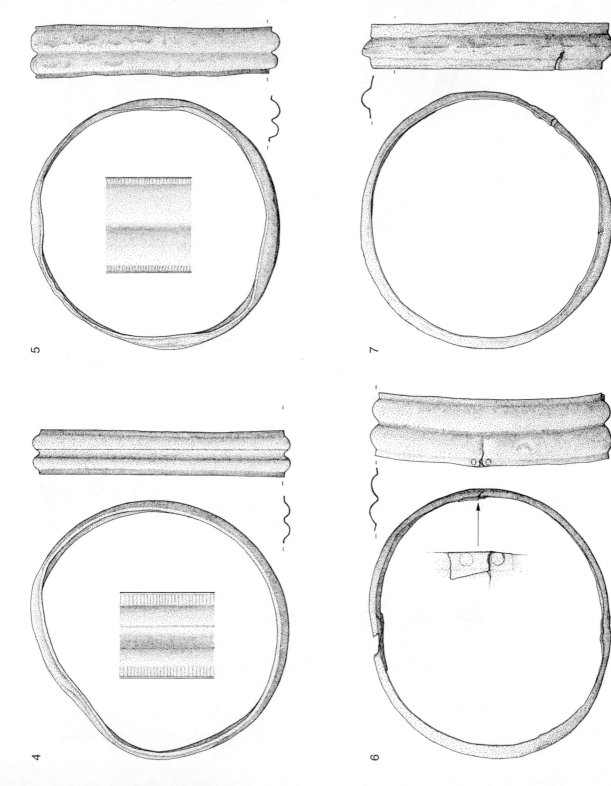

Figure 12: Nave hoops (Nos. 4–7) (scale 1:2). Details of nave hoops (Nos. 4–6) (scale 1:1)

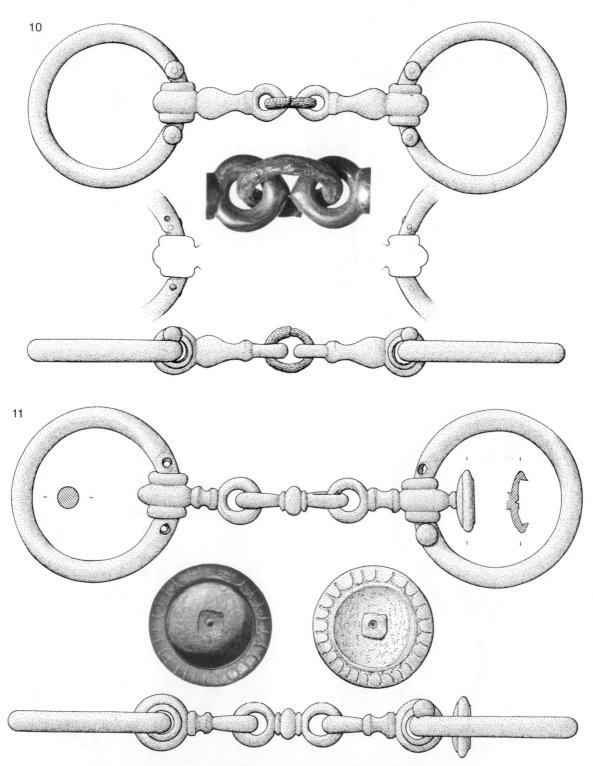

Figure 13: Three-link bridle-bit (No. 10) (scale 1:2): detail of central link (scale 1:1);
three-link bridle-bit (No. 11) (scale 1:2): detail of decorative roundel (scale 1:1)

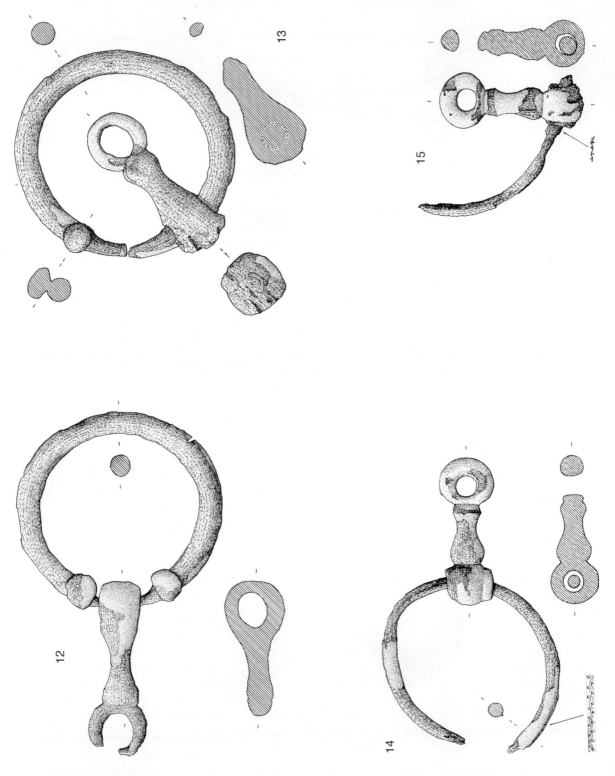

Figure 14: Three-link bridle-bits (Nos. 12–15) (scale 2:3)

16

19

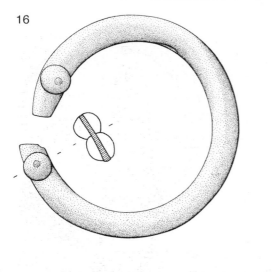

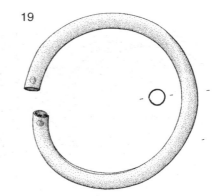

17

20

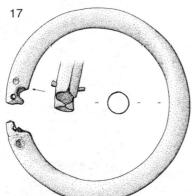

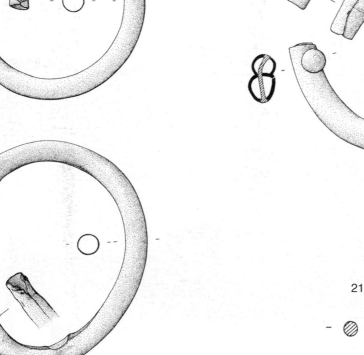

18

21

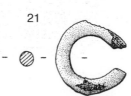

Figure 15: Rein-rings (Nos. 16–20); ring (No. 21) (scale 2:3)

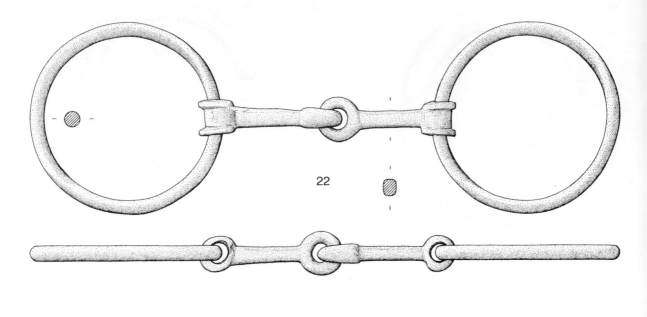

22

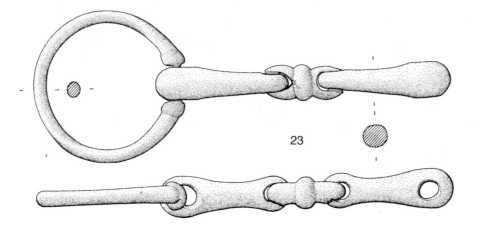

23

Figure 16: Two-link bridle-bit (No. 22) (scale 1:2); three-link bridle-bit of Irish type (No. 23) (scale 1:2)

24

Figure 17: Globular cauldron fragment (No. 24) (scale 1:2)

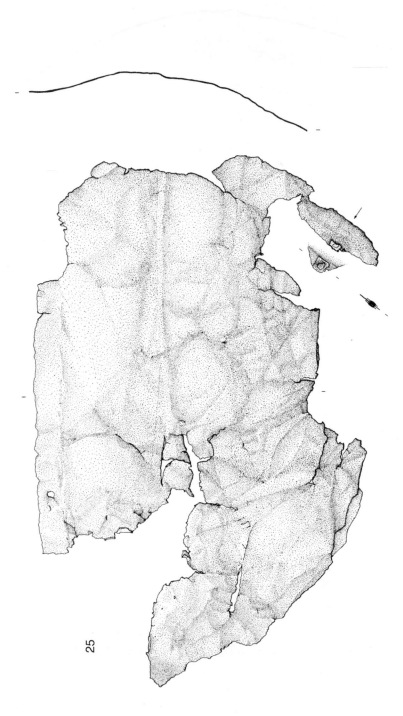

Figure 18: Globular cauldron fragment (No. 25) (scale 1:2)

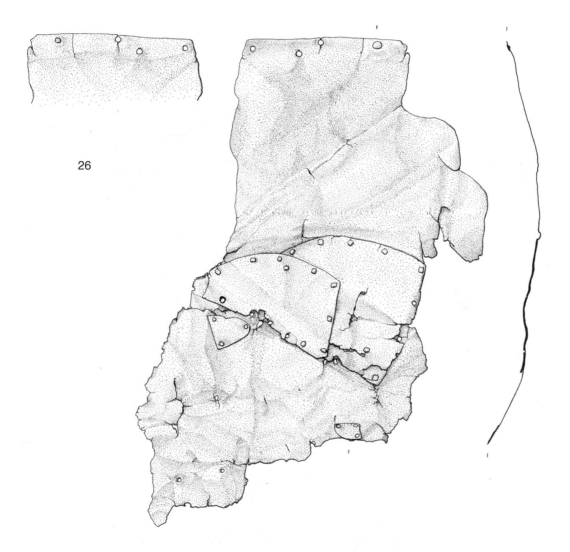

26

Figure 19: Hemispherical cauldron fragment (No. 26) (scale 1:2)

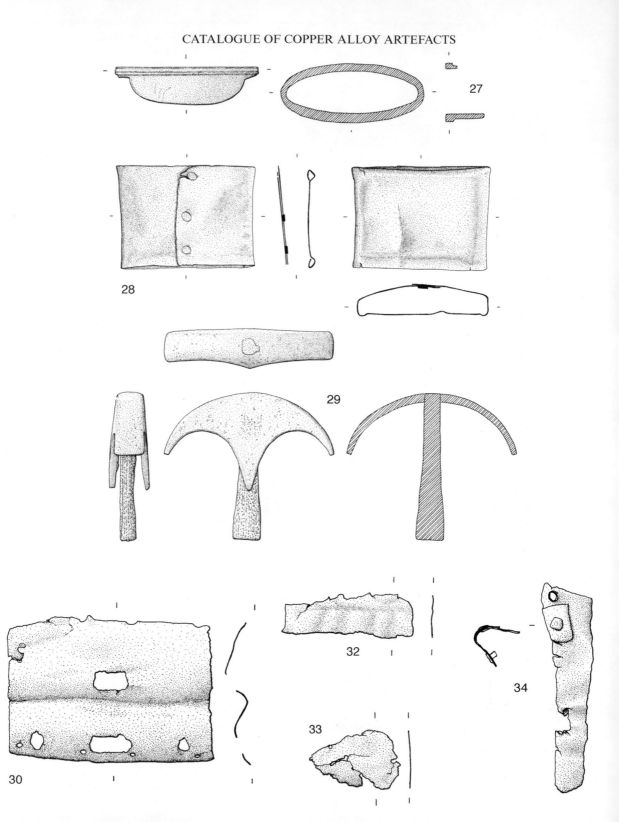

*Figure 20: Scabbard mouth (No. 27); probable scabbard or sheath binding (No. 28);
pommel (No. 29); cylinder (No. 30); sheet fragments (Nos. 32–4) (scale 2:3)*

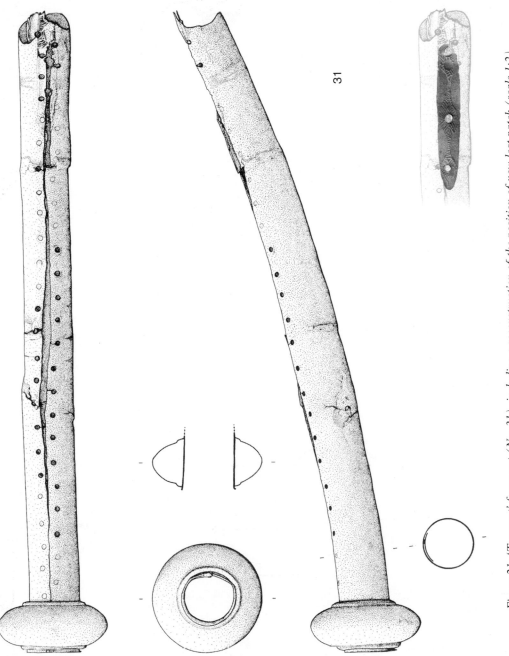

31

Figure 21: 'Trumpet' fragment (No. 31), including a reconstruction of the position of now lost patch (scale 1:2)

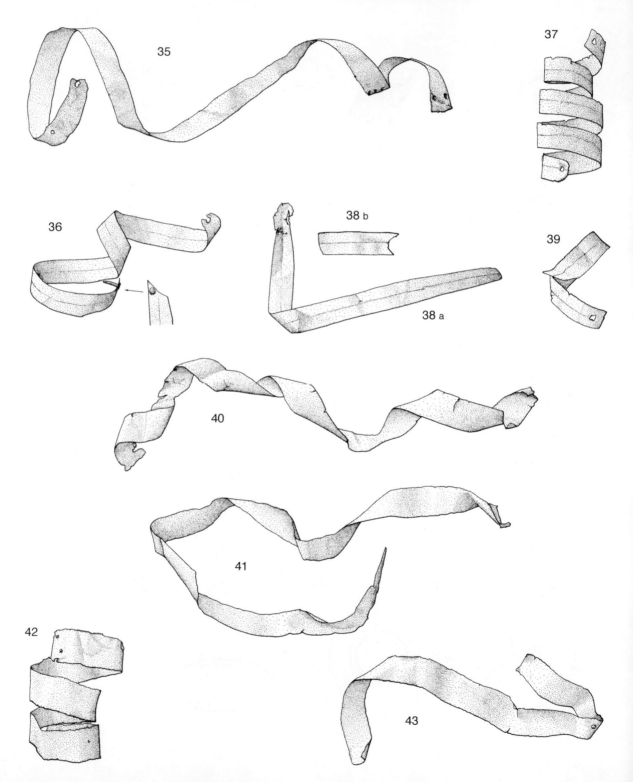

Figure 22: Coiled decorative strips (Nos. 35–43) (scale 1:2)

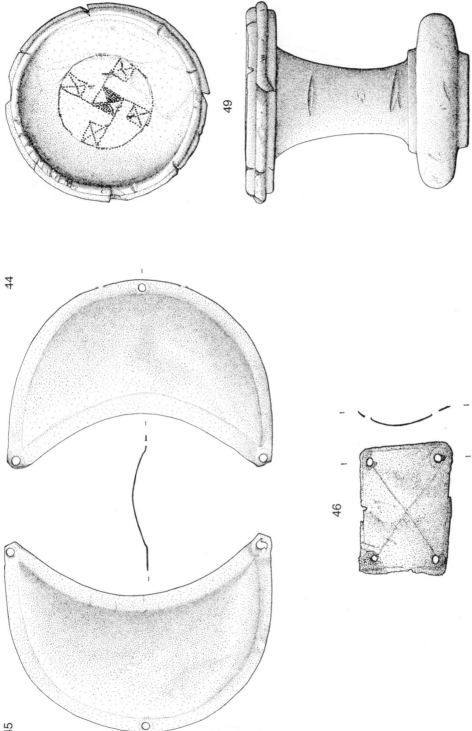

Figure 23: Bean-shaped plaques (Nos. 44–5); decorative curved plate (No. 46); so-called horn-cap (No. 49) (scale 1:1)

47

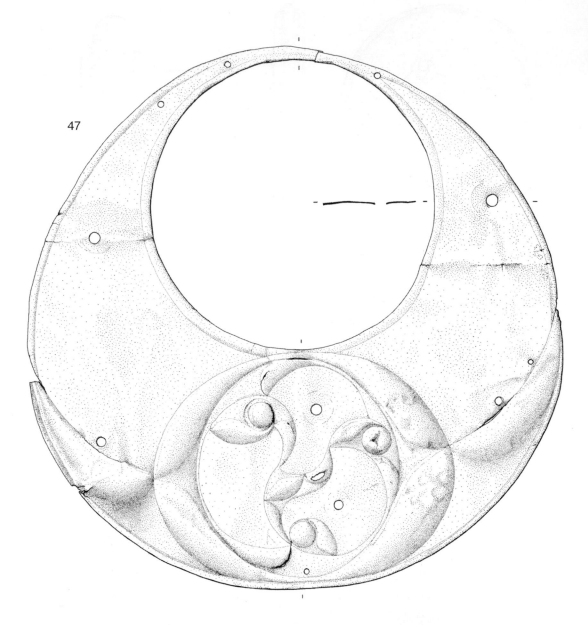

Figure 24: Crescentic decorative plaque (No. 47) (scale 3:4)

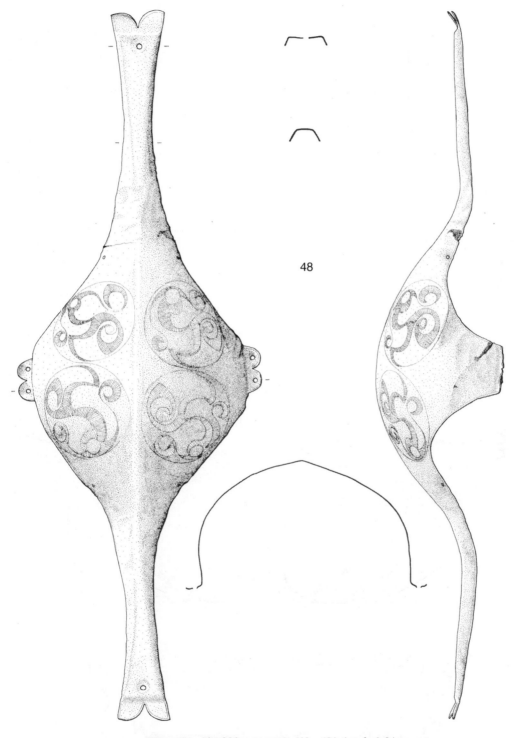

48

Figure 25: Shield boss mount (No. 48) (scale 1:2)

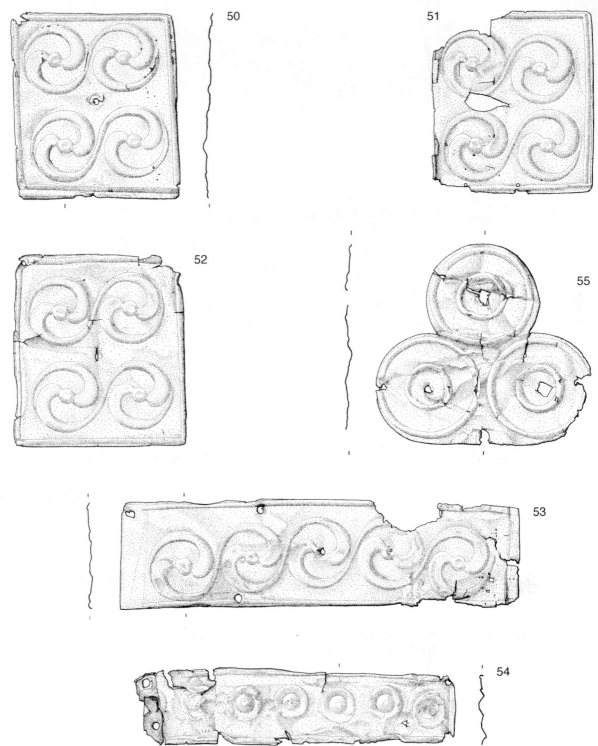

Figure 26: 'Square' plaques (Nos. 50–2); rectangular plaques (Nos. 53–4);
'tri-disc' plaque (No. 55) (scale 1:1)

PLATES

Plate 1: December 1940 (National Archives and Records Administration, Cartographic and Architectural Branch, USA, RG373 GX-12041 SD, Frame 546 23)

Plate 2: April 1942 (Central Register of Air Photography for Wales, Medmenham, H1 4/489 1PRV, Frames 46, 47, 48)

Plate 3: November 1942 (Central Register of Air Photography
for Wales, Medmenham, NLA/53 1PRV, Frames 2004, 1004)

Welsh Office   NLA/53.1.P.R.U.   13 November 1942   © Crown copyright

Plate 4: Detail of November 1942 aerial photograph (Central Register of Air Photography for Wales, Medmenham, NLA/53 1PRV, Frames 2004, 1004)

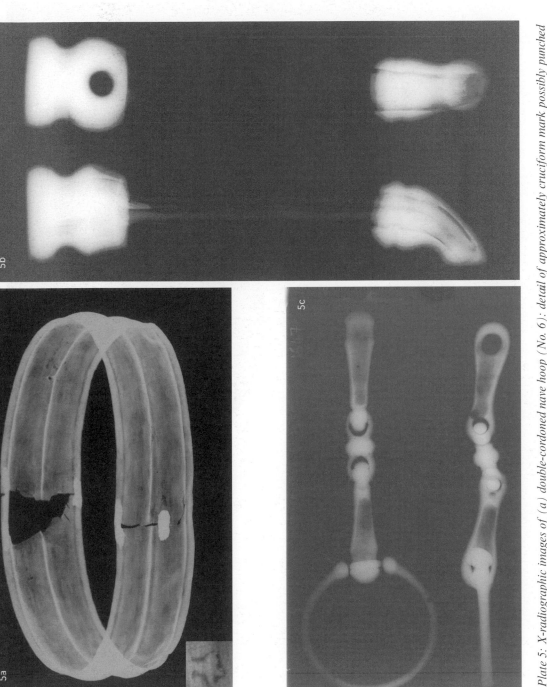

Plate 5: X-radiographic images of (a) double-cordoned nave hoop (No. 6): detail of approximately cruciform mark possibly punched on one of the cordons, (b) the 'vase-headed' linch-pin (No. 8) and (c) the three-link bridle-bit of Irish type (No. 23)

Plate 6: Shield boss mount (No. 49): (a) prior to conservation (c. 1944) and (b) after reshaping

Bibliography

Aitken, G. M. 1967. 'Third interim report on excavations at Whitcombe, Dorset', *Proc. Dorset Nat. Hist. Archaeol. Soc.*, 89, 126–7.

—— and Aitken, G. N. 1990. 'Excavations at Whitcombe, 1965–1967', *Proc. Dorset Nat. Hist. Archaeol. Soc.*, 112, 57–94.

Alcock, L. 1972. *'By South Cadbury is that Camelot ...': The Excavation of Cadbury Castle 1966–1970* (Thames and Hudson, London).

Aldhouse Green, M. 2000. 'On the road', *Brit. Archaeol.*, 52, 14–17.

Allason-Jones, L. and Bishop, M. C. 1988. *Excavations at Roman Corbridge: The Hoard*, (English Heritage Archaeol. Rep. 7, London).

Allen, D. F. 1963. *Sylloge of Coins of the British Isles: The Coins of the Coritani* (Oxford University Press, for the British Academy, London).

—— 1967. 'Iron currency bars in Britain', *Proc. Prehist. Soc.*, 33, 307–35.

—— and Nash, D. 1980. *The Coins of the Ancient Celts* (Edinburgh University Press, Edinburgh).

Allen, J. R. 1896. 'Notes on 'late-Celtic' art', *Archaeol. Cambrensis*, 51, 321–36.

—— 1905. 'Find of late-Celtic bronze objects at Seven Sisters, near Neath, Glamorganshire', *Archaeol. Cambrensis*, 60, 127–46.

Anderson, J. 1884–5. 'Notice of a bronze cauldron found with several small kegs of butter in a moss near Kyleakin in Skye: with notes of other cauldrons of bronze found in Scotland', *Proc. Soc. Antiq. Scotland*, 19, 309–15.

—— 1897–8. 'Notices of the pottery, bronze and other articles discovered during the excavations', *Proc. Soc. Antiq. Scotland*, 32, 453–71.

Anon. 1856. 'Catalogue of antiquities exhibited in the museum formed during the annual meeting of the Archaeological Institute, held at Chichester, in July, 1853', *Sussex Archaeol. Collect.*, 8, 281–344.

Anon. 1864–7. 'Various antiquities and coins discovered in the bed of the River Churn, near Cricklade, Wilts.', *Proc. Soc. Antiq. London* (2nd ser.), 3, 67–8.

Anon. 1866–8. 'Donations to the Library and Museum', *Proc. Soc. Antiq. Scotland*, 7, 7–10.

Anon. 1886. 'Thirty-eighth annual meeting', *Proc. Somersetshire Archaeol. Nat. Hist. Soc.*, 32, 1–90.

Anon. 1889–90. 'Purchases for the Museum', *Proc. Soc. Antiq. Scotland*, 24, 6–17.

Anon. 1893–4. 'Purchases for the Museum', *Proc. Soc. Antiq. Scotland*, 28, 237–43.

Anon. 1897–8. 'Donations to the Museum', *Proc. Soc. Antiq. Scotland*, 32, 55–6.

Anon. 1903. *Catalogue of the Collection of London Antiquities in the Guildhall Museum* (Guildhall Museum, London).

Anon. 1920–1. 'Donations to the Museum', *Proc. Soc. Antiq. Scotland*, 55, 10–24.

Anon. 1924. *Catalogue of the Well-Known Collection of Prehistoric Antiquities, etc.*

Chiefly from Ireland Formed by W. J. Knowles (Sotheby, Wilkinson and Hodge, London).

Anon. 1944. 'Valley RAF Station. Description of works carried out by the Ministry of War Transport as an agency service' (unpublished report, Ministry of War Transport, Valley).

Anon. 1968. 'Harlow Roman temple', *Current Archaeol.*, 11, 287–90.

Anon. 1992. 'Warrior burial found at Stanway', *Essex Archaeol. Hist. Newsl.*, 116, 9–10.

Anon. 1992–3. 'Warrior burial', *Colchester Archaeol.*, 6, 1–5.

Anon. 2000. *Portable Antiquities Annual Report 1998–99* (Department for Culture, Media and Sport, London).

Anon. 2001. *Antiquities Thursday 8 November 2001 at 10.30am and 2.30pm* (Bonhams & Brooks, London).

Anon. 2003. *Portable Antiquities Scheme. Annual Report 2001/02–2002/03* (Department for Culture, Media and Sport, London).

Archaeological Survey of Northern Ireland 1966. *An Archaeological Survey of County Down* (HMSO, Belfast).

Armstrong, E. C. R. 1923. 'The La Tène period in Ireland', *J. Royal Soc. Antiq. Ireland*, 53, 1–33.

Arslan, E. and Vitali, D. 1991. 'Catalogue and site index', in Moscati *et al.* 1991: 701–96.

Atkinson, D. 1942. *Report on Excavations at Wroxeter (the Roman City of Viroconium) in the County of Salop 1923–1927* (Oxford University Press, for the Birmingham Archaeological Society, Oxford).

Atkinson, R. J. C. and Piggott, S. 1955. 'The Torrs chamfrein', *Archaeologia*, 96, 197–235.

Austin, D., Bell, M., Burnham, B. C. and Thomas, J. 1990. 'Caer Cadwgan, Cellan 1988–9', *Archaeol. Wales* 30, 44–5.

Avery, M. 1990. 'Ulster archaeology in 1989', *Ulster J. Archaeol.* (3rd ser.), 53, 1–2.

Bagnall Smith, J. 1999. 'More votive finds from Woodeaton, Oxfordshire', *Oxoniensia*, 63, 147–85.

Bailey, G. B. and Cannel, J. 1996. 'Excavations at Kinneil fortlet on the Antonine Wall, 1980–1', *Proc. Soc. Antiq. Scotland*, 126, 303–46.

Bailey, J. B. and Haverfield, F. 1915. 'Catalogue of Roman inscribed and sculptured stones, coins, earthenware, etc., discovered in and near the Roman fort at Maryport, and preserved at Netherhall', *Trans. Cumberland Westmorland Antiq. Archaeol. Soc.* (2nd ser.), 15, 135–72.

Barber, J. and Megaw, J. V. S. 1963. 'A decorated Iron Age bridle-bit in the London Museum: its place in art and archaeology', *Proc. Prehist. Soc.*, 29, 206–13.

Barnes, I. 1985. 'The non-ferrous metalwork from Hunsbury hillfort', Northants (unpublished dissertation for postgraduate diploma in post-excavation studies, University of Leicester).

Barrett, J. C. 1989. 'Further problems in the Iron Age of southern Britain', *Scot. Archaeol. Rev.*, 6, 1–3.

—— 2000. 'Redefining the perimeter', in Barrett *et al.* 2000c: 83.

—— Downes, J. M., Freeman, P. W. M. and Musson, C. R. 2000a. 'The excavated areas', in Barrett *et al.* 2000c: 153–78.

—— Downes, J. M., Macdonald, P., Northover, P., O'Connor, B., Salter, C. and Turner, L. 2000b. 'The metalworking evidence', in Barrett *et al.* 2000c: 291–301.

—— Freeman, P. W. M. and Woodward, A. 2000c. *Cadbury Castle Somerset: The Later*

Prehistoric and Early Historic Archaeology (Eng. Heritage Archaeol. Rep. 20; English Heritage, London).

Bates, S. 2000. 'Excavations at Quidney Farm, Saham Toney, Norfolk 1995', *Britannia* 31, 201–37.

Bateson, J. D. 1981. *Enamel-Working in Iron Age, Roman and Sub-Roman Britain: The Products and Techniques* (Brit. Archaeol. Rep. Brit. Ser. 93, Oxford).

Bayley, J. 1984. 'Roman brass-making in Britain', *Hist. Metall.*, 18/1, 42–3.

—— 1990. 'The production of brass in antiquity with particular reference to Roman Britain', in P. T. Craddock (ed.), *2000 Years of Zinc and Brass* (Brit. Mus. Occas. Pap. 50, London), 7–27.

Becker, C. J. 1948. 'Die Zeitliche Stellung des Hjortspring-Fundes', *Acta Archaeol.*, 19, 145–87.

Bedwin, O. 1981. 'Excavations at Lancing Down, West Sussex 1980', *Sussex Archaeol. Collect.*, 119, 37–56.

Behn, R. 1954. *Musikleben im altertum und frühen mittelalter* (Hiersemann Verlag, Munich).

Bellows, J. 1880–1. 'On some bronze and other articles found near Birdlip', *Trans. Bristol Gloucestershire Archaeol. Soc.*, 5, 137–41.

Besly, E. 1995. 'Short cross and other medieval coins from Llanfaes, Anglesey', *Brit. Numismatic J.*, 65, 46–82.

Bevan, B. (ed.) 1999. *Northern Exposure: Interpretative Devolution and the Iron Ages in Britain* (Leicester Archaeol. Mono. 4; School of Archaeological Studies, University of Leicester, Leicester).

Birchall, A. 1965. 'The Aylesford-Swarling culture: the problem of the Belgae reconsidered', *Proc. Prehist. Soc.*, 31, 241–367.

Bird, J. 1989. 'Romano-British priestly regalia from Wanborough, Surrey', *Antiq. J.*, 69, 316–18.

Bishop, M. C. and Dore, J. N. 1988. *Corbridge. Excavations of the Roman Fort and Town, 1947–80* (Hist. Build. Mon. Comm. England Archaeol. Rep. 8, London).

Black, E. 1985. 'A note on the Farley Heath sceptre-binding', *Surrey Archaeol. Collect.*, 76, 140–2.

Blockley, K. and Blockley, P. 1989. 'Excavations at Bigberry, near Canterbury, 1981', *Archaeol. Cantiana*, 107, 239–51.

Boon, G. C. and Lewis, J. M. (eds) 1976. *Welsh Antiquity. Essays Mainly on Prehistoric Topics Presented to H. N. Savory upon his Retirement as Keeper of Archaeology* (National Museum of Wales, Cardiff).

Bourke, C. and Crone, D. 1993. 'Antiquities from the River Blackwater II, Iron Age metalwork', *Ulster J. Archaeol.* (3rd ser.), 56, 109–13.

Bourke, L. 1996. 'A watery end – prehistoric metalwork in the Shannon', *Archaeol. Ireland*, 38, 9–11.

Bowen, E. G. and Gresham, C. A. 1967. *History of Merioneth*, volume 1, *From the Earliest Times to the Age of the Native Princes* (The Merioneth Historical and Record Society, Dolgellau).

Boyd Dawkins, W. 1902. 'On Bigbury Camp and the Pilgrims' Way', *Archaeol. J.*, 59, 211–18.

Bradley, R. 1978. *The Prehistoric Settlement of Britain* (Routledge & Kegan Paul, London).

—— 1984. *The Social Foundations of Prehistoric Britain: Themes and Variations in the Archaeology of Power* (Longman, London).

—— 1987. 'Stages in the chronological development of hoards and votive deposits', *Proc. Prehist. Soc.*, 53, 351–62.

—— 1990. *The Passage of Arms: An Archaeological Analysis of Prehistoric Hoards and Votive Deposits* (Cambridge University Press, Cambridge).

—— 1995. 'The head of the river', *Antiquity*, 69, 168–9.

—— and Gordon, K. 1988. 'Human skulls from the River Thames, their dating and significance', *Antiquity*, 62, 503–9.

Brailsford, J. W. 1953. *Later Prehistoric Antiquities of the British Isles* (The Trustees of the British Museum, London).

—— 1962. *Hod Hill*, volume 1, *Antiquities from Hod Hill in the Durden Collection* (The Trustees of the British Museum, London).

—— 1975a. 'The Polden Hill hoard, Somerset', *Proc. Prehist. Soc.*, 41, 222–34.

—— 1975b. *Early Celtic Masterpieces from Britain in the British Museum* (British Museum Publications Ltd., London).

—— and Stapley, J. E. 1972. 'The Ipswich torcs', *Proc. Prehist. Soc.*, 38, 219–34.

Branigan, K. and Dearne, M. J. 1991. *A Gazetteer of Romano-British Caves and their Finds* (Department of Archaeology and Prehistory, University of Sheffield, Sheffield).

—— and —— (eds) 1992. *Romano-British Cavemen: Cave Use in Roman Britain* (Oxbow Mono. 19; Oxbow Books, Oxford).

Breeze, D. J. 1982. *The Northern Frontiers of Roman Britain* (Batsford, London).

Brent, J. 1867. 'An account of researches in an Anglo-Saxon cemetery at Stowting, in Kent, during the autumn of 1866', *Archaeologia*, 41, 409–20.

Brewster, T. C. M. 1971. 'The Garton Slack chariot burial, East Yorkshire', *Antiquity*, 45, 289–92.

—— 1975. 'Garton Slack', *Current Archaeol.*, 51, 104–16.

—— 1980. *The Excavation of Garton and Wetwang Slacks*, microfiche report (Prehist. Excav. Rep. 2; The East Riding Archaeological Research Committee, Wintringham).

Britnell, W. 1989. 'The Collfryn hillslope enclosure, Llansantffraid Deuddwr, Powys: excavations 1980–1982', *Proc. Prehist. Soc.*, 55, 89–134.

Brothwell, D. 1986. *The Bog Man and the Archaeology of People* (British Museum Publications, London).

—— and Bourke, J. B. 1995. 'The human remains from Lindow Moss 1987–8', in Turner and Scaife 1995: 52–61.

Brown, A., Brown, K., MacGregor, A., Moorey, R., Northover, P. and Sherratt, A. 1987. *Antiquities from Europe and the Near East in the Collection of the Lord McAlpine of West Green* (Ashmolean Museum, Oxford).

Browne, A. 1802. 'An account of some ancient trumpets dug up in a bog near Armagh', *Trans. Roy. Irish Acad.*, 8, 11–12.

Browne, M. 1888. 'Evidences of the antiquity of man in Leicestershire', *Trans. Leicester Literary Philos. Soc.* (new quart. ser.), 1/ix, 7–37.

Brunaux, J. L. 1988. *The Celtic Gauls: Gods, Rites and Sanctuaries*, trans. D. Nash (Seaby, London).

—— 1991. 'The Celtic sanctuary at Gournay-sur-Aronde', in Moscati *et al.* 1991: 364–5.

Bryant, S. R. and Niblett, R. 1997. 'The late Iron Age in Hertfordshire and the north Chilterns', in Gwilt and Haselgrove 1997: 270–81.

Budd, P., Scaife, B., Taylor, T. and Thomas, R. G. 1994. 'Untangling the web: some new views on the origins of prehistoric metallurgy', *J. Hist. Metall. Soc.*, 28, 98–102.

—— Haggerty, R., Pollard, A. M., Scaife, B. and Thomas, R. G. 1996. 'Rethinking the quest for provenance', *Antiquity*, 70, 168–74.

Budge, E. A. W. 1903. *An Account of Roman Antiquities Preserved in the Museum at Chesters, Northumberland* (Gilbert and Rivington, London).

Bull, W. F. 1911. 'Romano-British finds near Kettering', *Proc. Soc. Antiq. London*, 23, 493–500.

Bulleid, A. and Gray, H. St. G. 1911. *The Glastonbury Lake Village: A Full Description of the Excavations and the Relics Discovered. 1892–1907*, vol. 1 (The Glastonbury Antiquarian Society, Glastonbury).

—— and —— 1917. *The Glastonbury Lake Village: A Full Description of the Excavations and the Relics Discovered. 1892–1907*, vol. 2 (The Glastonbury Antiquarian Society, Glastonbury).

Burley, E. 1955–6. 'A catalogue and survey of the metal-work from Traprain Law', *Proc. Soc. Antiq. Scotland*, 89, 118–226.

Burns, J. 1969. 'A bronze cauldron of the Iron Age from Elvanfoot, Lanarkshire', *Glasgow Archaeol. J.*, 1, 29–34.

Burrow, I. 1981. *Hillfort and Hill-Top Settlement in Somerset in the First to Eighth Centuries AD* (Brit. Archaeol. Rep. Brit. Ser. 91, Oxford).

Bushe-Fox, J. P. 1916. *Third Report on the Excavations on the Site of the Roman Town at Wroxeter, Shropshire 1914* (Rep. Res. Comm. Soc. Antiq. London 4, London).

Carr, G. and Knüsel, C. 1997. 'The ritual framework of excarnation by exposure as the mortuary practice of the early and middle Iron Ages of central southern Britain', in Gwilt and Haselgrove 1997: 167–73.

Carson, R. A. G. and O'Kelly, C. 1977. 'A catalogue of the Roman coins from Newgrange, Co. Meath, and notes on the coins and related finds', *Proc. Royal Irish Acad.*, 77C, 35–55.

Carter, S. and Hunter, F. 2003. 'An Iron Age chariot burial from Scotland', *Antiquity*, 77, 531–5.

Caruana, I. D. 1990. 'The small finds', in M. R. McCarthy, *A Roman, Anglian and medieval site at Blackfriars Street, Carlisle: Excavations 1977–9* (Cumberland Westmorland Antiq. Archaeol. Soc. Res. Ser. 4, Kendal), 83–196.

—— 1997. 'Maryport and the Flavian conquest of northern Britain', in Wilson 1997a: 40–51.

Case, H., Bayne, N., Steele, S., Avery, G. and Sutermeister, H. 1966. 'Excavations at City Farm, Hanborough, Oxon.', *Oxoniensia*, 29/30, 1–98.

Casey, P. J. 1981. 'Lydney Park Roman temple', *Trans. Bristol Gloucestershire Archaeol. Soc.*, 99, 178.

—— and Hoffmann, B. 1999. 'Excavations at the Roman temple in Lydney Park, Gloucestershire in 1980 and 1981', *Antiq. J.*, 79, 81–143.

Chamberlain, A. T. 2003. 'The human bones', in Field and Parker Pearson 2003: 125–6.

Champion, T. C. 1985. 'Written sources and the study of the European Iron Age', in T. C. Champion and J. V. S. Megaw (eds), *Settlement and Society: Aspects of West European Prehistory in the First Millennium B.C.* (Leicester University Press, Leicester), 9–22.

Childe, V. G. 1935. *The Prehistory of Scotland* (Kegan Paul, Trench, Trubner and Co., London).

—— 1940–1. 'Examination of the prehistoric fort on Cairngryfe Hill, near Lanark', *Proc. Soc. Antiq. Scotland*, 75, 213–18.

—— 1946. *Scotland before the Scots* (Methuen & Co., London).

Clark, G. 1966. 'The invasion hypothesis in British archaeology', *Antiquity*, 40, 172–89.

Clarke, E. D. 1821. 'An account of some antiquities found at Fulbourn in Cambridgeshire', *Archaeologia*, 19, 56–61.

Clarke, J., Egan, G. and Griffiths, N. 1995. 'Harness fittings', in J. Clarke (ed.), *The Medieval Horse and its Equipment c.1150-c.1450*, (Mus. London Med. Finds London 5; HMSO, London), 43–74.

Clarke, R. R. 1939. 'The Iron Age in Norfolk and Suffolk', *Archaeol. J.*, 96, 1–113.

—— 1951. 'A hoard of metalwork of the Early Iron Age from Ringstead, Norfolk', *Proc. Prehist. Soc.*, 17, 214–25.

—— 1954. 'The Early Iron Age treasure from Snettisham Norfolk', *Proc. Prehist. Soc.*, 20, 27–86.

Clinch, G. 1901. 'Early man', in H. A. Doubleday (ed.), *The Victoria History of the Counties of England: A History of Norfolk*, vol. 1 (Archibald Constable, London), 253–78.

Clogg, P. and Haselgrove, C. 1995. 'The composition of Iron Age struck 'bronze' coinage in eastern England', *Oxford J. Archaeol.*, 14, 41–62.

Coles, J. M. 1987. *Meare Village East: The Excavations of A. Bulleid and H. St. George Gray 1932–1956* (Somerset Levels Pap. 13, Exeter).

—— and Coles, B. 1996. *Enlarging the Past. The Contribution of Wetland Archaeology. The Rhind Lectures for 1994–5* (Soc. Antiq. Scotland Mono. Ser. 11 and Wetland Archaeol. Res. Project Occas. Pap. 10; Society of Antiquaries of Scotland, in conjunction with Wetland Archaeology Research Project, Edinburgh).

—— and Minnitt, S. 1995. *'Industrious and Fairly Civilized'. The Glastonbury Lake Village* (Somerset Levels Project and Somerset County Council Museums Service, Exeter).

Collis, J. R. 1968. 'Excavations at Owslebury, Hants: an interim report', *Antiq. J.*, 48, 18–31.

—— 1970. 'Excavations at Owslebury, Hants: a second interim report', *Antiq. J.*, 50, 246–61.

—— 1973. 'Burials with weapons in Iron Age Britain', *Germania*, 51, 121–33.

Coombs, D. 1992. 'Flag Fen platform and Fengate Power Station post alignment – the metalwork', *Antiquity*, 66, 504–17.

—— 2001. 'Metalwork', in Pryor 2001: 255–317.

—— and Pryor, F. 1994. 'An Early Iron Age bronze scabbard mount from Flag Fen', *Antiq. J.*, 74, 337–40.

Corcoran, J. X. W. P. 1952. 'Tankards and tankard handles of the British Early Iron Age', *Proc. Prehist. Soc.*, 18, 85–102.

—— 1956. 'The iron handle and bronze bands from Read's Cavern: a re-interpretation', *Proc. Univer. Bristol Spelaeol. Soc.*, 7, 46–50.

Corder, P. and Hawkes, C. F. C. 1940. 'A panel of Celtic ornament from Elmswell, East Yorkshire', *Antiq. J.*, 20, 338–57.

Corrie, A. J., Clarke, W. B. and Hunt, A. R. 1872–4. 'On a cave containing bones and objects of human workmanship, at Borness, Kirkcudbrightshire', *Proc. Soc. Antiq. Scotland*, 10, 476–99.

Cotton, J. and Wood, B. 1996. 'Recent prehistoric finds from the Thames foreshore and beyond in Greater London', *Trans. London Middlesex Archaeol. Soc.*, 47, 1–33.

Cowell, M. R. 1990. 'Scientific report', in Jackson 1990: 69–80.

Cowley, L. F. 1947. 'Report on the animal bones', in Fox 1947a: 97.

Craddock, P. T. 1978. 'The composition of the copper alloys used by the Greek, Etruscan and Roman civilizations', *J. Archaeol. Science*, 5, 1–16.

—— 1980. 'The composition of the copper alloys', in Pryor 1980: 65–76.

—— 1986. 'Three thousand years of copper alloys: from the Bronze Age to the Industrial Revolution', in P. England and L. van Zelst (eds), *Application of Science in Examination of Works of Art* (Museum of Fine Arts, Boston), 59–67.

—— and Meeks, N. D. 1987. 'Iron in ancient copper', *Archaeometry*, 29, 187–204.

Crawford, O. G. S. and Wheeler, R. E. M. 1920–1. 'The Llyn fawr and other hoards of the Bronze Age', *Archaeologia*, 71, 133–40.

Creighton, J. 1995. 'Visions of power: imagery and symbols in late Iron Age Britain', *Britannia*, 26, 285–301.

Crew, P. 1984. 'Bryn y Castell hillfort – a late prehistoric ironworking settlement in north-west Wales', in B. G. Scott and H. Cleere (eds), *The Crafts of the Blacksmith* (UISPP Comité pour la Sidérurgie Ancienne, in conjunction with the Ulster Museum, Belfast), 91–100.

—— 1985. 'Bryn y Castell', *Archaeol. Wales*, 25, 20–4.

—— 1989. 'Excavations at Crawcwellt West, Merioneth, 1986–1989: a late prehistoric upland iron-working settlement', *Archaeol. Wales*, 29, 11–16.

—— 1990. 'Late Iron Age and Roman iron production in north-west Wales', *Trivium* 25, 150–60.

—— 1998. 'Excavations at Crawcwellt West, Merioneth 1990–1998: a late prehistoric upland iron-working settlement', *Archaeol. Wales*, 38, 22–35.

—— and Salter, C. 1993. 'Currency bars with welded tips', in A. Espelund (ed.), *Bloomery Ironmaking during 2000 Years: Seminar in Budalen, Sør-Trøndelag, Norway August 26th–30th 1991*, vol. 3, *International Contributions: Smelting and Excavation in Budalen* (University of Trondheim, Trondheim), 11–30.

Cronyn, J. M. 1990. *The Elements of Archaeological Conservation* (Routledge, London).

Crummy, P. 1993. 'Aristocratic graves at Colchester', *Current Archaeol.*, 132, 492–7.

Cuming, H. S. 1859. 'On Celtic antiquities exhumed in Lincolnshire and Dorsetshire', *J. Brit. Archaeol. Assoc.*, 15, 225–30.

Cunliffe, B. 1971a. *Excavations at Fishbourne 1961–1969*, vol. 1, *the site* (Rep. Res. Comm. Soc. Antiq. London 26, London).

—— 1971b. *Excavations at Fishbourne 1961–1969*, vol. 2, *the finds* (Rep. Res. Comm. Soc. Antiq. London 27, London).

—— 1974. *Iron Age Communities in Britain: An Account of England, Scotland and Wales from the Seventh Century BC until the Roman Conquest* (Routledge & Kegan Paul, London).

—— 1978. *Hengistbury Head* (Paul Elek, London).

—— 1987. *Hengistbury Head, Dorset*, vol. 1, *The Prehistoric and Roman Settlement, 3500BC–AD500* (Oxford Univer. Comm. Archaeol. Mono. 13, Oxford).

—— 1991. *Iron Age Communities in Britain: An Account of England, Scotland and Wales from the Seventh Century BC until the Roman Conquest*, 3rd edn. (Routledge, London).

—— 1995. 'The Celtic chariot: a footnote', in Raftery *et al.* 1995: 31–9.

—— 1997. *The Ancient Celts* (Oxford University Press, Oxford).

—— and Poole, C. 2000. *The Danebury Environs Programme: The Prehistory of a Wessex*

Landscape, vol. 2, part 2, *Bury Hill, Upper Clatford, Hants 1990* (Eng. Heritage and Oxford Univer. Comm. Archaeol. Mono. 49; Institute of Archaeology, Oxford).

Cunnington, M. E. 1920. 'Notes on objects from an inhabited site on the Worms Head, Glamorgan', *Archaeol. Cambrensis*, 75, 251–6.

—— and Goddard, E. H. 1911. *Catalogue of Antiquities in the Museum of the Wiltshire Archaeological and Natural History Society at Devizes*, part 2 (Wiltshire Archaeological and Natural History Society, Devizes).

Curle, A. O. 1919–20. 'Report of the excavation on Traprain Law in the summer of 1919', *Proc. Soc. Antiq. Scotland*, 54, 54–124.

Curle, J. 1891–2. 'Notes on two brochs recently discovered at Bow, Midlothian and Torwoodlee, Selkirkshire', *Proc. Soc. Antiq. Scotland*, 26, 68–84.

—— 1911. *A Roman Frontier Post and its People: The Fort of Newstead in the Parish of Melrose* (Glasgow University Press, Glasgow).

—— 1931–2. 'An inventory of objects of Roman and provincial Roman origin found on sites in Scotland not definitely associated with Roman constructions', *Proc. Soc. Antiq. Scotland*, 66, 277–397.

Cutts, E. K. 1873. 'Notes on Roman and British remains found at Billericay in 1865, and Great Dunmow in 1864–65', *Trans. Essex Archaeol. Soc.*, 5, 208–18.

Daire, M.-Y. 1991. 'Amorica', in Moscati *et al*. 1991: 237–42.

Darbyshire, G. 1996. 'Pre-Roman iron tools for working metal and wood in southern Britain' (unpublished Ph.D. thesis, 2 vols, University of Wales Cardiff).

Darvill, T. 1987. *Prehistoric Britain* (Batsford, London).

Davies, J. A. 2000. 'The metal finds', in Bates 2000: 226–30.

—— and Williamson, T. (eds) 1999a. *Land of the Iceni: The Iron Age in Northern East Anglia* (Stud. East Anglia Hist. 4; Centre of East Anglian Studies, Norwich).

—— and —— 1999b. 'Introduction: studying the Iron Age', in Davies and Williamson 1999a: 7–13.

Davies, J. L. 1995. 'The early Celts in Wales', in Green 1995a: 671–700.

—— and Spratling, M. G. 1976. 'The Seven Sisters hoard: a centenary study', in Boon and Lewis 1976: 121–47.

Davies, S. M. 1981. 'Excavations at Old Down Farm, Andover: part II: prehistoric and Roman', *Proc. Hampshire Field Club Archaeol. Soc.*, 37, 81–163.

Déchelette, J. 1914. *Manuel d'archéologie Celtique ou protohistorique: Troisième partie second age du fer ou époque de La Tène* (Auguste Picard, Paris).

Demarez, L. and Leman-Delerive, G. 2001. 'A linch-pin of British type found at Blicquy (Hainaut, Belgium)', *Antiq. J.*, 81, 391–5.

De Navarro, J. M. 1943. 'A note on the chronology of the La Tène period', in Wheeler 1943: 388–94.

—— 1952. 'The Celts in Britain and their art', in M. P. Charlesworth and M. D. Knowles (eds), *The Heritage of Early Britain* (G. Bell and Sons Ltd, London), 56–82.

—— 1972. *The Finds from the Site of La Tène*, vol. 1, *Scabbards and the Swords Found in them* (2 vols, Oxford University Press, for the British Academy, London).

Denford, G. T. 1992. 'Some exotic discoveries at Silkstead Sandpit, Otterbourne, and the possible site of an ancient temple', *Proc. Hampshire Field Club Archaeol. Soc.*, 48, 27–54.

Denison, S. 2000. 'Burial in water 'normal rite' for 1,000 years', *Brit. Archaeol.*, 53, 4.

Dent, J. 1985. 'Three cart burials from Wetwang, Yorkshire', *Antiquity*, 59, 85–92.

Dobinson, C. and Denison, S. 1995. *Metal Detecting and Archaeology in England* (English Heritage and the Council for British Archaeology, York).

Donaldson, T. O. 1856–9. 'On some remains discovered in a Roman fort at Spettisbury, near Blandford, Dorset', *Proc. Soc. Antiq. London*, 4, 190–1.

Downey, R., King, A. and Soffe, G. 1980. 'The Hayling Island temple and religious connections across the Channel', in W. Rodwell (ed.), *Temples, Churches and Religion: Recent Research in Roman Britain with a Gazetteer of Romano-Celtic Temples in Continental Europe*, part 1 (Brit. Archaeol. Rep. Brit. Ser. 77(i), Oxford), 289–304.

Dryden, H. 1845. *Roman and Roman-British Remains at and near Shefford, Beds.* (Public. Camb. Antiq. Soc. 10, Cambridge).

Dryden, H. E. L. 1885. 'Hunsbury or Danes Camp, and the discoveries there', *Assoc. Architect. Soc. Rep. Pap.*, 18, 53–61.

Dungworth, D. B. 1995. 'Iron Age and Roman copper alloys from northern Britain' (unpublished Ph.D. thesis, University of Durham).

—— 1996. 'The production of copper alloys in Iron Age Britain', *Proc. Prehist. Soc.*, 62, 399–421.

—— 1997a. 'Iron Age and Roman copper alloys from northern Britain', *Internet Archaeol.*, 2 (*http://intarch.ac.uk./journal/issue2/dungworth_index.html*).

—— 1997b. 'Copper metallurgy in Iron Age Britain: some recent research', in Gwilt and Haselgrove 1997: 46–50.

—— 1999. 'EDXRF analysis of horse harness from the hoard', in Fitts *et al.* 1999: 38–40.

Dunning, C. 1991. 'La Tène', in Moscati *et al.* 1991: 366–8.

Duval, P.-M. 1973. 'L'ornament de char de Brentford', in P. -M. Duval (ed.), *Recherches d'archéologie Celtique et Gallo-Romaine* (Centre de Recherches d'Histoire et de Philologie, Geneva), 3–10.

—— and Hawkes, C. (eds) 1976. *Celtic Art in Ancient Europe: Five Protohistoric Centuries. Proceedings of the colloquy held in 1972 at the Oxford Maison Française. L'art Celtique en Europe protohistorique débuts, développements, styles, techniques* (Seminar Press, London).

Earwood, C. 1988. 'Wooden containers and other wooden artifacts from the Glastonbury Lake Village', *Somerset Levels Pap.*, 14, 83–90.

—— 1993. *Domestic wooden artefacts in Britain and Ireland from Neolithic to Viking times* (University of Exeter Press, Exeter).

Egloff, M. 1987. '130 years of archaeological research in Lake Neuchâtel, Switzerland', in J. M. Coles and A. J. Lawson (eds), *European Wetlands in Prehistory* (Clarendon Press, Oxford), 23–32.

—— 1991. 'Celtic craftwork at La Tène', in Moscati *et al.* 1991: 369–71.

Ehrenberg, M. 1980. 'The occurrence of Bronze Age metalwork in the Thames: an investigation', *Trans. London Middlesex Archaeol. Soc.*, 31, 1–15.

Ellis, B. M. A. 1985. 'Discussion of bridle harness and spurs', in J. N. Hare, *Battle Abbey: The Eastern Range and the Excavations of 1978–80* (Hist. Build. Mon. Comm. England Archaeol. Rep. 2, London), 171–3.

Ellis, H. 1848–9. 'Account of a gold torquis found in Needwood Forest in Staffordshire', *Archaeologia*, 33, 175–6.

Ellis Davidson, H. R. 1967. *Pagan Scandinavia* (Thames and Hudson, London).

Elsdon, S. M. 1989. *Later Prehistoric Pottery in England and Wales* (Shire Archaeology, Princes Risborough).

Eogan, G. 1991. 'Irish antiquities of the Bronze Age, Iron Age and early Christian period in the National Museum of Denmark', *Proc. Royal Irish Acad.*, 91C, 133–76.

Evans, A. J. 1890. 'On a Late-Celtic urn-field at Aylesford, Kent, and on the Gaulish, Illyro-Italic, and Classical connexions of the forms of pottery and bronze-work there discovered', *Archaeologia*, 52, 315–88.

—— 1894–7. 'On a votive deposit of gold objects on the north-west coast of Ireland', *Archaeologia*, 55, 391–408.

Fabech, C. 1991. 'Booty sacrifices in Southern Scandinavia: a reassessment', in P. Garwood, D. Jennings, R. Skeates and J. Toms (eds), *Sacred and Profane: Proceedings of a Conference on Archaeology, Ritual and Religion. Oxford, 1989* (Oxford Univer. Comm. Archaeol. Mono. 32, Oxford), 88–99.

Feachem, R. W. 1957–8. 'The 'Cairnmuir' hoard from Netherurd, Peeblesshire', *Proc. Soc. Antiq. Scotland*, 91, 112–16.

—— 1965. *The North Britons: The Prehistory of a Border People* (Hutchinson, London).

Fell, C. I. 1936. 'The Hunsbury hill-fort, Northants: A new survey of the material', *Archaeol. J.*, 93, 57–100.

Fell, V. 1990. 'Pre-Roman Iron Age metalworking tools from England and Wales: their use, technology and archaeological context' (unpublished M.Phil. thesis, 2 vols, University of Durham).

Field, N. 1983. 'Fiskerton, Lincolnshire', *Proc. Prehist. Soc.*, 49, 392.

—— 1986. 'An Iron Age timber causeway at Fiskerton, Lincolnshire', *Fenland Research*, 3, 49–53.

—— and Parker Pearson, M. 2003. *Fiskerton: An Iron Age Timber Causeway with Iron Age and Roman Votive Offerings* (Oxbow Books, Oxford).

Figgis, N. P. 1999. *Welsh Prehistory: Catalogue of Accessions in the County and Local Museums of Wales and Other Collections* (Atelier Productions, Machynlleth).

Fitts, R. L., Haselgrove, C. C., Lowther, P. C. and Willis, S. H. 1999. 'Melsonby revisited: survey and excavation 1992–95 at the site of the discovery of the 'Stanwick', North Yorkshire, hoard of 1843', *Durham Archaeol. J.*, 14/15, 1–52.

Fitzpatrick, A. P. 1984. 'The deposition of La Tène Iron Age metalwork in watery contexts in southern England', in B. Cunliffe and D. Miles (eds), *Aspects of the Iron Age in Central Southern Britain* (Oxford Univer. Comm. Archaeol. Mono. 2, Oxford), 178–90.

—— 1992. 'The Snettisham, Norfolk, hoards of Iron Age torques: sacred or profane?', *Antiquity*, 66, 395–8.

—— 1994. 'Objects of copper alloy', in Thorpe and Sharman 1994: 47–9.

—— 1996. 'A 1st-century AD 'Durotrigian' inhumation with a decorated Iron Age mirror from Portesham, Dorset', *Proc. Dorset Nat. Hist. Archaeol. Soc.*, 118, 51–70.

—— 1997. *Who were the Druids?* (Weidenfield and Nicholson, London).

Flouest, E. 1885. 'Le char de la sepulture Gauloise de la Bouvandeau, commune de Somme-Tourbe, Marne', *Mém. Soc. Ant. Fr.*, 66, 99–111.

Foster, J. 1980. *The Iron Age Moulds from Gussage All Saints* (Brit. Mus. Occas. Pap. 12, London).

—— 1986. *The Lexden Tumulus: A Re-appraisal of an Iron Age Burial from Colchester, Essex* (Brit. Archaeol. Rep. Brit. Ser. 156, Oxford).

—— 1991. 'Gussage All Saints', in Moscati *et al.* 1991: 608.

—— 1995. 'Metalworking in the British Iron Age: the evidence from Weelsby Avenue, Grimsby', in Raftery *et al.* 1995: 49–60.

Fowler, P. J. 1960. 'Excavations at Madmarston Camp, Swalcliffe, 1957–8', *Oxoniensia*, 25, 3–48.

Fox, A. 1959. 'Twenty-fifth report on the archaeology and early history of Devon', *Trans. Devon. Assoc. Advance. Science Liter. Art*, 91, 168–77.

—— and Pollard, S. 1973. 'A decorated bronze mirror from an Iron Age settlement at Holcombe, near Uplyme, Devon', *Antiq. J.*, 53, 16–41.

Fox, C. 1923. *The Archaeology of the Cambridge region: A Topographic Study of the Bronze, Early Iron, Roman and Anglo-Saxon Ages, with an Introductory Note on the Neolithic Age* (Cambridge University Press, Cambridge).

—— 1927. 'A settlement of the Early Iron Age (La Tène I sub-period) on Merthyr Mawr Warren, Glamorgan', *Archaeol. Cambrensis*, 82, 44–66.

—— 1932. *The Personality of Britain: Its Influence on Inhabitant and Invader in Prehistoric and Early Historic Times* (National Museum of Wales and the Press Board of the University of Wales, Cardiff).

—— 1943. *The Personality of Britain: Its Influence on Inhabitant and Invader in Prehistoric and Early Historic Times*, 4th edn. (National Museum of Wales and the Press Board of the University of Wales, Cardiff).

—— 1944a. 'Early Iron Age discovery. Life in Anglesey 2,000 years ago. History from relics', *The Times*, 49798, 2.

—— 1944b. 'An Early Iron Age discovery in Anglesey', *Archaeol. Cambrensis*, 98, 134–8.

—— 1944c. 'An Early Iron Age discovery in Anglesey', *Trans. Anglesey Antiq. Soc. Field Club*, 27, 49–54.

—— 1944d. 'Life in Anglesey 2000 years ago. An Early Iron Age discovery', *Antiquity*, 18, 95–7.

—— 1945a. *A Find from the Early Iron Age from Llyn Cerrig Bach, Anglesey: Interim Report* (National Museum of Wales, Cardiff).

—— 1945b. 'A shield-boss of the Early Iron Age from Anglesey with ornament applied by chasing tools', *Archaeol. Cambrensis*, 98, 199–220.

—— 1947a. *A Find of the Early Iron Age from Llyn Cerrig Bach, Anglesey* (National Museum of Wales, Cardiff).

—— 1947b. 'An open-work bronze disc in the Ashmolean Museum', *Antiq. J.*, 27, 1–6.

—— 1948. 'Celtic mirror handles in Britain with special reference to the Colchester handle', *Archaeol. Cambrensis*, 100, 24–44.

—— 1952. 'A group of bronzes of the Early Iron Age in Yeovil Museum', *Proc. Somerset. Archaeol. Nat. Hist. Soc.*, 96, 108–11.

—— 1958. *Pattern and Purpose: A Survey of Early Celtic Art in Britain* (National Museum of Wales, Cardiff).

—— and Hull, M. R. 1948. 'The incised ornament on the Celtic mirror from Colchester, Essex', *Antiq. J.*, 28, 123–37.

—— and Hyde, H. A. 1939. 'A second cauldron and an iron sword from the Llyn Fawr hoard, Rhigos, Glamorganshire', *Antiq. J.*, 19, 369–404.

Fox, G. E. and Hope, W. H. St. J. 1901. 'Excavations on the site of the Roman city at Silchester, Hants, in 1900', *Archaeologia*, 57, 229–56.

France, N. E. and Gobel, B. M. 1985. *The Romano-British Temple at Harlow, Essex* (Alan Sutton Publishing, for the West Essex Archaeological Group, Gloucester).

Franks, A. W. 1866. 'Notes on the mirrors, &c. discovered in a cemetery near Plymouth', *Archaeologia*, 40, 510.

—— 1880. 'Notes on a sword found in Catterdale, Yorkshire, exhibited by Lord Wharncliffe, and on other examples of the same kind', *Archaeologia*, 45, 251–66.

Frere, S. S. (ed.) 1961a. *Problems of the Iron Age in Southern Britain* (Univer. London Instit. Archaeol. Occas. Pap. 11, London).

—— 1961b. 'Some problems of the later Iron Age', in Frere 1961a: 84–92.

Frey, O.-H. 1991. "Celtic princes' in the sixth century B.C.', in Moscati *et al.* 1991: 75–92.

—— and Megaw, J. V. S. 1976. 'Palmette and circle: early Celtic art in Britain and its Continental background', *Proc. Prehist. Soc.*, 42, 47–65.

Furger-Gunti, A. 1991. 'The Celtic war chariot: the experimental reconstruction in the Schweizerisches Landesmuseum', in Moscati *et al.* 1991: 356–9.

Gardner, W. and Savory, H. N. 1964. *Dinorben: A Hill-Fort Occupied in Early Iron Age and Roman Times* (National Museum of Wales, Cardiff).

George, T. J. 1917. 'Early man in Northamptonshire, with particular reference to the late Celtic period as illustrated by Hunsbury Camp', *Northampton. Nat. Hist. Soc. Field Club*, 19, 1–8.

Goodchild, R. G. 1938. 'A priest's sceptre from the Romano-Celtic temple at Farley Heath, Surrey', *Antiq. J.*, 18, 391–6.

—— 1946–7. 'The Celtic gods of Farley Heath', *Surrey Archaeol. Collect.*, 50, 150–1.

Gray, H. St. G. 1905. 'The 'Norris Collection' in Taunton Castle Museum', *Proc. Somersetshire Archaeol. Nat. Hist. Soc.*, 51, 136–59.

—— 1913. 'Trial excavations at Cadbury Castle, S. Somerset', *Proc. Somerset. Archaeol. Nat. Hist. Soc.*, 59, 1–24.

—— 1924. 'Excavations at Ham Hill, South Somerset', *Proc. Somerset. Archaeol. Nat. Hist. Soc.*, 70, 104–16.

—— 1926. 'Excavations at Ham Hill, South Somerset. Part III', *Proc. Somerset. Archaeol. Nat. Hist. Soc.*, 72, 55–68.

—— and Bulleid, A. 1953. *The Meare Lake Village: A Full Description of the Excavations and the Relics from the Eastern Half of the West Village, 1910–1933*, vol. 2 (printed privately, Taunton).

—— and Cotton, M. A. 1966. *The Meare Lake Village: A Full Description of the Excavations and the Relics from the Eastern Half of the West Village, 1910–1933*, vol. 3 (printed privately, Taunton).

Green, B. 1962. 'An Iron Age pony-bit from Swanton Morley, Norfolk', *Proc. Prehist. Soc.*, 28, 385–6.

Green, C. 1949. 'The Birdlip Early Iron Age burials: a review', *Proc. Prehist. Soc.*, 15, 188–90.

Green, M. 1986. *The Gods of the Celts* (Alan Sutton, Stroud).

—— 1991. *The Sun-Gods of Ancient Europe* (B. T. Batsford, London).

—— 1992. *Animals in Celtic Life and Myth* (Routledge, London).

—— (ed.) 1995a. *The Celtic World* (Routledge, London).

—— 1995b. 'The gods and the supernatural', in Green 1995a: 465–88.

—— 1996. *Celtic Art: Reading the Messages* (Weidenfeld and Nicolson, London).

—— 1998. 'Vessels of death: sacred cauldrons in archaeology and myth', *Antiq. J.*, 78, 63–84.

—— and Howell, R. 2000. *Celtic Wales* (University of Wales Press and Western Mail, Cardiff).

Green, S. 1991. 'Metalwork from Llyn Cerrig Bach', in Moscati *et al.* 1991: 609.

Greenwell, W. 1877. *British Barrows: A Record of the Examination of Sepulchral Mounds in Various Parts of England* (Clarendon Press, Oxford).

—— 1907. 'Early Iron Age burials in Yorkshire', *Archaeologia*, 60, 251–324.

Gregory, T. 1978. 'A bronze bowl from Upwell', *Norfolk Archaeol.*, 37/1, 134.

—— 1980. 'Two Iron Age linch-pins from Norfolk', *Norfolk Archaeol.*, 37/3, 338–41.

—— 1991. *Excavations in Thetford, 1980–1982, Fison Way*, vol. 1 (East Anglian Archaeol. Rep. 53, Norfolk Museums Service, Dereham).

—— 1992. 'Excavations at Thetford Castle, 1992', in J. A. Davies, T. Gregory, A. J. Lawson, R. Rickett and A. Rogerson, *The Iron Age forts of Norfolk* (East Anglian Archaeol. Rep. 54, Norfolk Museums Service, in conjunction with the Scole Archaeological Committee, Dereham), 3–17.

Gresham, C. A. 1939. 'Spettisbury Rings, Dorset', *Archaeol. J.*, 96, 114–31.

Griffith, M. and Crew, P. 1998a. 'Beddgelert, Cwm Cloch Farm', *Archaeol. Wales*, 38, 96.

—— and —— 1998b. 'Muriau'r Dre, Nantgwynant', *Archaeol. Wales*, 38, 96.

Grimes, W. F. 1939. *Guide to the Collection Illustrating the Prehistory of Wales* (National Museum of Wales and the Press Board of the University of Wales, Cardiff).

—— 1945. 'Maiden Castle', *Antiquity*, 19, 6–10.

—— 1948. 'A prehistoric temple at London Airport', *Archaeology*, 1, 74–9.

—— 1951. *The prehistory of Wales* (National Museum of Wales, Cardiff).

1961. 'Some smaller settlements: a symposium', in Frere 1961a: 17–34.

Gurney, D. (ed.) 1990. 'Archaeological finds in Norfolk 1989', *Norfolk Archaeol.*, 41/1, 96–106.

—— (ed.) 1993. 'Archaeological finds in Norfolk 1992', *Norfolk Archaeol.*, 41/4, 512–22.

—— (ed.) 1995. 'Archaeological finds in Norfolk 1994', *Norfolk Archaeol.*, 42/2, 221–9.

—— (ed.) 1996. 'Archaeological finds in Norfolk 1995', *Norfolk Archaeol.*, 42/3, 387–96.

—— (ed.) 1997. 'Archaeological finds in Norfolk 1996', *Norfolk Archaeol.*, 42/4, 539–46.

—— (ed.) 1998. 'Archaeological finds in Norfolk 1997', *Norfolk Archaeol.*, 43/1, 181–92.

—— (ed.) 1999. 'Archaeological finds in Norfolk 1998', *Norfolk Archaeol.*, 43/2, 358–68.

—— (ed.) 2000. 'Archaeological finds in Norfolk 1999', *Norfolk Archaeol.*, 43/3, 516–21.

—— (ed.) 2001. 'Archaeological finds in Norfolk 2000', *Norfolk Archaeol.*, 43/4, 694–707.

Gwilt, A. and Haselgrove, C. (eds) 1997. *Reconstructing Iron Age Societies* (Oxbow Mono. 71, Oxford).

Hall, G. R. 1880. 'An account of researches in ancient circular dwellings near Birtley, Northumberland', *Archaeologia*, 45, 355–74.

Harford, C. J. 1803. 'Account of antiquities found in Somersetshire', *Archaeologia*, 14, 90–3.

Harrod, H. 1855. 'On horse-trappings found at Westhall', *Archaeologia*, 36, 454–6.

Haselgrove, C. 1987a. *Iron Age Coinage in South-East England: The Archaeological Context* (2 vols, Brit. Archaeol. Rep. Brit. Ser. 174, Oxford).

—— 1987b. 'Culture process on the periphery: Belgic Gaul and Rome during the late Republic and early Empire', in M. Rowlands, M. Larsen and K. Kristiansen (eds), *Centre and Periphery in the Ancient World* (Cambridge University Press, Cambridge), 104–24.

—— 1989. 'Iron Age coin deposition at Harlow Temple, Essex', *Oxford J. Archaeol.*, 8, 73–88.

—— 1990. 'Stanwick', *Current Archaeol.*, 119, 380–5.

—— 1996. 'Iron Age coinage: recent work', in T. C. Champion and J. Collis (eds), *The*

Iron Age in Britain and Ireland: Recent Trends (J. R. Collis Publications, Sheffield), 67–85.

—— 1997. 'Iron Age brooch deposition and chronology', in Gwilt and Haselgrove 1997: 51–72.

—— 1999. 'Iron Age societies in Central Britain: retrospect and prospect', in Bevan 1999: 253–78.

—— Lowther, P. C. and Turnbull, P. 1990a. 'Stanwick, North Yorkshire, part 3: excavations on earthwork sites 1981–86', *Archaeol. J.* 147, 37–90.

—— Turnbull, P. and Fitts, R. L. 1990b. 'Stanwick, North Yorkshire, part 1: Recent research and previous archaeological investigations', *Archaeol. J.*, 147, 1–15.

Hatley, A. R. 1933. *Early Days in the Walthamstow District* (Walthamstow Antiq. Soc. Official Publ. 28, Walthamstow).

Häussler, R. 1998. 'Motivations and ideologies of Romanization', in C. Forcey, J. Hawthorne and R. Witcher (eds), *TRAC 97: Proceedings of the Seventh Annual Theoretical Roman Archaeology Conference which formed part of the Second International Roman Archaeology Conference, University of Nottingham, April 1997* (Oxbow Books, Oxford), 11–19.

Hawkes, C. F. C. 1936–7. 'The Needwood Forest torc', *Brit. Mus. Quart.*, 11, 3–4.

—— 1937. 'The excavations at Buckland Rings, Lymington, 1935', *Proc. Hampshire Field. Club*, 12, 124–64.

—— 1951. 'Bronze-workers, cauldrons and bucket-animals in Iron Age and Roman Britain', in W. F. Grimes (ed.), *Aspects of Archaeology in Britain and Beyond: Essays Presented to O. G. S. Crawford* (H. W. Edwards, London), 172–99.

—— 1959. 'The ABC of the British Iron Age', *Antiquity*, 33, 170–82.

—— and Hull, M. R. 1947. *Camulodunum. First Report on the Excavations at Colchester 1930–1939* (Rep. Res. Comm. Soc. Antiq. London 14, London).

Haworth, R. G. 1969. 'The bronze horse bits of the Irish Early Iron Age' (unpublished undergraduate thesis, Queen's University, Belfast).

—— 1971. 'The horse harness of the Irish Early Iron Age', *Ulster J. Archaeol.* (3rd ser.), 34, 26–49.

Hedges, R. E. M., Pettitt, P. B., Bronk Ramsey, C. and Van Klinken, G. J. 1998. 'Radiocarbon dates from the Oxford AMS system: archaeometry datelist 25', *Archaeometry*, 40, 227–39.

Hemp, W. J. 1917–18. 'Certain objects mostly of prehistoric date discovered near Beddgelert and near Brynkir Station', *Proc. Soc. Antiq. London* (2nd ser.), 30, 166–83.

—— 1928. 'A La Tène shield from Moel Hiraddug Flintshire', *Archaeol. Cambrensis*, 83, 253–84.

Hencken, H. O'N. 1932. *The Archaeology of Cornwall and Scilly* (Methuen & Co., London).

Hencken, T. C. 1939. 'The excavation of the Iron Age camp on Bredon Hill, Gloucestershire, 1935–1937', *Archaeol. J.*, 95, 1–111.

Henry, F. 1933. 'Émailleurs d'Occident', *Préhistoire*, 2, 65–146.

Herity, M. and Eogan, G. 1977. *Ireland in Prehistory* (Routledge and Kegan Paul, London).

Hill, J. D. 2002. 'Wetwang chariot burial', *Current Archaeol.*, 178, 410–12.

Hingley, R. 1990. 'Iron Age 'currency bars': the archaeological and social context', *Archaeol. J.*, 147, 91–117.

—— 1997. 'Resistance and domination: social change in Roman Britain', in Mattingly 1997: 81–100.

Hirst, D. 2001. 'Further finds from a Romano-British settlement', *Treasure Hunting* (Aug.), 45–7.

Hoare, R. C. 1827. 'Account of antiquities found at Hamden Hill, with fragments of British chariots', *Archaeologia*, 21, 39–42.

Hobley, B. 1966–7. 'A Neronian-Vespasianic military site at 'The Lunt', Baginton, Warwickshire', *Trans. Proc. Birmingham Archaeol. Soc.*, 83, 65–129.

Hodges, H. 1989. *Artifacts: An Introduction to Early Materials and Technology*, 3rd edn. (Duckworth, London).

Hodson, F. R. 1962. 'Some pottery from Eastbourne, the 'Marnians' and the pre-Roman Iron Age in Southern England', *Proc. Prehist. Soc.*, 28, 140–55.

Hooley, R. W. 1926–30. 'Excavation of an Early Iron Age village on Worthy Down, Winchester', *Proc. Hampshire Field Club*, 10, 178–92.

Horváth, L., Kelemen, M. H., Uzsoki, A., and Vadász, E. 1987. *Corpus of Celtic Finds in Hungary*, vol. 1, *Transdanubia*, trans. L. Bartosiewicz and A. Choyke (Akadémiai Kiadó, Budapest).

Hughes, H. 1909. 'Sword found at Gelliniog Wen, Anglesey', *Archaeol. Cambrensis*, 64, 256–7.

Hunter, F. 1997. 'Iron Age hoarding in Scotland and northern England', in Gwilt and Haselgrove 1997: 108–33.

—— 2001. 'The carnyx in Iron Age Europe', *Antiq. J.*, 81, 77–108.

Hurst, H. R. 1985. *Kingsholm: Excavations at Kingsholm Close and Other Sites with a Discussion of the Archaeology of the Area* (Gloucester Archaeol. Rep. 1, Gloucester).

Hurst, J. D. and Wills, J. 1987. 'A 'horn cap' mould from Beckford, Worcestershire', *Proc. Prehist. Soc.*, 53, 492–3.

Hutcheson, A. R. J. 1997. 'Native or Roman? Ironwork hoards in Northern Britain', in K. Meadows, C. Lemke and J. Heron (eds), *TRAC 96: Proceedings of the Sixth Annual Theoretical Roman Archaeology Conference. Sheffield 1996* (Oxbow Books, Oxford), 65–72.

Hutcheson, N. C. G. 2004. *Later Iron Age Norfolk: Metalwork, Landscape and Society* (Brit. Archaeol. Rep. Brit. Ser. 361; Archaeopress, Oxford).

Hyde, H. A. 1947. 'Report on certain wood specimens', in Fox 1947a: 98.

Jackson, D. 1993–4. 'Excavation of the hillfort defences at Hunsbury, Northampton, in 1952 and 1988', *Northampton Archaeol.*, 25, 5–20.

Jackson, J. W. 1910. 'Further report on the explorations at Dog Holes, Warton Crag, Lancs., with remarks on the contents of two adjacent caves', *Trans. Lancs. Cheshire Antiq. Soc.*, 28, 59–81.

Jackson, R. 1985. 'Cosmetic sets from Late Iron Age and Roman Britain', *Britannia*, 16, 165–92.

—— 1990. *Camerton: The Late Iron Age and Early Roman ironwork* (British Museum Publications, London).

Jacobsthal, P. 1944. *Early Celtic Art* (2 vols, Clarendon Press, Oxford).

James, S. 1993. *Exploring the World of the Celts* (Thames and Hudson, London).

—— and Rigby, V. 1997. *Britain and the Celtic Iron Age* (British Museum Press, London).

Jarrett, M. G. 1976. *Maryport, Cumbria: A Roman fort and its garrison* (Cumberland Westmorland Antiq. Archaeol. Soc. extra ser. 22, Kendal).

Jenkins, J. G. 1961. *The English Farm Wagon: Origins and Structure* (Oakwood Press, for the Museum of English Rural Life, University of Reading, Lingfield).

Jensen, J. 1998. *Prehistory of Denmark* (National Museum, Copenhagen).

Jessup, R. F. 1932. 'Bigberry Camp, Harbledown, Kent', *Archaeol. J.*, 89, 87–115.

Jobey, G. 1976. 'Traprain Law: a summary', in D. W. Harding (ed.), *Hillforts: Later Prehistoric Earthworks in Britain and Ireland* (Academic Press, London), 191–204.

Johns, C. 1971. 'Spur-shaped bronzes of the Irish Early Iron Age', *Brit. Mus. Quart.*, 35, 57–61.

Jones, J. D. and Stead, I. M. 1969. 'An Early Iron Age warrior-burial found at St Lawrence, Isle of Wight', *Proc. Prehist. Soc.*, 35, 351–4.

Jones, O. B. C. 1992. 'Aspects of Celtic decorative metallurgy' (unpublished M.Sc. thesis, Department of Metallurgy and Science of Materials, University of Oxford).

Jope, E. M. 1950. 'Two Iron Age horse bridle-bits from the north of Ireland', *Ulster J. Archaeol.* (3rd ser.), 13, 57–60.

—— 1954. 'An Iron Age decorated sword-scabbard from the River Bann at Toome', *Ulster J. Archaeol.* (3rd ser.), 17, 81–91.

—— 1955. 'Chariotry and paired-draught in Ireland during the Early Iron Age: the evidence of some horse-bridle-bits', *Ulster J. Archaeol.* (3rd ser.), 18, 37–44.

—— 1961a. 'Daggers of the Early Iron Age in Britain', *Proc. Prehist. Soc.*, 27, 307–43.

—— 1961b. 'The beginnings of La Tène ornamental style in the British Isles', in Frere 1961a: 69–83.

—— 1971. 'The Witham shield', *Brit. Mus. Quart.*, 35, 61–9.

—— 1976. 'The Wandsworth mask shield and its European stylistic sources of inspiration', in Duval and Hawkes 1976: 167–84.

—— 2000. *Early Celtic Art in the British Isles* (2 vols, Clarendon Press, Oxford).

Keller, F. 1866. *The Lake Dwellings of Switzerland and Other Parts of Europe* (trans. J. E. Lee, Longmans, Green and Co., London).

Kelly, E. P. 1993. *Early Celtic Art in Ireland* (Town House and County House, in association with the National Museum of Ireland, Dublin).

Kemble, J. M. 1863. *Horæ Ferales; or Studies in the Archæology of the Northern Nations*, ed. R. G. Latham and A. W. Franks (Lovell Reeve and Co., London).

Kendrick, T. D. 1939–40. 'A Celtic linch-pin', *Brit. Mus. Quart.*, 14, 77–8.

Kenyon, K. M. 1948. *Excavations at the Jewry Wall Site, Leicester* (Rep. Res. Comm. Soc. Antiq. London 15, London).

Kilbride-Jones, H. E. 1980. *Celtic Craftsmanship in Bronze* (Croom Helm, London).

—— 1994. A note on the date of the Battersea shield, *Studia Celtica*, 28, 1–9.

King, A. and Soffe, G. 1994. 'The Iron Age and Roman temple on Hayling Island', in A. P. Fitzpatrick and E. L. Morris (eds), *The Iron Age in Wessex: Recent Work* (Trust for Wessex Archaeology, on behalf of the Association Française d'Etude de l'Age du Fer, Salisbury), 114–16.

—— and —— 1998. 'Internal organisation and deposition at the Iron Age temple on Hayling Island', *Proc. Hampshire Field Club Archaeol. Soc.*, 53, 35–47.

—— and —— 2001. 'Internal organisation and deposition at the Iron Age temple on Hayling Island, Hampshire', in J. Collis (ed.), *Society and Settlement in Iron Age Europe. L'habitat et l'occupation du Sol en Europe. Actes du XVIIIe Colloque de l'AFEAF Winchester – April 1994* (J. R. Collis Publications, Sheffield), 111–24.

King, E. 1812. 'A description of antiquities discovered on Hagbourn-Hill', *Archaeologia*, 16, 348–9.

Klesius, M. 2000. 'Mystery ships from a Danish bog', *National Geographic*, 197, 28–35.

Klindt-Jensen, O. 1957. *Denmark before the Vikings* (Thames and Hudson, London).

Knüsel, C. J. and Carr, G. C. 1995. 'On the significance of the crania from the River Thames and its tributaries', *Antiquity*, 69, 162–9.

Kruta, V., Champion, S., Savory, H. N., Harding, D. W., Schwappach, F., Duval, P.-M. and Piggott, S. 1976. 'Discussion', in Duval and Hawkes 1976: 199.

Laver, P. G. 1926–7. 'The excavation of a tumulus at Lexden, Colchester', *Archaeologia*, 76, 241–54.

Leahy, K. 1995. 'An Iron Age strap-ring from North Newbald, Yorkshire', *Antiq. J.*, 75, 381–3.

Leeds, E. T. 1933a. *Celtic ornament in the British Isles down to AD 700* (Clarendon Press, Oxford).

—— 1933b. 'Torcs of the Early Iron Age in Britain', *Antiq. J.*, 13, 466–8.

Lethbridge, T. C. 1953. 'Burial of an Iron Age warrior at Snailwell', *Proc. Cambridge Antiq. Soc.*, 47, 25–37.

Lewis, M. J. T. 1966. *Temples in Roman Britain* (Cambridge University Press, Cambridge).

Lloyd-Morgan, G. 1991. 'Mirror handle', in Gregory 1991: 132.

Lowery, P. R., Savage, R. D. A. and Wilkins, R. L. 1971. 'Scriber, graver, scorper, tracer: notes on experiments in bronzeworking technique', *Proc. Prehist. Soc.*, 37, 167–82.

Lynch, F. 1969–70. 'Iron spearhead from Llyn Cerrig Bach', *Trans. Anglesey Antiq. Soc. Field Club*, 52, 243–6.

—— 1970. *Prehistoric Anglesey: The Archaeology of the Island to the Roman Conquest* (Anglesey Antiquarian Society, Llangefni).

—— 1991. *Prehistoric Anglesey: The Archaeology of the Island to the Roman Conquest*, 2nd edn. (Anglesey Antiquarian Society, Llangefni).

Lynn, C. J. 1977. 'Trial excavations at the King's Stables, Tray Townland, County Armagh', *Ulster J. Archaeol.* (3rd ser.), 40, 42–62.

—— 1988. 'Man-made ritual pool? The King's Stables, Tray', in A. Hamlin and C. Lynn (eds), *Pieces of the Past: Archaeological Excavations by the Department of the Environment for Northern Ireland 1970–1986* (HMSO, Belfast), 19–21.

—— (ed.) 1997a. *Excavations at Navan Fort 1961–71* (North Ireland Archaeol. Mono. 3; The Stationery Office, Belfast).

—— 1997b. 'Comparisons and interpretations', in Lynn 1997a: 209–30.

—— 2003. *Navan Fort: Archaeology and Myth* (Wordwell Ltd, Bray).

Macalister, R. A. S. 1929. 'On some antiquities discovered upon Lambay', *Proc. Royal Irish Acad.*, 38C, 240–6.

MacCormick, A. G. 1969. 'Three dug-out canoes and a wheel from Holme Pierrepont, Nottinghamshire', *Trans. Thoroton Soc. Nottinghamshire*, 72, 14–31.

Macdonald, P. 2000a. 'A reassessment of the copper alloy artefacts from the Llyn Cerrig Bach assemblage' (unpublished Ph.D. thesis, 2 vols, University of Wales Cardiff).

—— 2000b. 'The ironwork (excluding brooches)', in Barrett *et al.* 2000c: 122–32.

—— 2001. 'Wales: Late Iron Age model shield', *Portable Antiq. Scheme Newsl.*, 3, 9.

—— forthcoming. 'Perspectives on insular La Tène art', in C. Haselgrove and T. Moore (eds), *The Later Iron Age in Britain and Beyond* (Oxbow Books, Oxford).

—— and Young, T. 1996. 'Llyn Cerrig Bach: field survey 1995', *Archaeol. Wales*, 35, 20–4.

McEvoy, E. 1854–5. 'Urlingford: a magnificent specimen of the antique bronze cauldrons which seem to be peculiar to Ireland: and a St. Patrick's half-penny', *J. Royal Soc. Antiq. Ireland*, 3, 131–2.

McGrath, J. N. 1968. 'A report on the metallurgical examination of five fragmentary Early Iron Age sword blades from Llyn Cerrig Bach, Anglesey', *Bull. Board Celtic Stud.*, 21, 418–25.

MacGregor, M. 1962. 'The Early Iron Age metalwork hoard from Stanwick, N. R. Yorks.', *Proc. Prehist. Soc.*, 28, 17–57.

—— 1976. *Early Celtic Art in North Britain: A Study of Decorative Metalwork from the Third Century B.C. to the Third Century A.D.*, 2 vols (Leicester University Press, Leicester).

McWhirr, A. 1981. *Roman Gloucestershire* (Alan Sutton, Gloucester).

Mahr, A. 1937. 'New aspects and problems in Irish prehistory: presidential address for 1937', *Proc. Prehist. Soc.*, 3, 262–436.

Manning, W. H. 1972. 'Ironwork hoards in Iron Age and Roman Britain', *Britannia*, 3, 224–50.

—— 1977. 'Blacksmiths' tools from Waltham Abbey, Essex', in W. A. Oddy (ed.), *Aspects of Early Metallurgy* (Historical Metallurgy Society and British Museum Research Laboratory, London), 87–96.

—— 1983. 'The cauldron chains of Iron Age and Roman Britain', in B. Hartley and J. Wacher (eds), *Rome and her Northern Provinces: Papers Presented to Sheppard Frere in Honour of his Retirement from the Chair of the Archaeology of the Roman Empire, University of Oxford, 1983* (Alan Sutton, Gloucester), 132–54.

—— 1985. *Catalogue of the Romano-British Iron Tools, Fittings and Weapons in the British Museum* (British Museum Publications Limited, London).

—— 1995a. 'Ironworking in the Celtic world', in Green 1995a: 310–20.

—— 1995b. 'Ritual or refuse: the Harrow Hill enclosure reconsidered', in Raftery *et al.* 1995: 133–8.

Mariën, M.-E. 1961. *La période de La Tène en Belgique: le group de la Haine* (Monographies d'Archéologie Nationale 2; Musées Royaux d'Art et d'Histoire, Bruxelles).

Marshall, P. 2003. 'The radiocarbon dates for the human bones', in Field and Parker Pearson 2003: 127.

Martin, E. 1999. 'Suffolk in the Iron Age', in Davies and Williamson 1999a: 44–99.

—— Pendleton, C., Plouviez, J. 1999. 'Archaeology in Suffolk 1998', *Proc. Suffolk Instit. Archaeol. Hist.*, 39/3, 353–86.

—— Pendleton, C., Plouviez, J. and Thomas, G. 2000. 'Archaeology in Suffolk 1999', *Proc. Suffolk Instit. Archaeol. Hist.*, 39/4, 495–531.

—— Pendleton, C., Plouviez, J., Thomas, G. and Geake, H. 2001. 'Archaeology in Suffolk 2000', *Proc. Suffolk Instit. Archaeol. Hist.*, 40/1, 65–109.

—— Pendleton, C., Plouviez, J., and Geake, H. 2002. 'Archaeology in Suffolk 2001', *Proc. Suffolk Instit. Archaeol. Hist.*, 40/2, 201–33.

—— Pendleton, C. and Plouviez, J. 2003. 'Archaeology in Suffolk 2002', *Proc. Suffolk Instit. Archaeol. Hist.*, 40/3, 337–70.

Maryon, H. 1938. 'The technical methods of Irish smiths in the Bronze and Early Iron Ages', *Proc. Royal Irish Acad.*, 44C, 181–228.

—— 1949. 'Metalworking in the ancient world', *American J. Archaeol.*, 53, 93–125.

Mattei, M. 1991. 'The Dying Gaul', in Moscati *et al.* 1991: 70–1.

Mattingly, D. J. (ed.) 1997. *Dialogues in Roman Imperialism: Power, Discourse, and Discrepant Experience in the Roman Empire* (J. Roman Archaeol. Suppl. Ser. 23; Journal of Roman Archaeology, Portsmouth, Rhode Island).

Maxwell, G. S. 1989. *The Romans in Scotland* (James Thin, Edinburgh).

May, J. 1976. *Prehistoric Lincolnshire* (History of Lincolnshire Committee, Lincoln).

Megaw, J. V. S. 1968. 'Problems and non-problems in palaeo-organology: a musical miscellany', in J. M. Coles and D. D. A. Simpson (eds), *Studies in Ancient Europe: Essays presented to Stuart Piggott* (Leicester University Press, Leicester), 333–58.

—— 1970. *Art of the European Iron Age: A Study of the Elusive Image* (Adams and Dart, Bath).

—— 1976. 'An Iron Age sword with decorated scabbard mounts of Piggott's Group V from Thrapston, Northamptonshire', *Northampton. Archaeol.*, 11, 165–70.

—— 1991. 'Music archaeology and the ancient Celts', in Moscati *et al.* 1991: 643–8.

—— and Megaw, M. R. 1991–2. 'Celtic art: a reply to the editor', *Ulster J. Archaeol.* (3rd ser.), 54/55, 163–4.

—— and Merrifield, R. 1969. 'The Dowgate plaque: a bronze mount of the Belgic Iron Age from the City of London', *Archaeol. J.*, 126, 154–9.

Megaw, R. and Megaw, V. 1986. *Early Celtic art in Britain and Ireland* (Shire Publications, Princes Risborough).

—— and —— 1989. *Celtic art. From its beginnings to the Book of Kells* (Thames and Hudson, London).

—— and —— 2001. 'Expressiveness and communication: insular Celtic art through six centuries', *Antiquity*, 75, 433–6.

Merrifield, R. 1965. *The Roman City of London* (Ernest Benn Limited, London).

—— 1987. *The Archaeology of Ritual and Magic* (Guild Publishing, London).

—— 1995. 'Roman metalwork from the Walbrook: rubbish, ritual or redundancy?', *Trans. London Middlesex Archaeol. Soc.*, 46, 27–44.

Meyrick, S. R. 1830–1. 'Description of two ancient British shields, preserved in the Armoury at Goodrich Court, Herefordshire', *Archaeologia*, 23, 92–7.

Mortimer, J. R. 1869. 'Notice of the opening of an Anglo-Saxon grave, at Grimthorpe, Yorkshire', *Reliquary*, 9, 180–2.

—— 1897. 'The Danes' Graves', in Anon. (ed.), *Yorkshire Philosophical Society Annual Report* (Yorkshire Philosophical Society, York), 1–10.

—— 1897–9. 'The opening of a number of the so-called 'Danes' Graves', at Kilham, E. R. Yorks., and the discovery of a chariot burial of the Early Iron Age', *Proc. Soc. Antiq. London* (2nd ser.), 17, 119–28.

—— 1905. *Forty Years' Researches in British and Saxon Burial Mounds of East Yorkshire: Including Romano-British Discoveries, and a Description of the Ancient Entrenchments on a Section of the Yorkshire Wolds* (A. Brown and Sons, London).

Moscati, S., Frey, O.-H., Kruta, V., Raftery, B. and Szabó, M. (eds) 1991. *The Celts* (Bompiani, Milano).

Moss-Eccardt, J. 1965. 'An iron cauldron-rim from Letchworth, Herts.', *Antiq. J.*, 45, 173–7.

—— 1988. 'Archaeological investigations in the Letchworth area, 1958–1974: Blackhorse Road, Letchworth; Norton Road, Baldock; Wilbury Hill, Letchworth', *Proc. Cambridge Antiq. Soc.*, 77, 35–103.

Müller, F. 1991. 'The river site of Port Nidau', in Moscati *et al.* 1991: 528–9.

Munro, R. 1890. *The Lake-Dwellings of Europe: Being the Rhind Lectures in Archaeology in 1888* (Cassell and Company, London).

Musson, C. R. and Northover, J. P. 1989. 'Llanymynech hillfort, Powys and Shropshire: observations on construction work, 1981', *Montgomeryshire Collect.*, 77, 15–26.

—— Britnell, W. J., Northover, J. P. and Salter, C. J. 1992. 'Excavations and metalworking at Llwyn Bryn-dinas Hillfort, Llangedwyn, Clwyd', *Proc. Prehist. Soc.*, 58, 265–83.

Musty, J. 1975. 'A brass sheet of first century A. D. date from Colchester (Camulodunum)', *Antiq. J.*, 55, 409–11.

—— and MacCormick, A. G. 1973. 'An early Iron Age wheel from Holme Pierrepont, Notts.', *Antiq. J.*, 53, 275–7.

Mytum, H. 1989. 'Excavation at Castell Henllys, 1981–89: the Iron Age Fort', *Archaeol. Wales*, 29, 6–10.

—— 1999. 'Castell Henllys', *Current Archaeol.*, 161, 164–72.

Nash, D. 1976. 'Reconstructing Poseidonios' Celtic ethnography: some considerations', *Britannia*, 7, 111–26.

Nash-Williams, V. E. 1933. 'An Early Iron Age hill-fort at Llanmelin, near Caerwent, Monmouthshire: with a note on the distribution of hillforts and other earthworks in Wales and the Marches', *Archaeol. Cambrensis*, 88, 237–346.

Newton, W. W. H. 1852. 'Discovery of bronze vessels, &c., at Cockburnspath, Berwickshire', *Proc. Soc. Antiq. Scotland*, 1, 43–4.

Nicholson, S. M. 1980. *Catalogue of the prehistoric metalwork in Merseyside County Museums (formerly Liverpool Museum)* (Merseyside County Museums and University of Liverpool, Liverpool).

Nicklin, K. 1971–2. 'Stability and innovation in pottery manufacture', *World Archaeol.*, 3, 14–48, 94–8.

Norris, H. 1853. 'Antiquities and works of art exhibited', *Archaeol. J.*, 10, 246–8.

Northover, P. 1984. 'Analysis of the bronze metalwork', in B. Cunliffe, *Danebury: An Iron Age Hillfort in Hampshire*, vol. 2, *The Excavations, 1969–1978: The Finds* (Council Brit. Archaeol. Res. Rep. 52, London), 430–3.

—— 1987. 'Non-ferrous metallurgy', in Cunliffe 1987: 186–96.

—— 1991a. 'Analysis of Iron Age bronze metalwork from Llyn Cerrig Bach', in Lynch 1991: 392–3.

—— 1991b. 'Non-ferrous metalwork and metallurgy', in N. M. Sharples, *Maiden Castle: Excavations and Field Survey 1985–6* (Eng. Herit. Archaeol. Rep. 19, London), 156–62.

—— 1995. 'The technology of metalwork', in Green 1995a: 285–309.

—— and Salter, C. J. 1990. 'Decorative metallurgy of the Celts', *Materials Characterization*, 25, 109–23.

Nylen, E. 1958. 'The remarkable bucket from Marlborough', *Acta Archaeol.*, 29, 1–20.

O'Connell, M. G. and Bird, J. 1994. 'The Roman temple at Wanborough, excavation 1985–1986', *Surrey Archaeol. Collect.*, 82, 1–168.

O'Connor, B., Foster, J. and Saunders, C. 2000. 'Violence', in Barrett *et al.* 2000c: 235–42.

O'Dwyer, S. 2004. *Prehistoric music of Ireland* (Tempus, Stroud).

Oldeberg, A. 1947. 'A contribution to the history of the Scandinavian bronze lur in the Bronze and Iron Ages', *Acta Archaeol.*, 18, 1–91.

Orme, B. J., Coles, J. M., Caseldine, A. E. and Bailey, G. N. 1981. 'Meare Village West', *Somerset Levels Pap.*, 7, 12–69.

Owen, J. 1993. 'Iron Age linch pins from Tattershall Thorpe', *Lincolnshire Hist. Archaeol.*, 28, 68–9.

Page, W. 1911–12. 'Several objects lately acquired by the Herts. County Museum, St. Albans', *Proc. Soc. Antiq. London* (2nd ser.), 24, 132–4.

Palk, N. A. 1984. *Iron Age Bridle-Bits from Britain* (Univer. Edinburgh Dept. Archaeol. Occas. Pap. 10, Edinburgh).

Palmer, L. S. 1922. 'The Keltic Cavern', *Proc. Bristol Univer. Spelaeol. Soc.*, 1, 9–20.

Parfitt, K. 1990. 'An Iron Age warrior burial at Mill Hill, Deal', *Kent Archaeol. Rev.*, 99, 204–5.

—— 1991. 'Deal', *Current Archaeol.*, 125, 215–20.

—— 1995. *Iron Age Burials from Mill Hill, Deal* (British Museum Press, London).

—— 1998. 'A late Iron Age burial from Chilham Castle, near Canterbury, Kent', *Proc. Prehist. Soc.*, 64, 343–51.

—— 2000. 'Iron Age linch-pin: Thanington', *Archaeol. Cantiana*, 120, 375–8.

Parker Pearson, M. 2000. 'Great sites. Llyn Cerrig Bach', *Brit. Archaeol.*, 53, 8–11.

—— 2003. 'The British and European context of Fiskerton', in Field and Parker Pearson 2003: 179–88.

—— and Field, N. 2003a. 'Fiskerton in its local and regional setting', in Field and Parker Pearson 2003: 149–69.

—— and —— 2003b. 'The Fiskerton artefact assemblage', in Field and Parker Pearson 2003: 173–8.

Peake, H. 1931. *The Archaeology of Berkshire* (Methuen and Co., London).

—— and Padel, J. 1934. 'Exploration of three round barrows on Woolley Down, Berks.', *Trans. Newbury District Field Club*, 7, 30–48.

Peckham, J. 1973. 'The chariot horn caps of Britain' (unpublished undergraduate thesis, University College Cardiff).

Penhallurick, R. D. 1986. *Tin in Antiquity: Its Mining and Trade Throughout the Ancient World with Particular Reference to Cornwall* (The Institute of Metals, London).

Penn, W. S. 1959. 'The Romano-British settlement at Springhead; excavation of Temple I, Site C1', *Archaeol. Cantiana*, 73, 1–61.

Percival, S. 1999. 'Iron Age pottery in Norfolk', in Davies and Williamson 1999a: 173–84.

Petrie, G. 1833–4. 'Ancient Irish trumpets', *Dublin Penny J.*, 2, 27–30.

Philipson, J. 1885. 'Roman horse trappings', *Archaeol. Aeliana*, 11, 204–15.

Phillips, C. W. 1931. 'Final report on the excavations of Merlin's Cave, Symonds' Yat', *Proc. Univer. Bristol Spelaeol. Soc.*, 4, 11–33.

—— 1935. 'The present state of archaeology in Lincolnshire: part II', *Archaeol. J.*, 91, 97–187.

Piggott, S. 1950. 'Swords and scabbards of the British Early Iron Age', *Proc. Prehist. Soc.*, 16, 1–28.

—— 1950–1. 'Excavations in the broch and hill-fort of Torwoodlee, Selkirkshire, 1950', *Proc. Soc. Antiq. Scotland*, 85, 92–117.

—— 1952–3. 'Three metal-work hoards of the Roman period from southern Scotland', *Proc. Soc. Antiq. Scotland*, 87, 1–50.

—— 1959. 'The *carnyx* in Early Iron Age Britain', *Antiq. J.*, 39, 19–32.

—— 1968. *The Druids* (Thames and Hudson, London).

—— 1969. 'Early Iron Age 'horn-caps' and yokes', *Antiq.*, *J.* 49, 378–81.

—— 1970. *Early Celtic Art* (Edinburgh University Press, Edinburgh).

—— 1983. *The Earliest Wheeled Transport: From the Atlantic Coast to the Caspian Sea* (Thames and Hudson, London).

—— and Daniel, G. 1951. *A Picture Book of Ancient British Art* (Cambridge University Press, Cambridge).

Pitt-Rivers, A. H. L. 1887. *Excavations in Cranbourne Chase, near Rushmore, on the borders of Dorset and Wilts*, vol. 1, *Excavations in the Romano-British Village on Woodcuts*

Common, and Romano-British Antiquities in Rushmore Park (printed privately, London).

Pollard, A. M. and Heron, C. 1996. *Archaeological Chemistry* (Royal Society of Chemistry, Cambridge).

Probert, L. A. 1976. 'Twyn-y-Gaer hillfort, Gwent: an interim assessment', in Boon and Lewis 1976: 105–19.

Pryor, F. 1980. *A Catalogue of British and Irish Prehistoric Bronzes in the Royal Ontario Museum* (Royal Ontario Museum, Toronto).

—— 1992a. 'Current research at Flag Fen, Peterborough', *Antiquity*, 66, 439–57.

—— 1992b. 'Discussion: the Fengate/Northey landscape', *Antiquity*, 66, 518–31.

—— 1994. 'Flag Fen', *Current Archaeol.*, 137, 179–84.

—— 2001. *The Flag Fen basin: Archaeology and Environment of a Fenland Landscape* (English Heritage, London).

Quinn, M. 1994. *The Swastika: Constructing the Symbol* (Routledge, London).

Raftery, B. 1974. 'A decorated Iron Age horse-bit fragment from Ireland', *Proc. Royal Irish Acad.*, 74C, 1–10.

—— 1980. 'Iron Age cauldrons in Ireland', *Archaeol. Atlantica*, 3, 57–80.

—— 1983. *A Catalogue of Irish Iron Age Antiquities*, 2 vols (Veröffentlichung des Vorgeschichtlichen Seminars Marburg Sonderband 1; Vorgeschichtliches Seminar, Marburg).

—— 1984. *La Tène in Ireland: Problems of Origin and Chronology* (Veröffentlichung des Vorgeschichtlichen Seminars Marburg Sonderband 2; Vorgeschichtliches Seminar, Marburg).

—— 1987. 'The Loughnashade horns', *Emania*, 2, 21–4.

—— 1991. 'The island Celts', in Moscati *et al.* 1991: 555–72.

—— 1994. *Pagan Celtic Ireland: The Enigma of the Irish Iron Age* (Thames and Hudson, London).

—— Megaw, V. and Rigby, V. (eds) 1995. *Sites and Sights of the Iron Age: Essays on Fieldwork and Museum Research Presented to Ian Mathieson Stead* (Oxbow Mono. 56, Oxford).

Raftery, J. 1951. *Prehistoric Ireland* (Batsford, London).

—— 1963. 'National Museum of Ireland archaeological acquisitions for the year 1961', *J. Royal Soc. Antiq. Ireland*, 93, 115–33.

—— and Ryan, M. 1971. 'National Museum of Ireland. Archaeological acquisitions in the year 1968', *J. Royal Soc. Antiq. Ireland*, 101, 184–244.

Randsborg, K. 1995. *Hjortspring: Warfare and sacrifice in Early Europe* (Aarhus University Press, Aarhus).

Rankin, D. 1995. 'The Celts through Classical eyes', in Green 1995a: 21–33.

Read, C. H. 1909–11. 'A late Celtic bridle-bit of bronze found in the bed of the Thames', *Proc. Soc. Antiq. London* (2nd ser.), 23, 159–60.

Rees, S. E. 1979. *Agricultural Implements in Prehistoric and Roman Britain*, 2 vols (Brit. Archaeol. Rep. Brit. Ser. 69, Oxford).

Richardson, C. 1999. 'A catalogue of recent acquisitions to Tulie House Museum and reported finds from the Cumbrian area 1990–1996: part II: reported finds', *Trans. Cumberland Westmorland Antiq. Archaeol. Soc.* (2nd ser.), 99, 1–51.

Richmond, I. A. 1925. *Huddersfield in Roman Times* (Tolson Memorial Mus. Publ. 4; County Borough of Huddersfield, Huddersfield).

—— 1950. 'Stukeley's lamp, the badge of the Society of Antiquaries', *Antiq. J.*, 30, 22–7.

—— 1968. *Hod Hill*, vol. 2, *Excavations Carried out between 1951 and 1958 for the Trustees of the British Museum* (Trustees of the British Museum, London).

Rieck, F. 1994. 'The Iron Age boats from Hjortspring and Nydam: new investigations', in C. Westerdahl (ed.), *Crossroads in Ancient Shipbuilding: Proceedings of the Sixth International Symposium on Boat and Ship Archaeology. Roskilde 1991* (Oxbow Mono. 40, Oxford), 45–54.

—— 1999. 'The Nydam sacred site, Denmark', in B. Coles, J. Coles and M. S. Jørgensen (eds), *Bog Bodies, Sacred Sites and Wetland Archaeology: Proceedings of a Conference Held by WARP and the National Museum of Denmark, in Conjunction with Silkeborg Museum, Jutland, September 1996* (WARP Occas. Pap. 12; Wetland Archaeology Research Project, Exeter), 209–16.

Roberts, O. T. P. 2002. 'Accident not intention: Llyn Cerrig Bach, Isle of Anglesey, Wales – site of an Iron Age shipwreck', *Int. J. Nautical Archaeol.*, 31, 25–38.

Robinson, A. H. W. 1980. 'The sandy coast of south-west Anglesey', *Trans. Anglesey Antiq. Soc. Field Club*, 61, 37–66.

Rosenberg, G. 1937. *Hjortspringfundet* (Nordiske Fortidsminder, 3/1; Kommission hos Gyldendalske Boghandel – Nordisk Forlag, Copenhagen).

Rowlands, H. 1723. *Mona Antiqua Restaurata. An archæological discourse on the antiquities, natural and historical, of the Isle of Anglesey the Antient Seat of the Britiſh Druids* (Robert Owen, Dublin).

Rowlands, M. J. 1971–2. 'The archaeological interpretation of prehistoric metalworking', *World Archaeol.*, 3, 210–24.

Royal Commission on Historical Monuments (England) 1970. *An Inventory of Historical Monuments in the County of Dorset*, vol. 2, *South-East: Part 3* (HMSO, London).

Rynne, E. 1960. 'A bronze cauldron from Ballyedmond, Co. Galway', *J. Galway Archaeol. Hist. Soc.*, 29, 1–2.

—— 1976. 'The La Tène and Roman finds from Lambay, Co. Dublin: a re-assessment', *Proc. Royal Irish Acad.*, 76C, 231–44.

Savory, H. N. 1964. 'The Tal-y-llyn hoard', *Antiquity*, 38, 18–31.

—— 1966a. 'Armourer's mark from Llyn Cerrig Bach (Ang.)', *Bull. Board Celtic Stud.*, 22, 374–6.

—— 1966b. 'A find of Early Iron Age metalwork from the Lesser Garth, Pentyrch (Glam.)', *Archaeol. Cambrensis*, 115, 27–44.

—— 1968. *Early Iron Age Art in Wales* (National Museum of Wales, Cardiff).

—— 1970. 'The later prehistoric migrations across the Irish Sea', in D. Moore (ed.), *The Irish Sea Province in Archaeology and History* (Cambrian Archaeological Association, Cardiff), 38–49.

—— 1971. *Excavations at Dinorben 1965–9* (National Museum of Wales, Cardiff).

—— 1973. 'Llyn Cerrig Bach, thirty years later', *Trans. Anglesey Antiq. Soc. Field Club*, 54, 24–38.

—— 1974. 'An Early Iron Age metalworker's mould from Worms Head', *Archaeol. Cambrensis*, 123, 170–4.

—— 1976a. *Guide Catalogue of the Early Iron Age Collections* (National Museum of Wales, Cardiff).

—— 1976b. 'The La Tène shield in Wales', in Duval and Hawkes 1976: 185–97.

—— 1980. *Guide Catalogue of the Bronze Age Collections* (National Museum of Wales, Cardiff).

—— 1990. 'Celtic art: from its beginnings to the Book of Kells. By Ruth and Vincent Megaw', *Archaeol. Cambrensis*, 139, 83–5.

Schüle, W. 1969. *Die Meseta-Kulturen der Iberischen Halbinsel: Mediterrane und Eurasische elemente in Früheisenzetlichen Kulturen Südwesteuropas* (Walter de Gruyter and Co., for the Deutsches Archäologisches Institut Abteilung Madrid, Berlin).

Scott-Fox, C. 2002. *Cyril Fox Archaeologist Extraordinary* (Oxbow Books, Oxford).

Sheppard, T. 1907. 'Note on a British chariot-burial at Hunmanby, in East Yorkshire', *Yorkshire Archaeol. J.*, 19, 482–8.

Shortt, H. de S. 1947. 'Notes on prehistoric antiquities, previously unpublished, in the Salisbury and South Wilts Museum', *Archaeol. J.*, 104, 20–6.

Shotter, D. 1996. *The Roman Frontier in Britain: Hadrian's Wall, the Antonine Wall and Roman Policy in the North* (Carnegie Publishing, Preston).

Silvester, R. J. and Northover, J. P. 1991. 'An Iron Age pit at Holmebank Farm, Methwold', *Norfolk Archaeol.*, 41/2, 214–18.

Smith, B. and Neville George, T. 1961. *British Regional Geology. North Wales*, 3rd edn. (HMSO, for the British Geological Survey, London).

Smith, R. A. 1905. *British Museum: A Guide to the Antiquities of the Early Iron Age of Central and Western Europe (Including the British Late-Keltic Period) in the Department of British and Mediaeval Antiquities* (British Museum, London).

—— 1906–7. 'The timekeepers of the ancient Britons', *Proc. Soc. Antiq. London* (2nd ser.), 21, 319–33.

—— 1908–9. 'On a Late-Celtic mirror found at Desborough, Northants, and other mirrors of the period', *Archaeologia*, 61, 329–46.

—— 1909a. 'A hoard of metal found at Santon Downham, Suffolk', *Proc. Cambridge Antiq. Soc.*, 13, 146–63.

—— 1909b. 'Harborough Cave, nr. Brassington. II. Description of the finds', *J. Derbyshire Nat. Hist. Soc.*, 31, 97–114.

—— 1911–12a. 'On Late-Celtic antiquities discovered at Welwyn, Herts.', *Archaeologia*, 63, 1–30.

—— 1911–12b. 'The exhibits from Herts. belonging to the Herts. County Museum', *Proc. Soc. Antiq. London* (2nd ser.), 24, 135–7.

—— 1914–15. 'A series of thin bronze vessels including water-clocks of the Early Iron Age, discovered at Wotton, Surrey', *Proc. Soc. Antiq. London* (2nd ser.), 27, 76–95.

—— 1917–18. 'Specimens from the Layton Collection, in Brentford Public Library', *Archaeologia*, 69, 1–30.

—— 1925. *Guide to Early Iron Age Antiquities*, 2nd edn. (British Museum, London).

Smyth, W. H. 1846. 'On some Roman vestigia recently found at Kirkby Thore, in Westmorland', *Archaeologia*, 31, 279–88.

Spence Bate, C. 1866. 'On the discovery of a Romano-British cemetery near Plymouth', *Archaeologia*, 40, 500–9.

Spratling, M. G. 1966. 'The date of the Tal-y-llyn hoard', *Antiquity*, 40, 229–30.

—— 1970a. 'The late pre-Roman Iron Age bronze mirror from Old Warden', *Bedfordshire Archaeol. J.*, 5, 9–16.

—— 1970b. 'The smiths of South Cadbury', *Current Archaeol.*, 18, 188–91.

—— 1971. 'Further comments on the Iron Age cauldron from Elvanfoot, Lanarkshire', *Glasgow Archaeol. J.*, 2, 111–12.

—— 1972. 'Southern British decorated bronzes of the late pre-Roman Iron Age' (unpublished Ph.D. thesis, 3 vols, University of London).

—— 1975. 'Fragments of a lorica segmentata in the hoard from Santon, Norfolk', *Britannia*, 6, 206–7.

—— 1979. 'The debris of metalworking', in Wainwright 1979: 125–49.

—— 1989. 'A bronze linchpin and mini-terret', in W. Britnell (ed.), The Collfryn hillslope enclosure, Llansantffraid Deuddwr, Powys: excavations 1980–1982, microfiche supplement, *Proc. Prehist. Soc.*, 55, 54–5.

Stead, I. M. 1959. 'A chariot burial on Pexton Moor, North Riding', *Antiquity*, 33, 214–16.

—— 1965a. *The La Tène Cultures of Eastern Yorkshire* (Yorkshire Philosophical Society, York).

—— 1965b. 'The Celtic Chariot', *Antiquity*, 39, 259–65.

—— 1967. 'A La Tène III burial at Welwyn Garden City', *Archaeologia*, 101, 1–62.

—— 1968. 'An Iron Age hill-fort at Grimthorpe, Yorkshire', *Proc. Prehist. Soc.*, 34, 148–90.

—— 1971. 'The reconstruction of Iron Age buckets from Aylesford and Baldock', *Brit. Mus. Quart.*, 35, 250–82.

—— 1976. 'The earliest burials of the Aylesford culture', in G. de. G. Sieveking, I. H. Longworth and K. E. Wilson (eds), *Problems in Economic and Social Archaeology* (Duckworth, London), 401–16.

—— 1979. *The Arras Culture* (Yorkshire Philosophical Society, York).

—— 1981. *The Gauls: Celtic Antiquities from France* (British Museum Publications, London).

—— 1983. 'La Tène swords and scabbards in Champagne', *Germania*, 61, 487–510.

—— 1984. 'Some notes on imported metalwork in Iron Age Britain', in S. Macready and F. H. Thompson (eds), *Cross-Channel Trade between Gaul and Britain in the Pre-Roman Iron Age* (Soc. Antiq. London Occas. Pap. New Ser. 4, London), 43–66.

—— 1985a. *Celtic Art in Britain before the Roman Conquest* (British Museum Press, London).

—— 1985b. *The Battersea Shield* (British Museum Publications Limited, London).

—— 1986. 'Other bronze objects', in Stead and Rigby 1986: 125–40.

—— 1990. 'Whitcombe, burial 9, the grave goods', in Aitken and Aitken 1990: 73–5.

—— 1991a. *Iron Age Cemeteries in East Yorkshire: Excavations at Burton Fleming, Rudston, Garton-on-the-Wolds, and Kirkburn* (Eng. Heritage Archaeol. Rep. 22, London).

—— 1991b. 'Many more Iron Age shields from Britain', *Antiq. J.*, 71, 1–35.

—— 1991c. 'The Snettisham treasure: excavations in 1990', *Antiquity*, 65, 447–65.

—— 1991d. 'The Arras culture', in Moscati *et al.* 1991: 587–90.

—— 1991e. The Belgae in Britain, in Moscati *et al.* 1991: 591–5.

—— 1995. 'The metalwork', in Parfitt 1995: 58–111.

—— 1996. *Celtic Art in Britain before the Roman Conquest*, 2nd edn. (British Museum Press, London).

—— and Hughes, K. 1997. *Early Celtic Designs* (British Museum Press, London).

—— and Rigby, V. 1986. *Baldock: The Excavation of a Roman and a Pre-Roman Settlement, 1968–72* (Britannia Mono. Ser. 7; Society for the Promotion of Roman Studies, London).

—— and —— 1989. *Verulamium: The King Harry Lane Site* (English Heritage Archaeol. Rep. 12, London).

—— and —— 1999. *Iron Age Antiquities from Champagne in the British Museum: The Morel Collection* (British Museum Press, London).

——, Bourke, J. B. and Brothwell, D. 1986. *Lindow Man: The Body in the Bog* (British Museum Publications, London).

Stuart, J. 1819. *Historical memoirs of the City of Armagh, for a period of 1373 years, comprising a considerable portion of the general history of Ireland; a refutation of the opinions of Dr. Ledwich, respecting the non-existence of St. Patrick; and an appendix, on the learning, antiquities, and religion of the Irish nation* (Alexander Wilkinson, Newry).

Stuart, J. 1872–4. 'Notice of a bronze sword found in Carlingwark Loch', *Proc. Soc. Antiq. Scotland*, 10, 286.

Stukeley, W. 1718. 'Minute book of the Antiquarian Society', MS in the library of the Society of Antiquaries of London.

Sturt, G. 1923. *The Wheelwright's Shop* (Cambridge University Press, Cambridge).

Taylor, R. J. and Brailsford, J. W. 1985. 'British Iron Age strap-unions', *Proc. Prehist. Soc.*, 51, 247–72.

Thompson, F. H. 1965. *Roman Cheshire* (Cheshire Community Council, Chester).

—— 1983. 'Excavations at Bigberry, near Canterbury, 1978–80', *Antiq. J.*, 63, 237–78.

Thompson, H. 1993. 'Iron Age and Roman slave-shackles', *Archaeol. J.*, 150, 57–168.

Thorpe, R. and Sharman, J. 1994. 'An Iron Age and Romano-British enclosure system at Normanton le Heath, Leicestershire', *Trans. Leicestershire Archaeol. Hist. Soc.*, 68, 1–63.

Trow, S. D. 1988. 'Excavations at Ditches hillfort, North Cerney, Gloucestershire, 1982–3', *Trans. Bristol Gloucestershire Archaeol. Soc.*, 106, 19–85.

Turner, R. C. 1995. 'Discoveries and excavations at Lindow Moss 1983–8', in Turner and Scaife 1995: 10–18.

—— and Scaife, R. G. (eds) 1995. *Bog Bodies: New Discoveries and New Perspectives* (British Museum Press, London).

Tylecote, R. F. 1962. *Metallurgy in Archaeology. A Prehistory of Metallurgy in the British Isles* (Edward Arnold, London).

—— 1970. 'The composition of metal artifacts: a guide to provenance?', *Antiquity*, 44, 19–25.

Van Arsdell, R. D. 1989. *Celtic Coinage of Britain* (Spink, London).

Vouga, P. 1923. *La Tène: Monographie de la station publièe au nom de la commission des fouilles de la Tène* (Hiersemann, Leipzig).

Wainwright, G. J. 1971. 'The excavation of a fortified settlement at Walesland Rath, Pembrokeshire', *Britannia*, 2, 48–108.

—— 1979. *Gussage All Saints: An Iron Age settlement in Dorset* (Dept. Environ. Archaeol. Rep. 10; HMSO, London).

—— and Spratling, M. 1973. 'The Iron Age settlement of Gussage All Saints', *Antiquity*, 47, 109–30.

—— and Switsur, V. R. 1976. 'Gussage All Saints – a chronology', *Antiquity*, 50, 32–9.

Wait, G. A. 1985. *Ritual and Religion in Iron Age Britain*, 2 vols (Brit. Archaeol. Rep. Brit. Ser. 149, Oxford).

—— 1995. 'Burial and the Otherworld', in Green 1995a: 489–511.

Wakeman, W. F. 1883–4. 'Trouvaille of the Bronze and Iron Age from crannog at Lisnacroghera, Co. Antrim', *J. Royal Soc. Antiq. Ireland*, 16, 375–408.

Walter, R. 1853. Hamdon Hill, *Proc. Somersetshire Archaeol. Nat. Hist. Soc.*, 4, 78–90.

—— 1923. 'Some recent finds on Ham Hill, South Somerset', *Antiq. J.*, 3, 149–50.

Ward Perkins, J. B. 1939. 'Iron Age metal horses' bits of the British Isles', *Proc. Prehist. Soc.*, 5, 173–92.

—— 1940. 'Two early linch-pins, from Kings Langley, Herts., and from Tiddington, Stratford-on-Avon', *Antiq. J.*, 20, 358–67.

—— 1941. 'An Iron Age linch-pin of Yorkshire type from Cornwall', *Antiq. J.*, 21, 64–7.

Warner, R. B. 1976. 'Some observations on the context and importation of exotic material in 'Ireland, from the first century B.C. to the second century A.D.', *Proc. Royal Irish Acad.*, 76C, 267–92.

Watkin, J. 1995. 'An Iron Age shield from Ratcliffe-on-Soar', *Current Archaeol.*, 141, 336–40.

——, Stead, I., Hook, D. and Palmer, S. 1996. 'A decorated shield-boss from the River Trent, near Ratcliffe-on-Soar', *Antiq. J.*, 76, 17–30.

Watkinson, D. and Neal, V. 1998. *First Aid for Finds*, 3rd edn. (Rescue/UKIC Archaeology Section, London).

Webster, G. A. 1971. 'A hoard of Roman military equipment from Fremington Hagg', in R. M. Butler (ed.), *Soldier and Civilian in Roman Yorkshire: Essays to Commemorate the Nineteenth Centenary of the Foundation of York* (Leicester University Press, Leicester), 107–25.

—— 1982. 'Gazetteer of military objects from Cirencester', in J. S. Wacher and A. D. McWhirr, *Early Roman Occupation at Cirencester* (Cirencester Excavation Committee, Cirencester), 109–17.

—— 1983. 'The function of Chedworth Roman 'villa'', *Trans. Bristol Gloucestershire Archaeol. Soc.*, 101, 5–20.

—— 1986. *The British Celts and their Gods under Rome* (Batsford, London).

—— 1990. 'Part of a Celtic linch-pin', *Britannia*, 21, 293–4.

—— 1996. 'Harness strap junction', in Bailey and Cannel 1996: 318–20.

Webster, J. 1986. 'Roman bronzes from Maryport in the Netherhall Collection', *Trans. Cumberland Westmorland Antiq. Archaeol. Soc.* (2nd ser.), 86, 49–70.

Webster, J. 1995. 'Sanctuaries and sacred places', in Green 1995a: 445–64.

—— 1997. 'A negotiated syncretism: readings on the development of Romano-Celtic religion', in Mattingly 1997: 165–84.

—— 1999. 'At the end of the world: druidic and other revitalization movements in post-conquest Gaul and Britain', *Britannia*, 30, 1–20.

Webster, P. 1984. *Verulamium and St Albans: An Archaeological Guide* (Department of Extra-Mural Studies, University College Cardiff, Cardiff).

Wheeler, R. E. M. 1928. 'A 'Romano-Celtic' temple near Harlow, Essex; and a note on the type', *Antiq. J.*, 8, 300–26.

—— 1943. *Maiden Castle, Dorset* (Rep. Res. Comm. Soc. Antiq. London 12, London).

—— 1954. *The Stanwick Fortifications, North Riding of Yorkshire* (Rep. Res. Comm. Soc. Antiq. London 17, London).

—— and Wheeler, T. V. 1932. *Report on the Excavation of the Prehistoric, Roman and Post-Roman Site in Lydney Park, Gloucestershire* (Rep. Res. Comm. Soc. Antiq. London 9, London).

—— and —— 1936. *Verulamium: A Belgic and Two Roman Cities* (Rep. Res. Comm. Soc. Antiq. London 11, London).

Whimster, R. A. 1981. *Burial Practices in Iron Age Britain: A Discussion and Gazetteer of the Evidence c.700 B.C.–A.D. 43* (2 vols, Brit. Archaeol. Rep. Brit. Ser. 90, Oxford).

White, A. 1979. *Antiquities from the River Witham*, part I, *Prehistoric and Roman* (Lincolnshire Mus. Info. Sheet Archaeol. Ser. 12; Lincolnshire Museums, Lincoln).

Whitwell, J. B. 1966. 'Archaeological notes', *Lincolnshire Hist. Archaeol.*, 1, 33–53.

Wilde, W. R. 1861. *A Descriptive Catalogue of the Antiquities of Animal Materials and Bronze in the Museum of the Royal Irish Academy* (Hodges, Smith and Co., Dublin).

—— 1863. *A Descriptive Catalogue of the Antiquities in the Museum of the Royal Irish Academy*, vol. 1, *Articles of Stone, Earthen, Vegetable, and Animal Minerals; and of Copper and Bronze* (Royal Irish Academy, Dublin).

Wilkinson, T. J. 1987. 'Palaeoenvironments of the Upper Witham Fen: a preliminary view', *Fenland Research*, 4, 52–6.

Williams, D. 2000a. 'A newly-discovered Roman temple and its environs: excavations at Wanborough in 1999', *Surrey Archaeol. Soc. Bull.*, 336, 2–6.

—— 2000b. 'Wanborough Roman temple', *Current Archaeol.* 167, 434–7.

Williams, H. 1923. 'The Romano-British site at Rhostryfan, Caernarvonshire', *Archaeol. Cambrensis*, 78, 97–113.

Willis, S. 1999. 'Without and within: aspects of culture and community in the Iron Age of north-eastern England', in Bevan 1999: 81–110.

Wilson, D. 1863a. *Prehistoric Annals of Scotland*, vol. 1, 2nd edn. (Macmillan and Co., London).

—— 1863b. *Prehistoric Annals of Scotland*, vol. 2, 2nd edn. (Macmillan and Co., London).

Wilson, R. J. A. (ed.) 1997a. *Roman Maryport and its Setting: Essays in Memory of Michael G. Jarrett* (Cumberland Westmorland Antiq. Archaeol. Soc. Extra Ser. 23, Maryport).

—— 1997b. 'Maryport from the first to the fourth centuries: some current problems', in Wilson 1997a: 17–39.

—— 2000. 'On the trail of the triskeles: from the McDonald Institute to Archaic Greek Sicily', *Cambridge Archaeol. J.*, 10, 35–61.

Woodward, A. and Leach, P. 1993. *The Uley Shrines: Excavation of a Ritual Complex on West Hill, Uley, Gloucestershire: 1977–9* (English Heritage Archaeol. Rep. 17, London).

Wylie, W. M. 1852. *Fairford Graves: A Record of Researches in an Anglo-Saxon Burial-Place in Gloucestershire* (John Henry Parker, Oxford).

York, J. 2002. 'The life cycles of Bronze Age metalwork from the Thames', *Oxford J. Archaeol.*, 21, 77–92.

Young, S. M. M., Budd, P., Haggerty, R. and Pollard, A. M. 1997. 'Inductively coupled plasma-mass spectrometry for the analysis of ancient metals', *Archaeometry*, 39, 379–92.

Zirra, V. 1981. 'Latènezeitliche Trensen in Rumänien', *Hamburger Beiträge zur Archäologie*, 8, 115–71.

Index

Abercairney, Perthshire 93, 96
Agricola 151, 170
Akenham, Suffolk 39, 42
Alcester, Warwickshire 39, 42, 130–1
Alderton, Suffolk 39, 42
Aldridge, Staffordshire 11, 15
Almendilla, Cordoba, Spain 54
Alsópél, Hungary 137
Anglesey 1, 2, 152, 153, 156, 170, 172, 187,
    188, 189
Ardbrin, Co. Down 105, 106, 107, 109
Ardoch, Perthshire 12, 13, 14, 15, 21, 22
Arras, East Yorkshire 33, 42, 43, 46, 47, 48, 54,
    63, 64, 70, 158, 163
    see also Charioteer's Barrow; King's Barrow;
    Lady's Barrow; Yorkshire, East
Ashmolean Museum 16, 35, 41, 44, 73, 125,
    126
Attleborough, Norfolk 39, 42
Aughinish, Co. Limerick 81
Aylesford, Kent 147, 148, 149–50

Baginton, Warwickshire 12, 13, 14, 15
Baldock, Hertfordshire 45, 46, 48, 93, 94, 95,
    147, 148–9, 150
Ballyblack Moss, Co. Down 83
Ballyedmond, Co. Galway 93, 94, 95
Ballymagrorty, Co. Donegal 82
Ballymoney, Co. Antrim 92, 93
Bann, River, Coleraine, Co. Derry 73, 81,
    178–9
Barber, J. 55
Bardney Abbey, Lincolnshire 98, 99
Barking, Suffolk 47
Barmouth, Merionethshire 130, 134
Barrett, J. C. 184
Barzani, Amin 207, 208
Battersea, London 93, 94, 98, 99, 100, 107,
    108, 131, 132, 133, 137, 138
Bawsey, Norfolk 125, 126

Baydon, Berkshire 56
    see also Botley Copse
Beckford, Worcestershire 139, 143, 145
Beechamwell, Norfolk 35, 39, 42
Bench Cave, Devon 18
Beverley, East Yorkshire 26, 33, 57, 61, 64, 70
Bewcastle, Cumberland 92, 93
Bigberry Camp, Kent 18, 24, 35, 39, 41, 42, 43,
    44, 49, 57, 61, 140, 141, 144, 167
Billericay, Essex 129, 136
Birdlip, Gloucestershire 67–8, 95, 147
Birtley, Northumberland 18
Bishop Wilton, East Yorkshire 16, 17
Blackburn Mill, Cockburnspath, Berwickshire
    76, 93, 95, 171, 177, 185, 188
Blackwater, River 179
Blicquy, Belgium 39, 41, 42, 43
Board of Celtic Studies 6, 7
Bog of Allen, Co. Kilkenny 92, 93
bone
    animal 1, 6, 168, 169, 172, 173, 175, 176,
        177, 178, 180, 181, 182, 185, 186
    human 173, 175, 177, 179, 180, 181, 182
Borness Cave, Kirkcudbrightshire 103
Botley Copse, Berkshire 57, 61, 64
Brabham, Peter 207, 208
Bradford Peverell, Dorset 102
Brampton, Norfolk 12, 14
Brantham, Suffolk 45, 47
Bredon Hill, Gloucestershire 57, 61, 64, 71
Brentford, London 7, 139, 140, 143, 145
bridle-bits 5, 6, 19–20, 52–87, 124, 141, 144,
    178
    two-link 43, 52–3, 54, 70, 72–8, 79, 85, 156,
        173
    three-link 22, 23, 24, 52, 53–73, 74, 77, 85,
        86, 156, 160, 166, 169, 172
    derivative three-link 78–9, 85
    Irish three-link 52, 53, 64, 65, 69, 78, 80–7,
        156, 173, 188

Irish two-link 73
   miscellaneous 52, 79
   see also centre-links; rein-rings; side-links
British Museum 63, 71
brooches 13, 24, 25, 33, 74, 118, 158, 160
Broome, Norfolk 39, 42
Brough Castle, Westmorland 98–9, 100
Browne, M. 142
Brunaux, J. L. 181, 186
Bryn y Castell, Merionethshire 153
Buckland Rings, Hampshire 140, 141, 142,
   144–5
Burgh Castle, Norfolk 45, 47
burial deposits 12, 19, 25, 33, 43, 44, 47, 48, 54,
   61, 63, 64, 70, 73, 77, 100, 102, 118, 133,
   158–9, 167, 172, 179
Burns, J. 96
Burwell Fen, Cambridgeshire 140, 141
Bury Hill, Hampshire 12, 14, 16, 17, 18, 19, 24,
   39, 41, 42, 43, 66
Bushmills, Co. Antrim 106
Butterwick, North Yorkshire 12, 14

Caer Cadwgan, Cardiganshire 154
Caesar 171, 184, 187
Cairnegryfe, Lanarkshire 38
Camerton, Somerset 12, 14, 24, 25
Cardiff University 199, 200
Carlingwark Loch, Kirkcudbrightshire 71–2,
   76, 84, 92, 93, 94, 171, 177, 178, 185,
   188
Carlisle, Cumberland 12, 13, 14
'casket' ornament 5, 7, 115, 117, 121, 146–51,
   156, 166, 172, 188
Castell Henllys, Pembrokeshire 153, 154
Castellazzo di Palma di Montechiaro, Sicily
   123
Castleford, West Yorkshire 12, 14
cauldrons 88–97, 107–8, 159, 166, 172, 173
   Gundestrup cauldron 106
Cawston, Norfolk 39, 42
Cawthorn Camps, East Yorkshire 27, 31, 33,
   55, 60, 61, 64
Celtic Art in Britain before the Roman Conquest
   119
centre-links (of bridle bits) 52, 53, 54–5, 56, 58,
   59, 60, 65, 69–70, 78, 79, 85, 86–7, 166,
   173
Champagne 132

Charioteer's Barrow, Arras, East Yorkshire 26,
   60
Chedworth, Gloucestershire 114–15
Chelmondiston, Suffolk 45, 47
Chertsey, Surrey 133
Chesterholm, Northumberland 21
Chesters, Northumberland 18, 21–2, 98, 99,
   100
Chilly, Somme 182
Christchurch, Cambridgeshire 45, 47
Christie-Stokes, Lt. Col. C. J. 122, 144
Churn, River, Cricklade, Wiltshire 80
Cirencester, Gloucestershire 12, 14
City Farm, Hanborough, Oxfordshire 57, 61,
   64
Clarke, R. R. 54
Clevedon, Somerset 118
Colchester, Essex 12, 14, 15, 18, 37
   St Nicholas site 12
   Sheepen farm site 12, 16
Coleraine, Co. Antrim 178–9
Collfryn, Montgomeryshire 39, 42, 43, 45, 47,
   48
Conway, River, Denbighshire 84, 86, 87
Corbridge, Northumberland 12, 13, 14, 16, 21,
   22, 147, 150, 151
Corfe, Dorset 99, 100
Cork 'crown' 107, 108
Cornaux, Switzerland 175, 185, 186
Cors yr Ynys bog 1, 2, 4
Cotterdale, North Yorkshire 101, 102
Cowley, L. F. 168
Craddock, P. T. 165
Craig y Carnau, Anglesey 2
Crawcwellt West, Merionethshire 153
Culbin Sands, Morayshire 39, 42, 43
Cunliffe, B. 16, 18–19, 20, 25
Curle, J. 171
Cymyran, Anglesey 2

Daly, Tony 7
Danes' Graves, Driffield, East Yorkshire 26–7,
   33, 55, 60, 61, 64, 67
Darbyshire, G. 167
De Bello Gallico 171, 184, 185, 187, 188, 189
   171, 184, 187
De Navarro, J. M. 117
decorative motifs and ornament 6, 9, 10, 16,
   18, 20, 18, 22–5, 35–6, 42, 49, 63, 64, 70,

71, 72, 74, 79, 81, 83, 84, 88, 96, 98, 99, 100, 102, 104, 107, 110–16, 117–20, 122, 123–6, 127–30, 136–7, 139–40, 145, 160
  see also 'casket' ornament; pseudo-stitch decoration; swastika; triskele
Denmark 175
Deskford, Banffshire 178, 186
Deutsches Museum, Munich 106, 108
Diamond Hill, Killeshandra, Co. Cavan 106
Dinorben, Denbighshire 103, 153
Diodorus Siculus 184
Dirnveagh Bog, Co. Antrim 94, 96
Dog Holes, Warton Crag, Lancashire 59, 63, 64
Dolbenmaen, Caernarvonshire 122
Dolgellau, Merionethshire 84
druids, 186–7
Dublin, Co. 81
Dungworth, D. B. 163–5
Dunure 12, 14
Dürkheim 137
'Dying Gaul' 106, 108

Eckford 177, 188
Ellingham 12
Elmswell, East Yorkshire 100, 147
Elvanfoot, Lanarkshire 94, 96
Elvedon, Suffolk 74, 75, 147
Emain Macha, Co. Armagh 108, 177
Estrées-Saint-Denis, Oise 182
Eton, Berkshire 179
Evans, Arthur 171
Ewartley Shank, Northumberland 94, 96

Fabech, C. 184
Fairford, Gloucestershire 19
Farley Heath, Surrey 114, 115
Fishbourne, West Sussex 12, 13, 14, 15, 16
Fiskerton, Lincolnshire 180, 183, 185, 186
Fitzpatrick, A. P. 179, 184
Flag Fen, near Peterborough, Cambridgeshire 180, 183, 185, 186
Fordington, Dorset 74, 75, 77
Foster, J. 16, 20, 159
Fox, Cyril 1, 2, 4–5, 6, 9, 10, 23, 25, 28, 31, 38, 49, 51, 53, 54, 56, 66, 67, 68, 70–1, 73, 82, 88, 90, 92, 96, 98, 101, 104, 109, 112, 113–14, 115, 116, 117, 120, 122, 124, 126, 127, 129, 136, 137, 138, 143–4, 146,

147, 149, 162, 171, 174, 186–7, 188, 190, 207–8, 209, 212, 214, 236
France 26, 53
Fremington Hag, North Yorkshire 21, 22
Fring, Norfolk 45, 46, 47

Garton Slack, East Yorkshire 26, 27, 30, 31, 33, 57, 61, 64, 70
Garton Station, East Yorkshire 12, 14, 27, 33, 158
Gaul 181, 184, 185, 187, 188, 189
Gayton Thorpe, Norfolk 147
Gelliniog Wen, Anglesey 50, 51
Gillingham, Norfolk 14
Gilsland, Northumberland 74, 75
Glastonbury lake village, Somerset 12, 14, 15, 24, 32, 33, 42, 56, 57, 61, 62, 63, 67, 71, 73, 77, 95, 101, 103
Goring, Oxfordshire 140–1, 143
Gosbecks, Essex 182
Gournay-sur-Aronde, Oise 175, 181, 182, 183, 184, 186
Great Brackstead, Essex 133
Great Chesterford, Essex 147
Great Ellingham 12, 14, 15
Great Thurlow, Suffolk 40, 42
Green, M. 138
Greenly, E. 1, 210
Gregory of Tours 185
Grimthorpe, East Yorkshire 101, 125, 134
Guide Catalogue of the Early Iron Age Collections 190
Gussage All Saints, Dorset 8, 9, 10, 18, 19, 20–1, 22, 35, 36, 39, 44, 56, 57, 61, 64, 65, 66, 69, 71, 85, 86, 154, 159–60
Gussage-Bury Hill tradition 6, 16, 18–20, 25, 42, 63, 64

Hagbourne Hill, Berkshire 56, 57, 62, 64, 65, 67, 68, 69, 70, 71, 80
Hallstatt 132, 137, 138
Ham Hill, Somerset 50, 51, 57, 62, 64, 67, 76, 77, 79, 80, 103, 139, 140, 141, 142, 143, 145, 147, 149
Hammersmith, London 23, 24, 140–1
Harborough Cave, Brassington, Derbyshire 57, 62, 64, 69
Harlow 183, 186
Harrow Hill, West Sussex 182

Haselgrove, C. 189
Hawkes, C. F. C. 38, 92, 94, 95, 96, 141
Haworth, R. G. 80–1, 83
Hayling Island, Hampshire 56, 58, 62, 64, 65, 182, 183, 184, 186, 188, 189
Heathrow, Middlesex 182
Heighington, Lincolnshire 40, 42
Hemingstone, Suffolk 45, 47
Hemp, W. J. 132
Hengistbury Head, Hampshire 19, 56, 58, 62, 63, 65, 67, 70
Heron, C. 200
High Cross, Leicestershire 140, 141–2
Hingley, R. 183, 184
Hjortspring Kobbel, Denmark 175–6, 185, 186
Hoare, R. C. 139
Hod Hill, Dorset 12, 14, 15, 16, 17, 18, 23–5, 45, 47, 48, 76, 98, 99, 100, 101–2, 147, 149
Hodges, H. 7
Holme Pierrepont, Nottinghamshire 32, 42
Homersfield, Suffolk 40, 42
Honley, West Yorkshire 45, 48
horn caps, so-called 5, 6, 7, 103, 136–46, 156, 161, 172
horns 103–9
Horton, Dorset 139, 140, 142
Hradiště, former Czechoslovakia 106, 108
Hull, M. R. 38
Hundersingen 138
Hunmanby, East Yorkshire 12, 14, 15, 16, 27, 33, 45, 47, 48, 59, 63, 64
Hunsbury, Northamptonshire 12–13, 14, 15, 16, 17, 19, 27, 33–4, 45, 47, 48, 56, 58, 62, 64, 76, 77, 102–3, 167
Hunter, F. 95
Hutcheson, N. C. G. 62
Hyde, H. A. 190

Ingleton, West Yorkshire 71, 72
Ipswich, Suffolk 94, 96, 183
Ireland 53, 73, 80–7, 105–6, 107–9, 152, 155, 156–7, 176

Jackson, R. 12
Jacobsthal, P. 17, 137, 144
James, S. 185
Jones, J. A. 4
Jope, E. M. 5, 80, 133

Kenninghall, Norfolk 45, 47
Kermaria, Pont-l'Abbé, France 137
Kessingland, Suffolk 11, 15
Kettering, Northamptonshire 147
Kew, London 30
Kilberg, Co. Westmeath 83, 84
Killeevan, Anlore, Co. Monaghan 81
Killyfaddy Bog, near Clogher, Co. Tyrone 106
Kincardine Moss, Stirlingshire 93, 94, 95
King, A. 186
King's Barrow, Arras, East Yorkshire 23, 24, 26, 27, 31, 37, 39, 45, 47, 60, 64, 69
King's Langley, Hertfordshire 38
King's Stables, Co. Armagh 177, 185
Kingsbury, Warwickshire 40, 42
Kingsholm, Gloucestershire 40, 42, 43, 44
Kinneil, West Lothian 15
Kirkburn, East Yorkshire 27, 28, 30, 31, 32, 33, 36, 40, 42, 43, 45, 46, 47, 48, 59, 63, 64, 70, 118, 126, 158
Kirkby Thore, Westmorland 21, 22
Kirmington, Lincolnshire 12, 14, 16
Kishawanny, Co. Kildare 84
Krogsbølle, Denmark 175, 176, 186
Kyleakin, Skye 93, 95

La Bouvandeau 144
La Courte, Leval-Trahegnies, Belgium 46, 47
La Tène 175, 184, 185, 186
    Continental 23, 26, 46, 53, 54, 73, 83, 94, 98, 117, 131, 132–3, 137–8, 144, 167, 175
    insular 1, 5, 6, 16, 23, 42, 61, 63, 83, 92, 94, 95, 98, 99, 100, 101, 116, 117–19, 123, 129, 130, 131, 133, 134, 135, 136, 144, 149, 153, 154, 155–6, 157–8, 159, 160, 164–5, 178, 179, 184
Lady's Barrow, Arras 26, 27, 30, 31, 32, 33, 69
Lake Neuchâtel, Switzerland 138, 175
Lambay Island, Co. Dublin 98, 99, 100, 147
Lancing Ring, West Sussex 182
Langley Burrell, Wiltshire 45, 47
Lapworth, Warwickshire 40, 42, 44
Lea, River 179
Leeds, E. T. 8, 10–11, 52, 53, 73, 78
Leicester
    Jewry Wall 38
    Town Museum 141–2
Leigh, Worcestershire 40, 42
Lesser Garth, Glamorgan 161

Letchworth, Hertfordshire 93, 95
Lexden, Essex 147
linch pins 5, 19, 34, 37, 167, 179–80
  'vase-headed' linch-pins 5, 11, 20, 34–44, 47,
    49, 126, 156, 161, 166, 173
Lindow Moss, Cheshire 173
Lisnacrogher, Co. Antrim 115, 176, 185, 186
Little Cornard, Suffolk 45
Little Houghton, Northamptonshire 12, 14
Llanaber, Merionethshire 74, 75, 77
Llanfaes, Anglesey 87
Llanfair yn Neubwll, Anglesey 214
Llanfihangel yn Nhowyn, Anglesey 214
Llanmelin, Monmouthshire 154
Llanymynech Hill, Shropshire 154
Llwyn Bryn-dinas, Denbighshire 153, 154
Llyn Cerrig Bach, Anglesey
  concordance table 192–8
  dating of artefacts 25, 34, 49, 71, 72, 78, 87,
    97, 102, 103, 109, 115, 119, 126, 136,
    143–4, 150, 151, 157, 160–70
  manufacture of artefacts 34, 36–7, 49, 77–8,
    85–6, 91–2, 109, 146, 151
  metallurgical analysis of artefacts 155, 162,
    164, 165–6, 199–206
  as religious site 4, 5, 171–4, 183, 184, 185–9
  source of artefacts 82, 152–7
  topography of site 1–4, 173–4, 207–16,
    253–6
and *passim* contents of assemblage (copper
  alloy)
  bridle-bits, 5, 6, 202
  two-link 70, 74, 75, 77–8, 85, 156, 173, 224,
    242
  three-link 23, 24, 52–3, 56, 64–7, 69, 70–1,
    72, 78, 155, 161, 166, 169, 172, 173, 201,
    206, 220–3, 224–5, 239–40
  Irish three-link 64, 69, 70, 78, 80, 81, 82, 83,
    84, 85–7, 156, 173, 188, 242, 257
  miscellaneous bridle-bits 79–80
  centre-links 52, 64, 65, 66, 69–70, 86–7, 166,
    173, 202, 220, 221, 225, 239
  (possible) harness ring 49–51, 173, 202, 219,
    224
  linch-pin ('vase-headed') 5, 20, 34–7, 40, 41,
    42, 49, 156, 161, 166, 173, 219, 257
  mouthpieces 64, 65, 79
  nave hoops 5, 25–6, 27, 28–33, 34, 156, 166,
    167, 172, 202, 218–19, 238, 257

rein-rings 52, 53, 56, 64–5, 66–7, 68, 69, 70,
  72, 77, 85, 86, 156, 161, 172, 173, 201,
  202, 220, 221, 222, 223–4, 41
side-links 64–5, 66–7, 69, 70, 71, 77, 72, 77, 78,
  85–6, 172, 202, 220, 221, 222, 224, 225
stop-studs 67, 69, 70, 77, 85, 172, 220, 221,
  222, 223
terrets 5, 9, 10–11, 14, 15–16, 17, 18, 20–1,
  22, 23, 24, 25, 155, 161, 166, 173, 202,
  217–18, 237
cauldron fragments 5, 88–92, 94, 95, 97, 109,
  110, 166, 172, 173, 201, 202, 206, 225–7,
  229, 243–5
coiled decorative strips (or 'ribbons') 6, 88,
  110, 115, 121, 151, 161, 166, 170, 172,
  188, 201, 204, 229–32, 248
curved-horn or 'trumpet' fragment 5, 84,
  103–5, 107, 109, 156, 161, 172, 201, 204,
  228, 247
cylinder 102–3, 172, 204, 227–8, 246
decorative plaques or mounts
  bean-shaped plaques 1, 5, 116, 122, 134,
    232, 249
  'casket' ornament plaques 5, 115, 117, 121,
    146, 147, 149, 150, 151, 156, 161, 166,
    170, 172, 188, 204, 234–6, 252
  crescentic decorative mount 6, 115, 117,
    119–26, 129, 134, 145, 161, 172, 204,
    233, 250; curved mount 116, 233, 249
  shield boss mount 5, 6, 117, 119, 122,
    127–130, 131, 132, 133, 134, 135–66,
    161, 172, 204, 233–4, 251, 258
horn-cap (so-called) 5, 117, 136–7, 138–40,
  141, 143, 145, 156, 161, 172, 204, 234, 249
military equipment and weaponry
  pommel 5, 98, 101–2, 166, 172, 204, 227,
    246
  scabbard mouth 5, 98, 99, 100–1, 161, 167,
    169, 204, 227, 246
  (probable) scabbard or sheath binding 5,
    98, 101, 166, 167, 169, 204, 227, 246
shield-boss mount 98
sheet fragments 109–110, 166, 190–1, 201,
  204, 206, 228–9, 246
trumpet voids 118, 121, 126, 129
  contents of assemblage (other)
bone
  animal 1, 6, 168, 169, 172, 173, 190
  human 173

ironwork 1, 4, 5, 6, 34, 37, 65, 79, 98, 153, 156–7, 166–7, 168, 169, 172, 190, 220, 221, 222, 223, 224, 225, 227, 232
   medieval and modern items 1, 191, 208
Llyn Fawr, Glamorgan 97, 171
Lochlie Crannog, Ayrshire 78, 148
Loddiswell, Devon 40, 42
Loddon, Norfolk 45, 47
Loire, River 188
London, Dowgate 147
London, Great Tower Street 147
Long Stratton, Norfolk 12, 14
Lord's Bridge, Barton, Cambridgeshire 157
Loughbrickland, Co. Down 106
Loughnashade, Co. Armagh 103, 105, 106, 107, 108, 122, 177
Lound Run, Suffolk 92–4, 96
Lowery, P. R. 7
Lucan 187
Lydney, Gloucestershire 74, 75, 78, 147, 150, 151
Lynch, F. 5, 25, 122, 128, 167, 172

McGrath, J. N. 6
MacGregor, M. 7, 8, 11, 18, 23, 34, 38, 55, 92–4, 146, 155
Madmarston Camp, Oxfordhsire 80
Maiden Castle, Dorset 24, 25, 66, 73–4, 103, 139, 140, 141, 142, 143, 145
Manning, W. H. 102
Marlborough, Wiltshire 147, 149–50
Maryon, Herbert 28, 29, 92
Maryport, Cumberland 12, 13, 14, 15, 21, 22
Meare, Somerset 16, 17, 45, 46, 48, 56, 58, 62, 77, 103, 147
Megaw, J. V. S. 55, 128
Megaw, R. 107, 126, 149–50, 151
Megaw, V. 107, 126, 149–50, 151
Mela 188
Merlin's Cave, Symonds Yat, Herefordshire 37
Merthyr Mawr Warren, Glamorgan 154
Methwold, Norfolk 46, 47
Middlebie, Dumfriesshire 12, 14, 15, 16, 21
Middleton, North Yorkshire 131
Middleton on the Wolds, East Yorkshire 38
Mill Hill, Deal, Kent 19, 23, 24, 50, 63, 118, 158
Mill Plain, Hampshire 16, 17, 18, 20, 23
Minton, Treharne and Davies Ltd. 6, 104–5, 201, 206

Mirebeau, Côte-d'Or 182
Moel Hiraddug, Flintshire 122, 132, 133, 134, 147, 149
Mona Antiqua Restaurata 187
Morviller-Saint-Saturnin, Somme 182
mouthpieces (of bridle-bits) 64, 65, 77, 78, 79
Mouzon, Ardennes 182
Muircleugh, Berwickshire 12, 14, 16, 21
Müller, F. 175
Mullingar, Co. Westmeath 83–4

Nanterre, Marne 37
Nanteuil-sur-Aisne, Ardennes
National Museum of Denmark 81
National Museum of Ireland 86, 105
National Museum of Wales 1, 4, 168, 173, 190
nave hoops 5, 13, 25–34, 156, 161, 166, 167, 172
Needwood Forest, Staffordshire 24
Nether Denton, Cumberland 21, 22
Nettlestead, Suffolk 46, 47
New Cairnmuir, Peebleshire 24
Newbridge, Mid Lothian 8, 27, 76, 77
Newgrange, Co. Meath 83
Newstead, Roxburghshire 38, 148, 149, 150, 151
Norfolk 19, 154
Normanton le Heath, Leicestershire 98, 99, 100
Norris, H. 139
North Creake, Norfolk 148
North Grimston, East Yorkshire 50, 51
North Newbald, East Yorkshire 46
North Wraxall, Wiltshire 148
Northover, P. 6, 155, 201, 206
Norway 175
Nydam, Denmark 175, 176, 185

O'Dwyer, S. 106
Old Down Farm, Hampshire 19, 35, 40, 41, 42, 43
Old Oswestry, Shropshire 154
Old Windsor, Berkshire 20, 55, 60, 63, 64, 69, 70
Oriel Ynys Môn, Llangefni 5, 25, 30, 31, 52, 190
Orton Meadows, Cambridgeshire 98, 99, 100
Owen, Evelyn 52–3
Owmby Cliff, Lincolnshire 45, 46, 47
Owslebury, Hampshire 35, 40, 41, 42, 43, 44, 46, 48, 50, 51, 133

Palk, N. A. 53–4, 56, 73, 79–80
Parc-y-meirch hoard 8
Pattern and Purpose: A Survey of Early Celtic Art 117
Paulinus 4, 151, 162, 170, 189
Peckham, J. 142–3
Pentaun, Cornwall 29–30
Pentyrch, Glamorgan 80
Perkins, Ward 34, 37–8, 52, 53, 79
Personality of Britain, The 152
Petrie 'crown' 107, 108
Pexton Moor, North Yorkshire 27–8, 33, 52, 55, 60, 63, 64, 68
Piddlehinton, Dorset 46, 47
Piggott, S. 92, 98, 100, 101, 144, 166–7, 188
Pitt Rivers Museum, Farnham, Dorset 84
Plenderleith, H. J. 10, 88, 103, 127, 228
Plunton Castle, Kirkcudbrightshire 148
Polden Hill, Somerset 8, 13, 14, 15, 16, 27, 31, 33, 43, 52, 73, 74–7, 161, 167
Pollard, A. M. 200
Port Nidau 175, 185, 186
Posidonius 187, 188
Pryor, F. 180
pseudo-stitch decoration 6, 9, 10, 16, 18, 20, 22–5, 49, 63, 64, 67, 71, 218
Putney, London 139, 140–1, 145, 178

Quidenham, Norfolk 40, 42, 46, 47, 48

RAF Valley, Anglesey 1, 2, 4, 173, 174
Raferty, J. 80, 81, 83, 92, 95, 105, 108, 109, 155
Raglan, Monmouthshire 40, 42
Randsborg, K. 175
Ratcliffe-on-Soar, Warwickshire 130, 131
Read's Cavern, Burrington, Somerset 26, 27, 30, 31, 33, 34, 62, 67, 71
Rees, S. E. 167
rein-rings 24, 47, 52, 53, 55–6, 58, 59, 60, 61, 62, 63, 64–5, 66–8, 69, 70, 71, 72, 73–4, 77, 78, 79, 80, 81, 85, 86, 156, 161, 172, 173
Rezi-Rezicseri, Hungary 137
Rhostryfan, Caernarvonshire 148
Ribemont-sur-Ancre, Somme 181–2, 183, 186
Richmond, Ian 161
Rigby, V. 95
Ringstead, Norfolk 55–6, 58, 62, 63, 64, 65, 69, 70

Roberts, R. O. 25
Rodborough Common, Gloucestershire 148, 149
Romania 83
Roscrea, Co. Tipperary 105
Rowlands, Henry 187
Rushmore, Dorset 49

Saffron Walden Museum 18, 35, 41, 44, 46, 49
Saham Tony, Norfolk 21, 22, 40, 41, 42, 43, 44, 46, 47, 48, 74, 75, 77
St Arvans, Monmouthshire 40, 42
St Lawrence, Isle of Wight 50, 51, 98, 133, 134, 136
St Leonards Hill, Windsor, Berkshire 140, 141
Saint-Maur, Oise 182
St Rémy-sur-Bussy, Marne 132
Santon, Norfolk 27, 29, 31, 32, 33, 34, 38, 74, 75, 77, 92, 93, 94, 148, 149, 150
Savory, H. N. 5, 7, 53, 131, 133–4, 190, 201, 217
Saxthorpe, Norfolk 125, 126, 139, 140, 142, 145
scabbards 5, 6, 23, 24, 49–51, 98–101, 118, 137, 158, 161, 166, 167, 169, 178
Sena, Brittany 188
Seven Sisters, Glamorgan 15, 49, 160, 61, 182
Shannon, River 179
Sheepen, near Colchester, Essex 165
shields 5, 6, 24, 118, 127–36, 137, 138, 154
Shotesham, Norfolk 46, 47, 48
side-links (of bridle bits) 53, 54, 55–6, 57, 58, 59, 61–2, 64–5, 66–7, 69, 70, 71, 72, 73–4, 75, 77, 78, 79, 80–1, 82, 85–6, 172
Silchester, Hampshire 92, 148, 149
Silkstead, Ottebourne, Hampshire 20, 58, 62, 64, 148, 149
Sleaford, Lincolnshire 40, 41, 42
Smith, R. A. 32
Snailwell, Cambridgeshire 133, 148
Snettisham, Norfolk 24, 183
Snowdon, Caernarvonshire 161
Soffe, G. 186
Somerset County Museum 139
Somme-Tourbe, Marne, France 53, 54, 82
South Cadbury, Somerset 13, 14, 15, 16, 61, 63–4, 65, 102, 130, 141, 182–3
South Elmham St Mary, Suffolk 40, 42
South Walsham 12, 14

Spettisbury Rings, Dorset 90, 93, 95
Sporle with Palgrave, Norfolk 46, 48
Spratling, M. G. 5, 11, 15, 16, 18, 20, 30, 31, 34, 37, 41–2, 45, 46, 55–6, 68, 70, 77, 92, 94–5, 96, 101, 121–2, 127, 130, 134, 142, 144, 146, 148, 153, 155, 156, 157, 158, 160, 220
Springhead, Kent 19
Stamford Hill, Plymstock, Devon 71, 72
Stanfordbury, Bedfordshire 133, 148, 149, 150
Stanway, Essex 130
Stanwick, North Yorkshire 8, 13, 14, 15, 16, 21, 27, 33, 38, 40, 42, 43, 98, 99, 100–1, 148, 149
Stead, I. M. 5, 23, 34, 36, 42, 47, 54, 55, 63, 95, 100, 117–19, 122, 123, 127, 130, 131, 132, 133, 136, 144, 158
Stenstugan, Sweden 106, 108
Stichill, Roxburghshire 148, 149
Stoke Holy Cross, Norfolk 12, 14
stop-studs 67, 68–9, 70, 77, 80, 82, 85, 172
Stort, River 186
Stowting, Kent 21, 22
Strabo 171, 184, 188
Strand-on-the-Green, London 58, 62, 64
Stratton Strawless, Norfolk 74, 75
Suetonius 184
Suffolk 16, 17, 19
Sutton Benger, Wiltshire 46, 47, 48
Swanton Morley, Norfolk 20, 55–6, 58, 62, 65, 79
swastika motif 137–8, 145, 234
Sweden 175
swords 5, 98, 101–2, 118, 156–7, 166–7, 169, 172, 179–80, 190
Syon Park, Brentford, Middlesex 164

Tacitus 162, 187–8
Tacolneston, Norfolk 40, 42
Tal-y-llyn, Merionethshire 122, 123, 131, 132, 133–4, 160, 182, 201
Tattersett, Norfolk 40, 42
Tattershall Ferry, Lincolnshire 148
Tattershall Thorpe, Lincolnshire 19, 40, 42, 43
Tenbury Wells, Worcestershire 84
terrets 5, 8–25, 62, 144, 161
    Group I 12–16, 17, 18, 20–1, 22, 23, 25, 156, 166
    Group II 16–18, 20, 23, 25, 156

mini-terrets (so-called) 11, 39, 44–9
    tanged terrets 9, 11, 15, 20–2, 25
Thames, River 23, 24, 30, 58, 62, 64, 74, 75, 79, 98, 140–1, 142, 143, 164, 173, 178, 179, 185
Thanington, Kent 40, 42, 43
Thetford Castle, Norfolk 46, 47, 48, 71, 72
Thorsbjerg, Denmark 176
Thrapston, Northamptonshire 101, 178
Times 4
Toome, Co. Antrim 178–9
Toomyvana, Co. Tipperary 83
torcs 24, 118, 126, 183
Torrs Farm, Kirkcudbrightshire 107, 108
Torwoodle 13, 15, 16
Traprain Law, East Lothian 21, 22, 35, 40, 42, 43, 148
Tratman, E. K. 30
Trawsfynydd, Merionethshire 30
Trevelgue, Cornwall 40, 42, 43–4, 46, 47, 48
triskele motif 120, 121, 122, 123, 127–30, 136, 147, 149, 233, 234
Tunstall, Suffolk 59, 62, 65, 70
Twyn-y-Gaer, Monmouthshire 153, 154
Tywyn Trewan dune system, Anglesey 1, 2

Ulceby-on-Humber, Lincolnshire 19, 24, 59, 62, 63, 68, 69, 124
Uley, Gloucestershire 182
Upwell, Norfolk 92, 93

Vendeuil-Caply, Oise 182
Verulamium, Hertfordshire 24, 25, 98, 99–100, 115, 126
Vimose, Denmark 176
votive deposits 4, 5, 77, 100, 108–9, 115, 141, 142, 158, 159, 171–80, 183–9

Wainford Mill, Norfolk 46, 47, 48
Walbrook 179
Waldalgesheim, Germany 137, 143, 144, 145
Walesland Rath, Pembrokeshire 154
Waltham, Kent 12, 15
Waltham Abbey, Essex 167, 179–80, 183–4, 185
Waltham Chase, Hampshire 40, 41, 42, 43
Walthamstow, Essex 59, 63, 65, 69, 93, 94, 96
Wanborough, Surrey 115
Warburton, Lancashire 46, 47, 48
Waterhouse, C. O. 7, 120

Webster, Graham 187
Weelsby Avenue, Grimsby, Lincolnshire 8,
    9–10, 20, 61, 65, 74, 77, 139, 143, 154,
    159, 160
Weeting, Norfolk 35, 40, 41, 42, 43, 44
Welwyn, Hertfordshire 24
Wessex 18
West Acre, Norfolk 74, 75
West Coker, Somerset 59, 63, 67, 68, 71
Westhall, Suffolk 38
Wetwang Slack, East Yorkshire 27, 28, 31, 33,
    50, 59, 61, 64, 70, 73, 77, 158
Wheeler, R. E. M. 100, 141, 145
Whitcombe, Dorset 50, 98, 99, 100
Whitemills Moss, Dumfriesshire 94, 96
Wiggington, Hertfordshire 19, 35, 41, 42, 43
Wild, Jim 7
Wilderspool, Cheshire 13, 15, 20, 21, 22

Wilkins, R. L. 7
Winchester, Hampshire 24, 49, 148
Witham, River 23, 24, 98, 131, 178, 179, 180,
    185
Woodeaton, Oxfordshire 130
Woolley Down, Berkshire 140, 141, 145
Wormegay, Norfolk 92
Worms Head, Rhossili, Glamorgan 154
Worthy Down, Hampshire 76, 167
Wroxeter, Shropshire 38, 148
Wylye Camp, Wiltshire 74, 75
Wymandham, Norfolk 46, 48

Yorkshire 25, 37, 38, 54
Yorkshire, East 12, 18, 19, 25, 33, 37, 43, 44,
    47, 48, 54, 55, 61, 63, 64, 70, 73, 77, 118,
    152, 158, 163, 167;
Yoxall, Staffordshire 41, 42, 43